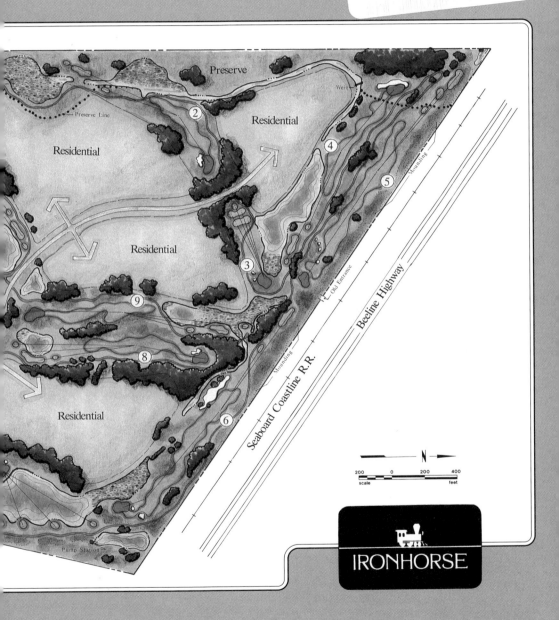

Preserve

2

Residential

Preserve Line

Residential

Residential

4

5

Weir

Mounding

3

9

8

6

Old Entrance

Mounding

Seaboard Coastline R.R.

Beeline Highway

Residential

200   0   200   400

scale   feet

N

Pump Station

IRONHORSE

DRIVING
THE GREEN

DRIVING THE GREEN

The Making of a Golf Course

John Strawn

HarperCollins*Publishers*

FIRST EDITION

Designed by Irving Perkins Associates, Inc.

Library of Congress Cataloging-in-Publication Data
Strawn, John.
    Driving the green : the making of a golf course / John Strawn.—1st ed.
       p.   cm.
    ISBN 0-06-016659-2
    1. Golf courses—Florida—West Palm Beach—Design and construction—Case studies.   I. Title.
    GV975.S68   1991
    712'.5—dc20   90-56183

91 92 93 94 95 AC/RRD 10 9 8 7 6 5 4 3 2 1

Contents

Characters

Alan Sher, retired button magnate with an option to buy 350 south Florida acres. Great place for a golf course, he thinks. Calls it Ironhorse.

Joshua Muss, rich, tough developer from Washington, D.C., looking for property in northern Palm Beach County. Takes on Ironhorse.

Bob Isakson, Muss's man at Ironhorse, a diligent lieutenant vexed by the complexity of south Florida's bureaucratic byways.

Arthur Hills, golf course architect, Sher's choice to design Ironhorse. Runs his busy practice from a small farmhouse outside Toledo, Ohio.

Mike Dasher, Hills's associate, based in Orlando. Happy to have the best job in the golf business.

Jon Harpman, Muss's nephew and Isakson's assistant.

Kenny Postell, the clearing boss. If it's green and has roots, by God, Postell can knock it down.

Kevin Phillipson, foreman for the excavating contractor.

Brent Wadsworth. His company is building Ironhorse. Wadsworth is Hills's best friend, Dasher's former boss. Hopes to build a flawless golf course.

Stu Britton, Wadsworth's superintendent. On the site from dawn to dusk, worrying about every detail, praying the rains will hold off.

Willie Owsley, Wadsworth's shaper. His mark on the landscape is the subtlest and at the same time the most critical. An old hand at building Hills's courses.

Roger Whitford, the golf course superintendent. His job is growing grass. He keeps the greens on the edge of death, a balancing act hard on the super's psyche.

Debbie Goss, an environmentalist with the South Florida Water Management District. Ironhorse will not make her list of favorite projects.

Michael Gordon, Ironhorse's lawyer, broker of the marriage between Sher and Muss.

Peter Aquart, civil engineer, native of Jamaica, calmly competent in a crossfire of small crises.

Howard Searcy, consulting engineer, peerless negotiator through the hazardous passages of public planning, author of Ironhorse's water management plan.

Pete Pimentel, head of the Northern Palm Beach County Water Control District and a major public ally of development in the county. His district issues bonds to pay for the construction of Ironhorse's water control facilities.

I

THE DEAL

1

The Button King in the Garden of Eden

ALAN SHER, the Button King, pumped my hand at the door of his penthouse apartment high above the Atlantic. He lives in the middle of a phalanx of tall condominiums, arrayed against the ocean like a nautical Maginot Line, that runs down Singer Island's narrow spine. Across Lake Worth to the southwest, the Sher apartment commands a grand view of West Palm Beach, and in the skies above Lake Okeechobee to the west, the wild lightning that signals south Florida's rainy season. The ocean rolled onto the narrow beach below, breaching the thin, diminishing shelf where sea turtles heave ashore to lay their leather eggs. Singer Island was named after a descendant of the man who changed America not so much by inventing the sewing machine that bore his name as by marketing it on the installment plan, creating consumer credit and the world that lives on time. Isaac Singer was the herald of the Age of Consumption, a Gilded Age Lee Iacocca.

Paris Singer, the son after whom the island is named, was a man of society, the lover of Isadora Duncan, and a paragon of the Palm Beach style. In 1918, he built a rest home at the west end of Palm Beach's Worth Avenue for shell-shocked veterans of the Great War. The architect Addison Mizner, a friend of Singer's, designed the

Touchstone Convalescents' Club in the eclectic neo-Mediterranean style that he would embellish over the next two decades in a flock of Palm Beach mansions. The war was over by the time Mizner finished construction. The Touchstone lured not a single veteran, shell-shocked or otherwise, to Palm Beach. Florida was a distant frontier then, no more accessible than Laramie, and not the magnet that seventy years of fabulation, Disney merged with Dante, have made it. Paradise was hard to get to if you didn't have your own railway car. Singer gave away the Touchstone's medical equipment, built a golf course on the grounds of his rest home, renamed it the Everglades Club, and nursed not veterans but Palm Beach's first and most exclusive country club. He bought up the land around it and abandoned good works for good times and tidy profits. They could, he told Mizner, make "Palm Beach the winter capital of the world." Paris Singer made golf indispensable to south Florida's social swirl.

Singer Island, due north of Palm Beach, is barely wide enough for its single row of high rises and looks from the air as if it would wobble in a good wind. In the midsixties, the Shers bought an apartment in one of the first Singer Island high rises, The Seagrape, a quarter of a mile north of their penthouse. They were just coming south for the season then. The only way onto the island was a drawbridge at the south end. The Button King hated the delays. Now there's a soaring four-lane bridge that the mast of the tallest sailboat passes under with ease. Singer Island is *less* rural than their Long Island home, but it has the sun and the warm sea and long, easy winters filled with lunches and golf and dinners and tennis and snacks and swims, the Singer style evolved and democratized.

On the night we met, Sher—pronounced "sure"—was voluble, relaxed, the picture of a happy man. His teeth were straight, his eyes clear, his drink stiff—three fingers of celebratory Stoli. He grinned in greeting, waved me in past the pair of thick enameled entry doors, across the zebra skin on the foyer floor, into the living room. Thinking of what was about to happen on a parcel of land lying eight miles west and nineteen stories beneath us, property he'd first laid eyes on four years before, prompted Sher's festive mood. As Paris Singer had seventy years before, the Button King was going to fix his social mark. And like the Everglades Club, Sher's project started as one thing but had become another.

In 1984 the Shers' daughter, Carrie Reese, was looking for a new place to board her three horses—Honey, Charlie, and a broken-down racing nag named The Colonel that she'd rescued from the glue pit. It was costing $600 a month to put them up in equine splendor at Burt Reynolds's ranch in Jupiter, twenty minutes north of Singer Island. Her dad heard about a piece of property for sale west of the Florida Turnpike, less than a mile from a big development called PGA National, where Carrie lived with her husband, Don, a golf pro trying to get back on the PGA Tour. Sher hoped he could buy or lease ten acres for Carrie's pet herd.

Sher loved the Grier Ranch the moment he drove in, with its commanding palms and pines, its feeling of bucolic isolation. These meadows look like fairways, he thought. The encounter was epiphanous: he had the vision. The fashion maven's instincts for a deal started to churn. "I'm not in there fifty feet, and my head was going back and forth like a tennis match. I knew what I wanted to do. It was like I got a message from God."

The appropriate use for this inviting Eden, he was sure, was not grazing cattle or pasturing horses, as the previous owner had done, not the moos and neighs of a playhouse ranch tucked onto the edge of West Palm's booming real estate market, but the queen of landscapes, the apotheosis of the developer's art, a golf course. That's why the golf architects Arthur Hills and Mike Dasher were at the Sher's penthouse, joining the small celebration. Sher had done what the voices said, hiring Arthur Hills and Associates to design a golf course for the Grier Ranch. Tomorrow, with the architects' walk-through, the golf course equivalent of a ceremonial ground-breaking, construction was finally going to get under way.

In his early sixties, Sher was semiretired from the button company his immigrant father had founded. Apart from service in the Coast Guard in World War II—seventeen when he enlisted, he was still in his teens when he sailed the north Atlantic in a destroyer escort and patrolled from Cape Hatteras to the north African coast—he had spent his whole life in what he called "the fashion business." Now, as he said, he was "completing the Tour—born in the Bronx, grew up in Brooklyn, raised the kids on Long Island, retired to Florida." The Shers' son, Richard, ran Sher Plastics from its Manhattan headquarters, but the old man kept in touch. Every morning, Sher called Richard. Even in exile, he was the Button King. He'd spent his life beating the bushes for customers, courting suppliers, sniffing for fashion's scent. "I was the first button man in Hong Kong," he bragged. "I taught them how to make a good button."

When he was still working full-time, he could barely stand the weekends. His game was tennis then, but even on the court he thought about buttons. His retirement was nearly as restless, until he hatched his golf course scheme. He'd finally found a substitute for the energy and will he'd devoted to the button business.

Within a few hours of seeing the Grier Ranch, Sher had christened his plan to develop a country club with a check to the realtor for $40,000, taking an option not merely on ten acres but on the entire property, 354 acres at $15,500 per, a five-and-a-half-million-dollar launch. He figured he'd put together a little financing scheme, get a development loan, and have a course underway in six months. "In a year, year and a half," he was sure, he'd tee it up with his pals on his very own golf course. He'd sell house lots to pay for the golf course and make a few bucks besides. The Button King had a very clear notion of what he wanted to do and an equally powerful uncertainty about what it would take to do it.

Sher named his project "Ironhorse," enjoying the way it combined the word for a golf club with the name of the animal that inspired his first visit to the ranch. Amtrak's passenger trains passed along the railroad tracks at the north end of the property several times a day. "Ironhorse" echoed the archaic for Sher, summoning images of the "casual, Western theme" he envisioned for his development. Two hundred houses, max. Luxury, but restrained, looped with taste. Exclusivity, privacy, staff who knew you by name. He designed a logo with a stylized locomotive rolling out above a giant horseshoe, a pair of crossed irons rampant on the nose of its steam tank. The name, however, came a lot easier than the deal. He could have floated a loan for a supertanker full of buttons, but to develop the most exclusive golf course community in Palm Beach County would take a little more than enthusiasm, even in the fired-up financial atmosphere of the unregulated Savings and Loan.

On many a night during the next several years, the Button King didn't sleep. Rising in a cold sweat at three in the morning, he would pad to the kitchen, the moon lighting his way. Visions of buttons, millions of buttons, an infinity of buttons pouring endlessly into a black hole plagued his sleep. "I'd think of all the sample cards I sewed, the rhinestones I pasted, the years and the buttons." Development costs breached the million-dollar mark. "And that," he'd say, "is a lot of fucking buttons." He would shake his head recalling this afflicted time, when the great fund of optimism that won him friends wherever he traveled threatened to dry up, leaving him with dwindling reserves of spiritual capital, not to mention the drain on his financial resources. His wife, Ardus, feared for his health. Not even the million-dollar view from his Singer Island penthouse could console him on these restless nights; there was no solace in its panoramas. The Button King was afraid of heights, but he was too rich to live any nearer the ground.

On the night we met, Sher believed Ironhorse's long, difficult gestation was behind him. Those scenes of woe had, he was confident, played to their final curtain. Happy in company, the Button King's natural state was convivial and hearty, a pesky bonhomie.

Hills and Dasher had been in the Sher penthouse before. Sher wooed his professional consultants, as if merely paying them was insufficient compensation for sharing his dream. Working for Sher was more courtship than drudgery. He liked to take the engineers and lawyers out to dinner, have them up to his apartment in The Reaches for drinks. The golf architects were used to his hospitality, and grateful for it. Their days were filled with travel, and a night with the Shers was a big step up from dinner at Denny's and a room at the End of the World Inn.

Hills sometimes stayed in the Shers' guest room, with its large and airy private bath and a perfect view of the western sky from its narrow terrace. Hills, as laconic as Sher was gregarious, found the Button King's praise irresistible. There was nothing Hills liked more than pleasing an enthusiastic client. Meeting successful people, he said, was high on the list of benefits in the golf course design business. When Sher said he was going to build the greatest golf course in Florida, there was no irony in his boast. "It should be good, Alan," Hills would say, guarded behind his enigmatic smile, waiting to see how well the course he had drawn was translated into reality before passing his own judgment.

Hills was a veteran of too many construction wars to think that his design alone, however well conceived, could meet Sher's glorified expectations. He didn't know yet who was going to build Ironhorse, so Hills was camped in the cautious range, hopeful but wary. The quality of the course builder would make as much difference to the way Ironhorse looked as the skill of its players affects the way an orchestra performs a composition. Sher had no doubt that Hills had designed nothing less than the centerpiece to "the perfect south Florida community." Hills was wily enough not to disagree when a client wanted confirmation that his course was, if not the best Hills had ever done, the best in West Palm, or in Florida, or in the southeast, or in the United States. In the golf world, the eighties were an era of accelerating expectations—better designs, better irrigation, better grasses, better maintenance, and a demand for courses so high that a job in the golf business was a ticket on the gravy train. And nobody in golf—not the developers, not the course builders, not the superintendents, not even the professional players—had a more self-satisfied and lucrative attachment to the golf boom than the architects.

Hills, even after more than twenty years in aggressive pursuit of a place among America's leading course designers, was a little stunned by the success he was now enjoying. *Golf Digest* wrote that he was the busiest golf architect in the United States. His fees were going up, but the phones at his office on the outskirts of Toledo, Ohio, weren't ringing any less. He was typically on the road four days a week, inoculated against jet lag by the force of his obsession to achieve. He was such a savvy traveler he'd found a secret parking space at the Toledo airport, one he guarded so zealously that not even his employees knew it existed. It saved him minutes on every trip. He was designing more holes at 35,000 feet than most golf architects managed on the ground.

Sher treated Hills as if he were the royal course designer, liege only to the Button King, but the truth was, Hills had forty other clients just as eager for his services. None, though, was as devoted as Sher to obliterating the line between friendship and professional service. Money nourished fellowship for Sher—the cash nexus bound his happy company.

Hills and Dasher had spent the day tramping through palmetto thickets laying out a course in Stuart, thirty miles north of Singer Island. Tomorrow they planned to walk the center lines of the proposed fairways at Ironhorse. Reviving with drinks, they were bouyed by Sher's exuberance. Mrs. Sher smiled elegantly from the far end of an array of sofas wrapped around a vast, glass-topped coffee table, its base a carved lion startled and tense, trapped under bowls of nuts and plates of cheese, its eyes locked on Mike Dasher's knee.

Offering me a drink, Sher crossed the white-lacquered oak floor to the wet bar. Florid, slightly stooped, heavier than he wished, Sher wore a light-blue checkered shirt with the top buttons—*his* buttons, one imagined—left undone, set off by a thin gold chain.

"If I'd known what I was getting in for," Sher said, handing me a glass, "I don't think I'd ever have tried this."

Ironhorse had created a network of associated professionals whose fees were a financial whirlpool, engineers and planners and lawyers willing to keep working as long as Sher's checks cleared but impervious to his risk. Hills, whose style was deliberate and cautious, tacked carefully into the winds of Sher's fervor, but the lawyers and land planners admitted in retrospect that Sher's enthusiasm seduced them into unconsciously suppressing their professional judgment. Sher had made his quest for Ironhorse's success so personal that he tended to read even the vaguest hint that there might be risks in building it as a sign of disloyalty, betraying the dream of the guy who paid their bills the day they crossed his desk and brought gifts when he visited their offices. His favorite gesture was to unstrap a Mickey Mouse watch from his wrist and press it on his companion as a kind of battle ribbon, a sign the recipient had enrolled in the campaign to build Ironhorse. These were diving watches, with quartz movements and red bezels, not cheap windup jobs. Sher was a hard guy to discourage. But the planners' and lawyers' best efforts couldn't keep the inevitable hazards from popping up, and Ironhorse was derailed more than once between Sher's epiphany and Hills's walk-through. Mrs. Sher, remembering the long and perilous four-year journey, sat in regal counterpoint to her husband's eagerness, calm and gracious in a well-turned way, tan, bejeweled, and beautiful.

Despite the shades of her classic New York accent, Mrs. Sher was not completing a tour through life identical to her husband's. Their paths had intersected in Dallas. Her style of speech was always protean, she said. In Texas she "you all"-ed. On Long Island she learned without trying to speak the language instinctive to the Button King, his tones and shrugs and phrasings flowing as naturally from her lips as they did from his. It came as no little surprise to later learn that she, as I am, is a native of southern Illinois. I detected not a single vestige of Little Egypt in her speech, none of the stretched-out vowels or homely consonants that will forever flavor my conversation. Her hospitality, though, had a familiar ease about it.

She was twenty-one, he twenty-five when they married. A mutual friend had given Sher her number, said to look up Ardus Cary the next time he was in Dallas. He was always glad he had. Once, waiting to pick her up for a date, he answered the phone in her apartment. "Who was that for?" Ardus asked after he hung up.

"Wrong number. Wanted Miss Freshborn or something."

"That's me," she said. "Ardus Cary is my *professional* name. My real name is Ardus Frischkorn."

"Well," Sher replied, "if I'd known your name was *Frischkorn* I'd never have asked you out."

"If I'd known your real name was *Sherashevsky*," she answered, "I'd never have accepted your invitation."

Now, forty years later, the Button King looked ready to launch. "Have you been there yet," he wondered, looking over his shoulder from the wet bar. "Have you seen Ironhorse?"

I'd been in Florida for about twenty-four hours and had spent half of that time with Hills and Dasher. We'd met at breakfast that morning, at the Holiday Inn in Stuart. I'd spoken with Hills on the phone, calling him from my home in Oregon to arrange a meeting. He had a deep and pleasant telephone voice, controlled and precise, carefully modulated. He gave me directions to the motel and said he'd call when he got in from Jacksonville. He forgot. I'd rung up his room at 11:30 P.M. to remind him that I was there. "Fine, fine," he said, and hung up.

Hills was in his late fifties, solidly built, with big hands and feet and a right eye that wandered slightly out of alignment behind clear-rimmed glasses. He had worn a Madras shirt, khaki pants, and gum-boots on the walk-through at the Stuart course, though the land we walked was dry. He had a distracted air about him, something more than simply concentrating on the job, as if he'd just been given a riddle that he couldn't quite answer. His manner in the field warded off casual questions. Dasher, on the other hand, seemed the giver of the riddles, the instigator, never at a loss for words, though not much given to small talk on a walk-through either. Thin and just under six feet tall, Dasher looked as if he'd just come in from bivouac, his reddish beard trimmed to a fashionable south Florida shadow. When he was working, Dasher's face had that flinty indifference movie cowboys affect, but when he said "it's beer-thirty" at the end of a working day, it was like putting heat on butter. The edges softened in an instant. There was an easy colleagiality between them, neither deference from Dasher nor commands from Hills.

When he had settled all his guests with drinks, Sher plugged a tape into the VCR. "You gotta watch this," he said. "Beautiful place."

An image flickered on the giant-screen TV that rose, like an ascending icon, from the gray-lacquered cabinet set against the apartment's outside wall. Recording his memorial to the land before it was transformed by the construction of Hills's golf course, Sher was his own Fellini—the Button King loose in the Garden. His red Porsche convertible crawled forward in first gear, subdued, across the railroad tracks as Sher recorded his arrival with a video camera slung over his right shoulder. Daisy, his skittish otter hound, rode shotgun. The images bounced as the Porsche strolled over the rails, the steel cattle gate at the entry flowing like a rainbow of electronic ribbons across the screen as the camera wiggled, then painted reality with its pause. The tape deck was digesting a bluesy rendition of Fats Waller's "Ain't Misbehavin'," but the director wanted to shift the mood. Changing tapes, he glided through the gate lubricated by the baritone caresses of Willie Nelson. "All of me, why not take all of me . . ."

A narrow paved road wound south, bisecting Ironhorse's 354 acres. Islands of Sabal palms and scrub pines floated in a sea of forage grasses that had grown shoulder-high until Sher leased the pastures. A small herd of Santa Gertrudis cattle grazed the meadows to the height of short rough. The golf course plan created for Ironhorse is indifferent to this road, which leads to a two-story brick house where the previous owners of the property lived. The golf course plan lays over the ranch like a palimpsest, just as the ranch erased wetlands to create dry pasture. The stable where Carrie's horses boarded was east of the house, just beyond the chain-link fence that kept the stock out of the front yard. All the pastures were theirs, an empire of grass. As empty as the pastures while Sher tried to get his golf course up and running, the house was going to serve as the job shack for Ironhorse, Ltd.

The domain we were entering is as flat as the rest of south Florida west of the Atlantic coastal ridge. It was part of the primordial flood plain of Lake Okeechobee. Like most of Palm Beach County, Ironhorse is only fifteen to nineteen feet above sea level. Inside the coastal ridge, south Florida is like a giant spoon, with the lake as its low point. It's tilted just enough to let water drain slowly south, through the Everglades, the river of grass. Without drainage canals and water control, Ironhorse and most of the rest of the land on the west side of the coastal ridge would be inundated a good portion of the year. Ironhorse's beauty is vegetative, not topographical.

As Sher the auteur approached the barn, the horses drifted over, sticking their noses into the Porsche, looking for a treat. Sher usually brought carrots. The lens's distortion pulled Charlie the quarter horse's mouth into a wide, silly grin. Oblivious in their tenantry, the horses were facing eviction when the big Cats came in to rip up the earth. Carrie once again was looking for her ten acres.

Sher ran the camera lovingly across the landscape. "See those wax myrtles there?" He pointed out some indifferent shrubbery in the foreground dwarfed by a canopy of pines. "A friend of mine bought two of those things from a nursery—one hundred and thirty-five dollars he paid! Look out there—we got millions of 'em!"

The trees communed with the sky, gave scale to the horizon. Hills, smiling shyly, looked up from the crackers and cheese to call the image filling the Shers' living room "Alan's Eden." Tomorrow I would see it, joining Hills and Dasher as they walked the clearing lines. Tonight though, it was time to eat and celebrate. Sher turned off the TV with one of a battery of remote controls clustered above the astonished lion. He rewound the tape on the VCR with another. He picked up the portable phone to dial Rafaele's, his favorite Italian restaurant, to have another place set. He hadn't expected me. Don and Carrie were meeting us there. It was late January, still in the tourist season. The maître d' greeted Sher as an old friend at the door.

Sitting to my right, Hills dined with the breathless intensity of a hungry adolescent. He spooned the dressing from his salad bowl, chased every pea across his plate. He ate pretty much the way he worked. Walking Willoughby, the infant course in Stuart where we'd spent the day, Hills trekked without rest, stopping only to survey the landscape, straining to translate his vision: seeing greens where thick underbrush grew, balls flying through stands of palms, shots skirting the edges of imaginary ponds. Questions confused him while he was working, derailed his concentration. An aural gap, a neural pause, clicked across his responses. He plowed through interruptions the way he ate—focused, engaged, indifferent to any mission but his own. The cadence of his speech was marked by odd pauses, stops and starts, as if he were constantly censoring himself or had learned English not in the crib but from a book that he had to consult before speaking. "Uh-huh," he would utter, distractedly, "uh-huh, uh-huh," an agreement without content, a mantra, resonant and deep, a verbal barricade tossed up against any further interrogation.

Dinner was restful and convivial—pasta and wine and chewy bread, punctuated by toasts to Ironhorse. Before serving dessert, the waiter whisked up the bread crumbs by running a little black box with brushes on its bottom across the red-and-white-checked tablecloth. "Damn," said Dash, "that thing works better'n a chicken."

By ten o'clock, Hills was ready to call it a day. Yesterday he'd been in Atlanta, visiting a job site north of the city where he was working with a Japanese developer, then had flown in last night to West Palm, rented a car, and driven to Stuart. Dash had driven down from his home in Orlando to meet Hills. They'd spent ten hours walking Willoughby in bright sunshine, motored the thirty-five miles back to West Palm, checked into a motel, showered, and then headed out to Singer Island to meet the Shers. Hills and Dasher agreed that a six forty-five breakfast date would give them plenty of time to eat and get to Ironhorse by eight the next morning. In the afternoon, Joshua Muss, the new general partner in Ironhorse, Ltd., was due in to check on the progress of the work.

MOST PEOPLE THINK that to build a golf course you just clear a few trees, toss out some grass seed, wait a couple of weeks to mow, and then set out the flag sticks. Dasher, who spends a lot of time in airplanes flying between job sites, says that when he tells an enquiring seatmate what he does for a living a common response is a sort of flaccid incredulity, like telling a joke nobody gets. "A lot of 'em say, 'I didn't know they *built* those things.' The real sophisticated ones ask me, 'Are you Robert Trent Jones or are you Pete Dye?' They *know* I ain't Jack Nicklaus."

When I took up golf a half-dozen years ago I shared that naive view. I was a golfing pilgrim, always looking for a new place to play. I liked variety. I played courses cut in the foothills of Oregon's Mount Hood, carved into sandy coastal dunes, tucked into bottomlands, cradled along creek beds. Enjoying their parklike settings, the cool emerald plains, I thought little about the shape or character of the courses themselves. I was preoccupied, too, with figuring out how to play. The kick-ass athletic bluster I'd learned as a schoolboy proved an unworthy approach to golf. I needed to hone my eye for subtlety and reprogram my sporting synapses, cultivating patience and tolerating caution. Playing a course called Three Rivers near Longview, Washington, forty miles north of my Oregon home, lifted my perceptual veil. I was seeing something new.

Three Rivers was built on ash the Army Corps of Engineers dredged from the Toutle and Cowlitz rivers near their confluence with the Columbia after the eruption of Mount Saint Helens in 1980. Three

Rivers had a reputation as a great place to play when it rained, and on most winter days in the Northwest it at least drizzles. The deep fill at Three Rivers soaked up water the way Congress absorbs rhetoric. "Designing a good golf course is five percent common sense and ninety-five percent drainage," I once heard an architect say, "and if you don't have enough common sense, put in more drainage."

The designer of Three Rivers had the drainage problem licked before he started. A half a dozen showers, three thunderstorms, and a minor deluge wouldn't begin to test the capacity of the great sandy sponge on which it sits. Three Rivers was the first course I ever saw that looked brand-new, that was obviously built from scratch. The young trees planted along its fairways were too small to affect play, so you could tee off in about a ninety-degree arc without getting in too much trouble. You could miss by two fairways and still have a second shot. There were occasional bare spots where the grass hadn't taken. A handful of ducks nested along the narrow shelves at the edges of its ponds, but they seemed vulnerable and lost in these wide-open spaces. As I played Three Rivers, I wondered why the first holes on each nine were par fives, why the finishing holes were so tough, and if it was a good idea to play the eighteenth hole into the setting sun. Why had the course taken the shape it did, followed the routing it took, played with the pace and rhythm it had? There was nothing to start with but an ashy plateau, a gray plain with not a single natural feature to emphasize or overcome. Evergreen hills rose off in the distance in every direction, the Cowlitz flowed by on the right of the back nine's outgoing holes, but there was nothing on the ground to suggest a shape the course might take. When I later had a chance to ask Robert Muir Graves, the California-based architect who designed Three Rivers, what the Kelso Elks Club, Three Rivers' owner, wanted for its new course, he said, "Their main interest, as I recall, was a bar that stayed open till two and seventy-five-cent drinks."

Graves gave the Elks a good golf course but left them on their own to run Happy Hour, a chance to confirm the old adage that a golf club is the only organization that can drink itself into solvency. Three Rivers was a revelation. It piqued my curiosity about how golf courses are designed and built. Graves had created a golfing venue from nothing, sculpting the dredged gray ash into a manicured landscape.

The American Society of Golf Course Architects (ASGCA), of which Jones was a founder and Graves and Dye both former presidents, may promote professional standards among its members, but it has no control over who can practice golf course architecture. It can decide who to admit to its august company, and it rarely does that without quarrel. Not every golf course architect belongs to the ASGCA—neither Desmond Muirhead nor Joe Lee, two architects well known for their work in Florida, is a member. Most of the big-name course designers are in the ASGCA, but that's a short list. In 1989, the ASGCA had only eighty-four full-fledged members, flanked by a couple of dozen associates who would join them after a two- to three-year probation.

It was through an inquiry to the society that I first heard of Hills. Though anonymous compared to the Joneses, *père et fils,* or Dye or Nicklaus, Hills was nonetheless working from coast to coast and border to border, in deserts and wetlands, in climates warm and cold, in terrain that ranged from the Rocky Mountains to the rolling hills of Kentucky's horse country. His best-known courses, though, were set in the smooth horizontal reaches of south Florida. Brent Wadsworth, the founder of the world's largest and best golf construction company, thought Hills was peerless working on flat ground.

There's a bit of a coals-to-Newcastle flavor to building a golf course in Palm Beach County. There are already more golf courses there than in any county in the United States—with 140 and counting, Palm Beach has more than many entire states. Aside from the fact that south Florida is the administrative capital of golf's imperial world, and that there's a greater concentration of golfers there than anyplace else, there's another good reason to choose south Florida as a place to watch a golf course in the making, as I wanted to do. A course built on flat ground, like Three Rivers or Ironhorse, shows the human touch more clearly than a course set on hilly ground, where the architect's artifice is sometimes difficult to detect. Before heavy earth-moving equipment liberated the golf architect from the limitations of natural terrain, much as the steel frame freed building architects to push giant towers toward the sky, golfers sought land "which resembles in character and contour links-land." An amateur golfer named Robert Hunter, writing nearly seventy years ago in the first American book on golf course design, thought avoiding wholly flat land, then as now the standard wisdom, was "a mistaken view. Not only some of the most popular but some of the most interesting courses have been made on flat land. As the greens can be placed anywhere, the layout in general should be without a flaw. The length of holes will not be governed by certain situations which must be used, but will be decided by ideal considerations . . . one can mould the surface at will, and create effects and problems which can but rarely be found provided by nature."

Sher assumed that Ironhorse's layout would be "without a flaw," but Hills was hardly operating in the pure realm of imagination. The constraints were not in the land, but in the juggling for space between the housing pods, as the land planners call the parcels devoted to housing, the excavated lakes, and the designated wetlands. The golf course at Ironhorse was a dialogue between real estate and recreation, not the unencumbered declaration of a golfing ideal. It's a lot easier to design a course on land devoted exclusively to golf, where you can avoid what land planners disparagingly call a sausage links, its fairways strung out in a long, meandering line so that from above they look like the green silhouette of a giant bratwurst chain. Three Rivers is what's called a "core course," a throwback to an earlier era in course design, where the holes are compact and contiguous, like a larval clutch. Most of the classic country club layouts, which didn't need to sell the land about them to justify their existence, are core courses. About the only core courses built these days are public or daily fee courses.

The National Golf Foundation (NGF), which has its headquarters in Jupiter, about ten miles from Ironhorse, is the propaganda arm of the golf business. Funded by the equipment makers and the course builders and architects, the NGF encourages golf's growth. People who know nothing else about golf are likely to have heard or read the NGF's prediction that we "need to build a course every day between now and the year 2000 to keep up with demand." Alerted to the dangers, we probably won't awaken one morning to the unpleasant realization that we're short on golf courses. Demand is surging as we enter the nineties, even as the impediments to building new courses proliferate. As Bob Graves says, "Anybody in the golf business who's not busy now should reevaluate his career plans."

In 1988, according to the NGF, 211 new courses opened in the United States. An additional 700 or more were in planning or under construction in the U.S. and a very large number under way around the world. The Japanese passion for golf has driven the price of country club memberships there into the millions—dollars, not yen—and at those prices, building a golf course can make economic sense even on land selling for hundreds of thousands of dollars an acre. The Japanese are pouring millions into golf in the U.S.—in 1990 a Japanese company bought Pebble Beach, one of golf's temples. The Japanese have spearheaded a course-building mania in Thailand, and Korea has taken the plunge, typically building courses with two greens per hole in hopes that the grass on at least one will survive the harsh winters. There is a golf building boom in Spain, 150 new courses underway in France, and more than a little interest in Scandinavia. "Swedish players are very careful with their expensive balls," a Swedish architect wrote to an American colleague, "and don't like too much water." Florida would be a Swedish golfer's idea of Hell. Robert Trent Jones, Jr., designed a course for Moscow seventy years after the American ambassador to St. Petersburg, David Francis, laid out Russia's first course, nine primitive holes in the little town of Viatka, where Allied diplomats enduring temporary exile staved off boredom with a daily round while the Whites and Reds slugged it out across the steppes for control of the Czar's disintegrating empire during the Russian civil war. Arnold Palmer's firm built eighteen holes in China. Golf is a strong cultural currency in the global marketplace.

Geoffrey Cornish, the Amherst, Massachusetts-based doyen of New England golf architects, keeps track of the worldwide boom in course construction. Along with Ron Whitten, an attorney in Topeka, Kansas, who moonlights as the editor on golf architecture for *Golf Digest*, Cornish wrote *The Golf Course*, a history of golf course architecture. Now in its third edition, *The Golf Course* has an appendix whose goal is to list every golf course ever built. Cornish estimates that of the 21,000 courses in the world, about 13,000 are in the United States. Forty were designed by Hills.

Ironhorse made the 1987 revised edition of *The Golf Course* when it was still a mote in Alan Sher's eye. When Cornish asked Hills for a list of his completed courses, he thought for sure Ironhorse would be ready for play by 1987. But in 1987 the Button King was having nightmares and Ironhorse was a bundle of drawings in a shipping tube in the basement of Hills's office. Sher, keeping his hopes alive, expected Ironhorse to take its place among the thirty-five new courses built in Florida in 1988. He was celebrating that belief the night we met. Ironhorse, by this reckoning, would be somewhere near the one thousandth course built in the Sunshine State.

A golf course takes time to build because there is dirt to move and there are lakes to dig and drainage pipes to install and grass to grow. The process of getting a golf course from the drawing board to the tee shots of the first happy foursome is difficult not merely because of the physical demands of the work but because the political and financial setting is complex and laden with hazards as difficult as any ever designed by Hills. I watched Ironhorse ascend along the edge of the Loxahatchee Slough, hard by the vast, flat wetness of the Everglades. I traveled deep into the land of golf.

2

Walkabout

WHEN HILLS and Dasher crossed the cattle gate at Ironhorse the next morning, company was waiting. Peter Aquart, whose engineering firm had calculated the storage capacity of Ironhorse's lakes and would plat the house lots whose sale the golf course was supposed to inspire, was leaning against the fender of the kind of job truck loggers in the Northwest call, with appropriate candor, a "crummy," looking over a large aerial photograph of the Ironhorse site with Debbie Allen. Allen, a landscape architect with Urban Design Studio, the land planners, was there to tag and identify specimen trees and locate donor sites for tree transplanting. It's possible to relocate pines with trunks up to eight inches in diameter using a tree spade, a bright-yellow hydraulically powered scoop whose four giant trowel-like blades encircle a tree and cut deeply into the soil, their tips digging at an angle to create an inverted cone. The spade then lifts the tree, its roots and compacted soil tightly compressed within the blades, and tilts it gently back onto the bed of the truck whose engine supplies the spade's power. The truck hauls the tree to its new home, digs a receptacle for the next transplant, and takes the dirt plug back to fill the hole left at the donor site. Cypresses even larger than the pines can, at least through the end of the spring, also stand the shock of transplantation. Quite large palms, which have none of the pine's delicacy, are easily moved. The palm's roots wrap in a loose spiral

19

that looks like braids of matted hair descending straight into the ground. The palms are as hardy as the pines are fragile. If a pine's roots are disturbed, or if the ground above it is compacted or if soil is loaded around its trunk, a pine will die. Palms can have dirt piled around them nearly to the top of their trunks, or be rudely pulled from the ground by a backhoe, dragged to a new home, heeled roughly into the ground, and still survive.

Superimposed over the aerial photograph Aquart and Allen were studying was a schematic drawing, sort of a stick-figure version of Hills's golf course. Early in Ironhorse's planning, UDS had done a map identifying eight basic clusters of plant types at Ironhorse. A hand-lettered note at the bottom of the map said, PRESERVATION OF MATURE PLANT MATERIAL IS AN OVERALL OBJECTIVE BECAUSE OF THE NATURE & THEME OF THE DEVELOPMENT.

During the past couple of weeks, surveyors from Aquart's company, using a small bulldozer to gnaw a path to sight down, had staked out the center lines for the fairways shown on this map and other drawings. Starting with the tee locations, the surveyors set markers every fifty feet along the ideal line of a golf ball's flight, wrapping red surveyor's tape around the tops of flat, lathlike stakes. On the sides of the stakes they wrote numbers indicating the distance from the tee—+ 50', + 100', and so on. Where the center lines turned at a slight angle right or left, the stakes bore the initials "DL" for "dogleg." Hills had a copy of the grading plan his Toledo office had prepared folded under his arm and checked it against the aerial photograph to locate himself. The old entry road across the railroad tracks, which would be used as a construction road while the course was built and then abandoned, ran between the future fifth green and sixth tee. In the aerial photograph, the road slithered from the north end of the site down to the house at the far south end, looking from above like the sepulcher of an ancient creek.

Hills and Dasher wanted the center lines located so they could walk the course's spine, its "route," to see what trees needed clearing and what could be saved. Everyone carried rolls of pink surveyor's tape to tag a set of initial clearing boundaries about fifty feet on either side of the center line. Debbie Allen hoped to identify salvageable trees within these clearing limits. Hills walked the center, while Dasher worked a perimeter, struggling through dense underbrush woven with myrtles, palmettos, and Brazilian peppers. Jon Harpman, a nephew of Joshua Muss's from Oklahoma starting his developer's apprenticeship at Ironhorse, tagged the side opposite Dasher. Educated at the University of Oklahoma, Harpman was teaching tennis at a country club in Oklahoma City when Muss summoned him to Florida. Shy and tentative and obviously well brought up, Harpman was eager, attentive, and good at introductions.

"Synchronize your Mickeys," Dasher called out, ready to plunge into the fray. It was going to be a long, hot day. We started at the first hole, fording a nearly dry drainage ditch just west of the road. Our path was cluttered with uprooted plants, mainly wax myrtles, as we began. The first hole is a dogleg right, a par four of 386 yards. There's a lake planned to the left of the first tee, and across the water will stand the clubhouse. The tenth hole runs parallel to the first, but it doglegs left rather than right. Separating these holes is a squat forest of myrtles floating on an ocean of muck. The plan shows a practice range succeeding here. The two nines roughly rotate in opposite directions—the front nine plays clockwise, the back counterclockwise. Both nines start and finish near the clubhouse, which is almost dead center on the site. They're not really loops, though, because they fold back on themselves at a couple of points. The front nine walks the north half of the property, the back nine the south.

The main entry bisects the two nines. Three holes cluster at the entry, so there will be no mistaking the impression that you're entering a world dominated by golf. The first and tenth holes play in a southwesterly direction if you hit the ball where you're supposed to, so the morning sun will never shine in the eyes of players starting early in the day, say about the time our walk-through began. It's a cloudless, bright, invigorating day.

There are a handful of obvious principles guiding golf course design, sort of the equivalent of making sure you get an elevator in a high rise rather than hard and fast rules about details like green size, or bunkering, or tee shapes, or even routing. These principles are easy to summarize. Avoid holes playing east and west, and take special care that the first hole and the finishing hole don't play into the sun. Keep the first and tenth tees and the practice range near the pro shop. It's a lot easier to keep track of the golfers and coordinate starting times when the staff can see the golfers. Aim the practice tee north to keep the sun at the golfers' backs. Make the two nines look and play about the same. Avoid back-to-back par fives and back-to-back par threes. A typical course has ten par fours, four par threes, and four par fives, for a total par of seventy-two, though there are fine golf courses with pars of seventy or seventy-one. Geoff Cornish thinks the first golf courses were simply single holes. The early links-land courses, "on common public land unrestricted by boundaries," had as few as five holes or as many as twenty-five. When the Old Course at St. Andrews was remodeled in 1764, paring its original twenty-two holes to eighteen, it established a pattern that nearly every course since has followed. As with other English measures, like the pound, the foot, and the hand, it's an arbitrary standard based on something real, a corporeal gauge. The idea of eighteen holes as somehow necessary and pure, as *ideal,* solidified in the nineteenth century, as the spread of golf coincided with the Industrial Age's worship of replicability and mechanical precision. By its appearance in the United States toward the end of the nineteenth century, golf seemed to its New World devotees as inevitably yolked to a playing ground of eighteen holes as American prosperity was to Destiny.

Some architects also subscribe to the getaway rule, which holds that you don't make the first couple of holes too tough. Avoid a long carry over water off the first tee, for example. Some people will top their ball into the lake, which means they'll have to tee up another shot, slowing down play. There's also the emotional toll of making triple bogey on the first hole to consider. As the British anthropologist Iona Opie once said in another context, there are often architectural solutions to psychological problems. Finally, never make either of the first two holes a par three. Short holes, oddly enough, take the longest to play, because the golfers on the tee have to wait for the group in front of them to putt before they can tee off. It takes a lot longer to putt than it does to hit a shot from the fairway, so play tends to bunch up at the par threes unless they're well spaced within the general progression of the course. No one likes a long wait on the first tee. That's about it for general principles. Every one of these rules is violated on some great golf course, but if you have a chance to follow them, it's a good idea. A golf course, like God, is in the details.

Hills wasn't thinking about general principles as he pushed down the first fairway, scanning right and left, turning back to ponder where he'd just been. I found it difficult from the start to get a fix on the scale of the holes, to hold their proportions in mind. When you're playing golf, you measure distance by the yard. A short hole is 150 yards long, a long one 550. The surveyors, however, were working in fifty-*foot* intervals. It was harder to walk fifty feet over these recently cleared center lines than to stroll fifty yards down a groomed fairway.

The vegetation lay in a jumble, like Pick-Up-Stix. There was a brutality to the clearing, even on this innocent scale. We climbed over the state tree of Florida, the Sabal, or cabbage, palm, bark thick and gathered, like the hide of an elephant or a rhino, and clumsily pulled our feet out of thick, clutching mud. Standing along this inaugural incision, I began to get a tentative sense of the scale of intrusion required to transform this flat canvas into the familiar and seductive landscape of golf. Clearing the center line was nothing compared to the annihilation that the clearing for the fairways would bring. The surveyors' small dozer scratched a path a few yards wide; the clearing contractor would flay open more than a hundred acres.

Debbie Allen worried that the dozers had already cut too wide a swath. Ironhorse didn't have a clearing permit yet. The surveyors' sight lines were not supposed to exceed five feet, she noted, but in places where the Cat had to back up and get a run at its target they were easily twenty to twenty-five feet wide. Dasher, wearing a straw boater, a white golf shirt, and brown braces to keep his Levi's up, shrugged off Allen's fretting. Hills took no notice at all. "Tie as high as you can," he called out to Harpman, barely visible behind a thick stand of cabbage palms, "so the dozers can see the ribbon."

You had to clear to build a golf course, and the amount of vegetation taken down so far, though rough and indecorous, was trivial when compared to the fields of vegetation that would eventually be cleared and burned. The front nine traveled across all of the representative plant clusters that Urban Design Studio—UDS for short—had identified. The first hole started across myrtle, then entered a mixed stand of large pines and palms, and finally plunged into a very dense stand of cabbage palms that ran from the dogleg to the green. They'd have to clear about 150 feet on either side of the center line to create enough room for the golfing corridors.

There were three exotic species growing widely around Ironhorse that Allen said would probably have to be eliminated as a condition of the construction permits. The Brazilian pepper that Dasher and Harpman had to occasionally fight through was a dark-green-leafed plant with bright red berries growing mainly along Ironhorse's drainage canals. There was a lot of it north of the first green and even more near the old entry road, by the fifth green and the sixth tee. It groped over the tops of young pines, growing in a wild profusion that violated the decorum of the native species. The Brazilian pepper, *Schinus terebinthifolius*, was introduced to south Florida as an ornamental plant, but turned pest when its seeds were spread by resident Florida mockingbirds, wintering robins, and, fittingly, an exotic bird escaped to the wild, the Indian red-whiskered bulbul. It grew best on disturbed soil, places where some or all of the native plants had been eradicated, usually near wax myrtle, *Myrica cerifera*. The pepper is a vigorous and opportunistic invader. Standing alone it grows ten feet high, its branches weaving into a thick tangle, but when it can hook a limb on a handy pine host it climbs to twenty feet or more. The pepper's presence suggested that the natural history of Ironhorse was more complicated than the flattering portrait on the Button King's memorial video.

Downed melaleuca trees, their exfoliating bark peeling like a stack of singed papers, also crisscrossed our path. *Melaleuca leucadendron* is an Australian native, sensibly known there as the paper-bark tree. It has an extraordinary capacity to absorb water and to survive drought and fire. It's also known as the punk tree because the feel of its spongy bark resembles that of a rotting or "punky" pine. I peeled back the orangish layers of bark from a fallen tree. They had a powdery feel, as if they had been dusted with talcum. They folded like vellum. Debbie Allen told me that John D. MacArthur, a millionaire insurance man and banker from Chicago who acquired tens of thousands of acres of south Florida wetlands before his death in 1978, had introduced the melaleuca to Florida, casting its seeds from an airplane. He hoped the trees would act as the biological equivalent of the drainage ditches that the Army Corps of Engineers and agribusiness tycoons were dredging across the wetlands, saving the expense of a dragline. The word "wetlands" was designated in the midsixties as a catchall term for all those fecund regions once variously known as swamps and bogs and marshes, miasmatic and drear, that generations of farmers and engineers did their best to destroy. The neutral "wetlands" was supposed to strip the old words of their pejorative baggage, but it signifies an even more horrible reality to developers, who want to cover their ears when they hear it. Wetlands are geographical whooping cranes, endangered and protected by federal law. You can't legally fill or drain a swamp anymore, and from a developer's point of view, as they're fond of saying, "If it's wet, you don't own it." In the old days standing water wouldn't inhibit a good Florida land-sales pitch, but in the modern era dry land was indispensable to development. Just about the only developable dry land west of the turnpike was acreage drained for agricultural use. Developers looking for dirt turned to old farms and ranches, like Ironhorse.

Dredges and pumps were the old mechanical ways to liberate land from beneath the water table. The melaleucas were more insidious, a biological gun cocked at the head of the Everglades. Unlike dredges and pumps, the melaleuca was not subject to regulation. No bureaucrat could stop its spread by denying it a permit. Impervious to statutes, the paperbark kept extending its range, and no one had figured out a way to control it. Biologists thought that with careful management it could be eliminated on a small scale at places like Ironhorse. In the long run, that might help halt its invasion.

If you knew anything about MacArthur's ruthless style and boundless ego, Allen's tale of the melaleuca's introduction was a plausible one, but it was apocryphal, just another episode in the MacArthur legend. Anyone who would first abandon his infant children and then, having accumulated millions, refuse to support them, as MacArthur had done, likely had it in him to destroy an ecosystem, especially old soggy marshes that weren't doing anybody a damn bit of good. MacArthur *had* transformed a considerable portion of Palm Beach County wetlands into marketable real estate in the sixties and seventies, but he was innocent of this particular plot to dry up the Everglades. The melaleuca was introduced long before MacArthur started buying up the huge tracts whose substantial remnants are now controlled by the John D. and Catherine T. MacArthur Foundation, dispenser of the so-called genius grants. Palm Beach Gardens, Ironhorse's nearest neighbor as the crow flies, is a MacArthur town.

Nowadays Florida's environmentalists look on the invasion of exotic plants with horror, but up to thirty years ago, when it was official policy to drain the wetlands, the argument was about who should get *credit* for bringing in the melaleuca. Members of a nineteenth-century religious community near Fort Myers called the Koreshan Unity were probably the first Floridians to grow melaleuca from imported seed.

The Koreshans were followers of the prophet Cyrus Teed, who called himself "Koresh" and imagined a New Jerusalem with ten million inhabitants rising along the Estero River on Florida's gulf coast. His metropolitan yearnings set a high standard for grandiose development, though no developer since, so far as I know, has adopted his marketing strategy, preferring straight cash to conversion.

Teed was a solemn-looking fellow with a square face who wore high collars and persuaded his small following not just to join him in creating the New Jerusalem but to surrender to his care all their worldly goods. Compared to marketing golf course lots, that seems like a tough sell. Under Teed's tutelage the Koreshans turned into good farmers and nurserymen, despite their urban origins, and created a thriving community of 125 souls. Until Koresh died, Koreshan children were reared apart from their parents, a practice borrowed from the British upper classes, who had raised it to a high art in the nineteenth century with the system of public schools. "British public schools fit a man for public life," wrote an alumnus, "and ruin him for eternity." The Koreshans were indifferent to public life, being without an empire to administer, but they were eager for eternal success.

Koreshan theology was part of the broad river of American utopianism that spawned the Shakers, Mormons, and other proselytizing communitarians. Even Ironhorse shares, in a small and unconscious way, in that old utopian impulse, secularized and inspired by profits rather than a prophet. Here's the very first line from Sher's original prospectus for Ironhorse: "The perfect South Florida community—it's a concept that has inspired countless dreams, endless discussions and numerous disappointing attempts." The Koreshans were familiar with dreams and disappointments.

What set the Koreshans apart was Teed's discovery—delivered to him during the same out-of-body "illumination" that revealed his name—that the universe is a hollow sphere with a circumference of 25,000 miles. We live on the inside. According to an official Koreshan chronicle, "the sun was an electromagnetic battery in the center of the sphere with a light and dark side revolving once every 24 hours." Using a machine Teed invented called the rectilinator, "the Koreshan geodetic staff" proved that the curvature of the earth is concave. This great proof was demonstrated on a beach in Naples, but no plaque or shrine marks the spot. Golfers might like the Koreshan geometries. I *think* you'd always be hitting downhill. Putts would roll toward the hole like a radish drifting to the bottom of a salad bowl. Drainage might be a problem, but a good Koreshan engineer with access to a rectilinator could work that out. Koresh strikes me as the totemic theologian of his adopted state, visionary of a seasonless and uniform world, isolated and contained, a place a lot like Florida.

Among Koresh's friends were his neighbor Thomas Edison, who might have helped him out with that electromagnetic battery business, and the intrepid plant explorer David Fairchild, an admirer of the Koreshans' gardens who stomped on their glory a bit by claiming in his autobiography that *he* introduced the melaleuca. He called it the "cajuput," raised it in his exotic garden near Miami, and helped "disseminate it throughout South Florida." Some people blame Fairchild now for the Brazilian pepper, too.

Once it got a foothold, the melaleuca set off across the wetlands at a botanical gallop, but it kept getting help it hardly needed anyway. A version of Allen's seeds-from-an-airplane story turns out to be true, but it doesn't involve MacArthur. Melaleuca seeds were dumped from light planes flying over the Everglades in the thirties, both to dry up the wetlands and provide food for honeybees. That was twenty years before MacArthur found his way to Florida. The honey scheme was a dead end. "Apiculturists at the University of Florida," a study from the late fifties dryly noted, "regard melaleuca honey as a most unpalatable commodity." "[T]he melaleuca," that study observed with clinical reserve, "is well adapted to its new habitat and is completely capable of naturalization without any artificial aid." The melaleuca was, in fact, the most successful invader of Florida since Andrew Jackson.

The melaleuca is wonderfully adapted to drought and fire. Rather than flowering seasonally, it stores its seed in pods for several years or until disaster calls on the mature plant to give its all for the species. When a melaleuca is burned it releases its tiny seeds, as it will also do when it is cut down. Eradicating it is tedious and difficult. It's a botanical Hydra—kill one, thousands more appear.

There were relatively few melaleucas at Ironhorse, but many Australian pines. The Australians, as they are called, are colonizing deciduous trees that were introduced to Florida, according to Allen, as windbreaks for citrus groves. There are a couple of species called Australians, but they look pretty much the same. Ironhorse's Australians are *Casuarina equisetifolia.* They grow on dry ground, so they don't compete much with wetland species like melaleuca and cypress. The Australians do especially well on spoil piles, dikes, and berms, any spot of dry land reaching well above existing grades. They grow rapidly, their wispy limbs ascending as their long needles droop. Instead of a crown that outlines the foliage around the tree's top, the sort of cauliflower shape of the native pines, the Australians grow out and up, as if they had been hung upside-down, shaken, and then replanted. Next to a native slash pine, *Pinus elliotti,* the Australians

look unkempt, wild punks at a finishing school. The parent Australians send out lateral roots close to the surface, runners that propa-
gate new trees. Dasher says they're lousy around a golf course because
the colonizing roots will push up through the turf grass. The roots run
just under the surface, and if you have the bad luck to land above one
when you're playing golf, you won't know it's there and may catch
your club on it.

As with the other aliens, unchecked the Australians would domi-
nate their invaded habitat. They are especially evident on the west
side of the property. Allen walked me through a stand of Australians
not far from where the second tee will go, standing atop the spoil
from a drainage canal. Nothing grew under its canopy, no birds nested
in its bows. A thick brown mat of needles cushioned our feet. Allen
picked up a handful. They were not degrading. Phytotoxic leeching
clears the ground of botanical competitors. No little creatures foraged
here. A dense stand of Australians is a kind of living neutron bomb.
"People love them," Allen said. "They say, 'Look, we've finally got a
real tree to grow in Florida.' "

Sher drove up about nine-thirty on one of the red ATVs he kept in
the barn, four-wheeled motorcycles whose large soft tires make them
as stable as a drunk on an escalator. Daisy the otter hound loped
along the perimeter of the clearing, avoiding contact with strangers.
Daisy was a dog without a mission, a random, curly-haired canine
missile who approached life in the grip of a profound trepidation. An
otter hound, judging by Daisy, is an anti-golden retriever, the genet-
ical invert of those loving animals. Perhaps her fear this day was not
biological but a reading of her master's mood. In blue jeans, cowboy
boots, and a Mets hat, Sher was subdued as he watched Hills looking
for the site of the third tee. He'd seen Ironhorse enough not to want
to join our trek. The ATVs were his preferred mode for perusing his
dreamland. He liked to take visitors for tours on them, gunning over
pastures and blasting across canals. Fun was at the heart of his in-
tercourse with Ironhorse, whether he was rumbling about on the
ATVs or thinking about playing golf. Two ATVs had been stolen, so
the fleet was down to two small Hondas. Security was lax since the
caretaker, who lived in an apartment above the barn, left the year
before. Nobody was growing marijuana anymore under the protec-
tive canopy of the trees, but there were piles of trash dumped here
and there, the ghostlike residue of an abandoned place. When you
see junk in somebody's yard, you think the occupants must lead

messy lives. The same abandoned debris can also make you wonder what drove those dwellers away. The rusting hulks of old appliances, rotting wooden crates, and tin-roofed sheds were destined for some random resting place under an Ironhorse fairway.

Sher offered to chase deli for lunch. Hills kept moving, pausing only long enough to smile and wave at Sher. Lunch would be good, he said, he'd like lunch. His technique, if it can be called that, was to look down at the folded drawing, then trace a line with his eyes across the horizon, then back to the drawing, checking foregrounds and backgrounds and summoning a fuller version of the holes to mind. The third hole was going to be a short par three, with a pond on its left and a parcel of zero-lot-line houses on its right. ("Zeros" are smaller lots with no side-yard setback. Tucking a house onto one side of a lot creates an illusion of space and reduces maintenance. Ironhorse's larger lots are called "estates," or sometimes "villas.") Despite what the drawings showed, what we were seeing was a raft of wax myrtles adrift in black muck, with an occasional dahoon holly or groundsel bush mixed in, proof, if the muck were not enough, that the ground on which we now stood had once been wetlands.

The muck made it impossible to walk the center line for the third hole, so we were skirting the perimeter, rounding the telltale wax myrtles when Sher showed up. The surveyors' dozer had gotten stuck when it tried to cut the center line, a rehearsal for the troubles the course builders would face. Dasher shook his head when he looked back at the muck. It helped explain the melaleuca's old appeal. Muck, Dasher said, would capture dozers the way a spider's web gathers flies, the struggle securing the prey. The thin surface of water standing on the muck made it shine like polished ebony. Muck was not as slick as marl, which would make a dozer's tracks spin, robbing it of its strength, so that a D8 Caterpillar riding on marl could barely knock down a sapling. Marl made clearing difficult, but muck was unforgiving to the heavy equipment that breached its fragile surface. Muck is organic, the product of years of slowly degrading marshy plants. The deposits in south Florida's wetlands are the accumulation of 10,000 years. Around Lake Okeechobee, the muck was thirty feet deep when farmers first started draining the Everglades a hundred years ago. Muck oxidizes when it's exposed to the air, and the thick deposits in the sugar-cane fields west of Ironhorse have, in some cases, shrunk to only six feet of soil. Dry muck can burn. Marl, on the other hand, is an inorganic mix of clay and calcium carbonate that

powders when it's dry. Most of the marl at Ironhorse is on the west
side of the property. Water tends to puddle above the marl's waxy
surface just as it accumulates above the saturated muck. In the sandy
soils, the water percolates through quickly. Wax myrtles love the
muck, so spotting myrtles helps landscape architects like Allen identify old wetlands. Almost anything will grow in muck. It looks like
potting soil. Not much grows on marl.

Where there wasn't muck, the dozer had turned back patches of
the thin soil to expose thousands of seashells, bleached white and
friable, packed in a loose sandy aggregate. It was the first evidence I'd
seen of the famous geological fact of south Florida's infancy, that this
is land only recently risen from the sea. There were large conchlike
shells, scallops, and the remains of tiny spiral-shelled augur mollusks
which seemed too improbably fragile to have survived.

Allen pointed out several small stands of *Taxodium distichum*, bald
cypress, their knees rising in the wet soil around them, looking like
a playhouse cemetery of tiny eroding brown tombstones. Botanists
aren't sure what these knees do, but the cypress is well adapted to
water—needs water, in fact, for its seeds to germinate—and the knees
may help nourish the plant during the wet season. One cypress head,
or cluster of trees, stood between the site of the first green and the
second tee, in wet, poorly drained soil of a type called Winder fine
sand. A scouting party of melaleuca was stalking its edges.

Much later in the day and a half a mile further south, nearer the
proposed site for the twelfth green, Allen spotted "the most beautiful
red swamp maple I've ever seen." She was grateful it was not on the
golf course, for it was much too big to move, and it would have
saddened her to see it destroyed.

After several hours, the flat, redundant landscape closed in obscurity to my unpracticed eye. Saw grass and myrtle, peppers and pines,
Sabals and cypress mixed in a botanical stew. In the Northwest, I'd
look for a mountain to get oriented, but the sole landmark at Ironhorse, only occasionally visible, was a large white smokestack about
two miles off to the south. Everyone was weary. As we walked back
and forth, following the route of the golf course across the land, I lost
all sense of direction. The land was flat, but you couldn't see very far
for the foliage. Even with the routing plan to guide me, I was having
trouble forming a sense of how the course sat on the landscape. I
could see the lengths of the holes, and noticed an oddity or two—that
holes five and six, for example, were back-to-back five pars and that

the seventh was a par three with a carry over water from the back tee that scaled at more than 200 yards, but because the lakes were not yet dug, where the plans showed open water we tramped across sedges and centipede grass, pushed through clinging vines, and stumbled over palmetto roots. Aside from a few isolated puddles, the only water we saw was drifting sedately through the drainage canals, drawn by a big pump up on the northwest corner that kept Ironhorse dry. We couldn't get across the big seepage canal on the west side and could only look from its east bank at the stakes the surveyors had set, their orange ribbons blowing in the breeze. Farther west of the seepage canal was the tall dike of the city of West Palm Beach's water-catchment basin, a 12,800-acre reservoir. Australian pines, staking out the high ground, pushed up from the crown of the dike. To see out across the catchment basin, you'd have to clamber up the dike and push back the Australians' limbs. It was, I later learned, an effort worth making. A great vista spread west, south, and north, fields of tall saw grass swaying under cypress hammocks. The basin would be a sanctuary for wildlife displaced by Ironhorse's construction and a nursery for the birds and reptiles that would recolonize Ironhorse once its lakes were dug and its marshes created.

The land to the west, between the seepage canal and the water-catchment basin, was identified on the plans as the preserve, a province off limits to development. According to the drawings, a few greens and tees had insinuated their way into the preserve, but Hills expected the golf course to merge unobtrusively into this tranquil buffer, the only place on Ironhorse not scheduled to bow to the dozer's power. The preserve was not precisely coterminous with the land enclosed between the catchment basin and the seepage canal, but the plan for the preserve acknowledged and built upon the wetter conditions prevailing across the canal.

At the pace Hills was setting, there was little to suggest the rhythm of the course, how it would play, or even what it would look like. We were either in narrow corridors of trees or in open meadows or skirting acres of myrtles. Hills seemed to know what he was looking for, but I was down to figuring out how many days filled with this many rays it would take to plant a noseful of melanomas. Dasher and Hills had both slathered on the sunscreen. I'd thought it odd that neither, despite his long hours every week in the sun, had much of a tan. In south Florida, dark skin is tasteful and chic, proof of adequate leisure and, one assumes, the wherewithal to engage the services of a first-rate dermatologist. But until you need the physician's knife, you bravely face the ozone-depleted sky, churn up the melanin production until you glow, and hoist your Perrier with a hand whose outer surface is slowly turning into leather. Hills and Dasher were there to work, indifferent to the emblems of prestige. I think I was getting dehydrated. The sun, high overhead, was no help getting oriented.

"Usually on something this rough," Dasher said, jumping off an uprooted Sabal palm, "you're out here by yourself." There was no reluctance to break, not even by Hills, when Sher got back with a sackful of corned beef sandwiches and a couple of six-packs of pop. We went back to the ranch house to eat. We'd "seen" most of the front nine.

Back at the house, Joshua Muss had arrived and was on the phone, sitting in an abbreviated beach chair eight inches off the floor. It was the only piece of furniture in the house. Muss had struck a deal with Sher several months before to take over Ironhorse, forming a limited partnership—Ironhorse, Ltd.—with his own development company, Joshua Muss and Associates, as the general partner and manager. He left no doubt who was in charge despite his lowly perch. Wearing a starched and monogrammed white shirt and rep tie, tan pants, and Gucci loafers, Muss looked like a slightly distended and stocky Paul Newman, his gray hair cut short, his jaw firmly set. No one spoke lest he interrupt Muss's call. Tucking the headset between his chin and shoulder, Muss pantomimed the need for a cigarette from his companion, a heavyset man with a blond pencil mustache, as short as Muss but much heavier, with powerful-looking forearms and well-tended hair, trained to let the sides give a power boost to the top. Bob Isakson lit a Camel and handed it to Muss with subalternly ease. Muss cupped the mouthpiece and ordered introductions. He may look like Newman, I thought, but Bob Hoskins could play a character with the perfect wound-up swagger needed to convey Muss. Isakson had just flown in from Dallas to see for the first time the project Muss had asked him to manage. Muss's nephew, Harpman, who said very little that morning, self-conscious in his working infancy, would be Isakson's assistant.

Hanging up the phone, Muss addressed the engineer, Aquart. "Did you redo the calculations on the fills for the parcels yet?"

The question put Aquart, a naturalized citizen from Jamaica with a prematurely graying beard whose speech bore traces of the island lilt, in a delicate spot. He didn't yet have the numbers Muss was after, which related not just to the golf course but to the roads and the house pads, the dirt on which to pour concrete foundation slabs. "I met with your boss about this in December," Muss added. Aquart was meeting Muss for the first time and had only been working on Ironhorse for a month. He wasn't sure what his boss had promised Muss, but improvised his way ahead. Muss used Aquart's hesitation to reinforce his own authority. "I don't want to move any dirt twice," he told him.

Aquart tried to deflect the interrogation. "The permits aren't ready yet, are they? We'll have the cut and fill by then."

"The permits are taken care of," Muss interjected. "I don't want to have to buy any dirt."

In five minutes Muss had instilled a sense of urgency that the morning's casual safari lacked and spiked whatever joy was attached to finally getting under way. This was not a party, it was a job. While Muss interrogated Aquart, the rest of the troop fell on the corned beef. Hills was ready for seconds, eyeing the remaining half of Dasher's sandwich, before Muss dismissed Aquart.

As it turned out, Muss's belief that the issue of permits was settled proved false. Isakson's main occupation for the next ten months would be gathering permits. But Muss was right to worry about dirt. There aren't many hills to cut down in south Florida and none west of the Atlantic coastal ridge. All the dirt for the golf course, the house pads, and the roads would have to come from digging holes in the ground, the by-product of creating the lakes engineered by Aquart and his colleagues to manage Ironhorse's storm water. Hills in turn had to integrate the lakes into his golf course. Bringing in dirt would cost at least four bucks a yard. Scraping fill out of ground you already owned cost only a third or less than the price of imported dirt.

Sher, listening, asked Muss if they couldn't market some of their abundantly redundant myrtles. "I don't think so," he replied. "Ask Debbie. She's my tree hugger."

Allen told Sher there was no market for his wild myrtles, that it would cost too much to prepare them to sell. The landscape plan, though, called for transplanting them in large numbers, so they were "plant material you won't have to buy." Some of the other species, the Sabal palms perhaps, might find a buyer, but it was unlikely when nursery stock, certifiably healthy, was available.

There was a poignancy to Sher's peripheral role in Muss's presence. It was as if he'd given a child up for adoption but still wanted to sing it lullabies and tuck it to sleep. Sher, the "crazy button man," as he called himself, had invented the idea whose appeal had summoned everyone to the ranch house, but instead of the dreamer in his restless sleep, casting visions, Sher was becoming a shadow, his dream transmogrified, dry bones clutched in Muss's fist.

3

The Genius of the Place

GOD'S COMMAND to build Ironhorse was not the first time He had whispered in Sher's ear. Art Hills wasn't Sher's first choice to design his golf course either. Nor was the Grier Ranch the unspoiled paradise a naive glance suggested, however persuasively Sher lamented the passing of its supposedly pristine splendor. "It's a shame, isn't it, those trees have to go," he said, looking across a tall stand of pines on the south side of the clubhouse site, "but how else you gonna build a golf course?"

Ironhorse's history—and its prehistory—is a tale of Florida development writ small. The first official notice of the land that would one day whisper its desire to Sher was an entry by the clerk of Dade County—a fragment of which later became Palm Beach County—on November 25, 1890. The land recorded was part of a tract of almost 350,000 acres conveyed to the Florida Coast Line Canal and Transportation Company by the trustees of the state's infamous Internal Improvement Fund. The Florida legislature in the spring of 1889 required the fund to transfer to the canal company 3,840 acres "of the lands held in reserve for the company" for each mile of canal dug between St. Augustine and Biscayne Bay, or present-day Miami. The Coast Line Canal was the ancestor of the Atlantic Intracoastal Waterway, the big ditch that runs the length of Florida's east coast. Ironhorse was part of the payoff for digging one hundred and thirty-four and a half miles, "no portion of it less than five feet in depth and fifty feet in width," from the west end of what was called the Haul-over Cut, north of Miami, up to Jupiter. Five years later, the canal company conveyed title to this property to the Florida East Coast Railway Company.

Henry Flagler, who more than anyone invented modern Florida, owned the Florida East Coast Railway. Ironhorse would be, in a way, a smaller, landlocked version of Palm Beach, the WASPy winter playground that adumbrated Flagler's version of the future. Henry James, no slouch in the snob department, thought the country club was American society's sole contribution to civilized life. Flagler was the colonizer of this cultural ideal, planting its flag in the derelict environs of south Florida. Paris Singer, with the Everglades Club, was its Saint Peter.

Flagler had been John D. Rockefeller's partner in the oil business. The cheap fuel that Flagler's enterprise helped supply, powering Henry Ford's inexpensive cars—bought, of course, on time—opened up Florida to tourism, though not for the sort of people Flagler's pricey developments wooed. Flagler's kind came on private railway cars—hauled along Flagler's tracks—or down from Newport on their yachts. Flagler didn't allow motorcars at all on Palm Beach, devising instead the quaint pedaled rickshaws known as "Afromobiles," vehicles powered exclusively by the muscles of African-Americans. These conveyances were still in use in the 1960s. One typical example from among the dozens of books promoting Florida, this one published in 1950, has a photo of a middle-aged African-American man peddling behind and above a smiling young woman in a dark dress, perched in a wicker chair mounted between the two front wheels of his vehicle. Flagler's prototype had the peddler up front, but that spoiled the view. In the photo the Afromobile's operator has on a tweed suit, a tie, and a pith helmet, his pant cuffs rolled up around his ankles to keep them away from the drive chain. There are no packages in the chair, no evidence of shopping. His passenger's bearing is stylized, the camera angle oblique. Hidden in the shadows, he was not *in* the background, he *was* the background. The photographer meant to make her look as if she belonged, on the way to her Mizner house, perhaps. He, on the other hand, would not stay the night. Only residents and guests remained on the island of Palm Beach after dark. Domestic servants with passes could stay—somebody had to do the dishes.

Palm Beach was a racist and anti-Semitic enclave, though not uniquely so in south Florida before 1960. In the twenties, a lady on the links wearing a knitted ankle-length pleated skirt and a broad-brimmed bonnet could pose for a photo in the fashion of amusing postcards, her club held above her head in a deliberate backswing, her left foot delicately arched above the sod, the ball she is about to strike teed up on the small upturned toes of her caddy's outstretched foot. A black child of perhaps ten, his hand covering his eyes in mock fear, he's toting a golf bag that reaches clear to the ground. A Palm Beach magazine reproduced this shot in 1989, with no sense of irony, as an example of local historical color.

When Flagler ruled Florida's roost, granting great public subsidies of land to stimulate private development was still common, as it had been elsewhere in the United States in the nineteenth century. It's how most of America's railroads were built. In Florida transferring public land to private hands was raised to a high art. Florida has a sort of viral energy, constantly creating more of itself. It's also the purist instance of the American genius for promotion. Flagler set standards that places like Ironhorse were emulating a hundred years after he first promoted his adopted state. Flagler, like Hills, was from Ohio.

Flagler's railroad eventually divested itself of most of its land grant, including the piece containing Ironhorse, but not before it logged off all the native pine to fuel its locomotives, clearing thousands of coastal and near inland acres. A lumber company held Ironhorse long enough to harvest whatever merchantable timber remained after Flagler's woodcutters finished with it, probably milling cypress logs. A mature bald cypress can grow 120 feet tall, but while the cypresses Debbie Allen found at Ironhorse were healthy, none was taller than forty-five feet. All the trees growing on Ironhorse today are less than sixty years old, excepting some of the commercially worthless Sabal palms, which may be as old as ninety.

In the Florida land boom of the early twenties, as speculation drove up prices and West Palm Beach's population quadrupled, the land that would be Ironhorse changed hands repeatedly, but was never divided into building lots. During the Second World War and into the early fifties, oil companies were drilling test wells all around Palm Beach and Martin counties, and both Gulf Oil and Humble Oil took leases on the property, but neither did any drilling.

Then, in 1967, John D. MacArthur bought Ironhorse. MacArthur made his fortune selling a brand of cheap mail-order insurance that almost never paid claims. Most of his clients were poor, paying a few dollars a month for their policies. They weren't very sophisticated about pursuing their claims. MacArthur employed thousands of salesmen and nearly as many lawyers. Based in Chicago—his brother, Charles, was the legendary newspaperman who wrote *The Front Page* with Ben Hecht and was married to Helen Hayes—John D. came to Florida in the midfifties after foreclosing on a developer's loan. He was a lender of last resort, charging usurious rates and quick to foreclose. He didn't have a staff of high-priced financial advisers either. He handled his business personally, guided by instinct. He made few bad choices and bargained hard. Seldom was a petitioner in a position to quarrel with his terms. He occupied the lending niche between a federal bank and the neighborhood loan shark.

During his last years, MacArthur lived in an apartment at the Colonnades Beach Hotel he owned on Singer Island, a couple of miles south of the Shers's penthouse. MacArthur owned most of the south end of the island, where he developed a marina and a small neighborhood of modest frame houses. Sher used to see MacArthur in the coffee shop at the Colonnades, sipping whiskey, smoking cigarettes, and talking on the phone. His insurance company, Bankers Life, was bringing in $200,000,000 annually in premiums by 1966 and paying out, at most, half of that in claims. MacArthur was the sole stockholder of his company. From his table in the Colonnades' coffee shop, MacArthur directed the purchase of land that by 1976 made him the largest landowner in Florida. He was the second wealthiest man in the United States when he died.

MacArthur was famous for philandering. He skinny-dipped on a stretch of beach just north of Singer Island that's now known as John D. MacArthur Beach State Park. Nude bathing is prohibited. Just above the park named for him is an exclusive residential golf course development called Lost Tree Village. The golf course at Lost Tree was the first anywhere to use the hybrid Bermuda grass called 419 developed at the United States Department of Agriculture's research station in Tifton, Georgia. Every time he drives by it Sher thinks not of the historical importance of Lost Tree's turf grass, but of the fact that hardly any Jews live there. "And why would they want to," he demands to know. "Why go where you're not wanted?"

MacArthur owned most of the land at the north end of the Loxahatchee Slough, the headwaters of the Loxahatchee River. The slough stretches south, encompassing the water catchment basin that forms the western boundary of Ironhorse. MacArthur owned just about everything there that wasn't public land.

MacArthur built three golf courses on property north of Ironhorse and east of the turnpike, even paying for an interchange so cars could get off at his property. He called it the JDM Country Club. Until it moved in 1981 to PGA National, just west of the turnpike, the Professional Golfers' Association, the organization representing club pros, was headquartered at MacArthur's club. JDM was sold in 1988 to a Philadelphia developer for $88 million, most of it in the form of a note carried by the MacArthur Foundation, with 46,000 acres still the biggest landowner in Palm Beach and Martin counties. Because of its huge holdings, the foundation is the biggest hitter in Palm Beach County development. MacArthur has the dirt. Neighbors like PGA National and JDM, and plans for other projects on nearby land once owned by the Foundation, encouraged Sher's belief that Ironhorse was a good place for his golf course.

Bob Grier, Ironhorse's penultimate owner, who made his money at the lower end of the development market, building trailer parks with boat launches and selling mobile home pads for a few thousand dollars, bought Ironhorse in 1971. It was Grier's acquisition that gave the property the character it had when Sher found it. Grier's widow and heirs sold it after he was killed in a car wreck.

Ironhorse has the shape of a rectangle with a triangle stuck on its northern end. It borders the water catchment basin on the west and the Beeline Highway along its diagonal northern boundary. It is surrounded on its east and south sides by the lands of the Solid Waste Authority, whose job it is to deal with Palm Beach County's garbage. SWA was part of the reason it took Sher so long to put together his development deal.

When Grier bought his ranch, it was at least 25 percent wetlands, the rest a mixture of wet and dry prairies. The wet prairies are a kind of transition zone, flooded a good portion of the year. In aerial photographs taken in 1965, six years before Grier bought the property, wet areas show up as dark amoebalike blotches, while the trees around them look vaguely cloudlike. By the time the county photographed the ranch again in 1973, drainage ditches invaded every wetland, a network of shallow trenches radiating across the ground, connected by a larger perimeter canal on the north, south, and east sides. There is nothing in the surrounding undrained land that looks even vaguely like the ranch's cleared and drained pastures. The water catchment area has cypress hammocks surrounded by thousands of acres of saw grass, but Ironhorse has only a few vestigial patches of *Cladium jamaicensis*, the great grass of the Everglades. Ironhorse was turning into pine flatwoods, a habitat uncommon in Palm Beach County a hundred years ago. The flatwoods need the dryer water cycle which drainage provides.

Following the cleared center lines on the walk-through with Hills and Dasher, we had slogged across narrow drainage ditches and looked at the preserve across the deeper and wider seepage canal on the west side of Ironhorse. The powerful pump Grier installed in the northwest corner kept the water drawn down well below its natural elevation. The landscape that seduced Alan Sher was created by Grier's drainage ditches as much as by nature. It was not a primordial Florida Eden but a third-generation mélange of biological transition zones and exotic invasion. It was still, for all of that, a very beautiful place.

Grier's father-in-law, a realtor who handled the ranch's sale to Sher, says that Grier's long-range plans for the property included a golf course. In the aerials, the pastures already look a lot like fairways. Today the drainage Grier did would violate federal statutes protecting wetlands, but twenty years ago it conformed with regulations guiding agricultural use, and that made Ironhorse possible. If 25 percent—or eighty-eight acres—had to stay as wetlands, it would have been a squeeze for the remaining 266 acres to yield both a golf course and enough building lots to make development financially feasible. The golf course takes another 120 acres, not counting the lakes, and by the time you factor in roads, not much is left. The effects of twenty years of drainage made it easy for Ironhorse's environmental engineer to demonstrate to the Army Corps of Engineers that Ironhorse was the custodian of degraded and moribund wetlands, with no duty to resurrect them. He proposed the creation of new wetlands instead.

West of the turnpike was beyond the pale in the early seventies. There was nothing out there but alligators, big white birds, and pickups on their way to the town of Okeechobee up on the northeast corner of the Big Lake. Walt Disney almost bought thousands of MacArthur's acres due north of Ironhorse when he was looking for a place to build Disney World. MacArthur was tough and difficult to deal with, and Disney was determined not to repeat the error he made in California when he neglected to buy up all the land around

Disneyland. MacArthur wanted to share in the peripheral development, so he and Disney couldn't strike a deal for the new amusement park. Disney then picked up 26,000 acres south of Orlando. PGA National, Ironhorse's northern neighbor, sits on acreage Disney considered buying.

Even without Disney's help, development had caught up to northern Palm Beach County by the time Sher saw the Grier Ranch. Sher hired a law firm to deal with the zoning and annexation issues, an environmental engineer to put together the water-use plan and gather permits, and a land-use planning firm—Urban Design Studio, Debbie Allen's outfit—to digest the site and find the corridors for golf. A lot of the professionals on Sher's team had worked on other tony local golf and real estate developments like Old Marsh, the Loxahatchee Club, and PGA National. Savvy in negotiating the bureaucratic byways, they were the top development firms in Palm Beach County. All that was left was hiring a golf course architect.

In 1985 nobody was hotter as a course designer than Pete Dye, who lived in nearby Delray Beach. Next to Robert Trent Jones, Dye was the world's most famous golf course architect who had not been a famous golfer, like Arnold Palmer or Jack Nicklaus. Dye, who works with his wife, Alice, until recently the only woman member of the American Society of Golf Course Architects, started designing golf courses in his native Indiana in the late fifties. His first efforts were undistinguished, but after a trip to Scotland in 1963, Dye inaugurated a reign of innovation unmatched in the work of any contemporary golf architect. Every course designed in the United States today owes a debt to the Dyes' Scottish hadj. Admiring the use of railroad ties as stabilizing sleepers on Scottish bunkers, he imported the look for bulkheads around lakes as well as bunkers. He worked the land more dramatically than predecessors like Trent Jones had, shrinking greens from the 12,000-square-foot behemoths common in the age of Trent Jones and Dick Wilson down to undulating surfaces of 6,000 square feet or less. He tolerated blind shots and hidden greens, abrupt edges and nearly shear bunker walls. He created great waste bunkers that sometimes skirted an entire fairway. His courses were subtle and tried to contain the good player's length off the tee not with longer holes, the response of Jones and others in the sixties and early seventies, but with tightened-down landing areas where the big hitters were sure to aim. The fairways were wide and accommodating for the tee shots of lesser players. He rarely bunkered the front of his greens, believing doing so hampered weaker players who needed room to run the ball up to the hole. He designed the fringes of the greens for tight mowing, so players could putt from off the edges. He was bold and tough, and his greens were treacherously sloped. Dye designed, as he liked to say, "on the edge of disaster."

Unlike most of his fellow architects, Dye does not draw. Nicklaus, with whom Dye had a brief collaboration in the late sixties, doesn't either. Great drafting technique is far from the most important arrow in an architect's quiver. Are Irving Berlin's tunes less hummable because he didn't read music? Only about half the members of the ASGCA are landscape architects with training in topography. Another 25 percent are schooled in turf management, agronomy, or soil science. The remainder are a potpourri. Dasher's a civil engineer. Dye was a hotshot insurance man before he took up course design. Both of the Dye sons also practice golf course architecture, and they learned on the job from their parents.

Dye creates as he goes, directing the earthwork and its shaping, installing the drainage, working the course onto the site. He and Alice move near the job for the eight or nine months it takes to build a course. He constantly fiddles with his creations, flying off on weekends from whatever project he is working on to rebuild a green on an earlier job. Sometimes it's to prepare the course for a tournament, but as often as not it's to reclaim a green that the new grasses and mowing techniques have made so fast they've tipped it over disaster's edge. In PGA Tour golfer Peter Jacobsen's phrase, modern putting sometimes feels like rolling marbles on a car fender. Dye's constantly trying to keep his greens in the limbo between impossible and merely nasty. Crooked Stick, a country club he organized in Indianapolis, has been in a more or less constant state of refurbishing since he laid it out in 1964. Crooked Stick is Dye's *Demoiselles d'Avignon*. "I don't know how the members stand it," he says of his tinkering.

Dye was Sher's first choice to design Ironhorse. "He sat in my apartment, with Alice," Sher says, "and told me how much he wanted to do this project. It was a great site, he said, and close to home." But later Sher heard rumors that Dye was going to do another course nearby, which turned out to be Old Marsh, and the courtship abruptly ended. Sher's memory of that episode was bitter and deep and differs from Dye's. Despite accelerating financial difficulties, the concatenation of impediments that kept Ironhorse from jumping up and running, Sher rejected deals that would have bailed him out of his expensive option, taking what his own lawyer called a ridiculously hard bargaining line, given his predicament, because of what that hard lesson taught. Sher says Dye wasn't straight with him, that when he asked him if he was going to design Old Marsh Dye said, "No." Dye says now he never wanted to do Ironhorse. "Who was going to play there," he asks? Dye likes to build courses with the strength to take on the touring pros. "That's just another Jewish country club, isn't it? Nobody'll play it."

Sher hadn't taken lightly losing out on his first attempt to build a golf course. His idea, he said, was to do an exclusive country club, give it a Scottish theme, not all pastel and tropical like these Florida courses, which were getting too crowded anyway, but traditional, *plaid*, with good service and a sense of ease. Bigger lots, nice houses, not so many members. Keep the membership under 300. He wanted the weight of the past without enduring the tedium of actual historical events. He'd always enjoyed his membership at Middle Bay, his club on Long Island, and wanted a similar feel in a warmer place. And if he made some money, the way Jack Haft and Bert Gaines had after they bought Frenchman's Creek from the MacArthur Foundation, who could complain?

Frenchman's was a MacArthur project with two golf courses and a marina that Haft and Gaines turned into a gold mine in the late eighties. It made so much money that when the time came to deal for Ironhorse, even someone as tough-minded as Josh Muss was swayed by Frenchman's example. When the MacArthur Foundation put Frenchman's up for sale, Muss bid half of what the successful buyers offered. He was happy to let the winners have it for such a ludicrous price, then watched it generate cash like Bolivian inflation. Frenchman's success helped pull Muss into the high-end market in northern Palm Beach County. His bid for Frenchman's showed he was already looking, and its thriving business sharpened his focus.

Sher was smitten even before Muss, a year before he discovered Ironhorse. He heard about a piece of property not very far north of the Grier Ranch and let his imagination loose, inventing the kind of club he wanted. Exclusive, but familiar. Rich, but not stuffy, solid but young at heart. "I know fashion. I know what people want. That's my business." Knowing nothing, however, about real estate, Sher asked the developer who'd sold him his Singer Island penthouse if he'd take a look at the property. Sher shared his vision, then left for New York. When he got back, a letter awaited him that was, in a way,

Ironhorse's preamble. The developer had decided to option the property with another group of investors, without Sher's help, thank you very much. They weren't really compatible partners, the developer decided, so it was better to separate before they got hitched. Where Sher envisioned instant camaraderie, the developer saw the hidden lineaments of an "ethnic club." Sher, he said, "wanted to create a Jewish Augusta National, and I just wasn't interested." Sher was stunned, angry, and embarrassed. He wanted more out of life than a good seat at the arena. He wanted to play. His initiation into the game began with real estate lesson number one: Dine, lest thou be eaten.

So Ironhorse was a second try, one he'd hoped his brother, Eugene, who was in woven labels, would join him in creating. Eugene, however, died, and little brother Alan was left to carry on alone. He called Craig Shankland, who'd once been the pro at Middle Bay, for advice. Sher wanted Shankland, whose English accent sounded great on the practice tee, as the pro for Ironhorse, too. Shankland's job was among the conditions Sher insisted on in any developer's deal. Shankland was a second-generation golf professional and a well-known teacher. When Sher solicited his help for Ironhorse, Shankland was working at a course in Coral Springs, north of Miami. Shankland's employer was a Tournament Players' Club (TPC) course, licensed by the PGA Tour as a marketing tool for developers. The TPC at Eagle Trace was a Westinghouse project. Art Hills, who had also done a Westinghouse course called Pelican Bay in Naples, was Eagle Trace's architect. Shankland had worked with Hills during Eagle Trace's construction and eagerly recommended him to Sher.

Sher invited Hills to take a look at the Ironhorse site in early May 1985. Hills listened carefully to Sher's hopes for his project. Sher was taken with Hills's modesty and cheered by his enthusiasm. When Dye had looked at the property, the response had been restrained. "Dye told me, 'Look, you don't need to sell buttons anymore, and I don't have to build golf courses,' " Sher remembered. " 'I just pick ones I like.' " Dye's coolness, his "maybe I'll do it, maybe I won't" attitude, as Sher saw it, argued against him, even if his fame was almost irresistible to a man of fashion. Sher and Dye leaned away from one another even before the Old Marsh contretemps.

Hills, on the other hand, listed in Sher's direction. That Ironhorse would be Hills's first job in Palm Beach County also appealed to Sher. Joseph Lee, Palm Beach County's third most famous golf course architect after Dye and Nicklaus, had been Sher's second choice to design Ironhorse, but Palm Beach County, Sher decided, was nearly at the saturation point with Joe Lee designs. Lee had worked on the three courses for MacArthur at JDM, which was just around the corner. Nicklaus, the most famous local course designer, was never in Sher's plans. It wasn't just Nicklaus's million-dollar design fee, it was where he hung his hat. Living as he did at Lost Tree was enough to disqualify Nicklaus in Sher's eyes, even if he had no evidence that Nicklaus was an anti-Semite. The Miami *Herald* did a series on anti-Semitism in south Florida's country clubs that Sher Xeroxed for friends. Sher was a cultural Jew, a nonobserver who peppered his speech with Yiddish phrases and was ever vigilant for ethnic slurs. He never bar-mitzvahed. He married a shiksa and thought the black folks living along Blue Heron Road, whose houses he drove past on the commute between Singer Island and Ironhorse, were too lazy to work. But he knew that eating trayf didn't make him any less a Jew as well as he knew that he had no ethnic test for friendship. A local disaster was sure to get his checkbook working. He paid the utility bill for a disabled couple threatened with the loss of their apartment. He helped an elderly lady rebuild her house after a car plowed through it. And Nicklaus, besides, had done a new course, called Loxahatchee, very near Ironhorse. Sher wanted something special.

Sher liked Lee very much, but was searching for a little more pizzazz than he believed the courtly Lee would provide. When Lee visited Ironhorse, Sher was fond of recalling, he called it "a Garden of Eden." How can one improve such a landscape, unless the implication is that God's creation was complete except for a golf course. How could He forget? You really did eat the apple. But it's just routine flattery, and Lee happened to say it first. Hills echoed Lee when he called Ironhorse "Alan's Eden."

Lee designs golf courses without ostentation or deception and among the leading architects represents a rather pure version of traditional design. A timber bulkhead, à la Pete Dye, may creep in here and there, but for the most part a Joe Lee course unfolds with stately deliberation. The tees sit gently and serenely above the fairways, aiming at unambiguous targets. Large bunkers, white sand flashed up their faces, proudly announce themselves. They're always visible. You'd never run up over an innocent-looking swale and find yourself in a hidden hazard on a Joe Lee course. The mounding is graceful and soft, all in the manner of Lee's mentor, Dick Wilson, a top course designer in the two decades after World War II. The greens typically are heavily bunkered in Wilson's amoebic style, trying to look like the depressions Scottish sheep dig into the landward side of sandy hillocks along the links-land to escape the chill of the wind off the sea. By this logic there should not be bunkers in the face of a mound oriented toward the prevailing wind. If sheep are smart enough to turn their backs to the breeze, the architects inspired by their natural intelligence should do no less. Lee's courses, in their modest way, honor the sheep's style.

The idea that a beneficent nature built the first and best courses, in primevel links-land along the Scottish coast, appeals to golf historians' sense of the game's place and provenance. Rees Jones, the younger son of the modern era's most influential designer, Robert Trent Jones, describes St. Andrews as without "artificial characteristics. Mother nature was its architect." Geoff Cornish says of his profession's aim, "We're trying to create land forms like those found on the links." A biographer of golf course architect Donald Ross, a Scotsman who migrated to the U.S. at the turn of the century and lived through two golf building booms before his death on the cusp of a third, called the North Sea the "real architect of Dornoch Links," in Ross's Scottish hometown. And there is a certain truth to that, even if Old Tom Morris, to whom Ross was apprenticed as a young man, actually laid out most of Royal Dornoch's holes. As Cornish points out, Old Tom didn't have heavy equipment available to create landscape illusions, so he looked for green sites among the natural mounds and earthen glyphs.

Scotland was the one place God didn't forget to provide for golf, and who better than a nation of righteous Presbyterians to avail themselves of this ordained game? Golf, in this devoutly Calvinist way, is a spiritual matrix, a ceaseless intersection of human will and grace. The golf course architect is a kind of priest who divines the landscape. "Natural green sites," Cornish says, "are a joy to behold." The architect just makes a lot more money than a conventional preacher, at least the kind who works behind a pulpit rather than before a camera.

Most golfers perceive the playing ground neither as inspiration nor theology but as a kind of background, the way a reader regards the layout of a magazine page. If you're getting the idea, the messenger recedes into the background. No popular magazine publishes more weighty articles than *The New Yorker*. Its elegant typeface and quiet graphic style tell you the message is in the prose. *Rolling Stone* publishes thoughtful and substantial pieces, though shorter and less dense than *The New Yorker*'s, but it surrounds them with a loud and aggressive visual style to let a reader indifferent to the writing get some sense of the magazine's content. Golf course design works in a similar range. Lee is a traditionalist, Dye an innovator pushing golf architecture to new limits. Hills admires Dye most among his contemporaries. Hills's work borrows from Dye and was influenced by Dick Wilson.

Cornish says, "You have to be able to identify who designed the course when you walk on it," but I think that's a tough maxim to follow. Someone like Robert Bruce Harris, who built moon-shaped bunkers set out thirty feet from his greens for ease of maintenance is a cinch to identify, but you can't easily tell a Trent Jones course from a Dick Wilson, or, to dip into the profession's obscurer ranks, a William Diddle from a Charles Mahannah. When Cornish says that one of his former colleagues could tell which superintendent in charge of construction built a course, that strikes me as more plausible. In the fifties, the kind of expertise Cornish's axiom implies was useful to a number of New England country clubs, across whose grounds government engineers had drawn the interstate highway system. If the members didn't have the pull to get the road rerouted, the government moved to acquire the property. After a flurry of course building in the roaring twenties, the twenty-five years after 1929 saw the loss of 2,000 courses to the cumulative effects of the Depression, the World War, and the interstates.

Donald Ross was the greatest figure in golf design in the first half of this century and a very busy man in the twenties, when he had 3,000 men working for him building courses. Ross led an industry that was putting up 600 golf courses a year, a pace today's National Golf Foundation would find exhilarating. There are "Donald Ross" courses, though, in places he never set foot, built by his associates. It's like the difference between a Rembrandt and a work *signed* by Rembrandt but painted by one of his talented apprentices, like Carel Fabritius or Aert de Gelder. Art historians with a lifetime of study under their belts still argue over the authenticity of old masters. A golf course is not always easier to read than a painting, especially if someone works eclectically, as Art Hills does. A Donald Ross course, to finish off this analogy, is more valuable than a course done by one of his lesser associates, so Cornish made a little cottage industry of appearing as an expert witness on behalf of the owners of Ross courses at condemnation hearings when the government was acquiring the right-of-way for the interstate highways. If you owned an authentic Ross, it was worth more than a "Donald Ross."

Dye's courses have a distinctive look, but forgery is not a crime in course design, and some of Dye's imitators approach the look of the master. Nicklaus often speaks in the Dye vernacular. The Dyes' younger son, P.B., does a great imitation—some would say gloss—of his father's style. The other Dye son, Perry, who developed a firm shrewdly called Dye Designs, lately sold to a Japanese company, plays on his clients' knowledge of his father's fame. This is a kind of standard use of the patrimony in golf architecture, pioneered by Robert Trent Jones, Jr. Perry Dye's sales pitch, according to his mother, is pretty simple. "There are two kinds of courses," he tells his potential clients, "Pete Dye courses and *imitation* Pete Dye courses. Do you want a phony or the real thing?" If you believe in diamonds, it's hard to wear cut glass.

Unlike Dye's use of motifs, the absence of a particular, repetitious style has been, until very recently, a deliberate part of Hills's method. He likes being adaptable, finding what he can in the site rather than imposing, in cookie-cutter fashion, a standard solution. He's made the absence of a style into a virtue, recalling Alexander Pope's imperious aesthetic, in his Epistle to the Earl of Burlington, written in 1731:

> In all, let Nature never be forgot.
> But treat the Goddess like a modest fair,
> Nor overdress, nor leave her wholly bare;
> Let not each beauty everywhere be spied,
> Where half the skill is decently to hide.
> He gains all points, who pleasingly confounds,
> Surprises, varies, and conceals the Bounds.
>   Consult the Genius of the Place in all;
> That tells the Waters or to rise, or fall;
> Or helps th' ambitious Hill the heavens to scale,
> Or scoops in circling theatres the Vale;
> Calls in the Country, catches opening glades,
> Joins willing woods, and varies shades from shades;
> Now breaks, or now directs, th' intending Lines;
> Paints as you plant, and, as you work, designs.
>   Still follow sense, of every Art the Soul,
> Parts answering parts shall slide into a whole,
> Spontaneous beauties all around advance,

Start even from difficulty, strike from Chance;
Nature shall join you; Time shall make it grow
A Work to wonder at . . .

That's what Sher wanted at Ironhorse—a work to wonder at, a landscape whose parts slid into a whole, surrounded by spontaneous beauties—greens, fairways, and luminous lakes. Hills was eager to see that he got it. The first thing Hills did back in Toledo after visiting Ironhorse was draft a letter to Sher: "We looked at a very attractive site, secluded, very natural, well-drained, stands of beautiful trees, large natural open areas . . . all the features to create a golf course different from so many of the heavily sculptured, big mounded courses found on the lower East Coast. What you can have is a more natural course which apparently has very little disturbed from what is there now. In my opinion," he coyly advised, "you will have a course of exceptional beauty if you select the architect who will take advantage of your unique site to create such a course."

This was exactly what Sher wanted to hear. Hills suggested that Sher look at a couple of his courses in Naples, and if Sher liked what he saw Hills could start designing Ironhorse in mid-June. Hills added, in typically measured phrases, that he wanted to "insure your comfort level as to our ability to do what we feel confident we will do . . . namely, create an excellent, distinguished, highly regarded golf course and community."

Hills had designed so many courses on Florida's southwest coast by 1985 that Pete Dye called him "the mayor of Naples." He'd worked on fourteen projects altogether, although three were executive courses and one was a par three layout. Quail Creek had thirty-six holes. Wyndemere had three nines. Bonita Bay, the best known and most widely admired of his gulf coast courses, was planning to add thirty-six more holes to its existing eighteen. Hills urged Sher to visit Bonita Bay and The Wilderness Club, where "some of the elements" he expected to incorporate in Ironhorse existed. Early in the summer of 1985, Sher and Shankland made the four-hour drive across Alligator Alley from West Palm to Naples.

The Wilderness Country Club, finished in 1974, was Hills's fourth course in Florida. He was only designing two or three projects a year in those days and could spend a lot more time on the sites. Wilderness was the brainchild of Paul Frank, who had grown up on the property when it was a working ranch and wanted to retain most of its greatly various native vegetation. Hills would stay in Naples for three or four days at a time while he was building Wilderness, directing the dozers during the clearing, marking trees to save, fine-tuning his design as he went, playing a little golf in the afternoon, having a couple of drinks in the evening—very much the style of work and living that Dye has maintained by doing only one or two courses a year. Hills had more direct control over the construction of Wilderness than he would later when Arthur Hills and Associates was doing a dozen jobs at once.

Wilderness was not a "heavily sculptured, big mounded course," but much subtler, with long, graceful movement in the fairways, larger greens than those planned for Ironhorse, and an occasional aggressive bunker of the type Hills later abandoned, more in the style carried forward by Joe Lee than the flat-bottomed, Dye-style grass-faced bunkers Hills was doing by the time Sher visited Naples. Built in the era of condos, The Wilderness Club has a series of apartment buildings tucked back among the trees surrounding its fairways. The condos take up less land than single family dwellings, so Wilderness has an uncluttered, tidy feel missing in courses with housing hunkered on all sides. "You play the golf course," Sher said, "and you never see the condominiums."

Sher liked Wilderness, but Bonita Bay clinched the Ironhorse job for Hills. Cut through acres of wetlands, Bonita Bay has less maintained turf than any course Hills has ever designed. Instead of fairways running from tee to green, many of Bonita Bay's tees are set in marshes so that the tee shot is a forced carry across wetlands to an abbreviated fairway. A typical golf course of 150 acres has about 110 acres of turf, but Bonita Bay threads across 200 acres, only 65 of them planted in grass. The rest is in native vegetation, much of it attractive habitat for birds—ospreys, egrets, herons, pelicans, and an occasional roseate spoonbill. The magazine *Audubon* praised Bonita Bay for its kindness to the site, and Bonita Bay's developer turned the careful environmental planning into a marketing success, putting out a promotional newspaper called "The Natural Life." Bonita Bay's original developer, who died before the golf course was built, made his fortune in yogurt and natural foods. Like the Button King, he was not the sort of developer who grew up chewing dirt and fighting city hall. "I don't know if this is a course you'd like to play every day," Sher told Shankland, looking across a lake to the twelfth green, "but it's beautiful."

By the time they started back to West Palm, Sher had made up his mind to hire Hills for Ironhorse. Hills's design fee was $115,000 plus expenses. The preliminary design phase would take sixty days and include four visits to the site. In preliminary design Hills would "develop a number of eighteen-hole plans with a practice area, including the schematic planning of parking areas, drives, clubhouse location, a maintenance facility location and the relationship of the above items to the residential areas." He'd have to get together with Urban Design Studio to create the preliminary designs. He made arrangements to come back to West Palm in early June to work on the routing with UDS. Sher, in the meanwhile, sicced the lawyers on annexation and zoning approvals, while the engineers and environmental consultants mapped out a water-management plan. All Sher had to do was tidy up the financing and everything would roll. Hope was high when Hills climbed on board. By the time he'd finished the preliminary design, Ironhorse was drifting into choppy waters.

4

Be Careful Where You Aim That Sucker

A golf course architect is a lot like a howitzer. You've got to be careful where you aim that sucker.

MIKE REDD, a land planner in West Palm Beach

THE PLANNING for Ironhorse proceeded quickly. By October Sher had a seventy-page appraisal of his "proposed golf course subdivision," a neatly printed and bound fifty-page prospectus, and a clip for his scrapbook from the Palm Beach *Post* reporting unanimous approval for his "low-density development" by the Palm Beach County Commission. Against his lawyer's advice, Sher asked its approval for only 230 housing units. Noting that development in the northern county lagged because the MacArthur Foundation held so much of the land, the appraiser nonetheless concluded that Ironhorse was the "highest and best use of the subject property." It ought, in other words, to make money. Sher's commercial instincts were sound—with approvals in hand, the golf course built and the land developed and ready to sell, Ironhorse was, the appraisal concluded, worth $18,000,000 given the 1985 real estate market in Palm Beach County. Not even six months had passed since Sher had written his first check for the

Ironhorse option. He had the hottest scooter on the block and he was ready to race. The appraisal was ammunition in his hunt for development money, but with the package he'd assembled for Ironhorse he couldn't imagine the money men not lining up to throw dollars at his conquering feet. Developing, though, is like farming—every new crop springs from hope, but dry winds or summer storms leaven it with worry. Sher still faced a season of bad weather. In the fall of 1985, though, he was plowing the ground for Ironhorse with the tractor on full throttle.

The eleventh page of the prospectus was a copy of the site plan, designed by UDS. The preservation buffer anchored the western boundary, while the golf course held sway around the other three sides. Those two features of Ironhorse's land plan would remain constant, even as the golf course and the siting of the housing pods migrated and evolved over several generations of preliminary plans. The land planners' job is to produce an abundance of *premium* house lots, which is not the same as getting the most houses on the site. You can't beat a grid for efficiency, after all, but there's not a straight street on a housing development in Florida these days, and it's not because of the lay of the land. Curvy streets look better—more refined. And you can't get a premium lot on a grid—every one is the same. Maybe the corner lots are a little better, but who wants the grandkids playing in an intersection? Any lot on the golf course, in real estate parlance, is a premium lot. Anything on a lake is a premium. Anything with a western view is a premium. If you can look over the golf course across a lake at the sunset, you are triply "amenitized," and boy, are you gonna pay. The more of these lots the land planner can generate, the more likely he is to find developers camping on his doorstep.

The land plan, like the course design, follows a few elevator-in-a-high-rise rules. Put golf holes all around the perimeter to buffer the houses from roads and neighbors. Ironhorse's plan did that, making a virtue out of the need to keep its million-dollar houses out of the range of gravel spitting off the tires of trucks barreling down the Beeline Highway. Avoid residential cul-de-sacs. Don't make the golfers cross any roads. On a site with changes in elevation, put the houses on the hills and route the golf course through the valleys. That way you preserve the views, avoid crowns on the fairways, and keep the storm water in its natural courses. Ironhorse gets plenty of storm water but has no hills or valleys. The perimeter berm, all of thirty feet above sea level, is the closest thing to a peak at Ironhorse.

UDS had good vegetation to work with at Ironhorse and a planning agenda with some troublesome features. The land planners' entry treatment would have to include a crossing gate at the railroad tracks, not an ideal threshold. The lands of the Solid Waste Authority abutted Ironhorse to the south and east. The aim of the land plan was to establish Ironhorse as an enclave, a private island in a public sea.

The land planner is not the same as the landscape architect, even though the same person or firm often does both jobs. The land planner does the site plan, figuring out what goes where—houses, golf course, clubhouse—while the landscape architect decides what planting style and earth forms will create the project's "look." The site plan is the structure, the landscape plan the details. If the project was big enough to do in stages, the planner would do a master plan.

The golf course controls a development's appearance, so the style of planting on the course needs to agree with the landscape scheme. Hills would later complain that Ironhorse's plan for a formally planted entry, for example, competed with the look of the native vegetation he was emphasizing on the golf course. A course Hills designed near Atlanta, The Standard Club, borrows from Bonita Bay a wild and unkempt look around the tees and mown turf kept to a minimum. The tee boxes are surrounded by unirrigated patches of fescue, weeds, and native grasses that brown out in the summer. The golf course superintendent at The Standard Club now cultivates plants he used to chemically destroy. He lets crabgrass go to seed where it's out of play. He harvests broom sedge seeds and casts them amidst the unmown fescue. Growing weeds for a golf course superintendent is like a preacher encouraging sin—all his training goes against it. The Standard Club's look wouldn't work if the course was surrounded by formally planted flower beds. There is one formal bed, but it's in the center of an enormous doughnut-shaped practice green, hard by the clubhouse, part of a separate tableau, isolated from the golf course.

The same land plan can be dressed several ways, so the golf course designer and the landscape architect need to hold hands. Frenchman's Creek has an elaborately landscaped berm around its perimeter, a formal, stylized garden that needs a lot of maintenance. A lawn of thick-bladed Saint Augustine grass runs up from the road to planting beds, tidy with bark mulch, whose edges are contoured along the undulating berm. The height of the mounds is constant. Berms converge from two directions at the entry, where Frenchman's pretensions soar. There's an artificial waterfall cascading over imitation rocks, imported palms, and lavish flower beds. It makes a statement. Across a bridge, curved to reduce car speed to a crawl, is the ubiquitous south Florida gatehouse security apparatus—clipboards, walkie-talkies, and uniformed guards. It's like entering a military base in a country that hasn't gone to war for three generations and can't quite remember the martial formalities.

The same land plan might erect a fence or stone wall or plant a hedge. The "look," in any case, is not the plan, though at Ironhorse, the idea from the beginning was to ride the horse you roped. Sher loved Ironhorse because of its trees. Hills wanted to feature them around the golf course and integrate them into the housing as he had done at The Wilderness Club. The land planners wanted to keep them, too, but it was going to be easier said than done. The golf course needed a hundred acres cleared, the drainage lakes at least another thirty-four. The preserve was fifty-four acres. There was no way a golf course, several miles of roads, a clubhouse, a dozen lakes, and 230 houses were going to rise on Ironhorse without sacrificing some timber. There were three strategies for saving trees.

First, everyone agreed to the native look. Rather than Frenchman's style of formal plantings on its perimeter berm, Ironhorse would transplant palms, pines, palmettos, and myrtles from the site and let them grow, spread, adapt, or die as any natural plant cluster would. That would save a lot of trees and bushes. Debbie Allen and the other UDS landscape architects knew Ironhorse's vigorous upland species would do best on the high dry berm. Unlike Frenchman's berm, which required constant maintenance, Ironhorse's would be only indifferently managed. After one year of temporary irrigation the plants were going to be on their own. This was an example of a style of landscape planting newly named "xeriscape," or landscaping with native plants adapted to the local water cycle. Despite its heavy annual rains, Florida is threatened by periodic droughts. Drawing too deeply from wells in dry times would allow salt water to invade south Florida's great freshwater aquifers, so the South Florida Water Management District regulates water use. Ironhorse couldn't pump a puddle without South Florida's approval. Slash pines, Sabal palms, and other native plants are adapted to the swing between hot, wet summers and dry winters. Ironhorse was not going to import royal or other costly specimen palms, it wasn't going to install formal beds of exotic plants, but instead planned to reproduce the clusters of dry prairie plants common to the site. The one plant that could not survive without irrigation at Ironhorse was grass, and without grass there's no golf course. Xeriscape stopped at the lawn. Hills was not fond of the arboretum look on a golf course and thought flower beds less appropriate than thistles, so he concurred with UDS on the landscape look. Hills is a landscape architect and land planner as well as a golf architect and knows the language their practitioners speak.

Landscape architecture is the name Frederick Law Olmsted gave to the profession he more or less invented in the last half of the nineteenth century, one his firm, managed later by his son and stepson/ nephew (Olmsted married his brother's widow and adopted his nephew) and their successors, carried into the second half of the twentieth century. With his partner, Calvert Vaux, Olmsted created New York's Central Park. He'd already been appointed to supervise the park's construction when his design was chosen in a competition. He worked on Central Park on and off over several decades, struggling against attempts to compromise his and Vaux's design—mixing uses, which he detested, or planting those dreadful formal beds. Central Park launched Olmsted's career. He designed parks for Philadelphia, for Boston, for Buffalo, Detroit, and Montreal. He laid out the campuses at Stanford University and the University of California at Berkeley, designed Prospect Park in Brooklyn, the South Side Parks of Chicago, and advised the creators of San Francisco's Golden Gate Park. Trying to create a name for this new profession he was practicing, Olmsted chose the prosaic "landscape architect" over the grandiloquent "rural embellisher"—otherwise, Hills and his colleagues might be known as golf course embellishers.

A great advocate for the salutary effects of parks and open space, Olmsted was a short, stocky New England–bred college dropout who struggled and failed as a farmer, wooed but did not win—he was thirty-seven when he finally wed—and despaired of ever freeing himself of financial dependence on his wealthy merchant father. Success came to him first as a writer.

On a trip to England with his brother, John, in 1850, Olmsted saw an urban park for the first time—Birkenhead, outside of Liverpool. We take city parks so much for granted that it's hard to imagine the powerful effect discovering Birkenhead had on Olmsted. Interested in horticulture, a contributor to journals on agricultural improvement, an experienced nurseryman, Olmsted had read the proponents of the picturesque, a Romantic style of gardening, before he sailed for England, but he was still unprepared for the great impression Birkenhead, as a *public* garden park, made. Designed by Joseph Paxton, famous for his Crystal Palace, the showpiece at London's Great Exhibition of 1851, Birkenhead was an ancestor to Ironhorse.

What Olmsted saw at Birkenhead was sort of a Victorian equivalent of a golf course without holes. Strollers meandered across its great lawns and along its garden paths, admired its specimen trees, and cooled down on the banks of its two artificial lakes. Painterly scenes of the lakes, of a rockery, or of meadows grazed by sheep were framed by openings in the trees or between mounds, contriving to create for the viewer the effect and feeling of a "natural" place, but one managed, not wild. Nature left to its own devices was a bit unruly. Paxton avoided flower beds and formal plantings. They ruined the scale, trivialized the grand effect. Some park committee of horticultural enthusiasts was always trying to add flowers, to the despair of Paxton, just as developers who insisted on planting flowers around tees were the bane of Hills and Dye.

Paxton shaped spoil from the lakes into hills, then planted their tops to add emphasis to the change in elevation—exactly the treatment planned for Ironhorse's perimeter berm. It took a thousand men two years to build Birkenhead, but the developer recovered his investment with a quick sale of the house lots around the park. By royal decree—the Victorian equivalent of a permit or a "condition for development"—the park was a public place. Birkenhead, as the amenity for the lots surrounding it, is both aesthetically and commercially Ironhorse's great-grandpa. It demonstrated the scale on which the landscape could be transformed and anticipated the building of the first "inland" golf courses in England by several decades.

In the book about his English travels that first brought him note, Olmsted wrote of Birkenhead, "Five minutes of admiration, and a few more spent in studying the manner in which art had been employed to obtain from nature so much beauty, and I was ready to admit that in democratic America, there was nothing to be thought of as comparable with this People's Garden. Indeed, gardening had here reached a perfection that I had never before dreamed of."

Olmsted admired the closely cropped turf, the deliberately shaped earth, and the orchestrated plantings, but the companionable mingling of the public, gentlemen and tradesmen, ladies and maids, was to him the real proof of Paxton's genius. Before Olmsted could put his English discoveries to use, he had to invent his occupation. In the

eight years between his English tour and the beginning of his work
on Central Park, Olmsted traveled in the American South, writing a
series of newspaper articles on slavery that he later collected into two
books. In *Journey in the Seaboard Slave States,* Olmsted told how he
toured lowland plantation regions that were, more than a century
later, completely transformed by golf. Even the dramatic aftermath of
the Civil War barely exceeded the repercussions of golf's coming to
the residents of the Sea Islands, an irony Olmsted would have appreciated. Olmsted's principles of planning and design lay over resort
developments like Hilton Head, Dataw, and Skidaway Islands as fully
as the spirit of Thomas Jefferson hovers over American politics.

Pinehurst, the granddaddy of American golf resorts, the North
Carolina home of Donald Ross, whose Pinehurst Number Two is a
golf shrine and one of Hills's favorite courses, was planned by Olmsted and Associates. Mrs. Edward Hartford's 4,000-acre preserve outside of Charleston, the Wando Plantation, was one of the hundreds of
private estates designed by the Olmsted firm. Once a slave plantation,
its great oak-lined entry was preserved in Olmsted's plan. Wando
Plantation had a nine-hole golf course by an unknown designer, a
swimming pool, a large brick-walled garden, and a mansion whose
image shimmered in a long reflecting pool that aimed like an arrow
at the front gate. The mansion burned down in 1942, and the property was sold to a veneer company, which logged off its hardwood. It
was sold again and made into a pine plantation. The tree farmers
poisoned but were unable to kill the ancient oaks. In the late eighties
the Dunes West Development Corporation bought Wando and hired
Hills to design a golf course, parts of which he lay atop its abandoned
predecessor. The reflecting pond, its broken banks restored, is a cross
hazard on the back nine. Hills has designed a half-dozen sea island
courses.

The old Olmsted office in Brookline, Massachusetts, now an his-
toric site run by the National Park Service, is desperately under-
funded, and its caretakers worry about the condition of the 150,000
drawings. Among the 149 "country clubs, resorts, hotels & clubs" the
Olmsted firm planned were The Country Club in Brookline, Timu-
quana Country Club in Jacksonville, another Donald Ross course,
and Bobby Jones's and Alister Mackenzie's Augusta National. Bal-
tusrol and Essex County in New Jersey and the Hempstead Country
Club on Long Island, with golf courses either designed or remodeled
by A. W. Tillinghast, were Olmsted clients. Olmsted and Associates

did the master plan for Asa Chandler's great Atlanta suburb, Druid Hills, where Mike Dasher grew up and *Driving Miss Daisy* was filmed, and Ottawa Hills in Toledo, where a youthful Art Hills trimmed hedges and mowed lawns. The Olmsteds did a master plan for West Palm Beach in the twenties, but it was never followed. Private estates like the Wando Plantation harked back to the work of the English master gardeners, Capability Brown and Humphrey Repton, who were, through Joseph Paxton, the true ancestors through Olmsted and Associates of every contemporary landscape designer. Golf architects are their kissing cousins. Charles Blair Macdonald, who coined the name "golf architect" in 1901, was acquainted with the writings of Repton and quoted from them approvingly in his memoirs. He was the first American to study golf design, revisiting the Scottish links, where he had learned to play as a schoolboy in the 1870s, so that he could adapt the essential features of the links' best holes for the American courses he laid out from scratch.

At the turn of the century, Harvard established the first academic program for the study of landscape architecture, inspired by the nearby example of the Olmsted firm and the availability of its partners to serve as adjunct faculty. Converted to a technical exercise, formalized and codified, landscape architecture lost the social edge Olmsted found so appealing at Birkenhead. "Olmsted had great faith," the editor of his papers wrote, "in the ability of his art to have an effect on society, and in particular to provide a sense of community. His great parks and park systems were to be spaces common to all residents of cities, where all classes could mingle free from the competitiveness and antagonisms of workaday life."

Olmsted's work was the headwaters for a great flowing river of planning and design. He was far from the first person to plan anything in America—Europeans imposed "order" on the New World from the beginning, after all, while the Native American affinity for shaping the earth produced mounds and effigies that astonished the settlers who came upon them. There's even a golf course in Newark, Ohio, built on Hopewellian mounds that once covered four square miles. "There has been surprisingly little mutilation in the course of converting the grand ceremonial center of a vanished people into a place of public amusement," an historian of the Mound Builders wrote. "[T]he low flat-topped mounds within the octagon serve now to test the ingenuity of golfers, and the flags emerging from the holes do little to detract from the beauty and splendor of the scene. One walks through the golf course, with its flawless green carpet of grass, so stirred by the size and symmetry of the ancient site that one scarcely has emotion left to object to the use to which it is put today."

Ritually sculpted earth is scattered all over the Midwest and the Southeast, pyramids, serpents, and conical hills that mostly had a funerary function. Golf courses share the ancient continental urge to shape the earth, only instead of providing a repository for bodies draped with weapons and trinkets to ease their passage into the next world, the earth shaped for golf nourishes the hope of breaking par. Golf is a secular rite.

William Penn, James Oglethorpe, and the Puritans imposed order on the New World, and the federal land survey has since our country's beginning laid its great grid across the United States, organizing settlement. Still, it's a long step from a city on a hill to a suburb in a swamp. Olmsted's reformist hopes may have vanished from his profession, but his principles still guide our sense of what a pleasing landscape looks like. The parks movement of the Progressive Era took up the reformist yoke the landscape architects shrugged off, fighting for small green spaces in the cities to relieve the dreariness of industrial life and to combat delinquency. In the Depression, the two streams merged once again, when the government was among the few solvent institutions and the planners' best client. Great public projects, like the TVA, gave the planners an opportunity on a scale that would have given Olmsted pause. Great national parks were created. Whole towns were removed to make way for reservoirs in the Tennessee Valley. Replacing them was a planner's dream, if sometimes a nightmare for the displaced. The planner for The Wilderness Club and Quail Creek in Naples cut his planner's teeth in the TVA, training under Depression-era veterans. After leaving the TVA but before hanging out his private consulting shingle, Bill Vines was the public planner for Collier County, Florida. That's the standard apprenticeship, the bridge to private work—when you know how the bureaucracy works and who to talk to, you're valuable to your clients.

The WPA and the CCC, New Deal public works agencies, carried on Olmsted's ideals, building country parks and roadside picnic facilities all over the United States. In addition to employing artists, writers, historians, and photographers, people like Walker Evans and James Agee, as the employer of last resort the WPA managed to find work for course designers like Robert Trent Jones and Donald Ross during golf's long nadir. The WPA—and its predecessor, the FERA—built 313 new golf courses and remodeled 389 more. It built the Scarlet and Gray courses at Ohio State University, designed by Alister Mackenzie, though his untimely death meant they had to be built from plans alone, without Mackenzie's supervision. The WPA built the George Wright Muni in Boston, designed by Ross. New Orleans' City Park courses were built by hand by men who would otherwise have been on relief. A WPA press release in the summer of 1939 announced "that golf as a popular recreation has survived the depression triumphantly due to the cooperation of the municipalities and the Federal government. . . . Golf courses, from a technical point of view, provide almost ideal work projects for the unemployed as unskilled laborers can be used in the clearing, grading and landscaping of grounds." The WPA even got Bobby Jones, the greatest golfer of the age, to act as an unpaid spokesman and consultant, and his view on golf's social benefits echoes the Olmstedian doctrine that the path to social improvement runs through parks. "Recreational facilities represent an investment which will return growing dividends in health and national well-being," Jones said. "Outdoor sports, and golf in particular, because it promotes sportsmanship as well as physical sturdiness, are a benefit in which all should have a chance to share." Jones resisted, however, the patriotic urge to invite the hacking masses to Augusta National, one of very few private courses built during the Depression.

About half a dozen times every year since 1984, Bob Graves and Geoff Cornish have run a two-day seminar on golf course architecture. It was from them I learned the handful of basic guidelines, the elevator-in-a-tall-building rules, that a well-laid-out golf course won't violate. Usually the audience for their road show is a group of golf course superintendents—the people the British still call greenkeepers—but once a year they descend on Cambridge, the wellspring of landscape architecture, to share their accumulated wisdom with a select group at the Harvard Graduate School of Design. Graves flies in from California, while Cornish drives over from Amherst, in western Massachusetts. The seminar I attended was supposed to start at 9:00 A.M. on a morning that fell by appropriate coincidence during the week the United States Golf Association (USGA) was staging The Open at The Country Club in Olmsted's Brookline, but Graves announced a short delay while our hosts tried to find a key that would open the cabinet with the slide projector. Cornish said, with polite conviction, that the superintendents handle the preparation for the seminar a little better, "but then Harvard's only been in education for three hundred years."

The supers take a test after their seminars, and if they pass get a document attesting to their acquaintance with the basic principles of course design from the Golf Course Superintendents Association of America, their professional organization. The Harvard crowd get certificates, too, VE RI TAS seal and all, but it's pretty much a straight cash transaction, no proof of learning required. Most of the attendees at Harvard are landscape architects, either honing up on course design for a subdivision or hoping that their tutors will reveal the secret path to fame and riches and a fabulous career as a golf course architect.

Cornish and Graves wear the official red plaid blazers of the American Society of Golf Course Architects, and have a practiced, easy instructional style, The Geoff and Bob Show. They're both past presidents of the ASGCA, and Cornish is the custodian of the profession's history. Like most golf course architects—but unlike Graves or Hills— Cornish learned his craft from a practicing course designer. Stanley Thompson, Cornish's mentor, was Canadian, a founding member of the ASGCA, and the first employer and partner of the young Robert Trent Jones. In those days, the limited shaping on a golf course was produced by a horse or mule pulling a scraper or, as it was sometimes called, a flipper pan. These pans were like giant flour scoops with wheelbarrow handles. The teamster would pull the handles up to gather earth, then drag the full scraper on its smooth bottom to the dumping spot and lift the handles to deposit the dirt. Cornish remembers that Jones, who is short, had trouble lifting the handles on the pan high enough to dump its load. Another of Thompson's young associates teased Jones, telling him he'd never make much of a golf course architect if he couldn't get any better at flipping a pan. Fifty years later, when he published his book on the history of golf course architecture, Cornish called the entire period after World War II "The Age of Robert Trent Jones."

Cornish was a fresh graduate of the University of British Columbia in his hometown of Vancouver when Thompson recruited him in 1937 to work on a course there called Capilano. Cornish hadn't planned on making golf architecture his career, but it provided him an opportunity he welcomed. When Cornish was mustered out of the Canadian Army after World War II, the prospects for resuming his career in golf design were not bright. Cornish was seeing more courses disappear than built—about 2,000 were lost between 1929 and 1957. Cornish took a teaching job at the Stockbridge School, the pioneer turf science program at the University of Massachusetts—he was trained in soil science—and slowly worked his way back into course design. By the 1970s, he was the dean of designers in New England, running a busy practice from his Amherst home with the help of his wife, Carol. Despite his association with Thompson, it took Cornish a while to persuade the ASGCA to accept him as a member, but the same year the society finally invited him to join it made him its secretary and handed over the minutes of its previous meetings. Wondering if he'd been blackballed—after all, he'd been associated with course design for nearly thirty years—Cornish searched the society's records, but they noted only that his previous applications were "incomplete." Cornish became the twenty-second member of the ASGCA, joining Pete Dye, Bob Graves, Ed Seay—the designer for Arnold Palmer—and Rees Jones in the class of 1967.

The origins of golf, like courtship, cuisine, and other basic cultural practices, are obscure, anonymous, lost in antiquity. But *designing and building* golf courses is, relatively speaking, an infant practice. Only 600 people in all of human history, according to Cornish's researches, have designed golf courses. History has had more kings than that. A child born any time in the last hundred years was more likely to find the cure for a disease than to design a golf course. The first golf course designers are roughly the grandfather's generation to architects of Cornish's age. Cornish's mentor, Thompson, was of the generation that bridged the ancients and the moderns. If the founding fathers of golf architecture were the profession's George Washington, Cornish and his cohort—no women among them—were of Lincoln's time. Nearly every golf course architect can reckon a line of descent from some pioneering predecessor. Joe Lee learned from Dick Wilson, who in turn acquired his trade working as a construction superintendent for Howard Toomey and William Flynn, proprietors of a flourishing design practice in the twenties. Donald Ross apprenticed to Old Tom Morris before he emigrated to the United States, and passed on his craft to a half-dozen associates. Frank Maples, for example, was a construction superintendent for Ross and was the greenkeeper at Pinehurst. His son, Ellis Maples, was a president of the ASGCA. His grandson, Dan Maples, born at Pinehurst, follows the family profession. Another architect trained by Ross, Skip Wogan, was the father of the contemporary New England course designer, Philip Wogan. Tracing these lines of descent echos the "begats" after a bit, which seems not inappropriate to a world that imitates the creation—microgenesis, pocket Edens, gardens of earthly delight.

Bob Graves and Art Hills are among the few course designers not anointed by an established predecessor. Graves and Hills were college fraternity brothers, both graduates in horticulture from Michigan State, but neither knew the other hoped one day to design golf courses. Graves's father was a dentist. "That didn't help much in my profession," he says, "but I've got good teeth." Graves is, however, connected by marriage to golf architecture's most illustrious line, the patrimony of Robert Trent Jones. Don Knott, the chief designer in Robert Trent Jones, Jr.'s, Palo Alto, California office, is husband to a Graves daughter. Jones, Jr., or Bobby, as distinguished from Trent, his father, is a salesman and a promoter more than a draftsmen, but he's not shy about taking credit for whatever work comes out of his office. Cornish says Bobby Jones and his brother, Rees, "are the only two people in the profession not surprised to have their jobs."

Hills, like Dye, is a self-created, self-taught course designer, though never the innovator Dye has been, sticking instead to more traditional modes of design. At Ironhorse, he expected to build a solid, dependable members' course, accepting as his challenge the task Dye disdained. UDS's site planners specified the golfing corridors, then asked Hills for comments and amendments. Even land planners who have worked on golf course projects sometimes don't really understand the work golf architects do, which is one of the reasons Cornish and Graves like giving their seminar at Harvard. During the construction of Ironhorse, after one of his site visits I went up to Hilton Head with Hills for a meeting with the planners and developers of a new course there, perhaps the last imposed on that golf-saturated island. The planners and engineers presented an elaborate scheme with some fancy engineering to handle effluent—that is, sewage water—traveling through the site's considerable marshland, with the dual attraction of cleansing the water and preserving the wetlands. The housing pods perched on the highest points, and a handful of archeological sites, among them the elaborate earthworks of a Union fort, constructed by the labor of former slaves, or as they were known during the peculiar legal limbo between the beginning of the Civil War and Lincoln's Emancipation Proclamation, "contrabands," dotted the property. The golf course was routed on this plan, right down to the lengths of holes and the locations of tees and greens even though Hills, the golf course architect, was seeing it for the first time. The "common view" of building architecture, according to Witold Rybczynski, is of "something refined, something superfluous, that is added to plain buildings to make them 'interesting.' " Hills was presented with a routing that left him to fiddle with the details, as it were, to trick up the greens, place the bunkers, and specify the plantings, as if that were the job of the golf course architect. Hills, though, thinks the routing is the course's spine, its strength, and no amount of legerdemain around the greens can overcome the deficiencies of a mediocre routing, any more than a new suit lets a tone-deaf man sing on key. But as his style in these meetings is restrained and deferential, Hills asked a few questions about how firm the routing was and, hearing that he had some flexibility, took it under advisement. Similarly, for Ironhorse the routing of the course was a dialogue between UDS and Hills.

Hills, Cornish, Graves, and every other golf architect run up against the recurrent hope among land planners that there must be compatible uses for all those acres devoted to golf. Couldn't we use the cart paths for jogging, they wonder, or put horse trails along the perimeter of the fairways? You could, Graves says, if the runners, riders, and horses are willing to don armor. You just can't trust the golfers to keep the ball on the fairway. Charles Fraser, whose Sea Pines Plantation on Hilton Head accelerated golf's conquest of the sea islands, has a plan to develop golf courses as part of larger public sports complexes that would open the fairways to runners early in the morning, before the golfers attacked, but that's still in the dream stage. Golf courses don't invite general use, any more than an interstate highway, despite all that good smooth concrete, welcomes skateboards.

Ironhorse was constrained above all by its entry, off the Beeline Highway and across the railroad tracks. The plan Sher expected to follow when the county approved his subdivision squeezed the golf course into tight corridors, with no parallel holes. Twelve holes worked around the perimeter, retaining the open feeling of the Preserve and the adjoining lands, but that left six canyon holes, nestled amid housing. Unless an expensive overpass was built, golfers would have to cross the road right at the main entry. To get to the clubhouse, they'd have to drive the entire length of the property, which would tend to clutter traffic. The interior portion of the golf course skirted the road, bringing it dangerously within range of a big slicer's drive on the two finishing holes. It's better to have the clubhouse nearer the entry, so the traffic around the residences is kept to a minimum, and as Graves told his Harvard seminar, it's always better to keep roads on the left if you must have them near the course. Most golfers are right-handed, and a right-handed slice sails in that direction, a hopeless and ruined flight, a helpless flutter. Cars skirting the right side of a hole risk intercepting sliced shots. The original Ironhorse site plan was not a triumph of the land planner's art, but that wasn't why Sher had so much trouble developing it. The plan could always be modified. No, Sher got stuck because he couldn't close a deal, and he couldn't close a deal because Ironhorse, despite the wide road labeled MAIN ENTRANCE on the site plan, didn't really have an entry. The easement granted by the railroad was not permanent, but permitted only at the railroad's sufferance. Sher had been set to close on an acquisition loan with an Ohio savings and loan, enough money to exercise his option and pay off the Grier heirs, when the title insurance company dropped the boom. There was no right-of-way onto the property. As the S&L read the county's approval, Ironhorse had entry rights off Jog Road, but Jog Road not only wasn't built yet along Ironhorse's eastern property line, it hadn't even been dedicated yet by the Solid Waste Authority or accepted by the county. The county left it up to the CFX Railroad to decide if it would grant rights-of-way at both the old entry and at Jog Road, but said that if the railroad would only grant one crossing it *had* to be at Jog. The S&L read that to mean that there was no public access to Ironhorse. It cost Sher a loan broker's fee of $40,000 to make this discovery. Jog Road didn't exist, so you couldn't come in on Jog. The railroad hadn't granted a permanent easement for the old entry road, so it could withdraw its permission to cross. When asked later how tough it was to deal with the railroad, Ironhorse's lawyer said, "When I call them, I can't even get them to admit they *work* for the railroad." Furthermore, the county might still say no, it would only approve an entry off Jog, which would hold up any development of Ironhorse until Jog was built, and no one could predict when that would happen. Despite its rosy prospectus and positive appraisal, Ironhorse the PUD—planned unit of development—wasn't worth much if you couldn't get to it. That's when Sher's long nights began.

5

Flight of the Bird Lady

NINE MONTHS after Hills saw Ironhorse, the prospect for building his first West Palm Beach golf course was meager. Sher, his optimism battered by a tepid response to Ironhorse's development plans, was like a tired swimmer in the middle of a lake. No proximate refuge beckoned, no beacon shone. Every distant shore seemed just out of reach. Hills added another worry, alarmed that the construction scenario envisioned by Sher's project manager, an old hand in Palm Beach development who'd worked on PGA National and Breakers West, would subvert the golf course. "If we follow his ideas," Hills wrote Sher, "we will lose the opportunity to build a course as good as or better than Bonita Bay or The Wilderness. His way will destroy the natural islands [of vegetation] which I want to keep for you." Hills almost begged Sher for his support. Contrary to what the project manager and the consulting environmental engineer were saying, Hills wrote Sher, "The course can be staked and surveyed without destroying everything in the line of play. Had we done what they suggest, Bonita Bay would not be what it is today."

Hills wanted Ironhorse to borrow some of the look of Bonita Bay and to a lesser degree perhaps The Standard Club in Atlanta, placing tees and even greens in settings which, whether natural or not, conveyed the impression of evolving from the existing landscape. What Hills wanted to avoid was the great pushed-out open spaces of the

typical south Florida golf course, the kind of unimaginative and te-
diously repetitive holes characteristic of, for example, PGA National's
courses. The project manager and the engineer were thinking about
ease of construction, while Hills was lobbying hard for a chance to
build another course with the beauty, strength, and integrity of Bonita Bay. "If we are to produce the kind of course you want," Hills
insisted, "one which will be singularly attractive and therefore enhance all values we must respond to the drainage work with exceptional care and imagination!" The exclamation point was not casual.
Hills's letters to his clients were, generally, pithy and precise. He
wanted Sher to absorb and contemplate his warning.

Before he could spend a whole lot more time worrying about
Ironhorse's drainage, though, Sher needed to get its financing in
place. He fired the project manager and retrenched, shearing expenses, but he couldn't find a developer or financial partner willing
to share his vision. Potential partners feared the effect of the Solid
Waste Authority's proximity, and while usually admitting, as one
courted developer put it, "to being earlier romanced by the site,"
begged off consummation when they couldn't satisfy themselves that
there would never be even a hint of contamination, olfactory or
otherwise, from either the Dyer Landfill—Mount Trashmore, the giant landfill just east of the Turnpike—or the new SWA incinerator
designed to replace Dyer. And Sher was still driving a hard bargain.
Michael Gordon, Sher's savvy and practiced lawyer, a self-proclaimed
master of the development deal, was stumped by Sher's stubborn-
ness. "He wanted *all* his money back, fifty percent of the profits, and
say-so over the density and the golf course and the clubhouse
design—that's the mentality I was dealing with."

Gordon introduced Sher to several candidates, but his demands
erased their interest. They were coming to the movies but wouldn't
hold hands. By the spring of 1986, half a dozen developers had
turned down a chance to buy into Ironhorse. The problem of access
to the property had not been resolved and the Grier widow and
heirs were eager to close, despite kindly feelings toward Sher and
his plans for the ranch. The purchase-money note between Sher
and the Grier estate, amounting to just under $4 million, was due
in August 1987. Sher's investment, now well into seven figures,
was looking risky. It was then, in the fall of 1986, that Joshua Muss
learned of Ironhorse.

Ironhorse came to Muss's attention, and he to Sher's, in a roundabout way. A friend with an apartment in the Shers' Singer Island building worked for Equitable Life. Sher asked him if his company might have an interest in the acquisition and development—A and D—financing for Ironhorse. Equitable wasn't interested, but knew of a British outfit looking for investment property in south Florida. Sher met with a representative of the British company, who toured the site and, like nearly everyone regaled by the Button King, found his ardor fetching and his land and plan appealing. His company, however, he was obliged to tell Sher, had a sedate and cautious operating style and acted only with great deliberation. Always careful moving into a new market, it was especially wary of one as volatile as south Florida's. Impulse and speed, the watchwords of the aggressively acquisitive, were not in its vocabulary. It would take at least two years for it to act on a purchase like Ironhorse. Sher was hoping for a quicker closure, an antidote to the disquieting apparition attending his sleepless nights, the nightmarish image of his hard-earned treasure sinking into Ironhorse's ravenous black muck, button by button by button, dropping with the rhythm of a dirge into the darkness. Well, Sher's visitor said, he knew of a developer in Washington, D.C., who was looking for high-end property to develop in Palm Beach County, someone with experience, deep pockets, and resolve, a man who, upon seeing a deal he liked, could act, decisively and alone, without the impediment of a board of directors that required persuasion or the restraint of investors with the power to reign him in. Muss, Sher heard, ran his own show.

Muss, as it turned out, shared a slightly muted version of Sher's faith in Ironhorse as a lasso waiting to fling around the neck of northern Palm Beach County's wild horse of a luxury housing market. Muss wanted more lots to sell. Ironhorse's original zoning was for very low density—only 230 homes. Muss agreed with Sher that "Ironhorse has very good prospects for being a successful real estate venture," even priced a bit under Sher's grand projections and without the beach club Sher planned on several acres he'd purchased on Singer Island. Muss was interested only in the Grier Ranch's 354 insular acres. Half-acre lots, he thought, "should be priced at $150,000, zero lot lines at $100,000, and club memberships at $30,000." At those numbers, projecting a five-year sellout, money could be made—in the neighborhood of $9 million. Muss told Gordon that he was interested in pursuing a deal. But he hoped there was a way to generate more lots to sell. He would look to the professional team assembled by Sher, which he expected to keep on board, to find them.

Gordon, tired out by Sher's intransigence, angry that he'd turned his back on deals that Gordon not only thought were generous and doable but that he'd pulled personal strings to arrange, met Muss two weeks after Sher had. His first impression was not exactly propitious. "He's a Nazi," Gordon remembers thinking. "I hated the guy." Muss, in the meanwhile, looked on Sher's demands with a certain detachment—this was not a deal Muss had to make, but Sher's ne-gotiating room was running out. Muss hadn't gotten where he was ignoring labored breathing across the negotiating table, and while expressing a serious interest in Ironhorse and sharing an outline of his plan to develop it, he hardly came courting. Muss quickly realized that Sher "wanted someone to put up the money and sit back, and I said, 'Not this Jewish boy.' "

Muss took a tour of Ironhorse on the ATVs with his friend and associate, Robert Judelson, cofounder of a company called Balcor, a pioneer in real estate investment trusts managing assets of about one and a half billion dollars when Judelson and his partners sold the company to Shearson—later acquired by American Express—in 1982, for $180 million. Balcor would, as it turned out, supply the bridge financing to purchase the ranch from the Grier Estate.

Sher thought Muss looked "more like a financial guy than a developer—Madison Avenue." Sher took Muss and Judelson on the ATV tour, bouncing over the pastures, splashing through the drain-age ditches, taking in the views. "They had a ball," Sher recalls. But Muss wanted more houses at Ironhorse than Sher thought com-ported with his dream, so, while not entirely turning his back on Muss, Sher kept looking. Arvida, a major Florida developer, wanted to buy the property for a development with much higher densities, but Sher, "still looking for my dream," also turned Arvida's offer down. He pursued a joint development deal with a Palm Beach developer—let's call him Mr. Miller—the kind of guy who's at pains to conduct his social life in full view of the gossipy reporters for "The Shiny Sheet," as the locals call the Palm Beach *Daily News.* A bon vivant with a reputation earned early in his career for refusing to sell his houses to Jews, Miller publicly effected a change of heart that people like Mike Gordon never found convincing. "When all the Gentiles moved out," Sher says, describing the impulse for Miller's conversion, "and the rich Jews moved in, he joined the antidefamation whatever and started getting humanitarian awards." Miller brought a very wealthy Canadian businessman, a man whose sail toward good fortune was launched over a sea of whiskey, to look at Ironhorse, and once again the ATV tour produced pleasure but no deal. Gordon, who despised Miller and thought the risks of dealing with a man he described as a "total psycho" were much greater than Sher could or should bear, erected a big barricade in the middle of this avenue. "I made him hate me," Gordon says. "I killed the deal."

SHER WAS NOW less than six months from a reckoning with the Grier estate. In early February, Muss wrote Sher a very cool note. He'd heard about the talks with Miller. "At one point I thought we had an agreement," he wrote, but given Sher's pursuit of other deals, "I have put my interest in this project on the shelf. I am sure you can understand that."

Gordon continued with his "one hour of therapy every day with Alan," trying to raise him from the doldrums. Sher called Gordon every morning. Tension ruled. "It's March," Gordon remembered. "They're closing in on us in August. Alan's finally starting to give in. So I called Muss."

Now, at last, the deal got serious. Sher's vision of an Ironhorse that, as Muss put it, was supposed to "look like Beverly Hills" was not one Muss could share. He hoped and expected to work "additional units into the plan," but still tap the luxury market. Ironhorse was, Muss knew, a bit of a "stretch. Most of my work," he said, "has been selling Chevrolets—*new* Chevrolets." Now he was ready to market Cadillacs. He didn't see a whole lot of difference. "It's not as if I decided to go manufacture motor launches." And he was indifferent to Sher's enthusiasm. These two were "*beyond* the opposite ends of the spectrum," one of the lawyers said, "and maybe that's what let them do the deal. Sher wanted the ultimate toy, but Muss had no emotional attachment to this or any other project." Willing to adopt Sher's development team, Muss specifically agreed to use Hills, Gordon, and, when the course was built, to hire Craig Shankland, the professional golfer who had advised Sher early on, as the director of golf. Muss didn't know Hills—he wasn't much of a golfer, for that matter, an eighteen handicapper whose goal when he played these days was "to only lose one or two balls"—but didn't think Hills's relative obscurity mattered. Nicklaus or Dye, he thought, could attract attention to a project, but if you didn't have a marquee name it was sufficient to have someone competent. Hills clearly qualified. The proximity of SWA didn't bother Muss, either. "I've sold under high-tension lines, next to industrial parks," he later reflected. "If there was a noxious odor, I'd have turned it down."

Ironhorse's insularity appealed to him. By early April, Muss and Sher had agreed to make a deal and by the end of May had hammered out most of its details. Balcor would loan money to satisfy the mortgage coming due for Sher, and Muss would take over the project. Immediately he had Urban Design Studio rework the master plan. He wanted the clubhouse in the center of the site rather than stuck way back in the southeast corner, as the original plan had it. He wanted the entry off Jog Road rather than the Beeline Highway. And he wanted higher density—325 houses rather than 230. By the middle of May, Urban Design had submitted a revised master plan to Palm Beach County. Hills had revised the golf course to fit the new corridors. At the end of July, the Board of County Commissioners would vote its final approval of the new plans, the appropriate county agencies having reviewed it in the meanwhile. In a memo to Muss and Sher in May, UDS outlined a schedule. Construction on the golf course would begin in mid-October 1987. It would be ready to grass by April, ready to play on November 1, 1988—two years later than Sher had originally expected, but soon enough.

AND THEN ALONG CAME the Bird Lady.

Ironhorse's new plans sailed through the county's staff review. With a few modifications, it said, "This proposal will be consistent with the requirements of the Comprehensive Plan and local development regulations." The town of Riviera Beach—pronounced "Rivera" by natives like Burt Reynolds, but "Riviera" by newcomers like the Shers, whose Singer Island home was jurisdictionally in Riviera Beach—had agreed to provide water and sewage service to Iron-horse, even though they shared no contiguous boundaries. A wealthy development like Ironhorse was a welcome addition to Riviera Beach's tax base. Riviera Beach was mostly African-American and poor, but it had bonding power and was eager to annex Ironhorse. That was fine with the county.

The Palm Beach Board of County Commissioners had first approved a master plan for Ironhorse in February of 1986. The proposal to amend it, everyone told Sher, was simple and routine. Even with 325 houses on its 354 acres, Ironhorse was well within the definition of "very low-density housing" that both its zoning and the previous approval required. The county's conditions of approval were all simple to meet. At worst they'd take a little time. The county wanted to make sure that the landscape code requirement of one tree "preserved or planted for each 1,500 square feet of residential lot area" was met. No problem. The planners thought moving the entry to the Jog Road side was an improvement. The board stated, however, that "the plans submitted do not reflect any mitigation to cover the loss of cumulative functional values associated with impacted wetlands," so before it approved final plans the county wanted to see how Ironhorse planned to handle its wetlands. Aside from clarifying the amount in traffic fees it expected Ironhorse to pay—with more houses there would be more people using the roads—the county had few conditions. It asked for a six-foot berm on the south and east sides to make sure no surface water would spill from Ironhorse onto SWA property. Finally, as its last condition, that "no modification shall be made of the western reserve area [the preserve] except as necessary to comply with required state and federal permits." The planning commission recommended approval of Ironhorse's petition by a vote of five to none and forwarded it to the Board of County Commissioners.

Alan Ciklin, a colleague of Michael Gordon's who had handled Ironhorse in its infancy, invited Sher to his office to listen to the board's deliberations. The meetings were transmitted over a public information telephone line as a convenience to the lawyers, who could monitor the meetings, wait until it was time to appear, and then stroll down the street to the county office building to take care of business. The lawyers were sure they didn't need to appear. Approval was strictly a formality. The county had consented to the idea of Ironhorse a year and a half before, and the amendments to the master plan from the county's point of view were minor. The golf course still took up about 160 acres, the lakes another forty or so. There were a few more houses, but still fewer than one per acre over all. Sher and Ciklin sat back to enjoy the elimination of this final hurdle. Once it was cleared, Muss would arrange to pay off the Grier estate and Sher could start sleeping again. Urban Design Studio sent a representative to the board meeting to answer any questions the commissioners might have about Ironhorse's request. Howard

Searcy, the engineer whose firm had designed the water-management plan and was negotiating for all the permits with the Army Corps of Engineers, U.S. Fish and Wildlife, and the South Florida Water Management District, came along specifically to discuss the preserve or any questions about water management. Sher settled into a chair and cocked his ear to the speakerphone.

"The next hearing item is Number 54, Petition 85-112 (A), the petition of Alan Sher." Sher grinned and winked at Ciklin, leaning back in his chair, looking as if he had just heard the world's best joke. As usual, he was dressed casually, in shorts, knit shirt, and tennis shoes, his mottled pate a monument to his long hours in the Florida sun. Ciklin, handsomely tailored and calm, happy for this client whom he'd come to think of as a friend, smiled back. Having shared the travails, they were ready for a triumph, however simple.

"In spite of what may seem to be some negative locational attributes," the UDS spokesman assured the commissioners, "we feel that this is an excellent site; and, again, it's an already approved PUD. The piece of property is isolated and, of course, that's enhanced by the catchment area and the . . . what *we* feel . . . the well designed resource recovery plant. The property has good access. The road conditions in the area are good; and we're not within a flood hazard area."

Sher thought all this sounded great. He'd known all along what a great site Ironhorse had. What a relief, he thought. It's really going to happen. They're talking about the thing that *I* created, about my idea.

"We've redesigned the site to enhance these inherently good site attributes; take advantage of the natural vegetation on the site; and to improve our isolation from both Jog Road and the Beeline Highway . . . The proposed golf course is a championship level, 18 hole golf course . . . We have a 9.3 acre clubhouse site in the center of the PUD, which will provide a swimming pool, tennis court and social amenities for the residents . . . we are in full agreement with all of the conditions recommended; and respectfully request your approval."

The chairman asked if there were any public comments. Ciklin didn't expect any. There hadn't been any at the planning commission, nor were there any objections when the original master plan was approved. After a pause, Sher heard the chairman say, "Would you give us your name for the record, please," followed by a woman's voice speaking in the accents of Sher's native New York.

"For the record," she said, "my name is Rosa Durando. I wish to discuss this petition at length . . ."

Sher looked to Ciklin, slightly alarmed. It's the Bird Lady, Ciklin told him. She objects to *every* development. Don't worry. She's like the boy who cried "wolf." Sher settled back to listen.

"This is one of those plans," Ms. Durando said, "that look good on paper, but should never really have gone any further. It was a bad development to begin with; and it's even proposed worse now; and I would say that no matter what you people decide here today, I doubt that it will ever really fly. Only, I wish the Board of County Commissioners accepts the responsibility of a review of this.

"It's a very low lying, wet area, and I guess it really knocks into a cocked hat the fact that the Solid Waste Authority lowers land values . . . We see a very upscale community here that is much closer, completely surrounded by preserve area on one side and on two sides by a Solid Waste Authority that was sued extensively by the City of Riviera Beach and Steeplechase [a development just north and east of Ironhorse, on the opposite side of the freeway]."

Sher was no longer happy with what he was hearing. Yeah, Riviera Beach and Steeplechase had sued SWA, but they lost, just like the Audubon Society lost when it tried to stop SWA from building its garbage-fueled power plant. All the engineering reports said that the air and water—either the groundwater or the water impounded in the catchment basin—were not endangered by SWA, so why was she bringing *that* up again?

Ms. Durando pushed ahead. "I was dismayed at the time this came back and I saw it a week or so ago; and I went to the Solid Waste Authority, and they were surprised, because they hadn't been notified. I consulted with Pete Pimentel [of the Northern Palm Beach County Water Control District] on whom this whole thing is keyed out and he said, gee, I haven't heard from them in a year and a half . . . Pimentel agreed that the Northern Palm Beach County Water Control District could manage the drainage if they could get the water to them, and that depended on a permit from DOT [Department of Transportation] on their canal . . . and they would have to get permission from them. Those letters were sent off, but the final permission was never in writing and that's why Pete Pimentel said he officially can't say that they will accept them. That matter hasn't been cleared up . . ."

As he listened to Rosa Durando explain in her rapid and breathless tones exactly why the City of Riviera Beach was ill equipped to annex Ironhorse—a judgment Muss would come to agree with—Sher felt bewilderment. Who *was* this woman, and why was she doing this to him?

Rosa Durando was there because of water, and birds, and a fear that her beloved Florida had turned its back on both. She had studied agriculture at the University of Kentucky, finding in those folded hills around Lexington a world that made New York a happily fading memory. She went to work for a couple of equine parasitologists— "going through ten miles of intestines every day"—and then discovered a gift for breaking yearlings. She finished an M.S. in zoology and then signed on for the gypsy life, working with thoroughbreds, making the circuit from Kentucky to South Carolina to New York. She went to work for a Florida trainer and found the place she felt was home. In 1960 she bought twenty acres on the edge of the Everglades, way west of any residential development. There were gladiola farmers in the neighborhood, but they didn't seem to mind the cypress heads and summer flooding, planting their bulbs in the dryer uplands. There was a three-acre pond on her place and seasonal swamps. Wood storks and roseate spoonbills fed on her lands. She rescued worn-out racers and let them graze on her pastures. She was, in her love of wildlife, a kindred spirit with the Shers' daughter, Carrie Reese, whose deliverance of the racehorse called The Colonel had, in a roundabout way, ushered in Ironhorse. Now the Bird Lady was threatening to show Ironhorse the door.

In the early seventies, the county dug canals west of her place, and "within a year my whole property drained out. My three-acre pond just got *sucked out*. Nobody would say why." She missed her water, longed for her birds, and vowed to learn why they'd gone. That's how she found out the whole drainage basin she lived in was, because of the county's drainage work, washing down South Florida's C51 Canal. It got her dander up. She joined The Audubon Society of The Everglades and took up the cudgel against the developers. Her birds still aren't back. Since she came to Florida, there's been an 80 percent drop in the number of breeding wood storks—only 500 nesting storks remain in the Everglades. Another endangered species, the Everglades snail kite, once nested and fed not far from Durando's house. In the drought of 1981, the kites started moving north, and she and a biologist from the Loxahatchee Wildlife Refuge went looking for them. Amid the trees and shallow ponds scattered among the windrows of spoil from an old shell-rock mining borrow pit, just east of the water-catchment basin—by coincidence the land SWA later acquired as part of its immense "resource recovery site"—they found the kites. When SWA bought the property, she fought its plans, but, when she found that its managers were serious about protecting the nesting birds on the property, dropped her opposition. She now saw SWA, which had set aside almost 400 of its 1,320 acres for wildlife, as a sort of grudging ally. It was protecting the rookery that harbored not only the snail kite but wading birds, vultures, and an occasional eagle. There were marsh rabbits, deer, and bobcats sheltered there, too. Her fears about Ironhorse were rooted in her deep suspicion of its experts. Howard Searcy, sitting near her, ready to defend Iron-horse's environmental plans, was to Durando just about the devil incarnate, even if she never could make him mad. "I insult him," she'd say, "but he just smiles. Someday he'll get his retribution," she imagines, knowing that in a world that rewards him well for his work it's riches alone that he'll gather in this life. "He's the central figure," she complains, "who destroyed all the wetlands with these develop-ments." And if Searcy is the devil, Pimentel—another "nice man," she says, "who's easy to believe"—is a junior Lucifer, "every word out of his mouth programmed by the MacArthur Foundation." She's used to jousting with windmills and is unafraid to stand alone.

"I'm going to refresh your memory," Durando said to the board, as if to answer Sher's astonished query. "One of the problems here is that [Ironhorse] is home definitely that we know to the Everglades snail kite . . . [SWA] realigned Jog Road because it was indeed going to impact a rookery that's on the Solid Waste property. Now, the kite has been documented by many agencies . . . It's not only a feeding area. It is a nesting area immediately to the south. We all know that now, and it's been documented.

"They talked originally about a fifty-four acre preserve area, [but] the Site Plan reduced it down to forty acres, plus in one place, the necessary berm looks like on the plan it is breached by the golf course, in one major place; and several other places along the pre-serve, there are golf—I don't know the right technology terms—but they're playing golf into the preserve area. I fail to see how the integrity of the purpose of this cypress head with the high water table is going to be protected if there is recreation in a buffer zone. I've always believed this buffer zone is small enough that it should have been absolutely inviolate as far as keeping the water head high and

keeping a berm on the east side of it. I don't think there should be golf
or any other recreation allowed in a preserve area.

"I've been on several bird counts at the Solid Waste site, one of
them in the evening about four to seven to count the kites as they
come in and they did come in from over this area. And let me tell you
the mosquitoes are horrendous. You're surrounded by marshland
that is very good for wildlife but very bad for human beings. The
mosquito populations are very, very high. I know what's going to
happen. There are going to be people who have worked hard, made
money and expect to live on a luxury level"—she was at least right
about that, Sher conceded—"surrounded on three sides by preserve
area, and they're going to want to spray. There's no question about
it, because I don't see how you can live there without spraying.

"That runoff is highly polluting. It will have to go somewhere,
someday."

The shallow irrigation wells Ironhorse was proposing also disturbed Durando. "I can't imagine what a shallow well will do to the
water catchment area in a time of very low water table."

"I think I've hit on all the salient points why I don't want to see this
increased today. Probably banks would like to see a larger concentration on paper to advance loans. There can never be shale rock in
here because obviously it's so low, they're going to need everything
they excavate in those ponds. The money is probably a big problem,
but I don't think you ought to enhance a developer's capabilities at a
bank to approve something that probably cannot happen physically.

"Thank you."

Rosa Durando sat down. Alan Sher jumped up. They were blocks
apart physically, but locked in a spiritual grapple. Ciklin told him not
to worry. She's an environmental gadfly. They know her. Snails.
Wetlands. Cypress head. Wellfield. Aquifer. Whatever she thinks will
summon sympathy. They know her speech. The board's a rubber
stamp. It's in the bag. Sher turned his ears to the speaker. Down the
street from the offices of Boose Casey Ciklin et al., the prominent
Palm Beach development lawyers, Howard Searcy gathered himself,
calm and modest, lean as Gary Cooper, the old gunfighter whose
wiles froze the hands of his enemies. He turned his familiar ruddy
face toward the commissioners, ready to rebut. He always took the
long view. He knew this was not a battle he could lose.

"Of the comments that Ms. Durando made," he began, in measured tones, "I think it's important to note that the permits that are

required before construction of this project can commence, are all in the process of being modified to meet the revised Site Plan that's before you today."

This was good strategy. Follow the rules and let *them* figure out where they've gone wrong. "With regard to U.S. Army Corps of Engineers and Fish and Wildlife Service, on January 6 there was a jeopardy opinion by the Endangered Species Section of U.S. Fish and Wildlife Service stating that based on the degraded quality of the wetlands on the site, that they felt like this project could be developed without placing the Everglades kite in jeopardy. That is the official opinion of U.S. Fish and Wildlife."

He was also working with the South Florida Water Management District to make sure that the shallow recharge wells for the golf course were placed as far away from the water catchment basin as possible and "demonstrate that the cone of influence during that period of time "—that is, when the lakes are low and Ironhorse has to pump from the wells to recharge the lakes it will irrigate from— "will not adversely impact the West Palm Beach Water Catchment Area . . . we think we'll have very little impact on the water catchment area. We've agreed to a list of conditions requested by the City of West Palm Beach. Those have not been changed. They will be complied with as per the previous approval; and the size, location and preservation of the buffer has not changed under the new plan.

"I think these are the salient points that need to be brought to your attention."

And with that Searcy sat down. Sher was still pacing. He looked at Ciklin again for reassurance. That answered the Bird Lady, didn't it? Now they'd vote, wouldn't they?

But there were more questions from the commissioners. "We have recently become aware," said one commissioner, "that where golf courses are owned independent that they can become a problem. Is Ironhorse going to be owned by the Association and the landowners?"

Yes, she was assured. The golf course is "part of the common area and would be maintained by them."

That may all be well and good, the commissioner replied, but, she added, "I don't think this is a good place for this development in the first place, and to be perfectly blunt, I'm not reassured by the Engineer's assurances that there won't be problems with either leachate or the irrigation wells, and I'm concerned about many of the same issues that Mrs. Durando is relative to the wetlands, the mosquitoes and the overall nuisance of the Solid Waste Authority's facilities being nearby; and the mosquitoes are absolutely awful; and I quite agree that, you know, I've lived in Florida since 1942, and the mosquitoes have been the bane of our existence, and where they are, and where the owners are able to institute a mosquito control program, they do it; and I can't tell you the number of sick birds I've taken care of from mosquito or secondary poisoning due to spraying. I just don't think it's going to work."

What was going on? Sher's earlier fears tickled his skin, like the chill of an IRS audit. The contentment he'd worn up the elevator to Ciklin's office was too thin to ward off this cool auditory breeze. He was pacing, barely able to believe the words that fluttered about his ears like the taunts of naughty children. *Mosquitoes!* First the bird, now a bug! He *loved* the bird, for crying out loud. God forbid we should see one. Just kidding! What was going on here?

Another commissioner pressed Searcy on the kite. "Has there been any sighting on the property of the kite?"

"It's never been sighted on the property," Searcy answered. The consulting biologist Ironhorse had hired to inventory its wildlife did not see any kites on his visit. South Florida's continuing drought seemed to have pushed them further north. "What is present," Searcy continued, "is the apple snail which is a food source; and the U.S. Fish and Wildlife Service requested that the Corps attach a condition to their permit that requires us to monitor the presence of the apple snail and also report any sightings of kites in the future, if they do exist."

"Since you've noticed that they are there, did they ask you to set aside that area to preserve the food for the feeding?" he was asked.

Not only are they setting aside the area where the existing apple snails were found, Searcy said, "in the mitigation plan in the waterway system there are going to be some shallow marsh areas that will promote the growth and development of the apple snail population in that area as well."

At last the board seemed satisfied on the wildlife issues, and no more environmental questions followed. But then the chairman began to press his staff on the traffic impacts, which led to a rather abstract and inconclusive debate—nothing to do with Ironhorse, really—about the models the county's planning staff used to determine the effects of new development. "It's damn frustrating to me," the chairman fulminated, "to spend the millions and millions of dollars that we're spending for staff and not be able to get at least one individual from staff at these very important meetings that are able to give us that comfort and that specifics. You know, we sat and approved a billion dollars' worth of budget and tremendous increases in Engineering, Planning, Building and Zoning, but still when you try and get specific impacts from decisions, it's like putting toothpaste back in a tube."

The preamble to this debate was the commissioners' realization in 1987 that they had accumulatively approved enough new development to add 500,000 people to the county's existing population of about 600,000. Palm Beach County then adopted its first growth control law, a revolutionary act in Florida, whose very essence is development. The law was a traffic ordinance, stipulating that as soon as a road was congested no new development could take place within five miles of it until after it was widened or a new road built. The county figured that just to catch up with the standards this statute imposed would take until 2005. In the meanwhile, one hundred people a day were moving to Palm Beach County.

The commissioners all knew that the county's planning staff was overworked. The county's director of zoning, when asked about all this later on, thought there was a hidden agenda in the bureaucrat's burden. "For many," he said, "it's self-serving to have a weak department. If you don't have the information, the battle of the anecdotes continues." That's what Sher was listening to, a setpiece skirmish over how and where to grow. On this day, the Bird Lady fired off the best stories.

Sher, buffeted by these inconclusive diatribes about the public weal, thought, that's all well and good for you to worry about, but this is my millions we're fooling with here and that's real money! His pacing was picking up speed. Ciklin thought he was going to jump on top of his desk. The voices whipping around the room were sounding more ominous by the second.

"For the environmental concerns that I've expressed," a skeptical commissioner was saying, "and because this development is like the hole in a doughnut of wetlands and wetlands that are going to be maintained as wetlands, I'd move denial of the Special Exception."

"Is there a second," asked the chairman?

The chair passed the gavel and seconded. The only commissioner who had not yet spoken summed up the board's irresolution. "I just don't have a comfort level with this. It just seems that there are so many areas that aren't answered; but—I don't know."

And with that ringing declaration of indecision resounding through the deliberative halls, the board voted three to one to deny Ironhorse its special exception and broke for lunch. Sher was stricken. "They denied it!" Ciklin, smooth and calm, said, "I think we miscalculated," and headed down the hall to summon the troops in "a scurry for reconsideration." Sher thought only of ruin. Mike Gordon joined Sher, sharing in his panic. He hadn't been paid yet.

And, of course, the Ironhorse professionals prevailed. One of Gordon and Ciklin's partners, an old hand at smoothing discord, rushed to meet the commissioners with box lunches tucked under his arm. An hour later one of the members who had voted against Ironhorse was ready to reconsider. "We feel it's kind of unfair to the owner of the property to suffer a denial . . . due to the inability on the part of the staff to answer some questions that the board had" was the way Urban Design's spokesman made his plea. Ironhorse *already had approval*—this was just a change in the plan, not in the use of the property. Let calmer heads prevail. Now, with their stomachs full, the commissioners voted first to reconsider and then, on the question of Ironhorse's special exception, to take it up again in thirty days. Meanwhile, the overworked planning staff would examine the all-important traffic volume issue.

So at the end of August, the special exception passed. The Grier estate, aware of the deal with Muss, didn't foreclose, waiting until September for Muss to complete the transaction. Muss, the "master of predevelopment exercises," as Gordon called him, had his high-end deal. He had managed to make time work for him—and time, Gordon says, "is the death knell of developers."

Ironhorse now belonged materially to Muss, but Sher was still the spirit hovering above it. He was "going to be whole again." He was getting reimbursed for all "the epileptic spending he did," a piece of the profits, and, he was sure, the right to pick the golf pro. Ironhorse the Golf Course. Now he could dream of birdies and drinks at the clubhouse bar, of watching the sun drop behind the range. Most of all, he could sleep, now that his dream of Ironhorse had gathered in its wings.

II

THE DESIGN

6

Fine Lines in Toledo

I SPENT A LOT of the summer of 1988 walking the grounds at Ironhorse, a copy of Art Hills's routing plan tucked under my arm, trying to discover what in the site might have inspired the shape or encouraged the features he planned for the golf course. What I saw mostly was an accumulated tension between Ironhorse's native south Florida flatness, its topographical ineffability, and the contours proposed in Hills's design. At Ironhorse, unlike a site with geologically derived shapes, the canvas was blank. Laying it out was a pure problem of design. Every bump, every swale, every mound and bunker grew first on a drafting table in Toledo, Ohio. Ironhorse had no gullies to ford or hills to level, just a flat receptive surface awaiting what Mike Dasher called the "sculpture by addition" that golf architects perform in south Florida. Ironhorse had lots of vegetation, but no movement in the ground. Ironhorse, in fact, wasn't moving anywhere.

Bob Isakson, the project manager at Ironhorse, struggling to get all his permits in line, complained endlessly about "this Florida." "I never saw a place like this for getting permits," he said daily, carefully recording his frustration in the three-ring notebooks that documented every call, every conversation, every memo and letter, compiling an official record with Nixonian exactitude, a dense package of rebuttals against faulty memory. Isakson knew how to cover his ass and struggled to keep the lines of discourse open. Muss, rarely visiting the site,

85

spent the time he devoted to Ironhorse—David Webber, Muss's right-hand man, estimated that Ironhorse took up no more than 10 percent of Muss's time—orchestrating its finances, fine-tuning the deal, getting all the horses to the starting gate. The salad days of easy acquisition and development money, the cash that the deregulation of the S&Ls unleashed, were over by the time Muss and Sher finally came to terms. Muss said later, "I didn't know how hard it would be to finance this thing. Six months before the deal I could have done it in two minutes, but by nineteen eighty-eight the failure of the S & Ls had left a vacuum. The banks whose business had been usurped by the S & Ls were hesitant to get back in. In January of nineteen eighty-seven," Muss continued, thinking back to when he and Sher had almost made a deal, "I could have gotten twenty-five million dollars without trying," but a year and a half later he was "sweating to get eighteen million."

While Muss was ironing out the finances, Ironhorse was abstract, its schedules ephemeral; the working days of its skeletal crew were spent chasing will-o'-the-wisps. Isakson regularly updated his carefully drawn time lines, showing the starting days for construction of the golf course, the clubhouse, the roads, sewers, and waterlines, until it dawned on him that this was a Sisyphean chore. Waiting to see which vehicle from his fleet the Button King would arrive in on his daily visit passed for excitement among the Ironhorse cast—Isakson, his assistant, Jon Harpman, and Matt Weeg, the sales manager for Ironhorse's real estate, who arrived from Hawaii in June and spent the next six months growing progressively more perplexed as he saw the date on which his first lot sale was likely to happen march further into the future as construction of the golf course was delayed, postponed, rescheduled. The odds-on daily favorite among Sher's automotive string was a four-wheel-drive red Range Rover, while the red Porsche showed up about as often as the Ferrari Testarossa—also red. The big black Benz swapped duty with the four-door Rover on days Sher brought along friends. His guests were always, in his mind, potential members of Ironhorse Country Club. "I think he's gonna buy," he'd say sotto voce to Weeg, or Isakson, or me, lips hidden behind his upraised wrist. He'd troop his companions back into Weeg's office, so Matt could practice his spiel. Colored renderings of the site plan hung on the wall of Weeg's office, once the master bedroom suite, which took up the ground floor at the west end of the ranch house. A golf course grading plan and an aerial photo pinned to the walls helped everyone get oriented. A similar set of drawings was thumbtacked in the dining room.

Isakson and Harpman had desks side by side in the living room, which was separated from the entry hall by a narrow wooden railing with thin turned balusters, a sixties' architectural touch that matched the shag carpet. The floors at the entry hall and the kitchen and the family room at the east end were of thick vinyl tile in a tasteful beige. Isakson's and Harpman's backs were against a wall of built-in hutches, used to store supplies and bear Isakson's carefully labeled collection of binders documenting the jobs he'd pushed, guides to contracts, procedures, building codes—the filaments that bound a project into a dense, controllable mass for a project manager. Isakson's smoking finally drove Harpman into the family room, at the opposite end of the house from Weeg's office, where his desk gave him a good view of anyone driving up. He shared this room of about 600 square feet with a small copying machine. Conversation richocheted between the hard floor and the vaulted ceiling. Harpman could look out the back through a wide pair of patio doors at a swimming pool in the last stages of decline, fossilizing from the top down as dense, bright-green algae formed a solid-looking, beautifully textured skin across its surface. You had to keep water in the pool or the shell would start to rise, floating in the groundwater like a phantom barge. It was cheaper to let nature reclaim it from above than mess with pulling it out. The land on which the house sat bridged two lots on the new Ironhorse plat, so the improvements were scheduled for destruction. In the meanwhile, the pool was an experiment in aquatic putrefaction.

Harpman's first defense against Isakson's thick cloud of Camel smoke had been a little fan clamped to a shelf behind his head, but curbing the air proved a lost cause, like trying to stop a surging crowd of Grateful Dead Heads with a really good deal on Barry Manilow tapes. Not even the air conditioner helped. Its supply ducts were in the ceiling, so its main effect was to hold the smoke at maximum inhalation height. Harpman wanted to stay close to Isakson so he could learn from his conversations, pick his brain about how to run a project, and ask him questions. Isakson started his construction career as a carpenter, and, like anyone who's spent too much time with his ear ten inches from a screaming Skilsaw, tends to talk with a volume that rivals traffic noise. When Isakson was on the phone, Harpman pretty much had to give up on any conversation of his own.

Moving his desk forty feet east gave both Harpman and Isakson a little privacy, even though there were no doors to close between them. Isakson sat out in the open, where no one could come or go without passing in review. Weeg had a door he could close, so on his occasional visits Muss tended to appropriate Weeg's office.

"You came down this road," Weeg would say to Sher's guests, drawing his finger down the white line on the aerial photo, "and we're here," pointing to a vague rectangle on the far left of the photo, which was hung with its western boundary to the top, the road bisecting its long axis.

"The entry road will be here, off of Jog," Weeg would point out, "which we should have open by next spring. The golf course will play to a par seventy-two, at sixty-eight hundred yards." Weeg's a tennis player, so these numbers are abstract to him. The lot prices are the figures he understands. The talk is that the lots will sell at first for $195,000—that's for a third of an acre, starting with the "least amenitized."

"If you sell off all your good product first," Weeg says, "you may sit too long on the lots that are left." The quicker the sellout, the less the interest cost on the development loan. "You're better off starting slow, building momentum, and then when sales take off you get the top price on the premium lots."

Weeg doubts that Sher's old friends will buy at Ironhorse, but he likes Alan and is happy to throw his pitch. Sher's enthusiasm, even as new impediments pop up to trip Ironhorse, radiates with enough heat to warm the coldest skeptic's heart. Late one morning Sher showed up with four elderly men, all residents of an older development near Boca, a place Sher described as "the Frenchman's of the sixties."

"None of these guys are moving anywhere," Weeg told Isakson, as he watched Sher's friends creak out of the Range Rover and idle up the front walk, "unless it's to a nursing home."

Weeg put on his best salesman's look, his boyishly handsome face trained to a sturdy smile, and shook each hand firmly as Sher made introductions. Isakson came around from his desk to welcome them. There wasn't yet a lot to do, but when there was these visits would lose their power to garnish a dull day. Weeg herded the visitors into the dining room, where they sat around the conference table, nodding in harmony as Weeg gave them the ten-dollar tour. "The clubhouse will be twenty thousand plus square feet, right here," pointing to nearly dead center on the aerial, "with plenty of parking, men's and women's locker rooms, a beautiful dining room, and a place to get a drink. Tennis courts here."

"The golf course, it's gonna be so great," Sher interjected. "Look at these holes here." He stood near the drawing, pointing vaguely. He wasn't really sure what hole was where, but had great faith in Hills and trusted his instincts. There was no doubt in his voice, even if his geography lacked precision. Sher could see great green carpets of grass running down to placid lakes, their surfaces wrinkled by a cooling breeze, flagsticks fluttering against the brighter green of the putting surface. He just wasn't sure where the tenth hole was going. In the lingo of the land planners, he couldn't "previsualize." He knew which lot he wanted, though, the one just across the lake from the eighteenth hole, with an unobstructed view of the clubhouse. In his mind, he was the head counselor at Camp Ironhorse, and he'd want to keep track of who came to play. His house would sit like a command post.

"On the west is the preservation buffer," Weeg continued as Sher came out of his reverie, "with the cart path here running along this berm that separates the preserve from the golf course. We're going for the natural look here. The architect is saving as many trees as he can, so it'll look mature when it opens. This land to the south and east is SWA, which will one day be a park, and this"—he ran his hand along the top of the aerial—"is the city water catchment basin, which will never be disturbed. So we're an island here, an exclusive, private island. Here's where Jog Road comes in"—he pointed along the eastern boundary—"and here's where the maintenance building goes. Which lot do you want?"

"So Alan," says one, "I got a question. Where does the garment factory go?"

Everyone laughed, and they headed out to repack the Range Rover for a tour of the grounds. Nothing had changed in the last six months, except a few test borings for soil samples and a study to see if there was any contamination left over from the ranching days, any chemicals leached into the groundwater. Only traces were found, mostly near the barn. Another environmental hurdle leaped. Days were passing, but the sense of urgency and mission with which the project began was softening into routines of boredom, long dull days only occasionally disturbed by uncertainty. Muss was struggling with the financing, while Isakson was waiting for approval of the water-management plan, annexation, and a permit to build the golf course.

After a couple of months I was starting to fear that Ironhorse would never get off the drawing board, that like the aborted cousins of the rockets we could see lifting off from Cape Kennedy, Ironhorse was going to get scrubbed, pulled off the launching pad, and hauled back to the hangar. It wouldn't be the first time a golf course was squelched. Hills designed a course on Fort George Island, Florida, in 1985, that was never built, even though the developer spent hundreds of thousands of dollars trying to deal with environmental and archeological restrictions. Dasher said he thought a half a dozen projects were probably contemplated, or even taken through some preliminary planning, for every one built. Ninety percent of the time the problem was money, but sometimes, as at Fort George Island, it was environmental. A course proposed for the Oregon coast was held up when an endangered butterfly was found breeding there. South of San Francisco, the discovery of another rare invertebrate stopped construction of a municipal course. "A spider, for crying out loud," one observer marveled.

HILLS HAD INVITED me up to Toledo to play Inverness, where he was a member, so I decided from what Isakson told me about the latest series of permitting delays that I wouldn't risk missing the first crunch of the dozer against pine bark by leaving West Palm for a bit. As it turned out, I could have stayed in Toledo for five months. I was as convinced as Sher that the first tree hitting the ground was of symbolic significance, and I wanted to be there to mark it. In the meanwhile, I'd take advantage of the delay to meet with Hills, look over his operation, and find out from Steve Forrest, Hills's first associate, whom I'd met at the ASGCA Convention in Bermuda that spring, how he managed to hold Hills's many projects together from Toledo while Art spent so much time in the field.

Hills hired Forrest as an intern in the summer of 1978, in the first flush of the resuscitation that finally reawakened the golf business after its collapse in 1974. A student at Virginia Tech in landscape architecture when Hills hired him, Forrest started drawing golf course routing plans when he was a boy. He still has drawings he did on the back of Marion Street Baptist Church programs when he was in junior high. It takes either a sense of destiny or unusual retentiveness to hang onto childhood doodles for twenty years. Forrest sent résumés to every golf course architect in the country, an early trickle in a steady stream of enquiries that's since risen to flood levels. Every golf architect gets a weekly batch of letters asking how to get started in the golf design business, frequently from golfers bored with their jobs—lawyers, salesmen, an occasional physician. Hills never discourages anyone from pursuing this hope, remembering his own struggle to get started. Hills knows, too, that Alister Mackenzie, the designer of Augusta National and Cypress Point, was a physician before he turned his hand to course design. Pete Dye sold insurance. Hills believes it when he says everyone should go after whatever opportunity he can imagine. But he had no jobs to offer until about ten years ago, just as, fortuitously, Forrest's letter came across his desk.

Hills interviewed two people for the job, deciding, as he recalled, that "one guy was a little more experienced and might handle the public a little better, so I called him and told him he had the job and all that."

Three days later a car with Virginia plates pulled up the driveway to Hills's office. Forrest climbed out the passenger side. His mom sat at the wheel. Tired from the 500-mile trip, Forrest pulled his suitcase from the trunk and looked over at the tiny back porch that's used as the main entry to Hills's office. Art watched Steve climb the steps, trying to figure out what to say when he came through the door. He'd called the wrong guy. Rather than embarrass him in front of his mother, Hills decided he'd give Forrest the job. Hills remembers thinking that Forrest would probably fail after a few weeks and he'd replace him with the person he thought he'd called. Forrest, as it turned out, was the perfect employee for Hills—orderly, calm, patient, pious, single, shy, self-effacing, and willing to work endless hours cheaply and without complaint. Eleven years later, married and self-confident, he runs Hills's little domain, the original associate, directing the work of five draftsmen and orchestrating the endless paper flow in and out of Toledo. Tall and thin, Forrest has a sweet smile and the sort of disposition Midwestern mothers describe as sweet. He plays golf as if it's a duty, with an acolyte's fervor but little skill. He's hard to rattle.

When Hills told me about hiring Forrest, he said, "Don't say anything to Steve about this," hinting that it might embarrass him. Then Forrest told me the story, without any prompting, laughing at its unlikely outcome. Art, though, doesn't remember telling Steve he was the wrong man, remembering only that "when I saw his mom there, what could I do?" Steve says Hills confessed his error right off the bat, but said he'd give him a chance anyway. Steve had enough gumption to accept.

On the morning of the second day I was in Toledo we were scheduled to play Inverness, but first we drove to Detroit, an hour north, so Art could meet with the superintendent and the greens committee at Oakland Hills to look at some tee renovations he'd suggested for these famous Donald Ross courses. Robert Trent Jones's "revitalization," as Herbert Warren Wind called it, of Oakland Hills's South Course for the 1951 U.S. Open inspired the taciturn Ben Hogan to say after he won with a final round of sixty-seven, "I'm glad that I brought this course, this monster, to its knees."

Ross, with his Scottish proclivity for discerning heavenly purpose, supposedly said when he first visited the land out of which he would fashion Oakland Hills, "The Lord intended this for a golf course." Oakland Hills looked benign rather than monstrous on the summer morning Art and I visited. As at Inverness, Oakland Hills's clubhouse view looks out toward the course across a wide swale. It's beautifully maintained, a striking parkland panorama.

Hills struggled with a way to tell the golf course superintendent that the trees and shrubs he'd spent the last twenty years planting along Oakland Hills's fairways made a wonderful arbor, but were something he'd rather not see on a golf course. Pictures of Oakland Hills, Inverness, and most of the other great old courses the USGA chooses for its championships taken right after they were built show only the faintest resemblance to their contemporary successors. In the old days, they were wide-open. Usually built on marginal farmland long since cleared of virgin forests, they bear about the same resemblance to today's courses that a corduroy road does to an interstate. Generations of plantings have tightened down the corridors and inhibit creative play. They take some of the randomness from the game, excise the fickle. The dictum that golf is not fair comports perfectly with a Scottish predestinarian fortitude, but sits less well with Americans, who abhor ambiguity and prefer domination to endurance. The courses designed by Ross, the Scotsman, seldom had trees anywhere near the landing area for drives. Ross is famous for his greens, which are often carefully preserved. When the greens at Ross's Pinehurst Number Two were rebuilt a few years ago, for example, every knob and bump was carefully charted before the old sod was lifted so the rebuilt greens could perfectly re-create the originals. The greens are the only feature of a course that get this worshipful attention. Nobody seems to much mind the slow and inexorable invasion of trees onto the margins of Ross's fairways. The East Course at Oak Hill in Rochester, New York, where Lee Trevino won his first U.S. Open in 1968, is a Donald Ross design transfigured by trees. "After the East Course was completed in 1926," according to William Davis in *100 Greatest Golf Courses*, "Dr. [John R.] Williams then planted thousands of trees and transformed an open, featureless piece of ground into the tree-lined test the world knows today."

Describing Oak Hill, Oakland Hills, or Inverness as an "open, featureless piece of ground" would not have pleased Ross. Old Tom Morris didn't design planting schedules for trees on his courses either. Ross's home course at Dornoch, in the northeast corner of Scotland, hasn't a tree in sight, nor would Dr. Williams's acorns have been welcomed on its sandy expanses. When the English started building inland courses toward the end of the nineteenth century, golfing traditionalists who abhorred a tree of any kind on a golf course thought the idea of playing golf in a forest made as much sense as a trombone in a string quartet. Bernard Darwin, the great scientist's grandson and Britain's greatest writer on golf, wrote of Romford in Essex in 1910 that it "is not particularly attractive, because in the first place it is flat, and in the second there are hedges and trees to be seen." "No course can be ideal which is laid out through trees," wrote Charles Blair Macdonald. "Trees foreshorten the perspective and wind has not full play." The ideal courses were, like Dornoch, whipped by the wind into shapes like frozen waves, the land leaning as if it were about to stumble, or molded into mounds, abrupt on the windward side with gradual slopes away from the breezes. The long shadows late in the day highlighted the links-land's mounds and craters, its tumbling and disorderly terrain. There was fate in the rolls the ball took on this ground. Skill at golf as a consequence had as much to do with tolerating the inevitable misfortunes that struck even the most accurate player as with simply hitting straight and long.

Americans wanted the ambiguity out of golf, so the American course evolved into what Art was seeing at Oakland Hills—perfectly maintained fairways from tee to green, mechanically groomed sand bunkers, and greens as smooth as the surface of a pool table, with the route of play set firmly within planted corridors. Hills was starting to

think that a shot of Scottish uncertainty would restore some reck-
lessness to golf. Pete Dye had been smitten earlier with the same idea.
My game was suited to wide-open spaces, so I was encouraged by
thoughts of playing on courses that could tolerate wild tee shots, as
Inverness once could.

The Inverness Club is a citadel of the golfing establishment. Its
clubhouse looks out over a great swale that rolls down below the first
and tenth tees and segues off to the southeast, where it becomes the
eighteenth fairway. There's a wonderful view of the tightly guarded
final green framed by the windows looking out from the darkly sober,
wood-paneled men's grill. Bob Tway holed out from the eighteenth's
right front bunker to derail Greg Norman in the 1986 PGA Championship. Its rich history colors one's perception of Inverness. Basketball players talk about the aura of Boston Garden, a place dense with
tradition, even though its baskets and the size and shape of the floor
are the same as any other court's. Even the least imaginative basketball player can summon forth memories of the idols who have drib-
bled across the Garden's parquet. Their spirits possess it. Golfing
ghosts haunt Inverness. There's a plaque hanging in the clubhouse,
dating from the twenties, thanking Inverness for opening its facilities
to professional golfers. As the presumed social inferiors to the members, the pros had to change shoes in the parking lots at the country
clubs where tournaments were held. Inverness broke with custom
and invited them into the locker room. A request from the Inverness
Club for advice on keeping its turf healthy had also inspired the
USGA to create the Green Section, its agronomic arm. Now the USGA
spends millions supporting turf-grass research and golfers play on
lawns that make the turf of a generation ago look like ground a
hungry herd of cattle has just passed over.

It was late in the afternoon, the sun breaking through clouds that
had dumped an inch of hail an hour earlier, when we got to Inverness. Waiting it out in the men's grill, we weren't sure we'd have time
to play, but the storm, which broke quickly, had cleared the course.
We wouldn't have anybody in front of us. Art and I both like to play
fast. Inverness was the first course I ever played that had once been
the site of a U.S. Open. This was also the first time Art and I were to
play together. The first hole and the tenth run parallel across a swale,
then up to a landing plateau, then down across another swale to
small greens tucked into the rising bank. A series of large, irregular
bunkers separates the fairways, gathering long hooks off the first

tee—assuming the golfer is right-handed, and courses are always designed for right-handed players—or slices from the tenth. I hit a three wood *over* the bunkers, landing almost on the tenth fairway. I had a fairly easy second shot, but hit my approach into the rough behind the green. Somehow scraping it on the green, I saved a par. Hit a good drive on two, pitched on the green, and made another par. I was playing much better than I expected. The third hole, a par three, didn't look or feel like the first two holes. Its elongated and kidney-shaped green was tucked around a lake, so if the pin was set high on the green the tee shot would have to carry over the edge of the water. Art told me this was one of four holes added by George Fazio when he rerouted the course for the 1979 U.S. Open. So much for revering Donald Ross. The Fazio holes were mediocre, but I was more interested in playing them than thinking about how out of character they were. The greens on the Fazio holes were bigger than the Ross greens. The remodeled series attacked the land, forcing it to yield, while the Ross holes adorned the landscape.

I don't know why, but I hit the ball well all that day. Art was more or less convinced after the front nine that I could actually play golf. I shot thirty-nine from the back tees. My only real strength as a player is off the tee, and when I'm driving the ball well the approach shots are so easy that even I can sometimes hit them. A good player like Art using my tee shots that day would have shot thirty-three. I managed to shoot forty-one on the back, losing a chance to break eighty when it took me two to get down from Tway's bunker, despite a drive that had left only a little flip sand wedge to the green. It took an unbelievably bad shot to hit that bunker. Still, Art thought eighty was a pretty good first time out at Inverness.

Toledo has the cachet of Peoria, and I hadn't expected to like it, but after a couple of months in the succulent, distended suburban clutches of south Florida I was ready for a little rust-belt realism. Inverness, well within the city limits, still recruits teenaged caddies, few of whom descend from the country club scene. An eager boy or girl can make several thousand dollars a season. The club also helps send several caddies to college every year with its Chick Evans scholarships.

My round at Inverness was only the second time I'd played with a caddy. The first was in Bermuda, at Mid Ocean, a course designed by Charles Blair Macdonald. Mid Ocean's fifth hole was borrowed from the fourteenth at Macdonald's National Golf Links on Long Island, a hole Geoff Cornish calls "truly a design original by Macdonald." Macdonald called his fourteenth at the National "Cape," a name now applied to every hole with its general character. The fourth, seventeenth, and eighteenth holes at Ironhorse will all owe a debt to this Charles Macdonald design. Mid Ocean's fifth is even truer to the Cape hole type than its eponymous predecessor. The tee, linked to the fairway by a bridge over a toe of Mangrove Lake, sits high above the water. The fairway's left edge skirts the lake along its entire length. The most direct line to the hole carries the greatest risk of landing in the water, but the more you lay back from the water the harder the approach shot to the green. The lake has a convex shape, which defines the dogleg. When architects today talk about setting up holes that "factor in the risk-reward ratio," what they really mean is a hole like the Cape. There is no ambiguity about the tee shot.

Mid Ocean sits on a high bluff along the sea, but it's not a linksland course. The wind, as in Scottish links, blows most of the time—and if there's nae wind, there's nae golf. Mid Ocean's soil and terrain are not linkslike, but instead have an inland feel with an ocean view. I shared a caddy at Mid Ocean with Mike Dasher. A bag on each shoulder, sweat popping out on his forehead, our caddy suffered not so much from the weight of our clubs as from the burden of our inept play. The day started badly for me when the starter refused to let me on the course because the shorts I was wearing were too—*short*. But these were Bermuda shorts, I protested, I bought them here, in Bermuda. "Too short, I'm telling you, sir."

He sent me in to see if George, the clubhouse man, might have an abandoned pair that would fit. When I asked George if he had any shorts with a thirty-four-inch waist he looked at me as if I had asked to sleep with his wife. Without comment, he reached behind his stores of shoe polish into what I thought was a stash of buffing cloths and hauled out a pair of knit polyesters in a stylish brown plaid that fit my thighs like tights and were a good two inches *shorter* than my proscribed pair. They clashed with my 100 percent cotton shirt. When I rejoined the foursome on the tee I felt as if I had committed some egregious breach of protocol. Here I was, playing one of the world's greatest courses in the company of three golf course architects—in addition to Dash, I was playing with Don Knott, chief designer in Robert Trent Jones, Jr.'s, office and Bob Graves's son-in-law, and Cabell Robinson, who before starting his own practice ran Trent Jones, Sr.'s, European operation—and I couldn't get dressed right. I rushed my first tee shot, pulling it onto the seventeenth fairway. I looked to the caddy for sympathy, but he refused to meet my glance. I was not sure I liked playing with a caddy.

But at Inverness, relaxed and properly attired, I discovered what the PGA Tour players know, that golf is best with a caddy. Mine was an eighteen-year-old boy who looked thirteen and who'd been lugging bags for several summers. He wore the dark pants and white shirt that Inverness requires. He knew the distances for every shot I had to hit and what side of the green to aim for. He raked the bunkers, cleaned the clubs, stood serenely by as I tried to advance the ball. Walking forward from the tee as we drove, well out of the line of fire, he marked every drive, no matter how errant. I liked playing with a caddy, however much it stirred my instincts against servitude. The caddies make a few bucks, and in their place today—a teenager looking for a summer job—I'd choose lugging golf bags out in the bright sunshine, giving myself a chance to meet some local mover and shaker who might help me get a real job later, over flipping hamburger patties for minimum wage. Golf carts did to caddies what Henry Ford did to hostlers, so there aren't many bag toters these days. Most clubs have given up even trying to provide caddies. Carts don't show up late, drink, or ask for more money. The American Society of Golf Course Architects was just one of many voices raised against carts in their infancy. "It is the belief of the Society," it harrumphed in 1955, "that the use of motorized vehicles to transport players is contrary to the spirit of the game of golf. The benefits derived by exercise and companionship are diminished by the use of such vehicles." Besides, they damage the turf and make it harder to design and maintain courses. Their use, the architects said, should be "limited to those with medical certificates."

Five years later, Tam O'Shanter Country Club, near Chicago, announced what the golfing press called "the revolutionary step" of replacing its caddies with carts. The PGA said that "the general trend to cars shuts off an extremely important source of future golf teachers and tournament players." When the resort at French Lick, Indiana, made a similar move, superannuated caddies hid in the bushes and shot out the tires of the golf carts driving by. Like displaced weavers who threw their wooden shoes into power looms to break the works, the caddies' turn to sabotage—from "sabot," a wooden shoe—was barely a hobble in progress's trot. Miles of dark ribbon will run the length of Ironhorse, a highway for its fleet. Golf carts can stretch the route of the course, elongating the distances between greens and tees, a not very subtle way of creating more golf course lots for the developer. The ASGCA has long since abandoned its principled stand against "the use of automotive transportation for playing." The same cultural impulse that makes clothes of natural fibers so popular is at work in golf, though, and some courses formerly requiring carts now let players walk. They just have to pay a little more for the privilege.

HILLS'S OFFICE WAS once the headquarters for his landscaping business. West of Toledo, it was way out in the country when Hills bought it, near black-bottom farmland rich with corn. Driving home from the office Art would pass the silica quarries that made Toledo a center for the manufacture of glass. An unobtrusively low wooden sign tucked under an evergreen announces to passersby on West Bancroft that Arthur Hills and Associates, Golf Course Architects, practice their arcane craft in this old farmhouse. There's not much drop-in traffic. An irrigation rep or a grass-seed salesman might make an occasional call, but more in the way of visiting than in selling hard. These are seemingly modest quarters for a professional organization working on the scale of Arthur Hills and Associates, but not unusual for a golf course architect. Bob Graves in California works out of a similarly small building behind his house in the East Bay. Geoff Cornish's office is a wing added behind his house on Fiddler's Green, near Amherst. Pete Dye's is wherever he hangs his hat. Muhammad always goes to the mountain. Hills meets his clients at the job sites or perhaps in the planner's or the developer's office. There's no reason for the clients to come to Toledo.

The driveway ascends a modest incline to a small graveled parking lot. Behind it a wooden outbuilding is giving in to the ages, its weathered wooden frame settling around a dry-set fieldstone foundation. This tolerated decay gives the place a rustic innocence. When he was in the landscaping business, Hills used to heel in trees and shrubs in the small fields along the side and the rear, warehousing them in the ground until his jobs were ready for plantings.

On our way back to the office from Inverness we drove through Ottawa Hills, a classic garden suburb in the Olmsted style with brick homes set well back from curving streets. Owens Corning and Jeep executives live here. Passing a young man unloading a lawn mower from the back of an old station wagon reminded Hills of a decrepit blue truck he once had. "It cost about four hundred dollars," he said. When his company was doing yard maintenance, he'd drive it out to the landfill to dump lawn clippings and debris. "The stuff would be steaming, decomposing. I'd be there at the dump with these black guys. One day I took a camera and had a guy take my picture next to that truck.

"We used these old reel mowers and I was always adjusting the blades. Not rotary mowers, but reels." Hills, at the wheel of his maroon Oldsmobile, looked across his shoulder at the kid pulling a rake from the station wagon and paused a moment, caught up in his reminiscence. He was, finally, secure enough in his success to let himself think about how far he'd come. "Future golf course architect," he said, smiling toward the boy.

Hills still more often than not identifies himself as a landscape architect, particularly in Toledo. There are times when this is a simple act of self-defense, a way to guard his time. On an airplane, he'd rather work than converse. A golf course architect is likelier to excite a seatmate's interest than a mere landscape architect. In first class, where he usually sits, given the simple demographics of the game he's more likely to find a golfer than in coach. He spreads out, unfolds a topo map, and goes to work. When you're doing a couple of dozen projects a year, you have to husband time. Besides, Hills is shy. I went with him to Friday lunch at the Rotary Club. "If it wasn't for Rotary," he said on the way, "I wouldn't know anybody in Toledo. I'm just gone so much."

When introductions were made around the table, and all the members and guests announced their names and occupations, Hills called himself a landscape architect. When someone asked, "Don't you do golf courses, Art?" he acknowledged, "That *is* mainly what we do," without any elaboration, not quite taking it as an accusation ("Don't you sell drugs, Art?"), but making no effort to trace the outline of his minor celebrity. No hint that the PGA Tour plays a tournament at one of his courses or that *Golf Digest* includes his work on its list of America's one hundred greatest courses. Hills has kept his profile low—slithering, really, merged with the horizon. He chose not to stick out at Rotary at all. Still, it struck me as a little ironic that Art was probably the only person in the room with a PR agent—except perhaps the young lawyer running as a Democrat in a local election, a liberal Daniel in this lion's den, glad-handing his way around the table looking for votes and campaign dollars. When he discovered I was from out of town, his hand, gripping mine, went limp with wasted effort. But these Rotarians were Hills's home folks, several men he'd grown up with, unimpressed in any case with their old friend Biff, the name his mother tagged him with as a boy still in use among the buddies of his youth.

Hills took his own work seriously and knew he had designed nice golf courses. Modesty fit him, merged with his controlled ambition. In it persisted a childhood diffidence brought on by crossed eyes that had required boyhood surgery and sustained by a father whom he felt he could never quite please. He'd made his way in a difficult and competitive job without any outside help, slowly, tenaciously—and, some said, with a big boost from the course builder Brent Wadsworth—working his way into golf architecture's top ranks. His name was not well known, even among golfers, but it was slowly penetrating into the golfing consciousness. Now that he'd hired a PR person, news items about Arthur Hills were cropping up regularly in the golf magazines, announcing course openings or deals struck for new designs. He was making more money than he had ever imagined possible, meeting the sort of successful people who appealed to him, traveling, putting his touch on the earth. Still, in Toledo he preserved his older, simpler identity as a landscape architect.

Hills had always been a good golfer. He played on the Michigan State team when he was an undergraduate and won the Ann Arbor city championship when he was twenty. He'd grown up surrounded by golf. His mother's family had a large plant nursery, not far from downtown Toledo, next door to the Ottawa Hills golf course. Art and his sister grew up in this hothouse demesne, which was large enough for Hills as a child to build his own little course. His parents were both golfers. Now retired and in their eighties, Ned and Marjorie Hills still play regularly. They moved to Fort Myers Beach, Florida, in the fifties and live in a bay-side house where Art and his wife, Mary, used to bring the kids every winter, when the Midwestern landscaping business was slow. The elder Hills were founding members of a course called Cypress Lakes laid out by Dick Wilson in 1960. Herb Graffis, who, along with his brother, Joe, created the National Golf Foundation, also belonged to Cypress Lakes. Graffis, who lived into his nineties, was a friend of the Hills and an eager supporter of their boy Biff's career.

Hills's office hasn't changed much since he bought it nearly twenty years ago. In the summer of 1988, he added a temporary building—a

job trailer—to relieve the congestion, setting it on cinder blocks behind the house. It had room for three drawing tables. The little house
was fine when just Art, his secretary, and Steve Forrest were handling
all the work, but now with John, Jodie, Brian, Spencer, Glenn, and
sometimes Chris there were just too many people for four small
rooms. Art worked upstairs, in a garret tucked beneath two gable
dormers. When he had to get work out Jeanne, his secretary, would
hold his calls so he could shut the door and keep the world away. The
entry room to his little suite had a drawing table, set high so that Art
needed a tall stool to work at it comfortably. Often he stood, his
pencil marking tracing paper laid smooth over a topo map with thin,
almost tentative lines. The stool was sandwiched between the drawing board and a flat worktable that was usually stacked with drawings. Sometimes Art kept one foot on the floor, cocking his hip on the
stool and leaning an elbow on the angled drawing board, working to
form the image of a golf course on paper. On some days when Hills
was on the road, one of the draftsmen would appropriate his drawing
table to escape the bustle below.

A second room, at the north end of the house, above the old living
room where Steve Forrest works, is Hills's inner sanctum, an inele-
gant room with a pair of desks whose tops are loaded with magazines, correspondence, and yellow tablets filled with notes. There's
also a less frequently used drawing table with a couple of bookshelves
attached to the wall above it. A red-and-black shag carpet covers the
floor, proof of Hills's indifference to fashion. Not that appearances
don't matter. Hills once suggested to Dasher that he rent fancier cars
when calling on clients, an idea Dasher had the good sense and
self-confidence to reject. "Art," he said, "don't you think the clients
would be happier knowing we're not nicking them for a fancy ride?"

"I suppose so," Hills responded, indifferently. And he was thinking
about image when he offered to pay for a nice golf outfit for each of
the younger employees after one of them showed up at a course
opening in clothes Hills thought were more suitable for a weekend
fraternity romp. While they were waiting for a plane in the Atlanta
airport, apropos of nothing Dash could determine, Hills said he was
thinking of establishing a company dress code. "What," Dash replied,
not sure he'd heard right? "A dress code?"

Hills said it was a little embarrassing for a company representative
at an opening to look as if he was out on a weekend furlough. "I
want a conservative look," Hills said, as his eyes surveyed Dash,

starting with his brown straw hat, his dark shades dangling halfway down the front of his white golf shirt, jeans held up by blue braces, and at the base, bearing the whole ensemble, a pair of brand-new black-and-white saddle shoes, the kind favored by teenage cheerleaders at consolidated schools. Dash had found his size on sale at a mall in Orlando. Hills laughed as he took in Dash's look. "Thinking of something like this, Art?" The employees were surprised by Hills's offer, and the boldest among them suggested to his fellows that if they were paid a little more they could handle their own wardrobes. He knew, he said, that Hills meant his offer kindly, but he couldn't help resenting it a bit. "I know how to dress," he said, "but this office isn't conducive to elegant dressing. If you have to get a print out of the basement you've got to fight through spider webs. Sometimes you're on your knees working on a drawing, or the lead erasures on your fingers get on your pants. But we know when it's appropriate to wear a suit and tie. Sometimes I think Art thinks we're younger than we are."

The bookshelves in Hills's office bear a little library of writings on golf course architecture, including a seldom consulted copy of *Golf Architecture in America*, written in 1927 by the designer of the Riviera Country Club in Los Angeles, George C. Thomas, Jr., another amateur designer of note. Hills thinks Thomas's book is pedestrian, "watered down and not very stimulating." A reprint of Bernard Darwin's *The Golf Courses of the British Isles* is sandwiched between Thomas's book and Bobby Jones's *Down the Fairway*. Jones endeared himself to golf course architects by always acknowledging that Alister Mackenzie was the course's architect and that he, Jones, who was merely the greatest golfer of his time and the owner of the place, contributed to its design purely as a consultant. The work was Dr. Mackenzie's. Today, a golfer of Jones's skill and fame, even if he didn't know a topo map from spilled spaghetti, could command enormous fees for "designing" a course. Jack Nicklaus has built perhaps the largest golf design business in the world after discovering that he could charge a million dollars for his services. The back pages of every golf magazine are filled with ads for real estate developments featuring Nicklaus courses. The landscape architects who draw the plans in Nicklaus's North Palm Beach office get little or no credit. Nicklaus's prominence as a course designer has caused no little resentment among golf architects, even as his fame has brought attention to the work itself. "Nicklaus is a great critic of course design," says one architect. "He changes things after they're done. From the point of view of the top golfer, he's surely the best critic of courses and holes in the world. Jack has several good ideas that make it more reasonable for the professional golfer to score, but nothing that works well for the average golfer." Jones was content to give Mackenzie his due at Augusta National, just as he did later when he commissioned Robert Trent Jones to design Peachtree in Atlanta.

Hills also owns two copies of Robert Hunter's *The Links*, published the year before Thomas's book, making it the first on golf design published in the United States. "To me," Hills said, "*The Links* is the bible of design. I consult it still. It's *always* stimulating."

One of his copies of *The Links* is wrapped in plastic, its binding broken, its light-green cover stained and damaged by water. The other, in a different binding, is in reasonably good shape. Its endpapers reproduce a site plan of the Old Course at St. Andrews sketched by Mackenzie in 1924. Referring his readers to Mackenzie's sketch, Hunter noted St. Andrews' routing deficiencies—"the worst," he wrote, among the "famous courses."

"Seven of the greens going out lie alongside of seven of the greens coming home. There are then not only many parallel holes"—which Hunter detested—"but most of the greens are of the double variety. Even the bunkers often do double service. Play to the seventeenth is often safest along the fairway of the second; and nearly all the canny golfers will use the fairway of the fifth when playing their second shots to the fourteenth. Play to the superb eleventh is across the fairway of the seventh. Of course all this is very bad. Many of the bunkers are hidden from view, and the long, wild hitter will more often than not find a good lie, while the accurate player who is the slightest bit off the line is frequently severely punished."

"It is rather difficult to explain," Hunter continued, why, despite these defects, "St. Andrews should be the one and only course which stands above and scorns all criticism."

"There is something in the very terrain which outwits us . . . we never have a sufficient variety of shots or quite enough skill and accuracy to play St. Andrews as we should like to play it, or indeed as we feel that one day we shall play it. That is, I think, what gives the old course its enduring vitality. It is the most captivating and unfair, the most tantalizing and bewitching, of all courses."

Hunter studied St. Andrews and the other great courses of the British Isles in the summer of 1912, five years after he took up golf, then still in its American infancy. He played mostly on Long Island and in Connecticut, near his home in Noroton. His favorite golfing companion was Finley Peter Dunne—Mr. Dooley—who was also a golfing companion of Charles Blair Macdonald. He was a friend and neighbor of Mark Twain, who thought of golf as "a good walk, spoiled." Hunter has dropped through history's cracks and is almost entirely forgotten—even his descendants have only a vague sense of who he was and what he did. Yet in his day he was a man of some fame, and not for *The Links*, which did not sell as well as Hunter's earlier work, even though it was published during the only golf boom in American history resembling in scope and intensity the one launched in the eighties. *Poverty*, published in 1905, was a best-seller and made Hunter a widely quoted authority on what today we would call the problems of the inner city. If he were around now, he'd be on *Nightline*. Hunter was a muckraking journalist and a crusading socialist until, disgusted by the excesses of Bolshevism, he forswore reformist politics after World War I for the tidier pleasures of golf. He moved politically to the far right of the Republican Party, holding views more in keeping with those of his golfing associates in the upper reaches of the country club circle. It helped that his wife was an heiress who could maintain him in the life-style he readily adapted. When his old comrades learned that he had written America's first book on golf course architecture, they probably felt like an old SDSer would if he discovered that Tom Hayden had, say, invented Nintendo.

Scribner's printed 3,030 copies of *The Links*, binding only 1,800, leaving it with 1,230 sets of unbound sheets as the Depression squashed whatever small market may have remained for a book on golf design. Polished apples were selling better than golf balls in 1933. Country clubs were fending off vagabond golfers, men who had lost their jobs and couldn't keep up with dues but kept trying to play as guests. They were like the engineers laid off by the aerospace industry in Southern California in the seventies, half of whom sat at home, usually in a dark room, drinking too much and watching TV, while the other half showed up for work every day to hang out by the water cooler and join their ex-colleagues for lunch and act as if the ax had stopped an inch from its fatal blow and hung suspended above their necks, in a limbo of clouded reckoning. I always thought the ones who went to work were the saddest, and the Depression-era golfers who tried to keep playing with their flush friends as their liquidity drained reminded me of the terminated engineers. In any case, nobody was spending much money on golf in the Depression, and Hunter's book wafted into obscurity.

In the late spring of 1935, an ad in *Golfdom*, the "Business Journal of Golf," announced that *Golfdom* had bought "a small number of unbound copies of *The Links* . . . and had them handsomely and durably bound." It was one of these *Golfdom* copies in the plastic bag in Art's office. Scribner's had sold *The Links* for $4.00. Nine years after it was first published you could get this "standard authority on golf architecture" for "$1.25, POSTPAID." *Golfdom* was published by the Graffis brothers. Herb Graffis, who died in 1989, was something of an idol to Hills. When Hills first met Graffis, he'd yet to design a course, but by the time Graffis died Hills's work was ubiquitous in southwest Florida. Graffis knew more about the golf business than anyone who ever lived, and Hills was grateful that he'd had a chance to know him.

Assuming that he earned a royalty of 15 percent on the sale of nearly 2,000 copies, Hunter's total return on *The Links* was perhaps $1,100. Hills found his copies of *The Links* in used bookstores when he was working on his degree in landscape architecture in the late fifties and bought them "for about a quarter each, I think." A mint copy today sells for at least $400.

Robert Hunter didn't need the money. His wife, Caroline, inherited perhaps as much as $12 million. Anson Phelps Stokes, Hunter's father-in-law, was an investment banker and sportsman who managed in the days before the income tax to accumulate a sufficiently large Gilded Age fortune to live in the cultivated luxury that his contemporary Thorstein Veblen called conspicuous consumption. Hunter moved to California in the early twenties, living first in Berkeley, where a dreadful fire destroyed all his papers and notebooks, including his manuscript and notes for *The Links*, moved next to Pebble Beach, then settled finally on an estate, staffed with servants, in Santa Barbara. At Pebble Beach, Hunter entered into a partnership with Alister Mackenzie, whose own small book, *Golf Architecture*, published in England in 1920, expressed a view very close to Hunter's. Together they worked to create several of the masterworks of California golf—Cypress Point, on the Monterey Peninsula, the Valley Club of Montecito, and the Meadow Club in Marin County, north of San Francisco. Mackenzie, who died in Santa Cruz in 1934, built ten regulation courses during his six years in California, as well as par three courses on the estates of Charlie Chaplin and Harold Lloyd.

Hunter worked with him on six courses, though he's rarely given any credit for the designs.

Given the fees contemporary golf architects command, the partnership of Dr. Alister Mackenzie of Leeds, England, and Robert Hunter of Pebble Beach was a bargain for its clients. They printed a SCALE of PROFESSIONAL CHARGES and CONDITIONS of AGREEMENT on a single sheet of thick stock using a lovely Baskerville typeface, which stated but two conditions of agreement:

"1. The general supervision which the architects will give the work is such periodical inspection by one or both of them as may be necessary to insure that the work is being carried out according to their plans and to their satisfaction; but constant supervision of the work does not form part of their duties and is not contemplated . . .

"2. In carrying out the work, the architects are empowered to make such deviations, alterations, additions and omissions as they may reasonably consider desirable in the interest of their clients, provided that no material addition to the cost is caused thereby."

Hills's procedures echo Hunter and Mackenzie's conditions, though his clients sometimes have difficulty accepting the fact that the drawings may not show in every particular what gets built. "Grades may be adjusted in the field by the Golf Course Architect," says a note printed in the lower-right-hand corner of an Arthur Hills grading plan, "in order to accomplish design objectives."

"The ever popular field adjustments," Dasher calls them, though Josh Muss, echoing complaints heard by landscape architects and course designers for a hundred years, would later wonder aloud just why it was, if field adjustments were so common, so necessary, he'd paid for such detailed plans. "Drawings were no more than memorandums the firm supplied to be referred to in getting on the ground a work of art requiring professional creativity and supervision" is how Laura Roper, Olmsted's biographer, summarizes his response to this dilemma. Mackenzie and Hunter avoided this problem in part by not bothering with much in the way of drawings. A sketch of the routing plan and the features around the greens, drawn in Mackenzie's rough style, was about all a client could hope for.

Mackenzie repeated the standard wisdom—"The finest courses in existence are the natural ones"—but put his hand to work transforming the land nonetheless. Hunter, on the other hand, wrote the prescription for Ironhorse sixty years before it was built. "[N]ot only some of the most popular but some of the most interesting courses have been made on flat land . . . ." Hunter wrote. "With plough and scraper one can mould the surface at will, and create effects and problems which can but rarely be found provided by nature."

Ironhorse was, for Art Hills, a chance to work without the constraints of nature. There were limits, though, especially the hard contours of commerce. Hills had to get a golf course on land that "maximized amenitized premium lots." He had to squeeze the golf course into the land plan. Hunter's book wasn't much help on that score.

THERE ARE VERY FEW personal touches in Hills's office. It's just a place to work. Formally posed family portraits, requiring a wider and wider viewfinder as the years passed and the children kept arriving, are tucked among the books, and there are a few large framed photos of golf holes, but nothing to suggest that from here emerge the plans for a couple of dozen golf courses every year.

Hunter's book held a special place for Hills, and he wrote a paper about it when he was studying landscape architecture. Early in his life, Hills had expected to work in the family business. He studied horticulture at Michigan State, but by the fifties the hothouse tomatoes the family specialized in cost too much to grow, and when the land and buildings were sold Hills looked for something else to do. He started the landscape contracting business that stuck him with trips to the dump but kept the wolf from the door for his and Mary's growing family. Deciding he needed a degree in landscape architecture so he could work as a designer and planner as well as a contractor, Hills commuted to Ann Arbor several evenings a week for a few years to nail a second sheepskin to his wall. "I had, I dunno, maybe two or three kids when I started," he sort of remembered one summer night in Florida, relaxing with a beer after a long day walking around Ironhorse, "and probably four or five by the time I finished." In all, the Hills had eight children.

He was playing golf when he could, running the landscape business and working as a landscape architect and land planner, but ambitious for more. In 1967 he got his first chance to design a golf course, an eighteen-holer for a housing development southwest of Toledo called Berwyn, later renamed Brandywine. Not only did Brandywine give Hills a chance to design a golf course, it introduced him to the man whose career would spiral about Hills like the coiling of a double helix. Brent Wadsworth was, like Hills, a landscape architect and an avid golfer, but he chose to build golf courses rather than design them. Wadsworth Golf Construction, based in Illinois, built its first golf course in 1958. Wadsworth finished another course in 1960, and a third in 1961, all designed by Larry Packard of Chicago.

Packard had worked with Robert Bruce Harris, who, according to Geoff Cornish, was not simply a founding member but the inspiration, along with the Canadian Stanley Thompson, of the American Society of Golf Course Architects. Posing at Pinehurst for a formal portrait at the ASGCA's inaugural meeting in 1948, Harris stood between Thompson and Donald Ross, a hint of a smile across his wide face. He had the sort of dark, thick hair that Ronald Reagan made famous, and a mustache. In his tweed coat and V-neck sweater, he looked like a Scottish gent, though he was born in a little farming town in northern Illinois. Harris was a small, dour man with limited imagination and fixed ideas—like keeping bunkers well away from greens for ease of maintenance—whose courses are largely forgotten, if they have not been remodeled out of recognition. Because of their eccentrically placed bunkers and roundish greens, says Geoff Cornish, you can always spot a Harris course from the air.

Larry Packard's wife worked for Brent Wadsworth's father, who was a physician in Joliet. That's how Wadsworth met his future partner and discovered there was such a profession as golf course architecture. With a degree in landscape architecture from the University of Illinois, Wadsworth worked briefly for Harris before he and Packard went out on their own. "But there wasn't enough business in the late fifties to keep us both busy," Wadsworth remembers, "so Larry stayed in the design business and I decided to go into the construction side."

That was how Hills and Wadsworth met. Brandywine is not an undertaking that precursed greatness for either its designer or its builder, but it's playable, coursing over some nicely rolling ground that's lovely to look at in the fall and sometimes in the spring if heavy rains don't flood the creek that bisects the first, ninth, tenth, and eighteenth holes. The corridors are very tight, and on at least two holes it's possible to drive completely across the fairway into serious trouble—a creek in one case, woods in the other. The angles of the doglegs are too sharp. One and nine play into the morning sun; nine and eighteen finish in the sunset. Hills says there wasn't anyplace else to put the clubhouse. The site was tight, a limited canvas. It had a lot of nice trees on it and a creek that dominates the routing of the back nine. Brandywine's strongest feature is its largish greens, very much in the style that Dick Wilson and Robert Trent Jones were designing in the fifties and sixties. Hills, in keeping with the advice of his guru, Napoleon Hills, author of *Think and Grow Rich*, won't say a single bad thing about Brandywine. The author Hills—no relation to the golf architect—says he'll share with his readers the secret to prosperity he learned from the "canny" Andrew Carnegie, but he's never quite explicit about it. Every line, though, glows with good feeling. Art Hills's son says his dad pored over a copy of *Think and Grow Rich* so devotedly that its pages finally fell out. It's sort of prototypical New Age positive thinking. Art Hills definitely thinks on the plus side. I saw little in Brandywine that would have predicted Bonita Bay in southwest Florida or the wonderfully subtle course called The Champions, in Lexington, Kentucky, built on land with the roll of Brandywine but with few of its constraints or squeezed-down golfing corridors.

The jobs came slowly. Hills had started with an ad in the Toledo yellow pages and a desperate wish to succeed. It was nearly fifteen years before he hired Steve Forrest, but after 1980 his practice grew at an exponential rate. He hired Dasher, who'd been working for Wadsworth, then more draftsmen. There were long pauses on the way, days sitting in his office, wondering if the work would come, struggling to keep the faith. The long depression after 1974 was especially tough. He had kids in college—five, at one point, mostly at Notre Dame—but was getting few courses to design. He made a brief stab at establishing a design partnership with Nicklaus in the early seventies, as Dye and Desmond Muirhead had both done, but was rebuffed in a cordial but patronizing way by Nicklaus, who referred to Hills as a "young man," even though Nicklaus is ten years Hills's junior. The Shaker Run courses in Middletown, Ohio, were the start of a strong run of projects that got a tremendous boost from The Club at Pelican Bay, a Westinghouse development in Naples, Florida. His commission for Eagle Trace, another Westinghouse project, grew out of Pelican Bay. "That really got us going," Hills says, "an opportunity for better projects, on better sites." Soon after, Hills met the Button King and took on Ironhorse.

*   *   *

HILLS DOES TWO KINDS of drawings from which the draftsmen work—the sketches on yellow tracing paper over the topo maps and very rough, schematic renderings, almost doodlelike, on yellow legal pads. Along the left margin he'll list the holes by number, with a note alongside describing its difficulty. Here's a typical list, though not for Ironhorse, whose initial sketches somehow escaped Steve Forrest's files. The holes are out of order in Hills's sketch, and only the back nine have yardages.

#1—easy
#2—not easy
#3—long
#4—not easy
#5—easy
#7—tough
#8—fairly easy
#9—med.
#6—med.
#10—long-430
#14—tough-160-10
#11—med.-535
#13—not easy-365 + 5
#12—med-210
#15—med.-455 + 15
#16—long, tough 390 + 20
#17—med.-570-10
#18—tough-425- 10

Filling the rest of the page are tiny drawings of each hole, showing line of flight, tees, greens and bunkers, and tree masses. These sketches are done after the basic routing has already been determined and look very much like the work of early architects like Mackenzie and Ross, who were not trained draftsmen but instead used simple abstractions, like dots for sand, or little lines in a row, like pickets, for mounds, or cloudlike shapes indicating trees, and notes, saying "Cypress" or "work on this." Hills makes another list of holes to check for "strategy"—are there choices from the tees, which way should the slope of the green be oriented, how are the bunkers placed? Then a third list relates green size to the strategy and difficulty of the hole. A long hole, for example, might get a large green, while an easy hole

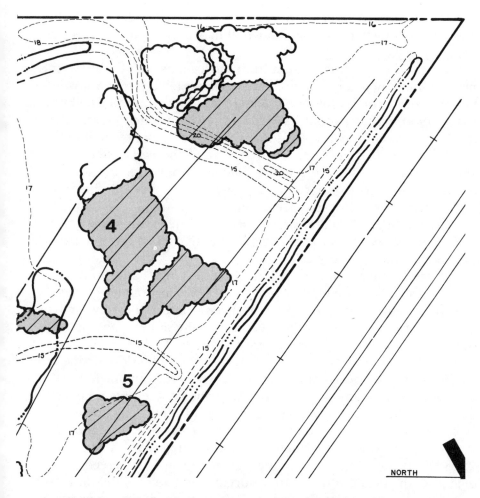

Detail of the clearing plan. (*Courtesy Arthur Hills and Associates*)

gets a medium-sized one. The elevation of the green is also attended to here—raised greens are harder to build well and harder to play, but may be the only way to create much difficulty or interest on feature-less property.

Hills transfers the information from the legal pads onto the tracing paper, which then goes to a draftsman, whose job it is to work Hills's doodles into a comprehensive grading plan. Medieval monks illuminating manuscripts cannot have known tedium much greater than that experienced drawing a grading plan. Brian Huntley, a graduate of Ohio State, still in his early twenties and the best golfer among Hills's associates, did the grading plan for Ironhorse. Because the ground is so flat, Ironhorse was pretty simple, but on sites with changes in elevation of sixty feet or more, the contour lines compress like drawn blinds. The draftsman starts with the existing topographical map, over which a Mylar sheet is laid. Every contour line has to be copied, and where grades are changed the new contour lines connected to the existing elevations. If, for example, as at Ironhorse, a tee is designed for an elevation of twenty-two feet (above sea level) and the existing grade around it is at seventeen feet, the drawing will show the size of the tee and the steepness of the slopes. The closer the lines are together, the more severe the grade. In this case, if each contour line represents one foot of elevation and the slope of the tee banks is "one to one"—for every foot down it goes out one foot—the contour lines are drawn almost touching one another. Even on a site as plain as Ironhorse, there are thousands of tiny, squiggly contour lines on the grading plan. Huntley drew each one by hand. The greens are shown without detail on the grading plan. A note says, "See GS-1" or "GS-2," meaning "green sheet." The green sheets elaborate the detail of the putting surfaces and any nearby bunkers, along with drainage details. The grading plans are drawn at a scale of $1'' = 100'$, while the green sheets are produced at thirty scale, or $1'' = 30'$. All the greens are drawn on a standard printed form, with four axes across the green enabling the draftsman to draw sections, from front to back, side to side, or on either diagonal. These are especially useful to the contractor.

Hills sketches the green on a blank grid, which is then reduced in scale and blended into the landscape in the grading plan. Once all the new contours are established, the information is again transferred to a green sheet, with its shelfs, dips, and rolls all formally described in terms the dozer operator can follow. It can take three weeks for a draftsman to produce grading and drainage plans and several more days to fill in the details on the green sheets. There is a lot of erasing going on. The men draw with the bottom of the table roughly at the height of their pubic bones, and the detritus of all the erasures gathers on their trousers. They call it getting fuzz balls.

Drawing quickly turns to drudgery, especially among people trained as landscape architects, as all Hills's employees are. They want more responsibility, more chances to work in the field. Hills is reluctant to give up control. There is an almost worshipful attitude toward Hills, who's a stern ruler despite his diffident manner, but it's stifling under a blanket of resentment. A tiny rebellion was brewing during my visit to Toledo. In the end, it would cost Hills three employees.

7

Dilemmas of Eminent Domain

ON NOVEMBER 21, 1988, at seven o'clock on a voluptuously bright south Florida morning, Kenny Postell of Robbinsville, North Carolina, drove a D8 Cat off its lowboy trailer, dropped the big blade down to where it could brush mud off a snake's back, and crashed off into the underbrush, smiling through his chew. His brass belt buckle glinted in the rising sun, the cast initials "CSA" locked across his belly, fixing his Dixie loyalties tighter than his britches. The Confederate States of America, Postell's home country. It was Postell's job to knock down the Sabal palms, pines, and wax myrtles growing where, according to Art Hills's plans, Ironhorse Country Club's fairways, tees, and greens were destined to fit. Any living thing within the clearing lines was doomed. The pesky exotics and the stately pines were equally condemned, victims of progress. Postell's business was scourging the earth in little pieces, making way for the future. He was a harbinger, the clearing boss, whose appearance foretold a special spring, a renewal wrought by the concentrated force of heavy equipment, long hours, and plenty of fuel oil. If it was green and in the way, Postell could topple and burn it. It was a skill he was proud of, even though he didn't operate much these days (and heavy equipment is always "operated," never "driven"), now that his job was pushing the work. Though not much past thirty, he'd already spent a working lifetime looking out on the world from the yellow steel cage of a bulldozer, breathing fried air and living far from home. Operating was hard on the back, jostled the kidneys, and was better done by young men, so if ambition let you climb off the tractor and save your aching bones so much the better.

I was happy to see Postell working through the underbrush, making the big Cat dance. There was such a graceful harmony in his control of the dozer that one forgot momentarily the scream of the huge diesel, running with the throttle wide-open, or the explosive crack of branches breaking, a sound like rifle fire, or the rhythmic clatter of the tracks as the Cat crawled back and forth and pivoted while one track locked and the other rolled ahead, carving its distinctive footprints in the ground. I was glad that some kind of work had finally started. The first schedule that project manager Bob Isakson had posted on the wall behind his desk showed Ironhorse opening for play in the late fall of 1988 or the winter of 1989, eight to ten months after I got to Florida. I'd been killing time walking the site, studying Hills's prints, trying to form a sense of what the course would look like when it was done. Alan Sher invited me to play golf with him at Frenchman's Creek, which had two nice golf courses originally designed by Gardner Dickinson and remodeled by Jack Nicklaus's company. Sher loved playing Frenchman's in the summer because no one else was there, and on those rare occasions he did run into another golfer he'd cut over to the next hole or change courses altogether. He couldn't stand to stop. Whatever subtleties of pace and rhythm an architect might design into a course were lost on the Button King, whose idea of a good day of golf was playing twenty-seven holes without interruption and finding a half-dozen balls. He loved leading the pack. Some days he played well, too, and despite arthritic hands and a bum knee could hit the ball a long way when he got his loopy swing in synch. On the days his swing was on furlough, Sher was in such misery that it was hard not to develop an empathetic slice. We'd make a little side bet, and Sher discovered in about thirty seconds how easy it was for him to pull up a chair and park inside my head. I play golf like a boy. My friend Don Otto, a teaching pro in Portland, watching another of my tee shots disappear in a great malevolent arc over the willow trees at my home course, Portland's Broadmoor Golf Club, shakes his head sadly and says, "Just like the Pee Wees." He thinks he's insulting me, but I take it as a compliment. I figured the only way to escape the constraints of a middle-aged neophyte's game was to learn like a child. So I lived to crush the ball off the tee, to hit a nine iron 160 yards. When I'd hear Pat Summerall whisper from my TV set, "Tom Kite's got one hundred and fifty yards to the hole and he's taking an eight iron," I'd say to myself, "What a wimp, Tom! Use your wedge!" Meanwhile, Kite's one of the ten best players in the world and I struggle to break eighty, but I bet the best drive I ever hit was longer than the best drive Tom Kite ever hit! I've been stuck for years at this primitive stage of development, as if it were my fate. Sher knew that instantly, so whenever we had a bet going and he was a hole behind he'd say to anybody who'd listen—a foursome at a nearby tee, or some ladies on the way to tennis, or if there weren't any golfers around the ground crew would do—"Watch this guy hit the ball! He hits it a mile, I'm telling you!"

So I'd obligingly step to the tee and hit a screaming duckhook so far out of bounds that we could hear tires squealing on Donald Ross Road as cars swerved to avoid my wayfaring Titleist. I'd tee up a second ball and block it so far right that if I did stay on the course my fourth shot was from so deep in the pines and palmettos that the best I could hope for was to scrape it back on the fairway and then play my heart out for a triple bogey. Sher would be shrugging his shoulders, palms upturned in mock consolation, his smile tucked in the folds of his *faux* frown. It only took me six months to figure out what he was doing. Swallowed the bait every time. It's the genius of a great salesman to work his customers, to fathom their psychological needs. Sher had no trouble diagnosing me on the golf course. It gave him a special pleasure to invade the poorly guarded perimeter of my golfing consciousness, to see that I didn't have a game yet but was bogged down in the primitive pleasure of watching a golf ball fly off the horizon. Playing golf was a good way for us to distract ourselves. We were both eager for Ironhorse to get under way, but Sher's concern was weighted by fear—he didn't have his money out of the deal yet. We spent a lot of time hanging out at the house, talking to Isakson and Harpman, riding the ATVs, walking the land. But until Postell started clearing, the land seemed immutable, and neither of us had much sense of what this great golf course was going to look like. Sher, at least, was certain it would be better than Old Marsh.

*   *   *

FIVE DAYS BEFORE P&J—Phillips and Jordan—Postell's company, started knocking down brush and trees, Mike Dasher and I had come down to West Palm Beach from Jacksonville to take a closer look at the clearing lines that Dasher and Art Hills had tagged nearly ten months before, in late January of 1988. Dasher wanted to make sure Postell didn't knock down more than he was supposed to. Dash's view of clearing combined a natural caution with the hard memories of experience. It was easier to come back and clear a tree in a bad spot than it was to transplant a tree where one had been eliminated prematurely. I hadn't expected to get back to Ironhorse until the end of the week, after the conclusion of a National Golf Foundation conference in Jacksonville called "Golf Summit '88," but when Dasher showed up at noon on the first day of the conference and told me he was heading on down to Ironhorse because they were ready to start clearing, I said I was coming with him. "You mean," he asked, "you don't want to stay and find out the real inside story on the golf business?"

At Ironhorse, a concatenation of improbable obstructions had held the work at bay all summer. Nothing dramatic until the Solid Waste Authority raised the possibility of condemning Ironhorse for extra space to store and separate its garbage, just niggling impediments, but cumulatively they had the stopping power of a stun gun to the spine. It seemed not impossible through most of the late summer and early fall that Ironhorse would stop dead in its tracks. Then Dash had arrived with the news I'd been hoping to hear. Ironhorse was getting under way. Besides, Summit '88 didn't hold much charm for Dasher.

He'd already, he said, "seen about four course builders I'd just as soon never see again asking me if they could get on our bid lists." The rumor that Arthur Hills and Associates was the busiest golf course design firm in the country collected the sort of potential collaborators Dasher had run into that afternoon, all of them, they assured him, admirers for many years of the great work of Arthur Hills. As a rule, Dasher kept his reply to a discreet "we're keeping busy" when confronted with the speculation that the Hills outfit was designing courses at a pace Donald Ross in his prime might have found tiring. Dasher sought to leave the impression that they were somewhere between being busy enough to stay in demand—clients don't want to hire someone who's not working, on the frequently reasonable assumption that there was a sound cause for the slack demand—but not so busy that he wouldn't be able to give *your* job the attention it deserved. Dash guarded his knowledge of how many jobs Art Hills had going and never turned away the opportunity to pitch new clients, but he wasn't eager to add any new names to his list of recommended course builders. Wadsworth Golf Construction, Dash's old employer, headed just about everybody's preferred builder's list anyway—Wadsworth was doing most of Jack Nicklaus's work, a lot of Tom Fazio's, and had done Arnold Palmer courses and Larry Packard courses and at least one course for Rees Jones and a host of other designers, but no architect's name was more closely linked to Wadsworth than Arthur Hills, and Dash was always happy to get Brent Wadsworth's bunch to push dirt for him. Even the head of the golf course contractors' trade group, which Wadsworth had never joined, called it the "best course-building company in the world." Dash knew the potential price an owner might pay for using an inexperienced builder. He also knew that a lot of course builders followed a path through booms and bankruptcies to new incarnations, a kind of contractor's karma. "One outfit I know's been bankrupt about four times and they keep coming back," Dash said. "Just rising from the dead."

By the end of 1987 Arthur Hills and Associates had done forty-five new courses, but by the spring of 1989, they had *twenty-one* courses under construction and another twenty-six on the drawing boards—more work than the firm had done in the twenty-one preceding years. No wonder Dasher was coy—at the rate Hills was going, in a dozen years he would design more courses than there were in his native Ohio.

Dash had an unusual attitude for an insider toward the golf business, an absence of the fervid religiosity that saturated the official view, especially now that golf was enjoying its extraordinary boom. Golf Summit '88 was the NGF's second conclave to survey the state of the game—or, more accurately, its commercial health—in three years. In a memo to the registrants, the head of the NGF, with academic caution, wrote that "Golf Summit '88 is shaping up to be a major and possibly historical event in golf." That was pretty qualified hyperbole for the golf business, but then the NGF had been trying for two decades to achieve its commercial ends by imitating the staid and cautious objectivity that the USGA had found so regally effective in exercising its control over *playing* golf.

I discovered that sending the NGF several hundred dollars qualified me as one of 400 "industry leaders," so I took my place among them, ready to endure the standard IRS half day of speeches before heading out for an afternoon round on one of the Sawgrass Resort's courses, among them Pete Dye's notorious TPC course, where the PGA Tour holds The Players Championship.

Hills and Dasher had also registered for Golf Summit '88, but only Dash was going to make it. He'd told me he would get there late, after checking in on a course under construction just across the border north of Jacksonville, in St. Marys, Georgia, at a Trident nuclear submarine base. David Robinson, the Naval Academy's basketball star, then waiting to join the NBA's San Antonio Spurs, was a construction manager on the project.

The Kings Bay course was one of the odder items in the Hills portfolio. An engineering firm in Atlanta that was designing a sewage treatment plant for the navy base contacted Hills about grading the effluent spray fields so they were in the rough shape of a golf course. Arthur Hills and Associates designed a golf course on the navy's 400-acre site, but instead of a plan with eighteen holes it designated eighteen "effluent spray sub-zones." Once grading and grassing were done, and the pipe laid underground to spray the aqueous effluent, the navy could *discover* a golf course. Dash went along with what he understood from the beginning was a charade. He wrote to the engineers early in 1987. "As you are aware, the effluent disposal area that we worked with your firm on for the Kingsbay [sic] Base looks remarkably like a golf course. This design enabled Kingsbay to satisfy their immediate need for an effluent disposal field as well as provide for the long-term need for golf facilities."

By then the navy was ready to abandon its ruse and build the golf course it had so conveniently detected. But a subcontractor on the job, who was losing money, called *The Atlanta Journal–Constitution* and blew the whistle. He said the navy had moved a half million yards of dirt that weren't necessary for the spray field. "It looks like it's in Scotland or something," he told the *Journal–Constitution.*

The navy played innocent, contending that it was only trying to keep separate the work done with appropriated funds—building a sewage treatment plant, for example, is something Congress is likely to tolerate—from that bought with nonappropriated funds, like a golf course. "It's all on the up and up," the navy spokesperson said, contending the navy was only trying to get "more bang for its buck."

"She said some construction workers may have believed the project was clandestine," the paper reported, "because the Navy instructed them not to refer to it as a golf course."

Having first acknowledged that maybe a little bit of money—perhaps $350,000, out of the $1.6 billion budget to make Kings Bay a Trident port—was spent inappropriately at Kings Bay, the Secretary of the Navy "directed the Commander, Naval Facilities Engineering Command to transfer any costs associated with the design and construction of the sewage spray irrigation system that could be remotely related to the golf course project from appropriated to non-appropriated funds. This project," he continued, "will provide a much needed recreational facility at a relatively remote site while providing us the additional fiscal benefits of operation and maintenance of a sewage spray irrigation system with non-appropriated funds."

So the navy got away with it, but it spent more money than it needed to, and in a very suspicious way. Had it designed the spray field and the effluent disposal system without a golf course, and priced it, then its case would stand a little more careful scrutiny. When it did go ahead with the conversion, it had to tear up and replace some drainage and irrigation pipe already in place, redo all the greens, and try to figure out how to get rid of the common Bermuda grass it had planted, which is pestiferous compared to the hybrid Bermudas southern golf courses now use. Common is leggy and big-leafed and very aggressive—fast-growing—and not at all as pleasant to play on as Tifway 419, a plant that was bred, just down the road in Tifton, Georgia, with public funding. The navy could have been honest about this from the start, but it wasn't. There's nothing special about the pipe used to carry effluent, and nothing unusual about Kings Bay's dirt, but it cost at least $3.6 million to "turn a pine forest into a spray field for disposal of treated wastewater" and then another $1.9 million to build a small clubhouse, acquire maintenance equipment, and convert the spray field into a golf course. That's $5.5 million for a military recreational facility. Ironhorse's fancy country club golf course would be cheaper to build.

Dash said the contractor doing the "conversion" was running into some problems getting the irrigation system to work again. The spray heads were expensive cast-brass models when the rest of the golf world was using high-impact plastic. It was a dedicated little family construction outfit doing the work, he said, figuring out where all the pipe was going and reshaping the greens. Dash was coming to Jacksonville after he finished up at Kings Bay.

On the way into the banquet hall at Summit '88 I ran into Bob Graves, the California course designer who taught the Harvard seminar on golf course architecture. We sat through the first morning's speeches at Summit '88, struck most by their vacuity. A geographer from Kansas expressed surprise that Mississippi had so few public golf courses per capita. It was as if it had never occurred to him that he was talking about a state where a large portion of the capitas were black and poor and it had been the avowed aim of the most powerful citizens of the state to keep it that way for most of the last one hundred years. I was reminded of what President Calvin Coolidge said when asked if he could account for the high rates of unemployment in the early twenties. "A lot of people," he replied, "are out of work."

We settled back for more wisdom on the golf boom. There was speculation about what might signal its end. "I remember how you can tell from last time," Graves whispered to me, recalling 1974. "The phones stop ringing."

By the time Dash showed up, I'd already listened to about all I could bear. The hotel accepted my explanation that an emergency required me elsewhere and let me take my bag back out of the room without charge. The NGF did well by me, though. I'd paid about a hundred bucks an hour to find out that there was money being made in the golf business. Heading south on I-95, I thought about the giant pot of gold that Ironhorse's developers saw at the end of their rainbow, but I didn't care about the money. I wanted to see some dirt moved, to witness the creation.

WHEN WE GOT TO IRONHORSE the next morning we met John Riley, the superintendent for Ranger Construction, the company that had contracted to do the clearing—Phillips and Jordan was a subcontractor to Ranger—the lake excavations and the rough-dirt moving for the golf course. Riley was a good old boy from North Carolina who had worked on more than a dozen golf courses, the most recent an Arnold Palmer design back in his home state. The first courses he had done were built in the early eighties at PGA National, Ironhorse's neighbor just to the north. Riley had brought along Postell, who was running the clearing operation, and Pat Painter, a "restoration biologist," as he styled himself, who had created a tree-moving subsidiary for Ranger that he ran pretty much as his private domain. It would be his job to relocate thousands of Ironhorse's trees by removing them from the land where the lakes, roadways, and the golf course were going and planting them on the perimeter berms that it would be Ranger's first task to build.

Because Ironhorse shared the same low, flat elevation with nearly every other acre between Lake Okeechobee and the Atlantic, these dikelike berms were essential for privacy. They would also block noise from the streets and the railroad. Painter was there, along with Riley and Postell, to review the construction schedule.

After introductions, the whole group, joined by Jon Harpman, headed for the first hole, a par four that would start west, then dogleg slightly north, or to the right. Its small green would encroach on the preserve by agreement with the regulators. The clearing line along the center of the fairway that the surveyors had made last January was our path. It was pretty rough in spots, crossing a drainage ditch up toward the tee, then through some downed Brazilian peppers, melaleucas and wax myrtles, occasional palms and pines. Surveyor's tape identified the trees that Hills wanted saved. Pink tape with the phrase TIMBER HARVEST BOUNDARY printed in thick block letters endlessly repeating down its length marked the outer edge of the clearing. (Surveyor's tape is thin vinyl ribbon, about an inch and a half wide, that tears easily but is sturdy enough to take a knot. It comes in a roll like masking tape, but it's not sticky. A range of colors, including two-tones, lets surveyors develop codes to tell people in the field what to do. Save anything tagged white, for example, or clear to the pink, stay away from blue, whatever.)

Painter wanted to identify the supply areas for his donor plant material, his Tree Spade Units, or TSUs. Just past the dogleg on the first hole, up toward the preserve area, there was a huge stand of cabbage palms. Ironhorse's environmental consultant and the biologist with the South Florida Water Management District (often referred to simply as "South Florida") planned to include part of this area in the preserve. Painter's tree spades could move a pine up to eight inches or so in diameter, palms of almost any size, smaller myrtles—which would colonize—along with the occasional cocoa plum or dahoon holly.

After struggling a few hundred yards down the first fairway, Riley and Postell started questioning the necessity for this group review of the clearing lines. Riley said, "I think we ought to wait 'til Monday to get a Cat in here so we can see a little better what we're doing."

In the nine months since it had been cut, the clearing line had grown over with vines and weeds. It was hard to see the tape.

"I'm gonna instruct my operator, when he gets in here," Postell said, "that if he sees any palms or pines within forty or fifty feet of the edge, save 'em."

Dash was not convinced that what they were doing was futile. He'd seen too many cases, he said, of clearing getting out of hand. You can't put back what you've knocked down. You could perhaps have Pat Painter put a smaller version back in, but it would be expensive. Dash said, prophetically, "I think we need to get a ribbon on these bigger trees anyway."

Riley and Postell weren't persuaded that they were doing anybody any good walking through underbrush, stumbling over roots, to look for pink ribbons. When Dash was out of earshot, Postell turned to Riley. "No more'n I know about building a golf course," he said, pausing to squirt a little tobacco juice for emphasis, "you got to have room to knock that ball from one end t'other to play, don't ya, Rile?"

"Sure do, Kenny," Riley agreed. "This here's a waste of time."

I asked Postell if any of this clearing would be difficult from what he'd seen. "Son, ain't nothing grows too big for us to knock down." He spit a brown ribbon, then spit again. Spitting is punctuation in Postell's speech. A little piff, like blowing a husk from off one's lip, is like a comma. Two spits is an exclamation point. "What gives us trouble is when it's wet, and any time you see that saw grass"—he pointed back behind and left of where we'd just walked—"it's soft. This is swamp here."

Kenny tried again to get Dash to put aside today's trek. "Mike, you can come in here and really start looking when we make the second pass. Getting through here today ain't benefitting us that much."

"We're gonna have the tree spades in here, you guys clearing," Dash responded. "I want to make sure we're not pulling anything out we want to keep."

Dash had worked with Kenny before, on the Willoughby job up in Stuart. The same triumvirate had been in action there that would swing through Ironhorse—clearing by Phillips and Jordan, Ranger moving the dirt, and Wadsworth building the course. Ironhorse and Willoughby had originally been scheduled to start at the same time, late in the spring of 1988. Willoughby had.

It was not that Dash didn't trust Postell; it wasn't that simple. He didn't trust a line of command, as it were, descending from him through Jon Harpman to John Riley to Kenny Postell and finally to the operators not to have a little distortion, maybe not as bad as what used to happen in the kid's game of gossip but something with the potential for mistakes that a few rolls of felicitously placed pink ribbon might avert. But Riley and Postell weren't buying. Claiming another meeting, they left, so the three remaining hands set out to stake the clearing, to check it against the line roughly staked ten months before. Dash walked the center line so he could keep notes and refer to the folded clearing sheet drawn in Toledo. He could check his print and sight back and forth down the center line to study the relationship of the clearing to the line of play. Harpman moved off to the right, and I climbed into the Sabal patch on the left, hoping I'd never hit a ball into this dense palm forest. I spent the next two days fighting my way across dense stands of palmetto, slogging through muck, grinding through myrtle, establishing a new intimacy with Alan's Eden.

PHILLIPS AND JORDAN was working with a short crew until more equipment arrived, just Postell—in his Carolina accent Postell's first name was "Keeney," with a hard accent on the first syllable followed by a soft drop on the second—and Charles Best, who was knocking down Brazilian peppers along the drainage canal Bob Grier had dug nearly twenty years ago up at the north end, along the railroad tracks. Best had been working for Ted Phillips, who owned Phillips and Jordan, for thirty-five years. He'd cleared for roadbeds and reservoirs, cane fields and orange groves, working from coast to coast. Pushing through redwoods on a highway right-of-way in northern California, he'd felt the forceful shadow of Shasta's great snow-capped peak but felt comfortable working on and around big hills. He wasn't fond of Florida's flatness. Since P&J had moved into Florida five years before, Best had worked exclusively there, but he still made his home in the hills of east Tennessee. Phillips and Jordan was a Smoky Mountain company, with its headquarters in Knoxville. Ted Phillips, like Postell, was from Robbinsville, a little town not far from the intersecting borders of Tennessee, North Carolina, and Georgia. This was once Cherokee land. There was a Cherokee reservation minutes from Robbinsville. P&J had Cherokee operators, even all-Indian clearing crews. Postell said, "some of them Indians are the best operators we got." There weren't any Cherokee operators at Ironhorse, but Mike

Dasher told me that P&J had an Indian clearing crew on the Wando Plantation job he and Hills were doing up by Charleston, South Carolina.

Sitting in his D8, Best worked with such economy that he seemed cast in place. He had been operating so long, he said, that sometimes "I don't think at all about what I'm doing. I'll even surprise myself some days when I see everything I've knocked down." His speech was slow, dry, and compact, almost monotonal. "Uh-huh," he'd say, taking a long pull on a Winston, listening to a tale, helping it end with a quick nod and a benedictive "by God." He kept a couple of two-liter plastic bottles of Dr Pepper stowed in a cooler behind his Cat's seat, and by day's end he'd have drained them, swallowing between puffs. After a few weeks a trail of bottles marched across the site, the flotsam of Best's passage. When he wasn't consulting the Dr, he was lighting another Winston. Best's cigarettes flowed in a steady arc from his lips to his lap, perched between the index and middle fingers of his gloved hand. There was a rhythm in his movements and a zenlike economy that made any animation hard to detect. All that smoking hadn't done a lot for his cardiovascular system, so skill here served necessity. Postell asked him one day, "Charles, how much you smoke?"

"I smoke four to five packs a day, by God," he said, his mouth barely moving in reply. "And I'd smoke more if I had time."

As the rest of his crew and equipment arrived over the next few days, Postell cruised the site in his gray Ford pickup, dropping into four-wheel drive to grind over muck and marl, laying out the work, checking the clearing lines, picking out the wet spots where the dozers might sink. Usually he worked seven days a week when the weather was good and P&J had a big job to knock off, and never fewer than six days, but he allowed as how something had come up so he was taking the coming weekend off. Getting married. Up in Virginia, at his girlfriend's home. "The hardest part of getting married for me," he said, looking over at his pickup, "is gonna be that eight-hundred-mile drive."

Phillips and Jordan started the clearing up at the north end of Ironhorse and would work its way south. It would clear the third, fourth, fifth, and sixth fairways and the lakes adjacent to them, so the dirt contractor, Ranger Construction, could start excavating the lakes. Then P&J would move slowly on south, clearing whatever was staked for it, until the job was done. Ranger, able to run its equipment across the cleared land, would start digging the drainage lakes, mining the raw material out of which Ironhorse would take shape.

It's NEARLY DECEMBER. Tropical storm Keith, now over the gulf, may move across south Florida. The air's too filled with moisture to absorb any sweat. Humidity makes the atmosphere palpable, a dense, thick coupling of skin and air. Dark smoke, with a kind of sickly sweet smell, drifts toward Ironhorse from the west. I think at first it must be from the landfill, but Postell, who's lit enough fires to qualify as an expert on smoke, says it's from sugar-cane fields burning to the west, over toward Lake Okeechobee.

Jon Harpman is talking to Postell in front of the Grier house. Kenny's dog, Molly, a brown mixed-breed bitch with just enough pit bull in her to discourage casual petting, is sitting in the cab of his pickup. Postell's got an elbow on the gray fender, and rolling his head around to look at me, runs his hand up the back of his neck to push his cap forward so the bill shades his eyes. "John," he says, "you're from out there in Or-e-gone," giving it the standard east of the Rockies mispronunciation. "How you like it here in Florida?"

I've been living in the Northwest for twenty years. Mount Hood and Mount Saint Helens anchor the view, white and solid and, from a distance, calm and reassuring. I told Kenny I wasn't real fond of Florida so far, that its monotony dispersed it, that its vistas were hard to comprehend, running off to the horizon like a line drawn across a page. I was having trouble getting a feel for the place. The weather granted a certain ease, but I hadn't yet found the key to liking Florida.

"Me, neither," he said, spitting a brown bullet over his left shoulder. His can of chew outlined a circle in the breast pocket of his light-blue T-shirt, like the shadow of a badge. "I'm from up in the Smokies, you know, up in North Carolina, and I like hills. I miss them mountains. I had an old boy from up home working for me down here, and I asked him, just like I did you, 'Cotton, how you like Florida?'

" 'Well, Kenny,' he said, 'if I had a house in Florida and a home in Hell, I'd sell my house and get on home.' Yessir." Postell laughed and spit, then pulled one eye shut, nodding in a deep parody of a wink. "Just *sell* my house and get on home."

It's just after first light. Postell's crew is at work by seven o'clock, cranking up the diesels at the sweetest time of day. Harpman, eager to do right with his first responsibilities but still with only a vague sense of what his job's about, comes early enough to unlock the gate, a boss's prerogative on a construction site. Kenny has a key, too. Sometimes Phillips and Jordan wants to work on a Sunday, and Jon's not quite that dedicated. He's taken up scuba diving in a serious way and likes to spend Sundays on the reefs. Harpman's a strong swimmer, good at all the country club sports—tennis, golf, and sweet talk by the pool.

Bob Isakson gets to the job about eight, driving in from his little efficiency apartment in West Palm Beach, on the second floor of a building run by a retired army man that has the tedious neatness of a military base, a quality that appeals to Isakson, whose stateside service during the early years of the war in Vietnam ran to operating motor pools. Isakson's wife and two children are still in Dallas, where the sclerosis of the oil business has blocked the flow of cash to the real estate market, taking the joy out of owning your own home. Figuring out what to do with a house you bought for a bunch more than you can get for it is like owning a prize bull when you're starving—do you feed it or eat it? A move to Florida for the Isakson family is complicated by the kids' school.

Isakson played golf with Alan Sher over the weekend at Frenchman's Creek. He hits the ball long and wild and swings so fast his grips smoke. Searching for his balls he got a good look at the houses going up along the golf course. Isakson said Frenchman's was selling houses at a rate that put them five years ahead of their projected sellout. That's the kind of progress that got Josh Muss's attention. Palm Beach County's growing so fast it can't keep up with the infrastructure. The state legislature has required every county to come up with a long-range plan, but Palm Beach County hasn't finished one yet. Every year Florida has to build the equivalent of a city the size of Portland, Oregon, to keep up with its population growth, even though its death rate exceeds its birth rate. Eight of the ten fastest-growing American cities are in Florida. When a baby's born, it usually has a place to go, it fits into an existing household. But the retired couple moving down from Akron needs a place now. That keeps the Florida economy roiling. Orlando, which had only the sun and acres of moribund orchards to recommend it when Disney moved in, is growing faster than West Palm, where Mickey almost landed. Disney's was the new way, family tourism, $500-a-day vacations with all imaginative requirements filled in advance. MacArthur's developments were a democratization of the earlier style, the Flagler way, retirement homes, vacation houses, and traditional recreations—golf first and foremost, and sailing and tennis and dinner parties. The Disney version of Orlando has as much to do with Florida as it has with Switzerland—it's an ahistorical place. West Palm Beach still specializes in inventing instant communities, but Disney is self-contained, a world of its own. People move to Orlando to service the millions coming to visit, and the migrants will, as people always do, create a way of life. And with them come, as in West Palm Beach, a need for water and roads and schools and housing and garbage collection. Especially potable water and solid waste disposal.

Ironhorse is surrounded on three sides by public lands, SWA on the east and south and the City of West Palm Beach's water-catchment basin to the west. SWA runs a large landfill east of the Florida Turnpike, the top of which is visible from Ironhorse, especially from along what will be the fourteenth and fifteenth holes. Between Jog Road and the turnpike, across from Ironhorse's entry, the major feature of the landscape is a shallow borrow lake of several hundred acres that SWA dredges to get fill for the Dyer Landfill. "Landfill" is not really a word that works in Florida. As Mike Dasher says, if you see a hill intruding on the horizon in south Florida, you know you're looking at a dump—a land*pile*. The water table is so near the surface you can't bury much, so to dispose of solid waste in south Florida you stack it. Dyer had nearly reached its capacity and was scheduled to close before 1990. It's where the northern part of Palm Beach County's refuse gathers. Dredges anchored in the borrow lake suck sandy soil up from the bottom into a slurry to pump under the turnpike. After drying it's spread over the refuse, building the SWA's artificial hill in accreting layers. SWA's mountain is a grand version of the technique Ironhorse will use to create its mounds, hummocks, and swales, throwing up dirt from a hole to make a dry place.

In the original plan for Ironhorse, the one closer to Alan Sher's idea of a small, *very* exclusive development—the newer, Mussian version of Ironhorse is just ordinarily exclusive—the entry was going to be off the Beeline Highway, on the north side of the property, over the existing railway easement now being used as the construction entry. The redesign to shift the main entry to Jog Road created a small problem of encroachment on SWA land. The Beeline runs at a diagonal on a southeast-to-northwest trajectory across Ironhorse's northern boundary. So that cars could turn perpendicularly rather than at an acute angle from Jog onto the Beeline, the northern end of Jog Road needed to turn out a little bit to the east. That turn then created a triangular sliver of land that was owned by SWA but contiguous to Ironhorse and, because its eastern border was defined by Jog, looked as if it belonged to the development. This was not land SWA needed or could put to use, so Muss wanted to buy it.

Negotiations for "the triangle" inaugurated a period of curiously tense interaction between Ironhorse and SWA, the culmination of which was an offer by SWA that, as Isakson witnessed to his own astonishment, caught Muss completely off guard. It is the guiding principle of Josh Muss's business life to be in charge, in control, *dominating*. There is little room in his psychic storehouse for subordination. He wears impatience like a uniform. As he had with Aquart, the project engineer, the first time I saw him in action, he kept his hirelings off guard by knowing, or appearing to know, more about their jobs than they did. No professional skill cowed him in the least. He hired engineers and planners, and he could fire them—they answered to him. That was Muss's style, and it had served him well. None of his employees was likely to name any children for him, but he marshaled a combat esprit that got things done. He was the general, mapping strategy, looking for ways to engage the enemy on his terrain, with his rules. But SWA, Isakson saw, caught him in the open.

SWA was not happy to see Ironhorse taking shape almost within its borders. The Dyer Landfill was about to close, but that didn't mean SWA was going out of business. On another part of its 1,320 acres, just to the south of Ironhorse—one would have an excellent view of it from the twelfth green and the thirteenth tee—SWA was building its administrative headquarters. And further south, already nearing completion, was a "state-of-the-art" trash-burning power plant, able when it was running at full capacity to generate fifty megawatts, or enough power for 30,000 homes.

Burning garbage doesn't get rid of it entirely, it just reduces its volume and concentrates its by-products. Combustion leaves an ash that SWA still had to dispose of. Creating plastic-lined pits, it figured that on its existing property it could store thirty years' worth of garbage, with a technique similar to that used at the Dyer site, alternating layers of ash with layers of dredged earth to create a series of hills. And just as the long-range plan was to convert Dyer into a park, with grass growing over the pile, eventually the transformation of the

SWA site would create a vast public playground—sailboats in the borrow lake, Frisbee golf across the artificial mesas, picnics and court- ship in the uplands planted above the residue of the county's incin- erated detritus. Ironhorse would then nestle amid this contrived nature, buffered from any future development. All in all, a wonderful- sounding plan, a technological solution to a solid waste problem compounded of ceaseless consumption, no serious recycling programs—Florida has no bottle bill, for example—and a rapidly growing population.

At the end of a meeting to discuss Ironhorse's purchase of the Jog Road triangle in the late summer of 1988, SWA dropped its bomb. Muss originally hoped to persuade SWA to trade the triangle he wanted for the trees Ironhorse had in abundance waiting for the clearing contractor. SWA could use them to landscape its property. Dyer had a small forest on its south side, a beautiful surviving ex- ample of native flora, a mixture of wetlands and upland vegetation that shielded the landfill from the highway. Except the Dyer forest wasn't vestigial, it was invented. Every tree—17,000 in all—had been transplanted, every wetland plant carried to the site not by the hidden hand of Mother Nature but by truck. As it continued to develop Dyer, SWA was going to need more and more palms and myrtles. Muss thought they could work a trade.

The triangle was one of several items on SWA and Ironhorse's joint agendas. They shared in the development of Jog Road, and Ironhorse needed easements to run its sewer and water lines across SWA prop- erty and enlarge the drainage canal that headed east along the Bee- line Highway toward a big South Florida Water Management District Canal so that it could handle the runoff from Ironhorse after a heavy rain. It's typical of the bureaucratic climate of south Florida that something as seemingly simple as arranging to move Ironhorse's storm water into the existing system of public drainage involved, in one way or another, the Army Corps of Engineers, the South Florida Water Management District, the Florida Department of Transporta- tion, Palm Beach County, the City of West Palm Beach, the Northern Palm Beach County Water Management District, and SWA, as well as the CSX Railroad, which, for bureaucratic sloth and pure indiffer- ence, put the public agencies to shame. So SWA and Ironhorse were, by the force of geography, locked into an enduring and risky part- nership.

SWA was potentially an impediment to Ironhorse's image, but

Ironhorse also pitched a fright at SWA. People who could afford to live at Ironhorse would not be either indifferent to any problems SWA might run into, or reluctant or unable to express their views. If not themselves lawyers, they'd know how to hire good legal talent. Ironhorse is SWA's only real neighbor. There are a couple of other developments within its olfactory range, but Ironhorse is the only one whose residents can really see SWA, who'll watch its trucks roll by on Jog Road, filled with the by-products of our disposable life. (In the summer of 1989, the smell from Dyer got so bad that some residents at PGA National, a mile or so north of Dyer, reported they couldn't sleep. The smell was partly from the methane that decomposition produces, but some improperly disposed sludge the county dumped spiked the aroma. It didn't last. SWA announced plans to install a citrus oil perfume system designed to mask the smell.)

Approached at eye level along the Beeline, Dyer looks like anything but a dump. The tree line is a typical native mix of Sabal palms, pines, and occasional cypress. There are myrtles, cocoa plums, and hollies along the margins of the water and saw grass and Spartina along the littoral shelves. The Dyer site looks like a miniaturized biological museum of south Florida. Ironhorse was a degraded site, a drained, expunged wetland where nature was creating a set of responses to a new hydrological reality. The low-lying ground north of the landfill looked like a remnant of undeveloped Florida, an unlikely companion to the rising monument behind it. But the truth is, the Dyer wetlands are as artificial as Art Hills's golf course at Ironhorse will be, the product of a Big John tree spade and Pat Painter, the "restoration biologist." Just as he's moved thousands of trees onto the SWA, he'll have his crews move thousands more at Ironhorse.

It's when one looks above the tree line at Dyer that the dump appears, a green wall of grass rising up a hill to the active face, where dumpsters drop their loads and dozers spread it in layers and compact it before covering it with dirt, kind of a strip mine in reverse. Hovering above the dump, great flocks of cattle egrets clamor over the bounty, watching the dozers stir the soup. Gulls stream in from the east to join them. Turkey buzzards, seasonal migrants from the north, enjoy this repast, and when they're not feeding they roost in Pat Painter's conveniently planted pines, gathering in such numbers that one wonders how the limbs can bear their weight, their hunched and vaguely ominous dark shapes outlined against the green hill. Ibis cruise over from the catchment basin to scrounge for

tidbits. Dyer is the world's greatest road kill, cultural carrion, a lay-
ered, suppurating beast, a prolific banquet, a succulent, fetid feast.
Generations of birds have fed off its flesh. When the landfill closes,
they'll disperse, memories of the easy life dimming. Until then, gray
gulls, white egrets, and dark buzzards turning in the bright-blue sky
above the dump point to its presence, a three-dimensional signpost.
Early on in my stay in Florida, when I was trying to get a feel for
direction and place, I'd find my way back to Ironhorse by looking
for the swirl of Dyer's flocks.

SWA made the first move to extricate itself, preferring, if it had to
have a neighbor, something like a little industrial park or a salvage
auto yard like the one across from Dyer on Haverhill Road. Everybody goes home at five, and there's no celebrated tranquillity for sight
or sound to disturb. And if there was a little smell in the middle of the
night, only the watchdog would notice, and he might find it savory.
If a dumpster were to lose a bit of its load in the breeze, it wouldn't
blow into the backyard pool of a million-dollar estate home, but be
caught instead in the wide net of a chain-link warehouse fence. The
big site SWA acquired was proving too small in the face of the county's growth, so it needed more room. The plan to create a second
disposal site in the south county—another trash-burning power plant
near Boca Raton—roused a huge popular antipathy. Neighbors pick-
eted the site, carrying signs saying DON'T DUMP ON US. SWA knew
its problems were compounding. The county's south dump, at Lan-
tana, closed in July 1988. Dyer had to take on the smelly sludge from
the Boca Raton sewage treatment plant as well as the additional solid
waste created by the delay in getting a new south county plant
opened. It had to get its new, and as it turned out undersized, garbage-
burning plant open and make sure it had plenty of room to bury the
ash. And it had to work on polishing an image tarnished by the
highly publicized opposition to its long-range plans. It was in that
context that SWA fooled Joshua Muss. When he went to talk to SWA
about buying its triangle, they said, we've got a better idea. How
about selling us Ironhorse?

Muss thought they were kidding. He tried a feeble joke. "You can't
afford it," he said. He knew the kind of money they thought the land
was worth. They wanted $20,000 an acre for the little triangle, more
than what Alan Sher had paid for the dirt four years ago, but a
pittance compared to what it would be worth with permits in place
to develop it, to say nothing of its value as developed property. Muss

had tried to play down the value of the triangle so he could get it from SWA cheap, but the SWA proposal put him in a tricky spot. When he and Isakson left the meeting, Muss was in shock. "They can't be serious," he said to Isakson.

"Well, Josh," Isakson opined, "don't forget eminent domain."

"Oh, shit," said Muss. It was an ominous time for Ironhorse and more days of worry for Alan Sher.

I MET MIKE GORDON on the top floor of the downtown West Palm Beach office building known, without affection, as Darth Vader, the same place where Sher had listened a year before to the Bird Lady's condemnation of Ironhorse. Gordon's building is black and slick and I think indifferently placed rather than ominous, a cousin to the high rises that stretch across the Dallas skyline. Buildings in Florida are not black, so Darth is a void among the lighter shades of the south Florida architectural palette. Still, inside it's just a contemporary office building that counts among its tenants the firm of Boose Casey Ciklin et al. Gordon orchestrated the deal that finally married Muss and Sher. But while Sher put his fortune at risk to try to make Ironhorse go, Gordon had nearly given his life.

Not long after he got access to the land, Sher bought his fleet of fast four-wheel-drive ATVs so he could carom around the place and show it off to friends and potential investors. Apart from the main paved road that ran from the Beeline Highway back to the house, a handful of paths, some engineered by the cattle moving from pasture to pasture, ran across the property. Sher loved to rev up the bright-red Hondas, peddle up to a high gear—there's no clutch on an ATV, so to change gears you let off the throttle and shift with your foot—and fly through the meadow grasses and over the shallow drainage ditches, water swirling in great arcs off the fat knobby tires. Sher's understanding of the mechanical properties of the ATVs was roughly the same as for the rest of his fleet—he knew on, off, fast, stop, and if it makes a funny noise take it to this guy I know who's the best mechanic in Florida. Speed makes Sher smile. Once he was driving his bright-red, twelve-cylinder Ferrari Testarossa to Ironhorse and squeezed it up to Mach 1 along North Lake Boulevard. He was waiting for the light to change at the Beeline when he saw a blue light coming up behind him from the east. He eased onto the shoulder. The blue light slid in behind, and a smiling deputy sheriff came alongside, the safety of his ballpoint pen clicked off. "I couldn't catch you," he said by way of introduction. "Got a license?"

"Do you play golf?" Sher wondered, looking up up up from a tan leather seat slung so low that it puts a driver's knee about chin high. Palm Beach County is the epicenter of the golf boom, after all, and there was always the chance that the healthy-looking fellow staring down at him was one of the thousands of frustrated hackers who didn't get to play as much golf as he would like because the majority of the eight million or so golf holes in Palm Beach County were private, for members only, inaccessible to the financially impaired. "I'm building this golf course just off the Beeline over here," Sher said, pointing vaguely northeast, "and I'm late for a meeting and I didn't know how fast I was going sorry how would you like to play my course when it's done whatah ya say come on over be my guest."

Sher got off with a warning and accepted the compliments on his Testarossa with a studied noblesse oblige. It is among the duties of the patron to approve the adoration of his objects. Nearly supine in the Testarossa's soft lap, Sher rolled on over to Ironhorse.

Ramming about Ironhorse in the ATVs he didn't have to worry about speed limits. Most of the time he knew where he was going. But Gordon, eager to please a wealthy new client, dressed perfectly à la Ralph Lauren for a day in the country, struggled with his ATV technique. Sher went faster than Gordon cared to go. He found himself straining to keep his bearings while trying to operate a machine that was cumbersome and foreign. Sher was racing ahead, Gordon fighting to keep up. Blindly Gordon plowed into a canal, went over the handlebars, and landed hard on his head, peeling back a thick flap of scalp. He stayed underwater an ominously long time. Sher, ahead of him, looked back at first with amusement, but then saw the blood and realized this might be a little more than a pratfall. When Gordon described his accident more than two years later, he was *still* mad. "Sher is crazy," he said, smiling over a drink at a corner booth in the private restaurant on the top floor of Darth Vader. "I had to keep going back to the hospital for weeks to have the wound debrided. It was not fun. I coulda been killed. Sher tells this story like I'm some kind of klutz, but he shouldn't have had me out there going so fast." It's true, Sher does think Gordon is somehow physically inept. When he tells the story of Gordon's kamikaze plunge into the drainage ditch, he usually yokes it to another story about Gordon falling in a swimming pool, exculpating himself with evidence of Gordon's clumsiness.

Gordon is convinced that no one but he could have put together the deal to bail out the water from Sher's sinking boat. He doesn't think he gets the credit for it he deserves. He fielded Sher's frantic phone calls every morning. A corollary of the famous real estate dictum that the three most important qualities in any piece of property are "location, location and location" is that there are never bad deals on good land, just bad timing. Muss's pockets were deep enough to insulate him from the minor irritation of a soft market or even a recession. The "upside was always there," as Matt Weeg said, and the downside only temporary. That was a salesman talking. There may not have been an underside to all this, but even the dealmaker himself couldn't forestall a public agency with the powers of condemnation.

By the early fall of 1988, it was obvious that something serious was holding up construction at Ironhorse. Bob Isakson complained endlessly about the complications of getting permits, and there were hints that Muss was having trouble putting together a financing package entirely to his liking, but until SWA reared up in the background all these delays seemed like simply confirmation of the developer's chronic complaints about bureaucratic restraints—permits and reviews and zoning and planning and all the associated paraphernalia protecting the public interest—that make it damn near impossible for a landowner to exercise his simple God-given property rights. If there's a tree on it, I can cut it down, if there's water on it, I can drain it off, if there's a hill on it, I can knock it down. If I can discern a dead president's face on the side of a mountain, I can blast and polish until it's exposed for all men to see.

But that's not how bureaucracies work, and anybody who has or ever had any power or authority knows it. Henry Flagler could drain swamps because there wasn't anybody to stop him, aside from a few dependent native people whose ancestors had lost their land when stronger armies came to claim it, or anyone who cared. But Flagler and his contemporaries were like a footprint on the sand compared to the Army Corps of Engineers and its schemes to capture and control water. The Corps could take the most spirited force of nature and given enough time and money break it, like a tough vaquero on a wild mustang. And when the Corps did it, the developers and farmers didn't have to pay. Everybody did. That's what is great about democracy—it not only encourages enterprise, it spreads the cost. Ironhorse may have had to jump through a few hoops, but there's a whole economy in south Florida that both invents hoops and offers guides on how to jump them properly. SWA had its own turf to defend, but it was hardly hostile to development. The bigger the garbage crisis, the more people are dependent on SWA. Institutions resemble living organisms—they want to perpetuate themselves. There's no evidence that the bureaucratic layers impede growth. It would make more sense to say that the bureaucracies *create* growth— with all its regulatory agencies in place, Florida's growing faster now than ever. The bureaucracies just spread the wealth a bit. Instead of my grading a road across my land, platting a few lots over the site, and putting out a FOR SALE sign, now I have to hire lawyers and planners and engineers and surveyors and biologists, all of whom are ultimately paid by the buyers of my now much more expensive lots. Typically, the professionals who are guiding me through the maze are the same ones who, if they didn't create the bureaucracy, at the least used to run it. The engineers worked for the Corps or the South Florida Water Management District; the lawyers and planners worked for the county or the city, often supervising the person whose help they now solicit to get their latest project approved. The sort of hostile language that still echoes through the conversation of the developer's minions is thoughtless, as if they haven't been initiated yet, they don't know the secret. Sophisticated developers like Muss know that regulatory agencies hold down the competition.

The question facing Muss when SWA floated the prospect of buying Ironhorse was explained by Gordon as we chewed on crudités at The Executive Club. Gordon took off the jacket of his gray-silk tailored suit as he launched the tale. He speaks rapidly and with great assurance, and he loves to please. He attends his own voice with great avidity. His speech is intelligently constructed, his stories full of detail.

Realizing its resource recovery unit—the solid waste incinerator— was going to be operating at maximum capacity from day one, the SWA was looking for a place to do a preliminary separation of the garbage. According to Gordon, this site would ideally have access from the Beeline as well as railroad service, but best of all it would be contiguous to the SWA. Ironhorse fit the bill perfectly.

Muss faced a real problem. First, there was the need for secrecy. Everybody involved in Ironhorse knew the Dyer Landfill and the SWA recovery plant were potential liabilities. More than one adviser to Sher in the early days advised against proceeding because of them. But Muss was willing to take the chance, as long as he could control the way the *perception* of Ironhorse's location was acquired. The last thing he needed was a public battle over SWA's attempt to take over his property. A well-managed marketing campaign, Muss was sure, could mitigate any doubts about SWA as a neighbor. He could make the proximity of SWA's lakes and wildlife areas as much a virtue as Ironhorse's parklike isolation. But if the buying public fixed an association between Ironhorse and the problem of garbage in its mind, the marketing would certainly be tougher. Muss had taken on this project in the first place because the potential profits were so great. He knew the risk. As he'd said in a letter to Sher as they were completing the financial arrangements that put Muss in charge, "Few people share our optimism and enthusiasm for this project." After his meeting with SWA, Muss called Gordon, telling him to set aside forty-five minutes for a meeting. "That was unheard of with Josh," Gordon said. "He'd come in for five minutes and we'd take care of business in the conference room or the reception area and Josh'd be on his way. He doesn't do lunches. He works."

Now he wanted time, and he wanted to see Gordon privately. When they met, Gordon said, Muss seemed stunned, uncertain of how to proceed. They decided, mainly at Gordon's instigation, to keep Sher in the dark for at least a week while they tried to resolve the dilemma SWA had placed at their feet. Muss was not emotionally tied to Ironhorse; it was a deal, a way to make money. Despite the lure of big bucks for a successful development, turning the dirt quickly and without risk for a tidy profit was not without appeal. The problem was finding the right price, one high enough to discourage SWA from buying Ironhorse, but not so high that it would initiate condemnation proceedings. Muss and Gordon wanted to find a price that was not unreasonable, that is, not so high that SWA couldn't give it serious consideration, and at the same time high enough that if it didn't discourage SWA it would still provide enough profit to satisfy Muss. If Ironhorse asked for some absurd amount, SWA could take them to court and probably get the property for less. But, as Gordon explained SWA's gamble, if it took Ironhorse to court in condemnation proceedings and the deliberations determined that the price Ironhorse offered to SWA had in fact been a fair one, SWA would be subject to paying damages, court costs, and lawyers' fees, making their decision much trickier. Gordon was feeling some personal ambiguity as he felt his way along. He had, after all, first been Sher's lawyer. When Muss took over Ironhorse, Gordon was part of the deal. He was in something of a compromising position. Sher was emotionally committed to Ironhorse. When Gordon asked Muss if it really mattered to him whether or not he sold, he said, as Gordon summarized it, "If I can make a nice profit now I would, but I'm not averse to developing."

Gordon calls Muss "The Surgeon" because he puts his deals together with such elegance and precision. Sher's the Mad Hatter. In this deal, because of his eagerness to get into the luxury market that's made so many developers rich, Muss had taken on more risk than he ordinarily would, but still less, according to Gordon, than most developers must.

Gordon called in a savvy appraiser to help them find the price, the point on the fulcrum that would give Muss enough profit to sell without regret but not so high that SWA would start condemnation and, at the best, tie them up in court for a year or two while God knows what happened in this red-hot high-end Palm Beach market. And they kept Sher in the dark. They didn't want anyone to know that SWA was even *considering* condemning Ironhorse.

BEFORE I LEARNED about all these SWA-induced maneuvers, I had driven over to see Sher at The Reaches. Ardus had told me over the phone that he was washing the cars, so I knew he'd be available for a while. The weather was what air conditioning is designed to imitate: seventy degrees, low humidity, the taste of a breeze. Alan was rinsing Ardus's new Jaguar convertible, a birthday present. It's black with a burgundy leather interior, long and dramatic and solid, and if it was a guy it would drink Glenfiddich and wear ascots. Alan was chamoising the last droplets off the hood, his chains banging on his chin, wearing shorts and a knit shirt. "My father always said, 'A guy who'd drive a dirty car would wear dirty drawers.' "

He climbed in the driver's seat and started the Jag, then felt under his hip with his hand. "Geez, there's a leak here somewhere—whenever I wash this thing the seat gets wet. Stay here a second," he told me. "I'll get the next one."

He ferried the Jag under the building and came back in two minutes with the Testarossa, pulling it out of the garage in a chorus of clearing throats. Driving the Ferrari keeps his mind off the enormous disappointment that's gnawing at his self-esteem. Muss has some money tied up in Ironhorse, but Sher's investment is personal. He wants Ironhorse to go, and everybody *knows* it. Sher is a nice man, a great salesman—his charm and instincts for knowing what people want built his company, wooed his wife, made his fortune. His father's aphorisms were his catechism, the wisdom that renewed him. "A customer would call my father and say, 'Where's my buttons? You said last week. I need buttons!' And my father would say, 'The last time I talked to you, Harold, your wife, Martha, she wasn't feeling well. How is she?'

" 'What's that got to do with anything? *Where are my buttons?*'

" 'Really, Harry, I'm surprised at you. What's more important, your wife's health or a few buttons?'

"And the customers would always laugh and my father would get the order out and everything's okay."

But over the last few weeks the well had started running dry. The old maxims were insufficient guidance against the strength of such a big gamble. "Oy, my stomach," he said, when I asked how he was. "I'm going crazy. I can't take this. I've always been a breadwinner and now I'm just spending money. Thank God my kids are doing well financially."

By this time Sher knew why Ironhorse was on hold, but I didn't, and he'd been sworn to secrecy by Muss and Gordon after they'd finally presented SWA with their price. They had invited Sher to lunch to let him in on the drama. "They can't do this to me!" Sher shouted when he learned what was afoot. "Fuck them! Tell them fifty million! We won't sell." Gordon herded him to the elevator to calm him down. Now he was biting his tongue when I pushed him to find out why there were so many delays. By this time Ironhorse was nearly nine months late getting started. Had the schedule pinned to the wall beside Bob Isakson's desk been followed, the course would have been done by the time I came by to watch Alan buff the fleet. I hadn't been able to figure out what was causing this latest delay. Hills and Dasher hadn't heard anything either, and Wadsworth was trying to figure out where Ironhorse would fit in its schedule. Its crew just up the road in Stuart was putting the finishing touches on Willoughby, but Wadsworth didn't know if it could just move that bunch down I-95 to Ironhorse or if it would have to find another crew to bring in. At Ironhorse there was a lot of bickering around the office about permits and rumors about Muss's financial package, but never a sense that the whole thing might come to a stop. As the summer dragged on, as days passed with a dreary dullness, Isakson, who'd worked on and off for Muss for more than twenty years, started to wonder if something sinister was going on. He'd moved from Dallas, separated from his family, taken on as his assistant the boss's nephew. Now the days were filled not so much with work, which Isakson was happy to take on, but with hours of waiting, wondering, and second-guessing, not just of the agencies whose permits were essential to getting under way but of Muss, who told Isakson what he wanted done but never confided in him. Isakson was often distressed after telephoning Muss at his office in Washington, D.C., taking a long pull on a Camel, stubbing it in his ashtray, and looking down through his half-circle reading glasses at the neat list of questions marching down the graph paper he liked to use for notes. He'd get through two or three items before Muss would hang up on him. No good-bye, no "Thanks, Bobby, we'll look at that later." Just the quick click of indifference. Isakson would hang up the receiver with controlled precision, struggling to keep a neutral look on his face, to bodyguard his feelings. He was so clearly loyal to Muss, so eager to do well and willing to work hard, that it was painful to watch him rebuked by Muss's inattention and contempt. But, just as the old Green Bay Packers learned not to take personally Vince Lombardi's lashings—"he treats us all the same, like dogs"—Muss's minions chose to accept his treatment.

A couple of days before, Isakson was pouring himself a cup of coffee in the kitchen at the office. We were wondering aloud, as usual, if Ironhorse the Construction Project would ever get under way. "If I didn't know Muss better," he said, "I'd think he was working Sher."

"What do you mean, working him?"

"I've seen this in Texas lots of times. A developer makes a deal for some dirt, then waits to pay. The seller starts getting nervous, worried about getting his cash. The buyer lets on he's having a little trouble with his financing, but if the seller will drop the price a little, he thinks it will work out. So now the seller thinks about all the time he's got in the sale, how long it would take to get a new buyer, the court costs to try to recover if the deal falls through, all that. So the seller drops his price. *That's* working. But Muss would never do that."

Besides, Muss had *already* closed on the property. Sher was still waiting to recover money out of his pocket and he wasn't earning anything yet, but he wasn't hanging out to dry as he had been the year before. Still, things had taken on such a Byzantine odor, I wanted Sher to tell me what was going on. I knew Muss wouldn't tell me. He didn't mind my being at Ironhorse as long as I didn't take up any of his time. He'd walk into the office when I was there and not speak to me, not even acknowledge my presence. If he had someone with him, more often than not he would ignore me when making introductions. It was a curious indifference, given that I was writing about a project in which he had such a personal stake. It helped me see him through Isakson's eyes, and Matt Weeg's, and David Webber's. He made them angry, but dominated their anger. He paid them well. They all insisted that he was loyal, that he'd never trick them. He *was* willing to keep them in the dark. But they were at some level desperate for approval, and his withholding it both repelled and attracted them. It was legendary among them that Muss *never* praised anyone, and they joked that Muss had almost said "good job" about something to Webber, but caught himself. "In twenty years," Isakson would say, "never thanks."

Sher was just the opposite. He was constantly cajoling, praising, passing out gifts, taking people to lunch, arranging golf dates. One of his lawyers called Sher "an as-fate-would-have-it kind of guy," who proceeds on faith and instinct. I wondered, now, if Isakson had not laid out a clue for me, suggesting despite himself that what he said Muss could never do was being done.

"Is Josh working you?" I asked Sher, as he aimed the hose on the Testarossa.

"What do you mean?"

I shared Isakson's generic tale of Texan deceit. He shook his head and rubbed a rag across the Testarossa's long equine fender. "No, that's not it. Muss wouldn't do that."

Like the rest of the fleet, the Ferrari had an Ironhorse plate on front, a casting of its new logo in black and brass: the silhouette of a steam engine above, its track a straight line across the plate, and the name below in stylized capital letters.

Sher was not forthcoming, a surprising reluctance in such a candid person. "I can't tell you," he said. "Something's happening, and I can't tell you. You'll find out, but not now. I can't say anything."

I had a package to mail. The Ferrari's nearly dry. "I've never driven the Testarossa," I mention, remembering Dasher telling me about a test drive he took down the Beeline.

"Here," he said, handing me the keys. "Take it down the street while I get the next one. But if you get out take the keys or you won't be able to get back in. You'll have to walk home."

The doors are wired to an electronic alarm activated by a little control on the key chain. I can remember that. I recline in the seat and head out of The Reaches. I'm not a car buff, but I want to drive this Ferrari *fast*. It's sullen at thirty-five. The steering responds to hints, to desire. Driving it is like being inside a muscle. I drove three miles down North Ocean Drive to the drugstore, which has a post office station, looking for a place to punch it just a bit. Just north of the Hilton I pulled the gear lever back down to second and pivoted my right foot forward just enough to feel the weight of the accelerator. In maybe a hundred yards I was doing seventy and it felt the same as twenty-five in the rented Cavalier. This car has the perfection of nature, of being ideally suited to the task of getting from here to there *quickly*. It feels above commerce, above traffic, above the rules of consumption, more art than thing, more an aesthetic experience than a technological one. Sher says, "It's like dancing with Cyd Charisse—you're touching the ground but you're above the clouds."

Once Sher heard an interview with a guy who had just won the lottery. Mr. Lucky knew just what he would do, he said. He would buy a Mercedes and a Porsche and a Jaguar. As he listened, Sher remembered thinking, I've got all of those, and a Ferrari and a Range Rover, too! He'd earned his lottery, he had the life he wanted. He wondered sometimes why he'd thrown the dice, taken the big gamble on Ironhorse.

The Mercedes was well lathered by the time I got back. Only the Porsche wouldn't get its bath today. It was at the shop. "Fifteen hundred dollars they told me—just regular maintenance and something clogged in the fuel line or something.

"I remember when my parents bought our first car. A four-door Buick convertible. Maybe they paid twelve hundred dollars for it. This was in the Depression. Then they did a bad thing. They dropped me at summer camp and without telling me beforehand they drove with my older brother to California."

A WEEK LATER, Sher heard the good news. SWA had decided to pass. Ironhorse was going to happen. Two months later, the first dozers pulled onto the site.

8

Prelude to Conflagration

PHILLIPS AND JORDAN's been on the job for nearly two weeks. While the dozers are heaping palms and pines in great piles along the fairways and in the lakes, Matt Weeg, Ironhorse's sales manager, and David Webber, Muss's right-hand man, are putting together what they call a "dog and pony show" for a group of salesmen from Gulfstream Financial Associates. Gulfstream will try to sell a "private placement" of $3 million in limited-partnership interests in Ironhorse, Ltd. Weeg and Webber have to tell these salesmen what it is they're peddling. Gulfstream has to prepare documents that will disclose, in the arcane language of real estate and the law, the risks investors face at Ironhorse, but Weeg and Webber want to emphasize Ironhorse's virtues.

The folding chairs set up in the old ranch house's family room face the pool with its bright-green coat of algae. Weeg has Hills's routing plan and renderings of the clubhouse set on easels up front to give the Gulfstream salesmen a sense of the final product. He spent the last couple of days putting up signs where the holes are going, nicely done up in sturdy white poster board. When the Gulfstream salesmen drive through the cattle gate the first thing they'll see is the Ironhorse locomotive in profile and under it, 5TH GREEN. If they're looking closely, they'll see that just across the road from the fifth green is the 6TH TEE. Weeg put up a sign indicating the clubhouse site and another for the practice range. Weeg's selling an idea, but the visual aides help him superimpose the Ironhorse scheme on what's still largely a bare and muted landscape. Hoping to control what the salesmen see and hear, Weeg asked Bob Isakson, Jon Harpman, and me to make ourselves scarce while he paraded the dogs and ponies. He doesn't want someone coming into the office complaining about SWA or Muss or anything that might embarrass his pitch.

P&J has five holes pretty much cleared, and parts of eight others, working around from the railroad entry toward the south and east. Yesterday Postell cleared the drainage ditch to the right of the entry road so the Gulfstreamers can see Weeg's signs at the third green, the fourth tee, and the fifth green. I doubt that these signs in the flat ground will convey much, but they suggest that whoever took the time to make them and put them up is trying.

Isakson and Harpman decide to spend their exile putting in wooden stakes every one hundred feet along the center lines of the fairways. Most of the original survey stakes lie piled and broken amid the drying vegetation P&J wants to start burning next week. Dasher's due down from Orlando tomorrow, and Isakson thinks the stakes will help him locate the limits for the second phase of clearing. I caught up with them at the eighth hole, and walked eight, nine, one, and two. They'd already done thirteen, fourteen, fifteen, and sixteen. Isakson, in long pants, boots, and a golf shirt, was dripping sweat. He stood on the tee holding the orange reel of a long cloth tape, while Jon marched out with the dumb end until Bobby read one hundred feet and hollered "Ho!" Jon drove in a piece of lath and walked ahead, pulling the tape while Isakson moved up to spray the top of the stake with Day-Glo orange paint and write the distance from the tee with a black marker: + 100', + 200', + 300', and so on down the fairway. The tape yoked them, a lazy yellow line dragging in the dust, hanging up on limbs, downed branches, and churned-up palmetto roots that look like the scat of a very big and vicious predator.

I caught up with Postell working over the myrtles where the big lake by the seventh hole's going. He's operating the wide-track D6. Ernest Conward Crisp, another Robbinsvillian, is working the heavier vegetation in a D8. I can hear him, but I can't see him. Kenny's crawling over a thin, dry skin of muck, the same stuff a P&J operator got buried in over by the third hole last Saturday. It took two pieces of equipment and a couple of hours to liberate the dozer. It was in clear up to the cage.

"You push you some of that little brush down in front of you,"

Postell said, explaining how to clear soft ground, "and ride on that. There's a thin layer of roots, six inches or so, on top of that muck, and you've got to stay on top of that. If you put your rake too deep, or try to push too much brush, you'll break through that root layer and down you'll go. You don't want to walk back on yourself either, or those tracks'll tear that top layer up."

Postell finished up the myrtles along the third hole Sunday and cleared along one of the house parcels where the zero-lot lines are going, just opposite where Wadsworth Golf Construction will set up, along the ninth fairway. Then he moved onto seven, which was not as tough to work as he had expected. It's mostly myrtles, except along the seventh green, which has a lot of peppers along the canal and a thick stand of Sabal palms near where the entry road goes.

"Pepper's the best clearing there is," Postell said, stepping down from the Cat. "It don't break up, it holds together when you move it, and the roots don't carry a lot of dirt so it burns real good."

Phillips and Jordan, according to Dasher, charges less than any other clearing contractor he's ever worked with or heard about. "Used to be," Dash said, "that a lot of the dirt movers would do their own clearing, but Phillips and Jordan came in here charging so much less that the rest of 'em figured they might as well cut up their clearing blades and sell 'em for scrap."

The key, says Postell, is getting all the dirt out so the piles can burn. "If you've got to get back in there and rerake after you've tried to burn," he said, "you're gonna lose money."

Postell doesn't see much sense in the stakes Isakson and Harpman are putting out. If the trees are tagged, he said, or if they just tell him what they want out, he'll get it. He never takes notes, rarely marks on his print. He seems to know what needs doing and when, and he is never distracted. Wherever he goes, there he is.

"They say we're supposed to be able to clear this in two passes," Postell said, standing on the dozer track, his arms folded, looking across piles of brush that dot the length of the property along the north end, parallel to the railroad track. "But not on an Art Hills course we ain't. Hell, no. Like on six, at that dogleg?" He pointed across about 200 yards of cleared myrtle to a narrow opening through a stand of pine. "We're only seventy-five feet wide through them trees and we need to be three hundred. You can't leave all those trees in the fairway. But with Art Hills, they'll take one out, and look at it, and then take another one, kind of pick at it. Hell, we had a machine and operator up at Willoughby I bet three months. That selective clearing probably cost the developer another hundred thousand.''

Driving one of Sher's ATVs, bouncing over palmetto roots and piles of dirt pushed up by dozer blades and tracks, I headed back for the house later in the afternoon. The dog and pony show was over. Picking my way across the sixteenth fairway, I saw fifty or more buzzards circling, riding heat currents reflected from the bare white ground. A dozen or so others either perched in the crazy jumble of a burn pile or hopped across the ground in a clumsy tumble, as if they were about to fall. None of their soaring ease flew with them to the earth. In the air they looked sleek and gentle, but on the ground dense, muscular, and determined, and they hopped or moved away without hurry or fear as I approached. Ironhorse was, during these few weeks of clearing, a carrion eater's banquet. Little dead critters littered the ground—snakes, a few small rodents, an occasional rabbit or raccoon, but mostly armidillos, whose defensive strategy of curling into a plated ball, which had worked so well for eons against predators with claws, beaks, and slashing canines, was trumped by the great turning steel feet of the dozers.

The caterer for the dog and pony show was clearing up, and Weeg and Webber were shrugging through a postmortem. Webber was in the dining room smoking his pipe, his feet on the table, the knot of his tie pulled down so he could open his shirt collar. He's a small man, but tight and full of energy, as if he imagines himself larger and lives compressed. Weeg, like Harpman a good athlete, moves with a physical ease, while Webber cuts across a room with his chest out like a spinnaker. They don't know how much good they've done with the Gulfstream salesmen. "These things are always like foreplay," Webber said. "When it's over, you wonder why you got involved in all the fuss. It's like Muss's definition of eternity . . .

"The time between when you come and she leaves.''

Muss's rare smiles are all edge, tight and formal, but there's mercy in Webber's grin, a bedrock of sympathy that redeems his imitation of his boss's curtness. Muss is class-bound, a glad-hander among his peers in the aristocracy of dollars but indifferent to his inferiors. He has no tolerance for chat. Webber, who calls Muss his mentor, is in the second generation of retainers to the Muss family. His parents worked for Muss's father, David Muss, first in their native New England and then in Illinois when the elder Muss started developing in the Midwest. Webber first worked for Josh Muss when he was fifteen and has worked for him on and off ever since. Muss went to Harvard. Webber, ten years younger, has a degree from Western Illinois.

Muss likes to imagine that he started at the bottom, sweating in the field, but his was the abbreviated apprenticeship of the company owner's son, a symbolic ascent. He didn't linger amid the practitioners of the manual arts. When he was discharged from the Marine Corps, Muss went to work for Winston-Muss, the company founded by his grandfather, as a construction assistant, much like the job he's assigned to Harpman at Ironhorse. Two years later Muss was vice president and director of the company, and by 1968, as his résumé modestly summarizes, "president of several of its subsidiaries." David Muss was a lawyer as well as a developer, a very handsome man to judge from the portrait in his son's Washington office, who owned shopping centers and commercial real estate but specialized in starter homes, something closer to Levittowns than fancy, private, gate-guarded communities like Ironhorse.

While Webber was working for Muss in Chicago in the late sixties Muss enrolled in an MBA program at the University of Chicago and decided all his key employees should attend. Classes met at night. Webber didn't like going and never finished, but Muss took his degree. There is universal agreement among everyone who knows or has worked for him that Muss is smart—"smarter than anybody else," as one former colleague put it. "You have to recognize opportunity and that begins with location in real estate and Muss could do that. He knows how to calculate risk. He takes in all that info and whirls it around in that computer and makes a decision."

One of Muss's assignments one semester in the MBA program at Chicago, Webber said, was to put together a business plan. One's grade depended on it. "Most of the people in the class wrote these long papers," Webber said, "but Muss turned in a single page with one sentence: 'Read the *Wall Street Journal* tomorrow.' And in the next day's paper there was an announcement that Winston-Muss had merged with Centex, the big Texas home-building company owned by the Murchisons. Josh had put that deal together."

As part of his agreement with Centex, Muss moved back to Texas in 1970—he had lived there when he was a teenager—and for the next five years was the chairman of the board of Centex Homes, a very large company in the most anarchic segment of the American economy, the home-building business. Like Winston-Muss, Centex built mostly for the starter market. Chevies, as Muss said, but *new*

Chevies. Isakson loved to tell what Muss did after leaving Centex. He enrolled at SMU Law School. "He'd send his secretary to take verbatim notes," Isakson said, "and the word got back to the dean that he had a job, so the dean called him in.

" 'Mr. Muss,' the dean says, 'we discourage students from working while attending law school full-time. I understand you have a job. What do you do?'

"So Muss tells him, 'I'm the chairman of the board and the chief executive officer of the Chase Manhattan Mortgage and Realty Trust,' and I guess that old dean just shut right up."

It harms these stories very little to know they twist the truth—they're not entirely apocryphal, but they build on legend. They're like Webber's quip that Muss had it easy in the marines because Congress wouldn't have had the nerve to declare war while he was in the service. Muss laughed when I repeated them. "Not true," he said. "Close, but not true." .

He did use the Centex deal as an example of how to prepare a business plan, but it was more than a sentence. The real law school story, he thought, was better than Isakson's. His secretary, who was taking notes for him while he was working in New York, approached a professor after a class to ask for clarification on a point. After he obliged, she told him she enjoyed his lectures. "He puffed up and asked her how she liked law school, and she said, 'Oh, I'm not going to law school, I'm just here to take notes for my boss.' And then she told him what I did, I guess. Nothing happened with a dean."

Muss finished his work for Chase in 1978 and then spent the next four years in Dallas, working in real estate and managing his investments. Then he took a stab at public life, which brought him to D.C., where he's been ever since. He has a horse farm in Virginia—he rides to hounds and shows horses—as well as residences in Florida, where he lives with his second wife. He has three grown children from his first marriage. Joshua Muss and Associates is on Pennsylvania Avenue NW, an easy walk from Muss's former White House office.

Muss was appointed by Ronald Reagan in 1982 to work in the Executive Office of the President as the executive director of the Property Review Board. His job was disposing of excess federal property. He spent two not entirely happy years in that post, avoiding the limelight. Ronald Reagan gave him a presidential portrait for his fiftieth birthday which hangs on his office wall. "It only looks like you've been trying to sell federal property for fifty years," his boss scrawled. After his White House service he formed both Joshua Muss and Associates and the law firm of Carmen and Muss. He's a member of the bar in Texas, Florida, and the District of Columbia. His office on Pennsylvania Avenue is spare, unostentatious. His desk is a beautiful antique cherry table. On the wall near his portrait from Reagan hang pictures of Muss with George Bush and with Sam Pierce, the famously neglectful HUD secretary.

While Weeg and Webber recovered from the dog and pony show, Muss huddled with the lawyer in charge of preparing the due diligence for Gulfstream. The offering required "full disclosure," but there was no point in scaring the money away. The Gulfstream brokers brought up two points about SWA: one, they'd heard that the ash, the by-product of the power plant, smelled, and two, that the plant would be down 20 percent of the time, garbage would accumulate, and *it* would smell. Webber said the marketing guys would have to handle these questions. Weeg said, as he would continue to, if a customer smells something you've lost. "What are you going to do, stick your nose in the air and say, 'Gee, I don't smell anything.' Or 'I've never smelled *that* before.' Good chance they'll believe you."

The memorandum for the Gulfstream offering, distributed two months later, said this about Dyer Landfill and the SWA, under the boldface heading RISK FACTORS: "At the present time, the Dyer Landfill emits fumes containing an unpleasant odor which, if the wind is from the southeast, may be discernable to individuals on the Property [i.e., Ironhorse]. It is not believed that any such emissions are harmful to anyone's health. It is anticipated that the Dyer Landfill will be closed permanently at the end of 1989, and the SWA has committed to converting the Landfill into a public park. Activities are already underway to begin this process. In connection with the final closure of the Landfill, the Landfill is likely to periodically emit a foul odor, although this process should be completed by late 1990."

And later, while acknowledging that with the "down time" inevitable in any new plant garbage might accumulate for a day, or two, or more, the memo says, "The General Partner has been assured by SWA that odor from the ash, if any, should not travel to the Property. The base of the landfill will have a double plastic liner to prevent contamination of underlying groundwater. Innovative disposal techniques, such as composting, are planned by the SWA in order to minimize and contain odors."

This is a problem Muss has been confident of overcoming from the start. Ironhorse is not terribly much farther as the crow flies from SWA than a new development to the west called Ibis Landing. Steeplechase, a subdivision without a golf course directly across the Beeline from Dyer, was selling well. PGA National and JDM—the latter built partially over a landfill—are very close by. Ironhorse is smaller— more "exclusive"—than any of its neighbors, and if SWA doesn't have too many trucks rolling down Jog Road it should maintain its tranquillity. SWA is the one unknown weighing on Ironhorse. Dash is due in the morning. It's late, and everyone's heading home.

CHARLES BEST, running a D8 with a root rake, was clearing along the railroad canal near the entry, but doesn't go too far east. "It's too soft down that end."

The D8 can knock down the largest pine or palm at Ironhorse with relative ease. The soil Best is working in is sandy and loose, and because it hasn't rained in a while it's pretty dry. The drainage canals seem almost stagnant. Unless the pump's on, water movement is barely perceptible.

Phillips and Jordan made its first equipment drop in a pasture just to the east of the entry road, not far from the third green. Three months from now, they'd have to float to stay where they are. P&J is staging in what's going to be, according to the engineer's plans, Lake Nine. Ironhorse's eleven lakes are arbitrarily numbered and have no relationship to the golf course. Lake Seven, for example, runs along the fourth hole, while Lake Four is on the seventh hole. This makes for a bit of confusion. After a while, as a sense of where the golf course runs across the property settles in, the lakes come to be identified by where they are on the golf course and the engineering numbers are used only to guide the work. Then people say, "Over on the lake by the twelfth hole" instead of "Over on Lake One." Golfers— especially poorer players—hate playing over water. Art Hills thinks there's no place for water on the ideal golf course, but here it's the only way to get dirt and control the storm water.

On the west side of the lake where P&J dropped its equipment will be the third green and the fourth tee; to the east the ninth tee; and to the north, near where Best is working, the sixth tee. There's a stand of pines between the lake and the tee that Dasher decided to save when he was tagging for the clearing. It's close to the lake edge. Dash thinks the trees will give some shape to the tee and help define the hole. Bob Isakson doesn't mind saving the trees, but he doesn't want to see any change orders, anything that will require the engineers to resubmit drawings. "I'll tell you how I feel about that after being at this place for nine months. Art Hills and everybody's had plenty of time to think about changes and now that we're ready to move dirt I don't want any messing with the plans."

If it's a matter of zigging or zagging a line by five or six feet, Isakson said, he would just go ahead and do it. That wouldn't really change the volume of the dirt coming out of the lakes or reduce their retaining capacity. But he doesn't want to see any redesigning going on now, he just wants to see the thing built. Dash wrote to remind him that the architect *has* to make field adjustments. The better the golf course, the more likely the lots will sell. Hills wanted Ironhorse to be as good as he could make it.

Phillips and Jordan will get the third, fourth, fifth, and sixth holes, along with the lakes near them, cleared first. In another couple of weeks they'll have enough cleared for Ranger Construction to start digging the lakes, the inauguration of the earth-moving phase. The first hauls of sand and shell will fill the canals and build the perimeter berms along the Beeline and Jog Road that give the golf course some privacy from the railroad and the streets. In theory there is a simple sequence to follow. Phillips and Jordan will clear two places, one where dirt goes and one where it comes from. Ranger will start digging and placing the dirt. When a section of the berm is done, Ranger's tree spades will go to donor areas and pull out trees for the berms. Again, at least in principle, Ranger will exhaust the donor areas before Phillips and Jordan moves in for the serious clearing. There are donor areas in lakes and fairways and on the house lots.

The logic of playing the golf course doesn't have any more connection to building it than the numbering of the lakes had to the golf holes. There is no need to start on the first hole. P&J wants to get out in front of Ranger by about two weeks, so there is no chance the dirt-moving equipment will catch up with the Caterpillars and have to sit idle. That's too expensive. Once it's there, you've got to keep that equipment operating.

Best is grinding up Brazilian pepper with the root rake, rolling it on the ground in front of him to keep the dirt out. He's hit a couple of Australian pines. "Heavy," he says, "like picking up iron. It'd make great firewood but who needs it down here?"

I stood behind the fifth green while Best worked around it. The brush moved, as if it contained a giant beast running through it in fear. After twenty seconds or so, I could see the outline of the dozer, a yellow shadow in the dense green brush. A faintly sweet smell of crushed foliage and sap, the perfume of clearing, lay in the breeze. It looked like fun, busting up the branches, tidying up the site.

DASH IS DRIVING down today from Orlando. It takes four hours on the Florida Turnpike, unless it's real early in the morning and the fuzz-buster's fine-tuned for cruising. Then he can lay the heavy foot on the little four-cylinder Taurus and pour down in three and a half. Dash moves energetically in traffic, something just short of bumper-car technique. He rolled up to the house at 9:00 A.M., ready to spend the day reviewing the preliminary clearing. I'd been there since six forty-five, enjoying the solitude of the sunrise before the diesels idled up to a full-blown scream. I liked to walk over to the canal where the twelfth tee's going to go and sit on the spoil pile from Bob Grier's ditch and look across into the pond between Ironhorse and the water-catchment basin. I'd watch the herons and the egrets and sometimes see a small alligator on the bank. There are apple snails in this pond. Their delicate shells, vaguely shaped like a tiny apple but smooth, their color blended striations of violet and gray, litter the south shore of the pond.

These mollusks are the main food of the snail kite, the small raptor whose curved beak is perfectly adapted for pulling the snail from its portable home. The snail kite, as Rosa Durando pointed out in the oration that made Alan Sher's heart flutter, is endangered in Florida, though the same bird—or at least some ornithologists think it is the same bird, while another opinion holds that the Everglades kite is a subspecies—thrives in parts of South and Central America. There just aren't many places left in south Florida where apple snails thrive, and without them the snail kite can't make it. In 1986, there were a record number of kites at the SWA site, 360 by official count, but an ongoing drought in south Florida forced most of them north by 1988.

As a condition for receiving permission to develop the property from the Army Corps of Engineers, Ironhorse was required to establish a program to monitor the apple snails and the snail kites. The Corps also asked Ironhorse to excavate a couple of shallow lakes in the preserve to create new habitat for the apple snails. The Army Corps of Engineers, which has statutory authority over federally defined wetlands, issued a permit for the development of Ironhorse in May of 1988.

There were a lot of jokes about what they would do if they saw a snail kite, but nobody faced the actual dilemma of a kite on the wing. The buzzards wheeling above the Dyer dump and cruising Ironhorse for carrion are protected, but the fine for shooting one didn't deter somebody at Ironhorse from pulling the trigger on one of these slow-moving, harmless birds. Its carcass lay where it fell, not far from the house. There's not a lot of risk for a poacher, unless you're dumb enough to take a boat into the water-catchment basin to cast for bass. Then the helicopters that patrol it are going to catch you, roust you out, and fine you, as a couple of guys working at Ironhorse later found out. But if you shoot the pigs and deer on the property, or knock a bird from the sky with a twelve-gauge, the chances of being caught are nil.

The SWA is monitoring its snail kites, part of a larger scrutiny of the environment by its staff biologist. But though the Corps' permit required Ironhorse to monitor the snail kite, it had no way of enforcing the requirement, so for the time being Ironhorse was ignoring it. Or if not Ironhorse, the Northern Palm Beach County Water Control District—either Northern, or the District, as it was called—which would eventually own the preserve, and along with its parts of seven holes of the Ironhorse Country Club. But that's jumping ahead of the story.

P&J's beat-up Suburban with Alonzo Wright at the wheel, silver duct tape holding down a sheet of clear plastic over the opening of the broken rear window, pulled up first today, Bill Stewart and Ernest Crisp resting in the cab. Ernest and Alonzo room together in a motel room with a kitchenette. Kenny and Charles pulled in about five minutes later. They both have trailers parked out at Wildlife Safari, a half-hour drive away from Ironhorse on a good day when there's not much traffic running. The roaring lions gave Best a few sleepless nights until he was satisfied they couldn't get at him. Postell had smelled out a back way to Ironhorse that avoided traffic, but it's longer and the roads aren't as good. "That's the great thing about being the boss," he said, smiling, as he closed the gate. "You can be late."

Postell can joke because he puts in a lot of uncompensated overtime. The P&J crew treat work as a kind of sanctified fate. It's what a man does, by God. A Sunday off every now and then's good for Postell, especially now that he's married, but he's here to pay off the rest of what he owes on the house he's building up in Robbinsville so he can climb off the dozer for good and head back to the hills.

Charles, Alonzo, and Bill smoked and drank coffee while the machines warmed up, getting ready for the day. It was raining hard north of West Palm, but still dry at Ironhorse. Charles said once in a while up in Georgia or the Carolinas they'd be clearing and run into an old unmarked cemetery. Usually there's a lot of illegally dumped trash on land they're clearing, especially near towns. Up at Willoughby there were a dozen or so abandoned cars. That place didn't have a fence, as Ironhorse does. Alonzo said he knew of cars "with bones in them" pulled out of canals in Florida. The easiest way to get rid of the cars they find is just to bury them, though there is probably a regulation on someone's books making that illegal. Down at Eagle Trace, the TPC course that Hills designed just north of Miami, there were a lot of old cars scattered about, so Dash told Art they ought to just work them into the mounding. Then when you were playing you could say, "Just take out a four iron and cut it around that fifty-four Buick up there on the right."

Ernest is a reader. He keeps a paperback with him, so when the dozer breaks down—and Phillips and Jordan's equipment tends to be on the old side, so the operators joke that P&J stands for "piece a junk"—or when he's watching a burn pile and is there more to make sure the fire doesn't get away than to tend it, Crisp—called variously by any of his three names, either "Ernest" or "Conward" or "Crisp"—will commence reading. Lunch is a good time for literature. He loves Westerns, nature books, and *National Geographic.* He used to like the *Reader's Digest.* Last year he read thirty books. "Never been a movie made," he says, "that can get you involved like a good book."

Charles Best had a good start on his first pack of cigarettes. Jim Bakker's arrest was the main subject of conversation. Best wondered if we'd heard about the preacher and the chicken. Country preacher kept showing up among his flock wanting a little poultry for his pot. This was starting to wear on his congregation. One fellow was down to a single scrawny chicken, and his wife said, "That preacher was by again today asking for more chicken."

"Fuck the preacher," he said.

"I did," she said, "and he's *still* wantin' more chicken."

The operators climbed up on their machines and went looking for trees to knock down, and I walked back up to the house to wait for Dash. Then he, Jon Harpman, and I went to survey the first pass of clearing.

*   *   *

"WE'RE SAVING eighteen for a while," Jon told Dash, "so they can get some trees out of it for tree spading." Dash was in the kitchen, pouring a cup of the good coffee Isakson had brewed. Jon was showing Dash on the clearing plan the route P&J was taking.

The eighteenth tee is a little ways north of the house, just off the old entry road. It looks like a tough hole on the plan, a par five with a tee shot over the edge of a lake to the right, sort of a modified Cape hole, like the fifth at Mid Ocean in Bermuda. The eighteenth green is near the tenth tee, and both are close to the clubhouse, in conformity with the basic design rules. The grading plan shows mounding behind the eighteenth green, to push shots hit out to the right back toward the green instead of letting them bounce up toward the clubhouse. Because the entry road we're using to get to the house/office runs across the eighteenth hole, and because there is a good stand of palms near the tee, Jon says they're going to wait to clear it and work around instead on the east and south sides.

"First thing we'll do," Jon told Dash, "is flag eleven. Then we'll walk the initial clearing."

Postell stopped by to tell Dash that he hadn't cleared the lakes yet around the thirteenth and fourteenth holes, down on the southeast corner, and was finishing the lake by the seventh hole. Ernest was clearing today on ten, while Kenny was going to finish up the lake called number nine on the engineering plan, water that's the background for the third hole and will have to be carried by tee shots on the ninth hole. It's the big lake on the left just past the construction entry, on the north side.

Dash, in blue jeans and braces, is wearing his Southern Trace golf shirt and a beat-up tan Southern Trace hat. Southern Trace is a new Hills course in Shreveport. Dash has grading and clearing plans folded under his arm and sunglasses hanging from a thin strap around his neck. We walked down the paved road a quarter of a mile or so and then cut west, or left, along an old ranch trail, "old" meaning from the Grier days, made sometime in the last two decades. There's a wetland a little further down on our right where one sometimes can see a family of otters slithering through the high grass. Their little home won't survive the construction, so they will probably migrate to the water catchment basin.

Five years ago there was a lot of wildlife at Ironhorse—deer and wild pigs chief among the bigger fauna and kites and herons and egrets and alligators. But during the years it took to get Ironhorse started, almost all of the larger animals were poached out. There are large-caliber rifle casings all about the place, as well as dozens of large plastic pots that once grew marijuana hidden under the canopy of peppers and pines.

The eleventh is one of seven holes that encroach into the preserve. The water on the golf course lakes is engineered at a control elevation of fifteen feet. When the water gets this high in the lakes, a pump up near the intersection of Jog Road and the Beeline will discharge it so that it will ultimately run into a South Florida Water Management District canal, which in turn will carry it into the Atlantic. In principle, then, Ironhorse's lakes will never rise more than fifteen feet above sea level, except during heavy rains. The fairways have to rise above the control elevation or they will take on water, so the lowest spot on the golf course is an elevation of about sixteen feet.

The preserve, on the other hand, has a control elevation of seventeen feet. When the rains come, the preserve will stay wet for a while as a large portion of it floods. Cypress grow well in this wet condition, as well as native plants like pickerelweed, spike rushes, the arrow-shaped leafed Sagittaria, and a variety of bulrushes. As the water gradually recedes into pools, it concentrates the little creatures living in them into convenience stores for roosting birds. Whether a preserve as small as Ironhorse's can make much difference is an open question. Before the Army Corps of Engineers undertook its great project to control the waters of south Florida in the late forties, rivers like the Kissimmee and the Caloosahatchee flowed freely into Lake Okeechobee, which served as a great expansive flood basin, slowly releasing the waters it stored into the River of Grass, the Everglades. The water then flowed on south to the sea in a shallow, very slow-moving, forty-mile-wide sheet. Okeechobee spread and shrunk with the seasons, sometimes in years of deluge stretching as far east as Ironhorse, more than forty miles from its modern, controlled eastern shore. By drawing down slowly and seasonally, Okeechobee orchestrated a process that the preserve is designed to imitate. As the flood-waters receded, the shrinking ponds filled with food for the great populations of wading birds. Everything meshed in a natural cycle. The birds bred as the waters drew down, and the concentrations of food made it easier for them to forage for their chicks. But the Corps of Engineers' work destroyed this water cycle, which was not convenient for the sugar farmers, tomato growers, and dairymen who tilled the rich muck opened to farming when the Everglades was drained. Instead of sustaining a cycle of wet and dry periods, the high dikes the Corps threw up around Okeechobee impounded the water, so that the engineers could release it steadily, year round. Some birds—especially the wood stork—had to work so hard to find food that they were unable to breed successfully. The egrets and herons were more adaptable, but the wading-bird population in general shrunk by 95 percent. By the time the biologists and the South Florida Water Management District figured all of this out, it was nearly too late for the wood storks and the kites.

Now there is more sensitivity to the risks to wildlife and some regulatory effort to preserve habitat, but a lot of jurisdictional limbo. The federal statutes on wetlands put the Corps in charge and created a complicated system of control. In order to get permission to develop Ironhorse, it was first necessary to inventory the wetlands and describe them for the Corps. Howard Searcy, the consulting engineer who once worked for the Northern Palm Beach County Water Control District, had been hired to design a water-management plan for Ironhorse and walk the permits through the Corps and the Florida Department of Natural Resources and the South Florida Water Management District.

The inventory of Ironhorse found that of its twenty-one identifiable wetlands covering nearly eighty-four acres, only 4.5 acres still had "good wetland habitat value." Between Bob Grier's drainage ditches and the invasion of exotic species, most of the "wetlands" had long since ceased to function. That meant the developer had pretty much a free hand to dredge and fill, which is what building a golf course would require.

The Corps of Engineers wanted to see if there was a way to restore the wetlands. Searcy intercepted that pass. "We disagree," he wrote to the Corps, "that it is the current owner's responsibility to restore these wetlands to their former characteristics." Between the dike thrown up to impound water in the catchment area and Grier's drainage canals, the property had long since been degraded, he argued. Besides, he urged, the mitigation plan, an attempt to create wetlands along the littoral shelves of the golf course lakes, would be a sufficient improvement over the pastures and mesic uplands at Ironhorse. As he wrote in a letter to the Corps, "The construction of the water control facilities and associated water bodies will provide a habitat superior to that which exists on the site at the present time." This echoes the Corps' belief that it can always do nature one better.

Searcy also had to convince the Corps that there were public benefits to building Ironhorse. "The project planned for this site," he wrote, "includes the development of a private golf club and associated middle and upper income residential units associated with the golfing facility. The citizens of the United States are increasingly seeking this type of housing . . . The market thus created provides a level of job activity for the construction industry and associated service industries in the South Florida area and is a key element maintaining a viable economy in the area."

The Corps bought this argument and issued a permit. It had U.S. Fish and Wildlife review the threat to wildlife—the "jeopardy" Searcy referred to in his rebuttal to the Bird Lady. But U.S. Fish and Wildlife, overworked and understaffed, especially after the budget cuts of the Reagan era, depended on Ironhorse's consultants to make its call. The local office of Fish and Wildlife had eight biologists and three secretaries to review and monitor all the endangered species and wetlands between Orlando and Key West. Nowadays there were many more smaller projects like Ironhorse and fewer big developments whose impact was easier to judge. The Fish and Wildlife biologist who approved Ironhorse "felt like we got a pretty good preserve area," but said there was still a lot of debate among his colleagues about the value of the mitigated wetlands. "If they give feeding habitat for wading birds, that's good. But some people think all they do is fill up with cattails and are useless except for red wing black birds." He was never on the site, and expected never to see it. Fish and Wildlife has little capacity to follow up on the roughly 1,000 projects it approves every year. "Agencies get on the treadmill to give all these developments permits but not to follow up. There's no agency geared up to check up on all the actions that have been taken. We don't do law enforcement."

The Corps asked only that Ironhorse develop the snail kite monitoring program and implement it within six months and create a ten-foot-wide shoreline fringe along the lakes, in total 4.36 acres—equivalent to the "good habitat" discovered in the wetlands inventory—to replace what construction would destroy. It also expected that Ironhorse would enhance the buffer preserve by, among other things, eliminating exotics and creating a six-acre marsh with good snail-kite habitat. The preserve was the key that unlocked Ironhorse's development.

*   *   *

BUT IRONHORSE would not own the preserve, or the lakes and canals and the pump station, and in the netherworld that evolved the Corps' conditions would fall between jurisdictional cracks. The lakes and the preserve belonged to the Northern Palm Beach County Water Control District, which would operate them in a happy partnership with Ironhorse.

Pete Pimentel runs Northern. In the old days, Northern was an agricultural improvement district, empowered by the State of Florida to sell bonds for money to drain wetlands. This was back in the era of the dike wars, when farmers would throw up higher and higher earthen ramparts around their property to keep it dry. The water they pumped out flowed onto less-defended lands. They were still fighting the dike wars when Howard Searcy was working as an engineer for the District, but that now seems a tale from an ancient age. Illegal dredges and fills are almost unheard-of today. The challenges to wildlife are subtler now.

Originally, Northern was a way to rationalize the drainage, to spread its costs among the taxpayers and bring down the dikes. But not many years later, the environmental costs of draining the Everglades and drawing down the water table to irrigate crops—dropping the water pressure let salt water flow into the aquifers—halted wholesale drainage. The agricultural improvement district transformed itself into a water-control district, still with the power to sell bonds. Under Pimentel's guidance, Northern created a cozy atmosphere for development. PGA National was the first country club development to take advantage of Northern's powers. Ironhorse affiliated itself with Northern as soon as Muss realized what it was offering. Isakson at first was suspicious of Northern, seeing it as another bureaucracy with which he would have to contend, but then realized Pimentel was an ally, that he was not one of those secret environmentalists with his own agenda ensconsed in a public agency but instead a solid friend of Progress.

The first step was to set up Ironhorse as a water-control district—Northern's Unit of Development Number 24. Then Northern could sell bonds to implement Ironhorse's water-control plan. Northern was required, as Searcy had been with the Corps of Engineers, to demonstrate a public benefit for Unit 24, but that was easy to do. It rains a lot in south Florida, up to one hundred inches in a year. On average, forty-two inches will fall each year between June and October. The purpose of a water-management plan is to make sure this water doesn't flood roads or dwellings. Undeveloped land is not at risk from flooding, but when you put in streets and houses, the water doesn't go straight into the ground any longer but instead accumulates on these impermeable surfaces. In Florida, a big storm can dump huge amounts of rain, so the catch basins and conduits that carry the storm water must be large. The engineers size them for a twenty-five-year flood and calculate the effects of a one-hundred-year storm, that is, a storm of a magnitude expected only once in a hundred years, a Hugo event.

The "major elements of the water management system," as the plan described them, were the interconnected lakes, which would fill under ordinary precipitation, and a large pump station to discharge excess water during heavy rains. The outfall pump would send the water into a small retaining lake, built on the triangle of land acquired from SWA, from which it would flow into a canal that eventually linked with the C-17 canal of the South Florida Water Management District. "Runoff from the unit," as the plan said, "will be routed to the canals and on-site lakes via sheet flow, swales, and stormwater pipe collection systems." The storm-water pipes pick up the water from the houses and roads, but the "sheet flows" and the "swales" refer not to the natural topography of the site—over its entire 354 acres, after all, Ironhorse ranges in elevation only between fifteen to nineteen feet above sea level, changes barely perceptible on the ground—but to the invented terrain of Hills's golf course design. In order to manage the water on the golf course—and water runs off turf more as it runs off roads than off native vegetation—it's necessary to dig lakes to hold the water. If you dig lakes, you need someplace to put the dirt, and the golf course grading plan is a handy rough guide for placing fill. So Ironhorse, in essence, gets the rough grading on the golf course done for free, through bonds sold by Northern. In exchange, Northern acquires title to the lakes and the pump station—and the preserve, which is also part of the water-management plan—and has perpetual access to them for maintenance. Ironhorse gives Northern a letter of credit equal to the value of the bonds and will, until houses are sold, have sole responsibility for the taxes Northern will impose both to retire the bonds and maintain its property. In principle, Northern will own the golf balls hit into its plentiful lakes.

The users of Ironhorse, as the taxpayers of Unit 24, will pay in the long run for the golf course and other "improvements," as Pete Pimentel carefully points out. It's a better way to achieve public scrutiny and a measure of control than simply issuing permits, which is the management technique of the Corps of Engineers and the South Florida Water Management District. Northern's plans are reviewed by its board and by the courts, all out in the open. This is not Chinatown, and Ironhorse is not the Owens Valley. Still, to accept a private, closed community of 325 houses, most of them vacation homes costing upward of a million dollars, a market open to perhaps 2 percent of the people, in a city that has some of the worst housing and desperate poverty in Florida, strikes me as a skewed reading of the public interest. On the other hand, there is no reason for a place like Ironhorse not to exist, and no one is faced with choosing between it and, say, a program to extend home ownership to low-income families. Ironhorse was not created by Northern, and Muss had the means to build it whether bonds were available or not. But as the developer of a nearby golf course project said of Northern's bonds, "I can't think of a reason anyone would turn them down."

ONCE NORTHERN'S BOND PROGRAM was in place the construction of Ironhorse could get under way. There was a public bid for the dirt work, won by Ranger Construction, one of south Florida's largest excavation contractors and a course builder itself. Ranger also bid on the golf course construction—the fine shaping of fairways and greens, installation of drainage and irrigation, and grassing—but was just barely higher than Wadsworth. So Ranger had the earth moving under a contract with Northern, while Wadsworth would build the golf course under a separate contract with Ironhorse, Ltd.

Ranger's contract covered clearing of the lakes and fairways—the work P&J was doing—excavation of the lakes, construction of the perimeter berms, and rough placement of the earth for the golf course. Wadsworth would have preferred to move the dirt itself. Hills didn't care who moved the dirt just as long as the work was done according to his plan, but he was happy that Wadsworth was low bidder on the golf course. Once clearing started, the idea was for Wadsworth to finish up the course in Stuart and jump down to West Palm—the same superintendent, the same shaper, the same pipe man. Dash wanted to stay on top of the clearing so Ironhorse could keep its schedule.

*   *   *

DASH AND JON HARPMAN looked over the tagging for the eleventh green, which was tucked up into the preserve, just south of the tenth green. On the routing plan, ten and eleven fought for space. Ten was a long par four, a very slight dogleg left that played nearly due west. Its fairway was parallel to the first hole; the practice range was sandwiched between them. Because a large house parcel—Parcel B on the plan—tucked up against the preserve, there was very little room for the eleventh hole. The back nine played roughly counterclockwise from the clubhouse, and ideally the eleventh hole would have turned south, playing toward twelve. Alister Mackenzie, in *Golf Architecture*, listed thirteen "essential features of an ideal golf course." The third of these held that "the course should be arranged so that in the first instance there is always a slight walk forward from the green to the next tee; then the holes are sufficiently elastic to be lengthened if necessary."

Ironhorse's routing violated this advice after the tenth hole. The players would have to walk back nearly parallel to the tenth fairway to reach the eleventh tee. Eleven's 6,000-square-foot green tucked into the preserve, separated from the tenth green by a thick forest of preserved pines and palms. A small stand of pines behind the eleventh tee would protect players from a bad shot from the tenth fairway, but players walking *toward* the tee would be briefly vulnerable. Dash thought that for two reasons there wasn't a real great problem, though. As a private course, Ironhorse wouldn't get a lot of play. The members would know to wait until the group in front of them was well off the tenth green before hitting. And second, it would take a hook or pull to hit them, and most bad players slice rather than hook. Even before the clearing was done Dash was already worried a bit about this difficult and tight constellation of holes.

A flock of ibis flew over, heading from the catchment basin to the dump. Dash told Jon, "Let's just do this in order" and headed off to the first tee. He wanted to get a sense of the clearing lines in the order the golf course was designed to play. There wasn't any clearing yet on one, but up around the green by the second hole P&J had started taking out some tall pines and palms. Along the edge of the lots were thousands of myrtles, but behind the green a good backdrop of tall trees. Dash told Jon to make sure P&J didn't head straight back behind the green when it moved between holes or when it cleared for the cart path. That would leave a big, unsightly hole in the backdrop. "What you want to do," Dash said, dropping to his knee to draw in the dirt, "is go out at an angle, so that from front or back it looks undisturbed."

Jon wondered if it wouldn't be a good idea to go ahead and clear to the parcel line up near the green along two, so he wouldn't have to clear again when the parcel was developed. "It's not important to the golf course that you clear this now," Dash replied, "but if you clear it you'll have to irrigate and maintain it. And some owners may want heavy myrtles between them and the golf course for privacy, instead of being wide-open all along their back property line."

Harpman said he'd wait on that. But looking to the right of the green, Dash said, "Slice off this corner of myrtle to give us a little movement in this line."

There wasn't much yet to see on two, so we walked ahead to three, crossing what will eventually be the road through Parcel D, in the far northwest corner. The second tee is in the preserve, and the fairway and green play between a housing parcel and the preserve. The third hole plays across the deep muck that captured first the surveyor's dozer, then one of P&J's. Wherever there is muck there was once an active wetland. Muck may be great for growing vegetables and sugar cane, but it's lousy on a golf course. It's slick when it's wet, it doesn't drain, and unless it's dry it won't support much weight. Ironhorse has to get it off the golf course. There are several areas of deep muck, besides number three. The range is mostly muck, and there is muck along the seventeenth hole, as well as in locations scattered among the parcels and the golf course. John Riley, the clearing superintendent for Ranger, says that if enough fill goes over the top of the muck it will bridge it, but if the grading plan calls for only a foot or so on top, they'll have to demuck before they can haul the fill and rough-grade. They can get rid of muck in the berms and in low spots on the golf course that are getting several feet of fill on top of them.

Harpman had already had P&J clear to the parcel line along three. Looking at it, Dash said, "As a rule, Jon, it's not good to do that."

The original clearing and grading plan called for the elimination of most of the trees south of the sixth tee, but looking across from the third tee beyond the green, Dash thought it would be better to save as many of those trees as he could, move the sixth tee slightly to the north, and give the third green a thick if somewhat deceptive back-drop. The trees were 150 feet from the back of the third green, across the toe of the lake, but from the third tee the compression of distance made them look closer.

The clearing lines from January were still in place along four and five. There was some new clearing up toward the green on five, but it hadn't yet been pushed very far west. There was a big stand of myrtle at about the first dogleg on number five that Harpman told Postell to save for donor material for the perimeter berm. Dash wanted to work on the sixth hole, which by now had been pretty well cleared through its center. The plan showed that the lake along the sixth tee was connected to the lake at the seventh hole by a long stretch of thirty-six-inch pipe. An earlier version of the plan had a canal along the north side of the sixth fairway—utilizing the route of Bob Grier's old drainage ditch—but the current version had the perimeter berm going on top of the old drainage ditch and a connecting canal running all along the right side of the fairway, water that would catch a slicer's ball before it jumped into somebody's backyard.

The only problem with Dash's plan was that the back tee for the *ninth* hole was north of the canal, so they'd have to figure out a way to get to it. Dash told Bob Isakson, who'd come out to check on things, "Build a little bridge."

Isakson grimaced, imagining going to Muss with a change order for an expensive bridge that had not been on the original plan.

"Hey," Dash said, catching Isakson's expression, "a bridge is going to be a hell of a lot cheaper than two hundred and sixty feet of thirty-six-inch pipe."

"That sounds good to me," Isakson said. "I'll have to tell Ranger not to get the pipe."

Dash told Isakson he would send the grading and clearing notes he was making up to Brian Huntley, who was in charge of drafting for Ironhorse in Toledo. He told Isakson he'd keep sending stuff to Huntley "till we get a plan that works. Not that this one wouldn't work, but revised to what's here."

Isakson asked, "What if Art wants to get out some trees you leave in? Is that a third clearing for Phillips and Jordan?"

Yes, Dash tells him, it is. "We're gonna be taking trees out till the end of the deal. 'That tree's gotta go,' or 'that one's dead.' That's just the way building a golf course goes."

"Fish and Wildlife says we need three dead trees for the red-tailed hawks."

"I don't mind saving dead trees," Dash said, "but we've got to decide where they're gonna be on the golf course."

While they were there Dash took a look at the trees behind the eighth green. On the original grading plan for Ironhorse, dated December 1987, a large mound loomed behind the eighth green. There was a lot going on at this junction of the golf course, formed about this lake. In plan, the golf corridors at the north end of Ironhorse form a large "T," with the fifth and sixth holes running one after another in a straight line forming its top and the eighth and ninth holes— eight running north, toward the line of play along five and six and nine turning back south toward the clubhouse—roughly perpendicular to five and six. The fourth hole is parallel to five, while the third green tucks in at the junction of the base and top of the "T." This is a busy golfing intersection. There are three greens—the third, the fifth, and the eighth—and three tees—the fourth, the sixth, and the ninth—all clustered in an area that could be contained in a circle with a radius of about 135 yards, a tiny region in a golf course's 120 or so acres. The trick for Hills is to shoehorn this much golf into a tight space without making the golfers feel as if they are on top of one another, so someone putting on the eighth green, for example, is safe from a really bad tee shot launched from the sixth tee. In the version of the course guiding the initial clearing, the pines behind the eighth green would disappear, replaced by a large mound shaped to hide the green from players going down the sixth fairway. But when he was looking at removing the pipe and putting in an open canal, it occurred to Dash to eliminate the mounding and save the trees and perhaps move the eighth green a little ways south, shortening the hole. Dash had already decided to move the third green twenty or thirty feet left along the line of play and didn't see any problem shortening the eighth hole.

Saving the trees behind the eighth green would help in another way. "We probably saved five to six thousand yards of fill by eliminating that mound," Dash said. Isakson was worried about having enough dirt. Not only did he have to build the golf course with the lake excavations, he had to get in his roads, the pad for the clubhouse, and the perimeter berm. The berm was on the margin of the golf course, not really in it, but it affected the look of the course. The higher the perimeter berm, the more comfortably the golf course sat.

Northern's contract with Ranger provided that it would get paid according to how much was actually dug and hauled. The engineers had sized the lakes, calculating how much dirt was needed on the golf course, the berms, and the roads, working both with Hills's grading plan and the land plan from Urban Design Studio. Using a topographical map of the original site, the engineers figured out how much dirt each golf hole required and then made sure the lakes were big enough to provide it. They wanted a balance between the cut and the fill, or perhaps a little too much dirt. The worst thing would be to come up short.

Ranger's bid had been $1,150,597. This included clearing forty-one acres for lakes—P&J cleared a lot more acres on the golf course and the parcels for Ironhorse under a separate contract—the installation of the pipes to connect all the lakes, the construction of the low berm along the east edge of the preserve, including the installation of an impermeable plastic liner, and, under Item 4, "Excavation and Fill Disposal," digging and hauling 606,000 cubic yards at a price of $1.38 a yard. The $818,100 for digging the lakes and spreading the dirt was what contractors call an "upset price," or a "not to exceed" price. If Ranger dug 610,000 yards instead of 606,000 yards, it wouldn't get paid for the extra 4,000 yards. So while Ironhorse—both the golf course and the development—needed all the dirt it could get, the excavation contractor wanted to make sure it didn't dig any oversized holes—everything on the big side was free. Isakson, who'd spent his life in the construction business, knew that Ranger would probably leave a little dirt in the lakes and from the first day was worried about running short.

When he finished with his notes Dash Fed Exxed them up to Toledo so Huntley could revise the grading plan. The revised version he sent down in early January had the sort of penumbral fade of heavy erasures, particularly around the "T"—eliminating the mound behind the eighth green, adding the trees by the sixth tee, drawing the canal and a bridge, relocating greens and tees.

Dash was heading up north, to Jacksonville and Atlanta, but he'd get back to Orlando in time for his Saturday skins game at Dubsdread. I decided to go up and meet him. I took the train, so I could see Ironhorse from a new vantage point. I'd seen it close-up from the air in Ranger's helicopter and from higher up in a descending jet, I'd walked every inch, bumped across it on an ATV, and surveyed it from the top of Charlie the quarter horse's broad back. The view from Amtrak was interrupted by the Australian pines growing along the railroad canal, but I could see the clearing at the north end. It was just after 7:00 A.M. when we whistled by, pushing up to cruising speed on the way to Okeechobee. I saw Kenny Postell, tiny in the distance, getting ready to fire up a burn pile in the fifth fairway. Ironhorse was ready to enter a new stage—conflagration.

9

Dasher and Dubsdread

THE FLORIDA HEADQUARTERS of the Arthur Hills empire is about ten feet square and sits just off the living room of Mike and Beverly Dasher's rehabilitated bungalow hard by the shore of Little Lake Fairview in a pre-Disney suburb of Orlando. A pair of rarely closed French doors separates the office from the house. The front window looks out past the garage Dash built right after he bought the house onto Greens Street, a narrow lane that avoids running head-on into the seventh tee at Dubsdread Golf Course by taking a quick jog about seventy-five yards past the Dashers' driveway. Sometimes when he's on the phone in the officette, Dash will hear the tattoo of golf spikes on his living room tile, so he knows that play has stacked up at number seven, a par five with a little pond out to the right that squeezes the fairway down so tight even big hitters have to lay up off the tee. Restless waiting to hit, Jimmy the P or Tony or Buddy or John Woodward or some other Dubsdread regular has detoured to the Dasher kitchen to expropriate a restorative brew. Until he and Bev tied the knot in 1989, Dash's lakeside cottage was an unofficial outer clubhouse for Dubs, an unconventional variation on the model of the Scottish golf clubs that are associated with a public golf course but not the same as the course itself. St. Andrews belongs to its eponymous town, for example, and the Royal and Ancient is but one of several clubs with privileges at golf's cradle. Dash's cottage welcomes the fellowship of the Plebeian and Modern. The wives and girlfriends of the Dubsmen sunbathe, swim, and sip chilled vodka on Dash's tiny beach or sail on Little Lake Fairview while the men rally forward in their unending assaults on Dubsdread's flat fairways and pushed-up greens.

It said a lot about Dash that he played on a course with character rather than glamour, a storied public course instead of a country club, a plain and eccentric layout whose rich history substituted for the pale contentments of refinement and grandeur. Dubsdread's chief eccentricity is that on the fifth, seventeenth, and eighteenth holes you've got to hit a shot across a public street. Prudent players check for traffic, but the regulars think only sissies doubt their swings enough to entertain the prospect of firing a bullet into the fender of a passing Chevy. Dubsdread's design would never pass muster in the present age. The American Society of Golf Course Architects already holds irregular sessions at its annual conventions to fret about architects' liability. They worry about cart paths that are too steep, or tees dangerously close to greens, or roads abutting fairways—anything affording an opening through which the lawyers might strike. Dubs was built in 1923, when it was assumed that anyone foolish or unfortunate enough to blast a tee shot into a passing car would instantly make it right with the victim. Tom Bendelow, one of the pioneering émigré Scottish course designers, a contemporary of Donald Ross and a golfing Johnny Appleseed credited with the design of more than 400 courses, laid out Dubsdread's original eighteen.

The photos on the walls of Dubsdread's official clubhouse, which has the rumpled élan of a speakeasy, date from Bendelow's era, when male golfers wore white shirts and ties and plus fours and women mostly waited on the patio for them to finish. Dubs is still pretty much a men's playground, but now they all wear logoed knit shirts and shorts with anklet socks, and when they take off their shoes after a round to bathe their dogs in Little Lake Fairview's cooling waters the contrast to their darkly tanned legs makes their white feet flapping in the gentle waves look like the suicidal thrashings of a school of some teratogenic and inedible fish flinging itself toward shore.

The tradition at Dubs is of tough players and ruthless bets, a subtle testing ground that challenges not so much a golfer's course management and comprehension of shot values and all those phrases that make playing golf sound like a weekend seminar on increasing his net worth but how well he can swallow when his ball is four feet from the cup and there are ten skins hanging on the vine. There's more dignity at stake than cash—a truly terrible outing might cost its author twenty bucks. The toughest part of a round at Dubs comes at the end, sorting out the tangled heap of wagers and presses, cut skins and side bets, a pitiless and noisy reckoning. Usually Scotty the CPA asserts his authority and masterminds the redistribution. The winnings cycle back through the bar. Dubs's restaurant has much-better-than-average golf course food, live music two or three nights a week featuring the dulcet phrasings of Stan the singing barkeep, plenty of cold beer, and pleasant places, inside and out, to sit and drink it.

When Dash first showed up at Dubs, he didn't make an altogether good impression on the regulars. John Woodward, who sells real estate and advises Dash on their joint citrus land deals—and who can live in central Florida without at least a small grove, particularly when the tax consequences have been carefully explained?—thought he was "kinda mean, even," when they first met. "Dash," Woodward says, "didn't seem to have a lot of diplomacy, I guess." Woodward is tall, lean, and prematurely gray and still moves with the athlete's grace that won him a scholarship to the University of Florida. He writes taut and vaguely autobiographical short stories in the first person, plays lots of golf, and lives with a feisty lawyer who's indifferent to his love of games but enjoys his gentle ways. Like a lot of the Dubsers, he's that rare bird, a native Floridian. Woodward says it took him a year to figure out what it was about Dash that set his teeth on edge and made him wonder if they'd ever be friends. "Mike always tells the truth. Most people, you ask them something, they tell you what they expect you want to hear, but Dash tells you what he thinks. If I told him I was thinking of taking up polo, he'd say, 'Hell, John, you don't even own a horse.' "

On those rare mornings he works at home, Dash showers and dresses just as if he were heading out on the road to remind himself that it's a business day. His contract with Hills pays a small salary and a considerable commission, so Dash is more like a free-lancer than an employee. Nobody tells him where to be or when to go, but he pushes himself enough to keep both him and Hills happy. He has a bowl of cereal, drinks his coffee, tells himself—and now Bev—goodbye, and walks across the dining room to his office. He's on the road about four days a week. He tries to make the Friday afternoon game at Dubsdread, but if he's stuck in Charleston, Atlanta, or West Palm Beach he'll make a late flight on Friday night so he's at least there for the Saturday skins game.

Dash plays golf with the company draw, the right-to-left shot that echoes Art Hills's preferred trajectory. He's not as good a player as Hills, but he hacks around to about a ten handicap and on a good day can threaten par at Dubs. Dash continues to claim, in the face of derisive skepticism from the Dubsers, that he was on Georgia Tech's varsity golf team. "I never said I *played* for Tech, I said I was *on* the golf team. That's a little too subtle, I reckon. I practiced with 'em, I just didn't get in any matches."

Dash's special golfing devil is the snap hook. He'll run the ball out in a harsh parabola headed for the left rough with a swing made to order for a dry west Texas course in mid-August, one with fairways dense as steel, bald rough, and no trees, somewhere out between Pecos and Odessa. But he plays instead where the grass grows so quickly the greens can slow down while a long putt's working its way to the hole and the tall Bermuda grass rough gathers up the ball the way dusk summons darkness.

On the Sunday I visited Dash he'd organized a group of Dubsers to drive west, hard by Weeki Wachee in Hernando County, to play the Hills course called Seville. Hills, who's modest about his work, told me Seville was a "hidden treasure." The superintendent at Willoughby, who's a good enough golfer to play in the Florida Amateur, said it was his favorite among Hills's courses. Dash, with less constraint, thinks it's "the best course in Florida." Wadsworth—whose Florida headquarters are only about forty-five minutes south of Seville, in Oldsmar, on the north side of Tampa Bay—built Seville, a project caught in developer limbo so far off the beaten path that a boiled-peanut stand one hundred yards from the entry was the only sign of civilized life for miles around. There was a Bates Motelish cast to Seville's isolation. You expected Anthony Perkins to sidle behind the counter at the little temporary clubhouse trailer to collect the greens fees. Except there weren't any greens fees.

The course, designed as the centerpiece of a 3,000-acre development, opened in 1987, but a year later there still weren't any houses under construction and nothing to suggest that building would start any time soon. Seville was sort of a pre-ghost town. The developer, Dash said, was an Iowan who was always a little vague about his long-range plans. You couldn't help but wonder if yet another Savings and Loan playing with the people's money wasn't behind Seville. (Hills told me much later, in confirmation of this suspicion, that Seville was about to join 200 other golf course properties on the Resolution Trust Corporation's inventory.) Seville's isolation reminded me of Stonebridge Ranch north of Dallas, perhaps the greatest of all S&L golf boondoggles, but there, at least, amid the Texas depression of the late eighties, one heard nail guns popping and saws screaming and watched carpenters walking plates, hanging joists, and running rafters. Hills and Pete Dye had designed courses at Stonebridge. Dye's course, according to the owner's instructions, was supposed to sum up all his wiles. They wanted a grand championship layout worthy of consideration by the USGA for the U.S. Open. "Pete's not interested in building a course anymore unless it's going to be the kind you can hold a major on," the engineer at Stonebridge said. Hills's course at Stonebridge, on the other hand, was supposed to be more forgiving, more of a "members' course." The owners satisfied themselves that Hills's ego was neither so fragile nor so consuming that he would try to compete with Dye to see who could design the tougher course.

Hills liked stopping by to see Dye's work on his trips to Stonebridge, but Dye never looked at Hills's work. The Stonebridge engineer told me Dye avoided the competition to stave off creative contamination, but Alice Dye says that's silly. "If he looks at somebody else's course," Alice Dye says, "they're going to ask him what he thinks, and if he doesn't like it, being Pete, he'll tell them. It might not be flattering. So he never looks, and if somebody asks him what he thinks, he can always say, 'I haven't seen it.' "

Dye's Stonebridge course had the hauteur of an Open venue, with vast expanses of turf—almost 300 acres, more than twice that of an ordinary course—on which a gallery of thousands could easily gather. It had wonderfully textured and photogenic orange-tinted sand in the bunkers, and a cornucopia of grasses—not just the Bermudas one would expect on a southern golf course, but fescue, centipede, and, inevitably on a course with pretensions, Penncross creeping bentgrass on the greens. The golf superintendent needed a crew of twenty-five to care for all this grass. The annual maintenance budget to keep it tidy was about three times the $500,000 that Steve Forrest told Bob Isakson to figure for Ironhorse's upkeep. My question, as I visited Stonebridge in the middle of the great Texas slump, was the same one any taxpayer would have. When I asked the engineer how they'd managed to pay for all this splendor—the clubhouse for the Dye course looked as if McKim, Mead & White had resurrected for one last grand gesture in their patrician shingle style—he said, conspiratorially, "The owners have deep pockets."

The pockets, of course, belonged to the public, but to reach in them one had to pass first through the Gibraltar Savings and Loan. Stonebridge, all 6,250 acres, consumed 330 *million* Gibraltar dollars. When the S&L failed, the taxpayers got stuck for $270 million. Designed for 27,000 houses, Stonebridge had sold 270 by 1989. Richard Strauss, the son of the long-time chairman of the Democratic Party, Robert Strauss, outbid Ross Perot for what was in 1984 called the Flying M Ranch. Perot threatened a lawsuit, so the Gibraltar bunch gave him $8 million to let bygones be bygones.

The government's seizure of Gibraltar late in 1988 added a fillip to what was already a pretty exciting story of greed and deceit. Gibraltar, with assets of $7.1 billion, was sold to Ronald Perlman. The government threw in a $5.1 billion guarantee "to cover the thrift's bad assets," as *Fortune* reported it, "and tax benefits worth $900 million." Perlman paid the government all of $315 million for this package. Strauss continued to earn a $2.9 million annual property management fee, until Stonebridge was finally put into bankruptcy. It comes as no surprise that when the government did finally find a buyer the price was nowhere near the losses Stonebridge represented. The federal government agreed late in 1990 to sell Stonebridge Ranch, with its two fabulous golf courses and clubhouses, its beach and tennis club and equestrian center, to Mr. Yukio Kitano of Osaka, Japan, for $61 million.

Seville was a sort of minor league Stonebridge. Nothing like the Texas millions were squandered here. What the clubs mostly shared was isolation. At Seville there was blue sky, acres of trees and green grass, and the only sound was the wind rustling the pines. Hills and Brent Wadsworth were giving some thought to buying Seville, which encouraged golfers to make the long drive over from Orlando or up from Tampa by charging only the rent on a golf cart to play. It was the best deal for golf in Florida, where the demand was so high by the late eighties that even mediocre courses like The Squire at PGA National, Ironhorse's neighbor, could get away with charging a $65 greens fee. Seville was nearly ten times the size of Ironhorse, but with nothing else around it felt like Yellowstone.

Dash had been urging the Dubsers to buy a lot at Seville and put up a bachelors' retreat, but an epidemic of marriages, among them his own, put a damper on that plan. Seville's lots were cheap, and Dubsdread, like all of Orlando's courses, was getting awfully crowded on the weekends.

The sand hills of central Florida are a pleasant topographical contrast to south Florida. There are unsightly phosphate mines near Tampa, but around Seville the white-fenced horse farms look more like Lexington than Lauderdale. Seville was built across a tree farm, twenty-year-old pines in tidy orchardlike rows, rooted in sandy soil. Hills's routing plan ran Seville's fairways diagonally through the pines, so when they're playing the course golfers won't look into the trees at right angles, a landscaping trick to mute the visual effect of their cultivated symmetry. Aside from their largely uniform size, the pine trees' orderly monotony is not oppressively evident.

Colonies of gopher tortoises had burrowed into the tops of the sandhills at Seville, destroying the nursery pines planted there. Without tree roots to secure them, the hills eroded into untidy gullies and grass-capped mounds of orangish soil. The developer expected the golf course to avoid these denuded regions, but Hills saw them as perfect golfing terrain. The owner had to arrange with the state to relocate the tortoises, a threatened species. Hills then had ground to work with that looked more than anything like Pine Valley in New Jersey, by universal acclaim one of the world's greatest golf courses. There are more acres of manicured fairway at Seville than at Pine Valley, but nowhere else are there greens complexes that come as close to Pine Valley's combination of artifice and indifference as there are at Seville. Because the soil was, when analyzed, nearly perfect greens mix, the creative opportunities were almost unlimited. Instead of having to carefully mix imported sand and peat and then lay it into the hole prepared at the green site, Wadsworth could just push up the local soil wherever Hills decided, run irrigation pipe, and plant grass. Dash says they rototilled a little peat into the greens to try to slow down the rate at which water percolated, but grass would grow just fine on the native soil. Seville was, therefore, a very cheap course to build—not much more than a million dollars, and most of that in installing the irrigation, at a time when courses costing $4, $5, or even, as at Stonebridge, $8 million were not uncommon. Hills left large areas unirrigated, providing water only on the fairways and a narrow margin of rough. He planted Bahia grass on the edges of the course and around many tees, assuming it would rarely if ever get mowed. Unlike Ironhorse, where water will come into play on thirteen holes and heavily influence the look of the course, Seville has only a single small irrigation storage pond to the right of the eleventh green. Seville's abundant natural contours, its rich topography, made digging lakes for fill dirt or for storm water retention unnecessary. The land is so high above the water table and the soil so permeable that dry wells or sumps—basically holes in the ground with pipes stuck in them and rock at the bottom—are adequate for draining Seville's low spots. It was a simple course to engineer and build once Hills found places for the greens.

There are no hazards at Seville, apart from the one little pond, because the eroded regions that spoke so loudly to Hills's imagination are all played as waste areas. The sandy, eroded terrain surrounding many of the greens, unirrigated and unkempt, irregularly colonized by clusters of native grasses, may look like sand bunkers from Hell, but this is really a primordial golfing realm. Seville touches golf architecture's historical roots more than most courses built during this golf boom, especially those in Florida. The self-consciously contrived "linkslike" courses that proliferated in the eighties, however genuine their intent to pay tribute to golf's Scottish origins, lay on the ground like captured giants struggling to rise, Gullivers fallen far from home. Seville, however, cozies up to its site the way a hawk lays against a breeze, effortless and calm, proving once again that a great piece of land can muscle its way past a limited budget better than bundles of cash can transfigure poor ground. Putting in a lot of bumps and mounds and planting unusual grasses may help an architect justify his giant fee, but they won't—and can't—automatically produce a good golf course.

When Hills first got the aerial photos and topo maps for Seville, Dash said, he saw that the contour lines in the eroded areas "just went nuts—they looked like an EEG for somebody not doing too good. Art did a preliminary routing before we got out there and saw what all it was. When he and I got in the field we started shifting things around. Obviously, you had more flexibility working on three thousand acres than you have at Ironhorse. If you were a little tight you could shift something five feet and nobody cared. At Ironhorse there's a lock on those parcel lines."

At a scale of one inch equals one hundred feet, it took two sheets of drawing paper six and a half feet wide and three and a half feet high to show the golf course at the Seville site in plan view. At the same scale, Ironhorse fits on a single sheet five and a half feet wide by three feet high. Existing grade meant little to Hills at Ironhorse—in order for storm water to drain, a golf course has to be built above the native ground, so all of its contours are artificial. At Seville, the elevations range from thirty-five to ninety-eight feet above sea level and the draftsman in Toledo had to strain his visual imagination to tie the new golf course contours into the existing grades. On Seville's grading plan, which has one-foot contour lines, the symbol for the existing topography has a little perpendicular mark every couple of inches, while the new contours are simply bold lines. With Hills's rough sketches of the greens and tees to guide him, the draftsman blended the existing and contemplated grades. Wadsworth could figure from the plan how much dirt to move. The ideal golf course is built in cut rather than fill—there's no chance you'll run out of dirt when you're cutting, and the fairways will run through valleys which, however subtle, help keep the ball on the course. Convex surfaces exaggerate the effects of a bad shot, while concave courses modulate them.

When they walked the site, Dash said, "Art and I found the best green sites and changed the course as we needed to fit them." They lengthened what is now the seventeenth hole to get its green back into a beautiful dune with pines on the left, but that made the hole a par five and created a blind third shot—or, for long hitters, an eyeless second. The blind shot didn't bother them—they put a tall pole with a marker flag well behind the green to aim at, and with sprinkler heads showing yardages, even a naive player would have a pretty good idea of the shot to hit—but making this hole a par five would give Seville a run of *three* consecutive par fives. On the original routing plan, the hole they wanted to elongate was the eighth. Nine and ten were already par fives. Nine was a tremendous dogleg left playing down and against the slope of a hill. A pushed-up plateau at its base would flatten the landing area and help keep shots from bounding with a gravity boost into the woods on the left. Not even the biggest knockers would reach the heavily guarded green in two. Eighteen was one of the "found" greens, atop an eroded hill. Ten, slightly shorter, didn't have as much bailout room on the right for someone fearful of the trees and had a less fearsome green, deeper and more commodious, but it, too, was a formidable three-shot hole nonetheless. Hills and Dasher didn't mind the consecutive par fives. Hills found the eccentricity intriguing, but the owner absolutely did not want three par fives in a row.

The solution was to switch the nines, front to back. The old num-

ber one was a short par four. They'd make *it* the tenth, and eight and
nine would then be seventeen and eighteen. A tough par five is
always a great finishing hole, and starting with a three-shot hole
encourages a speedy getaway. Finding better green locations was a
serendipitous invitation to fuss with the routing. Consecutive par
fives were no problem. "We had back-to-back par fives *and* back-to-
back par threes at Bonita Bay," Dash said. "That worked out okay.
You're trying to find the best holes you can out there."

To keep par at seventy-two, Dash and Hills changed the eleventh
hole from a par five to a par four and made the twelfth hole a longer
par four to push *its* green back into the dunes. With that, they had a
routing they liked and the suspicion that there was a great course
lurking in Seville's hills and pines. Dash has never doubted Seville's
greatness, but he doesn't talk about the course much because "its
condition is not very good, so we don't push people to go there."
Seville doesn't have a big maintenance budget, and mole crickets
have chomped through a lot of the unirrigated Bahia grass rough.
"That's the beauty of Bahia," Dash says. "The crickets prefer it so
they leave the Bermuda alone." The scruffiness doesn't bother Dasher
or Hills, but the clients they're courting may not share their tolerance
for letting natural biological processes work. Scottish golfers would
find nothing remarkable in Seville's unpolished spaces, but American
golfers still typically prefer unblemished lawns, so rather than scare
off potential clients with Seville's ruggedness Hills and Dasher serve
them up a course like Bonita Bay, which in contrast to Seville probably has Florida's most beautifully maintained turf, or Eagle Trace,
the host of a PGA Tour tournament, with coddled acres of perfectly
kept grass. Bonita Bay's superintendent gets teased about keeping his
course green by spreading wheelbarrows full of dollars down the
fairway. Bonita Bay's immaculate condition draws golfers, and golfers buy lots, and that makes the company rich, so it can spend more
money keeping up the golf course. "If there was a BMW pickup,"
Ironhorse's superintendent later joked, summing up his view of Bonita Bay's unrestrained maintenance style, "he'd buy it." Bonita
Bay's reputation helps sell Hills's services, as it did in getting him the
Ironhorse job, and both it and Eagle Trace are a lot easier to get to
than Seville. They're at the top of Dasher's list of Hills's projects to see
in Florida. Seville, though, is for Dash nonpareil.

Without houses to intrude, Seville plays in privacy, and even
though relatively tight corridors cut across the piney hills the course

feels open and inviting. Not every hole nestles in eroded repose, but enough do to give Seville its character.

The first hole—the original tenth hole—is a long, straight par five, across a great swale from an elevated tee to an elevated green. Completely surrounded by the weathered dunes, the first green plants a clear idea of what's ahead. The green itself is firm, with only a very narrow grass fringe, and balls hitting it on the fly tend to run over its back into the sandy waste. Sitting out in the open as it does, it's baked by the sun, and because it's a pushed-up green, built with native materials, it blends into its setting, with no harsh or abrupt edges. The Tifdwarf Bermuda on the greens had little thatch and seemed tentatively rooted in the first year of play, though the greens were smooth and putted true.

Dash says Seville was fun to build—if you didn't like the way a green looked or weren't satisfied it was in exactly the right place, you could just order the shaper back on the dozer and have him push the dirt around some more until it was where you wanted it. And if the rain or wind did a little free reshaping before the grass sprigs went down, that was fine, it helped give Seville its fit and let the same forces that shaped the natural features arrange the artificial ones.

ON THE DAY WE PLAYED it was clear and warm, hot but nothing like West Palm's brush of tropical pepper. It was my first time playing with Dash since Bermuda, and I was eager to redeem myself. My round at Inverness had fooled Hills into thinking I could play, but Dash had seen me at my infantile worst, livid and desperately unavailing in the face of Bermuda's epic winds, and knew I was nothing but a hack. The Dubsers were mostly good sticks, three and four handicappers who could post in the high sixties on a good day. They putted everything out, and had only a limited tolerance for incompetence. I tested their kindness, particularly Dash and the two partnered with us. They reined in their disapproval for a stranger, turning their backs in silent rebuke at another missed putt or a tee shot launched so deep into the trees that no one bothered with even a perfunctory search. By the fourth hole I was carrying two balls to the tee, a humiliating concession to the utter errancy of my swing. I tried harder the worse I got, and by the fifth hole I was shanking.

A shank is the symptom of a golfing psychosis, a vexation so mortifying that it projects its victim into a grotesque new plane of being, a wall of embarrassment from behind which one cannot imagine any escape. A shanked shot goes off at roughly a right angle to the line of play. It's not merely humiliating, it's dangerous. "This has never happened to me before," I lied, the fib so transparent no one bothered faking a sympathetic reply. The shanker is golf's leper, feared as contagious and deadly. Dash consoled me as we rode from green to tee. You can't shank a wood, he reminded me. Here I am, hoping on the way over—even sort of *expecting*—to break eighty, and by the sixth tee, on a course I loved at first sight, I'm looking at three figures on the scorecard for sure, assuming I have enough balls to finish. I'm breaking into a cold sweat every time I reach for an iron, freezing over the ball. I'm so tight I can feel blood dripping from my fingertips. God, I love golf.

DASHER, along with his brother, Pete, and his sister, Barbara, are probably the only people their age in the United States who grew up in a female boardinghouse. The Lullwater Home for Working Girls was Mike's grandfather's idea after he took a 20,000-square-foot mansion—a house nearly the size of Ironhorse's clubhouse—off the hands of an insurance company that had foreclosed on the mortgage during the Depression. The Lullwater had been built by George Adair, who helped Asa Candler, the inventor of Coca-Cola, develop Druid Hills—the Olmsted-designed Atlanta suburb where, as Dash's father puts it, "all the big dogs lived." Mike's parents met when his mother moved into the Lullwater in 1941. Celia Cleland and T. M. Dasher— also called Troy, his given name, and sometimes "Red"—married after he got home from the Pacific war, survivor of a sniper's bullet through his chest on Okinawa on Easter Sunday, 1945.

Mike remembers as a boy getting up at four-thirty A.M. to turn on the Lullwater's coffee machine. "I knew I didn't like doing it. The pay was bad, and the hours stunk." No one else in the family recollects this selfless contribution. Dash lived at the Lullwater until he was a sophomore at Georgia Tech. By then the Dashers lived in a house they had built next door to the Adair mansion. At its peak, T. M. recalls, the Lullwater "could accommodate eighty girls. And that's with linen, maid service, two meals. We had forty-five baths in the two buildings, so no more than two rooms shared a bath. Right after the war, all that was forty to fifty dollars a month, though we had some rooms as low as twenty. We had two housekeepers, a lady in charge of the kitchen, colored help—kind of low-paying, but quite an operation. We made a living."

T. M., which in Georgian sounds like a languorous pronunciation of "Tim," called a family meeting in 1970. "The boardinghouse business isn't what it used to be," T. M. opined, "and none of you kids want to hang around here, do you?" And the Dasher siblings replied, in perfect unison, "Naaaaawh, Daddy," so Dash, as he says, "dodged the boardinghouse business."

Apartments now occupy the corner of Ponce de Leon and Lullwater Roads, across the street from Candler Park, where Dash started learning to play golf on its nine-hole course when he was ten. "I was never a golfer," T. M. says, "never thought about a golf course. Didn't know if it was a good idea for Mike to spend all that time over there or not. But a fella told me, 'Red, you leave that boy alone. No young fella ever got in trouble on a golf course.' "

While in high school, Dash got a summer job picking rocks off the fairways during its construction at Mystery Valley, a course near home, and hatched the notion of building golf courses for a living. A half a dozen years later, in 1973, he took a degree in civil engineering from Tech, "and only flunked out once. I really majored in graduating."

"I'm at that point in my life where Daddy's telling me the best thing I can possibly do is go to work for a big company, get some of that serious service in there, and they'll take care of you. At that point, anything that man told me to do I was going to do the exact opposite. So right before I graduated I worked out a little program with my adviser at Tech—I got a list of every single golf course construction company in the U.S., got a form letter worked up on what was then state-of-the-art word processing equipment, and sent them all a letter. I think there were forty-six of them. I also contacted a couple of local architects. I got three replies.

"One of them was a guy who asked me to meet him at the Atlanta airport. 'If you want to learn the golf course construction business from the bottom of the ditch up, I'm your guy.' he said. 'Most of my people I pay two dollars and fifty cents an hour, but seeing as how you got that college degree and you're really interested in getting in the business, I might go two seventy-five.' He had a project going in Point Blank, Texas, I believe it was. Said to drive on out there. I said, 'Well, I may show up in Texas if nothing else comes along, but don't leave the light on.'

"Then another little outfit offered me six hundred dollars a month to work on a remodel at a course on the south side of Atlanta. That sounded better. Then I got a reply from Brent Wadsworth saying I needed to get down and meet his general superintendent, John Cotter, who was building a course in Macon. So I drove to Macon. It just so happened that the guy they'd hired to grow that course in was the guy who'd hired me to pick rocks at Mystery Valley. I figured I'd go see him first, and he could carry me to this Cotter fella.

"So I went in there, and the first person I saw was shoveling greens mix out of the back of a Cushman—asked him how I could get ahold of this superintendent I knew. He told me I'd find him down so-and-so, and I did, and we got in a pickup truck and drove all around the golf course looking for Mister Cotter. Finally we came back to the green where I'd started, and this guy in coveralls working out of the rear end of that Cushman was John Cotter, who's now the vice-chairman of Wadsworth Golf Construction. So we stood around a while kicking the ground, out in that Georgia heat, and in an effort to impress Mister Cotter I made a show out of reaching down and pulling a couple of stones out of the greens mix—giving a little demonstration of my rock-pickin' training.

"I guess I impressed him enough to get invited to an interview with Mister Wadsworth. This was September of nineteen seventy-three. He offered me a job. Eight hundred bucks a month. He mumbled something about a travel expense . . . his voice kinda trailed off, and I didn't catch the details, but I knew this was my best offer in the golf construction business. 'Okay,' I said. They'd just gotten the largest earth job they'd ever chewed off up in Chicago—an eighteen-hole muni called Highland Woods, designed by William James Spear, who, I later learned, was, like Brent and Larry Packard, a protégé of Robert Bruce Harris. I worked up there the whole fall of seventy-three, pounding grade stakes, shooting grades, laying out this thing.

"I could run a transit, shoot grades . . . I was just doing basic layout. Put out a lot of stakes, then look at it. We dug a twenty-five-acre lake in the middle of a peat bog. Dug it all with a dragline. Pushed clay over the peat, so the dragline could walk on it, then pull the stuff out. We worked that job all winter. That was a rude awakening for the kid.

"I was broke as a convict when I got out of school. My mother gave me two hundred dollars to drive to Chicago. I was in a motel for a week, then found a seventy-five-dollar-a-month apartment. I was squeezed. I asked the super on that job, 'Any way I can get an advance off this job?' and he said, 'Ain't you got any money, Mike?' They got me a check up there right away.

"This was a job with union operators . . . a different work environment. They had a shaper, a couple of scraper hands who later became pretty good shapers, and some laborers who worked for Wadsworth quite a while. That was a big job—with the usual tension and personality clashes that always go on when you get that many guys working that close on a job that long. I put in about eight miles of drain tile—small plastic stuff. Laying pipe on a golf course goes on about from the first day to the last.

"John Cotter took me to lunch once. That means we picked up a sack of hamburgers at McDonald's and ate them in the car driving back to the job. John asked me if I was interested in being an irrigation super. And I said, 'John, I really don't think I would. I like the dirt work better. To me that irrigation's just a job.' And he agreed with me, but they needed somebody and figured it couldn't hurt to ask. Then they found a little redo for me near there, in Lake Forest. This was in the late summer of seventy-four. I rebuilt four or five holes. Finished out the year there. Moved all the dirt, ran pipe, built the greens. They seeded them the next spring.

"Brent Wadsworth came to that job eight or ten times. He was the guy that owned the company. *Mister* Wadsworth. I was out setting string line for drainage pipe one day, and he came by and said, 'Mike, we've got something we want you to do.' I said, 'Okay, I'm right here, let me know.'

"He said, 'Mike, I'm going out to Colorado to bid this job, and I need you to do something for me'—and I'm thinking, sure, while you're gone you want me to watch the house or wash the car—and he says, 'I want you to fly out with me and give me a hand getting the backhoe together to dig some test holes.' And I said, sure, thinking, man, that'll get me out from under running any more of this damn string! He didn't really need me to go out there. It was an opportunity for him to get a feeling for who I was. That's Brent. It was my first airplane ride."

Dash worked fifteen months straight and had about two months vacation coming, so he jumped on his Yamaha TX 750 motorcycle and headed for Key West. When he was a boy, his parents had taken the kids for a vacation to Cuba, where Mike's mother was born, the daughter of Scottish émigrés. Dash's grandfather had run a fertilizer plant in Matanzas. The vacationing Dashers sailed on a ferry from Key West to Havana—it was the summer of 1958. Fifteen years later someone in Key West told him that same ferry ran to the Yucatan for a dozen years after Castro stopped commerce with the Keys. It planted the germ of an idea. Hell, he thought, if I can't go by ferry I'll two-wheel it. From Key West, it's *800 miles* of swallowing bugs before you even get out of Florida. Then Alabama, Mississippi, Louisiana, the gulf coast of Texas, and then a *long* ride south to the Yucatan. Dash has a little family Spanish—he called his grandmother *abuela,* and his mother is bilingual—so he could order cervezas and arroz con pollo and he figured out pretty quick what ALTO meant on those things that looked just like stop signs. In a month he made it as far as Mexico City and back. Still hasn't been to the Yucatan, but at Ironhorse he would see descendants of the people who built the great Mayan monuments he set out to visit busy laying sod, working not to push great pyramids up from the floor of the jungle but to hold in place the sandy slopes of Art Hills's golf course.

Reporting back to Wadsworth in April 1975, Dash worked next on a public course in Terre Haute, Indiana. Then in the spring of 1976 Dash went down to Skidaway Island, Georgia, to build nine new holes—his first job, start to finish, from clearing to grassing, as a Wadsworth superintendent. At Skidaway he fired somebody for the first time. "I had a bunch of laborers—they were half-assed, but they did show up. One guy was smarter than the rest, so I was kind of grooming him for a little responsibility, but Darrell was a party animal and couldn't always manage to get to work on time. He came in late one day, and I said, 'You want this job or not? 'Cause next time you're late your ass is gone.' We went through three or four more times of me giving him his last chance, and then he was late again. I was running a loader, bouncing around, getting madder, when he finally showed up. I climbed off that loader and said, 'Darrell, you're history!' Felt so good, I ran the rest of those assholes off. Even the guys I *couldn't* fire, the old operator hands, spent the rest of the day 'yes sirring' and 'no sirring.' Decided I liked being the boss."

The Magnolia course he was building was an Arnold Palmer/Ed Seay job, one of five courses Wadsworth would ultimately build at Skidaway, two of them designed by Hills. Palmer's first visit was on a hot summer day, the kind sweat bees live for. Sweat bees orbit about their victims' heads, drifting closer and closer, looking for a spot to land. They don't sting like a honeybee, but have an irritating buzz. Palmer's appearance attracted the standard retinue—the owner's rep, a couple of PR types, Dash, and his shaper. Everyone but Palmer was experienced at sloughing sweat bees. "You'd get the rhythm of that bee circling your head," Dash recalled, "strike up a conversation with someone, and then kind of lurch forward and duck away right when that bee's path got him swinging behind the other guy. After a while, you got where you could just sort of drop one off, casual as laying change on the table, and that's what was happening to Palmer. Nobody planned it, but everybody knew the trick except him. It was early in the job. We'd just about finished the clearing. I'd say, 'Arnold, what about this tree here?' And he'd go "Fine, fine," SWAT, SWAT, SWAT, knocking at those bees. By the seventh hole we could barely keep up with him, and he ran the ninth fairway with this *swarm* around his head. His driver was asleep in the back of the Cadillac. 'Get me to the airport!' he said. I don't remember if we saw Arnold again on that job or not."

By now Dash was making $850 a month plus another $250 for travel expenses and the ever popular Christmas bonus—"what made the difference between what you shoulda been making and what they were actually paying you. Biggest one I ever got was nine thousand. I was making in the midtwenties working ten months a year by nineteen seventy-six."

Mike's brother, Pete, came to work for him at Skidaway. "Pete knew how to work, even if he didn't know anything about golf courses. Still doesn't. But he showed up early the Monday he was supposed to in boots and jeans and a T-shirt, gripping a new pair of gloves. 'What you want me to do, Mike?'

" 'Pete,' I said, 'take this fifty dollars and drive over to Statesboro and bail out my scraper hands.' Wadsworth had this uncle and nephew duo who lived in Macon and commuted on the weekend in this old station wagon that they parked when they got here and slept in during the week. They were coming back Sunday night, both drunk, but the one driving didn't have a driver's license, so when they saw the trooper's light they tried to switch places on the fly. Somehow that well trained Georgia state trooper noticed, and hauled them both to jail. We called the sheriff and told him we figured they'd be better off working than sitting in jail, and he saw the sense in that, so we gathered all the cash we could and offered him fifty bucks to spring 'em. So Pete's first job for Wadsworth was being the bail bondsman."

After he finished building the Magnolia course, Dash took the first of what he calls his two sabbaticals from Wadsworth, this one five months traveling around the world, starting in New Zealand and Australia. There was a consumer law in Australia, he said, that required the seller to warranty any car sold for more than $500, "so there were a lot of four-hundred-ninety-five dollar cars for sale in Australia."

Dash bought a '58 VW Bus for the standard nonwarranty price and drove from Sydney to Perth. He'd planned to drive through Darwin— "sort of like going from Atlanta to LA by way of Edmonton"—but discovering that "the rainy season there is a serious meteorological event" took a more direct route. He spent a few days in the little town of Albany, a visit that coincided with Queen Elizabeth's Jubilee tour. "I had a long lens on my camera, so I climbed up on a roof to get some pictures. When they got out of their car, Prince Philip looked up and saw me, whispered to the Queen, and pointed up at me. Then they walked right by me, and I got pretty excited. My mom loved those photos—sent them to all her relatives in the U.K. 'Mike ran into the Queen in Australia.' Like me and the Queen were *tight*."

He went to Singapore, then to Scotland to visit his maternal relatives. While in Scotland, playing a different course every day with rented clubs, his thoughts inevitably turned to course design. Back home, Wadsworth rehired him, but his second stint wasn't as long as the first. In the fall of 1978, he took another sabbatical, this time to go back to Tech for a master's degree in civil engineering. He finished school in the fall of 1980, having gone back to work for Wadsworth for eight months in '79, when cash was running low.

"I had a lot of experience being in the field every day on these jobs, and from the point of view of the guy out there building things I thought the golf course architect had a kind of idyllic deal working. They come in there every couple of weeks, walk around, tell *me* what to do and then leave. Roger Packard [Brent Wadsworth's former partner is Larry Packard's son, who took over his father's practice. He's only four years older than Dash] would pull up onto this job I was doing in Chicago in his Corvette, hop out, wave his arms around a little bit, and leave me to deal with the mud and the blood and the beer and the whole deal. I realize the grass is always greener, but in this case the grass is a *whole lot* greener. I could go back to building. There's a lot of gratification in that. Kind of the Pete Dye approach, I guess. You're there, you start it, get it done, you chalk it up, and go on.

"The gratification's *all* at the end. There's *no* gratification in the process. It's all at the end. Then what you've got to look forward to is starting another one. Never's a harsh word, so I wouldn't say I'd never go back to building, but what I was toying with after I got back from that trip around the world was just saying, 'I'm Mike Dasher. I'm a golf course architect,' and going after some work. I knew that was possible. Then after a bit Wadsworth contacted me about going to work for Art.

"I wasn't gonna go back to pushing dirt around. Wadsworth said they knew I wasn't going to make a career out of being a construction superintendent. And from my vantage point, Wadsworth was already a top-heavy organization. The guys running the company were pretty young and seemed like hardly anybody ever quit. So they came to me with an offer. The way they explained it to me was, Art and Brent were pretty good friends, and they all respected Art, but he was always changing stuff on them. He'd say, 'Yes, this looks good, that looks fine,' and then the next visit he'd say, 'Lower that, or raise this' to the same work, and it was driving them crazy. It got to the point that when Art would make a change they'd ask him to initial it so when he came back he wouldn't change the thing again. So what else is new? Every golf course architect I ever worked with did the same thing. That's what a golf course architect *does*. But they thought Art could expand his career by having somebody selling in the southeast—Wadsworth could figure on getting a lot of that new work—but also they were thinking if they could get Art *out* of the field the work would go smoother.

"But Art's *still* not ready to give up that work in the field. So there was no immediate benefit for me being around. You can't have two guys supervising the shaping. The only way to do that is for me to be there when Art's there and then between his visits I can do things, but I'd have to let Art know what's going on. Otherwise, I'm gonna make a different decision than he's gonna make and he's gonna get pissed off about it.

"I have to be there when he's there so I know what he's doing so when he's *not* there I can keep it moving in that direction. If we're gonna make two different decisions—and in very few cases are you gonna make identical decisions because basically it's such an arbitrary thing—I try to follow Art Hills's principles of, say, smaller greens are better, or down closer to the water is better, to get the variety of being down low, and then maybe some up-high greens—that sort of thing. I can successfully do that, as long as in a phone conversation I mention, 'Art, on this hole we did such and such,' and he'll say, 'That's fine.' Or maybe he'll say, 'I really don't like that,' in which case I make a phone call to the job and tell them, 'We better do it the other way.' "

Hills and Dasher met at the Atlanta airport in September 1980. "He was really looking for a salesman and wasn't interested in giving up any of the board work, the designing of courses, or the field instructions. I said I wasn't interested in being only a salesperson, period. He said, 'If we do a good job of selling I think all that other will work out,' but he didn't promise anything."

Dash got a salary of $18,000, 20 percent of the fee for the jobs he sold, plus expenses and a car. Hills's fee then was $65,000. "I'm still at eighteen thousand," Dash says, but Hills's fees are at $250,000 and climbing.

Dasher's impression of Hills when they met was "the same as I have now. Low-key, quiet, hardworking. . . .the only thing is, his sense of humor didn't come out at that first meeting. Not real outgoing."

Dash wanted to set up an office in Atlanta, but Hills wanted him in Orlando to work the Florida market. "We were both right," Dash thinks now. "We've done a lot of good stuff in Florida, but we would have done more in the Carolinas if we'd been up here."

In 1983, Hills considered moving to Atlanta, and his wife, Mary, agreed to the move as long as Art handled all the details. Atlanta is the hub of the southeast, but Hills finally decided to stay put. His roots are deep in Toledo. When Hills told Dash that Mary's reaction to not moving "was like finding out she didn't have cancer, I said to him, 'Toledo must be a *very* nice place!' "

Dash started his new career making cold calls to engineers, land planners, real estate developers. "I'd just call and say, 'Can I send you something?' And at that time the situation was, 'Art Hills, who's that?' "

III

THE DIRT

10

The Fires This Time

Never judge a man until you've burned one of his piles.

—Charles Best

I CAUGHT THE TRAIN back from Orlando on Sunday afternoon. Three hours later I passed the spot where last Friday on my way up I'd seen Kenny Postell chunking a burn pile. Wisps of gray smoke curled off the ground not far from the copse of trees separating the fourth and fifth fairways. Postell had worked all weekend to make a good show. Monday morning the fellow Postell called "the bossman" was coming by to see how P&J was doing.

Scott Orr is another Robbinsvillian, a second cousin of the company's owner. Orr, who runs P&J's Florida operations from Mulberry, up near Lakeland, is getting his first look at Ironhorse from the ground. He reconnoitered it seven months before from Ranger's helicopter. "I never look at anything from the ground anymore," Orr says. We were standing on the fifteenth fairway. Postell, listening, responds, "Yeah, that's why you got me clearing all this swampland for nine hundred dollars an acre." Orr laughs and looks for a place to spit. He's known Kenny forever and taught him shop in high school. "Meanest kid there was," he says, while Postell crosses his arms and grins. Orr's not a whole lot older than Postell and was once an

189

operator, too. Knocking down trees helped get him through school. Graduated from Western Carolina and went home to teach, drawing top pay because he also coached the football team. Eleven thousand dollars, he remembers, the year he decided to give it up. Postell figures Orr's annual bonus with P&J will top five figures this year. The operators expect at least several thousand each. Orr says P&J makes sure that on these jobs far from home the men get plenty of overtime. "It costs them one hundred dollars a week to sleep."

Dash says clearing was the hardest work he ever ran into when he was building courses with Wadsworth. "When you're spreading dirt," Orr explains, "you might wait five minutes between loads, but when you're clearing it's always in front of you."

When the operators showed up this morning they could see their breath, and they all had on heavy jackets, hats or hoods that covered their ears, and gloves. Orr's visit brought out the hard hats. This bunch is not much for OSHA rules, or anybody else's for that matter. They don't strap in, rarely wear safety glasses or masks to filter the dust and fumes, and calculate that the fire marshal—the "smoke fairy"—preserves air quality to about the same degree that a truant officer safeguards culture.

After Orr tramped about admiring P&J's ravages, he met with Postell back at the ranch house. "This here's what you looked at when you flew over," Postell teased, pointing to the pastures on the aerial photograph of the preconstruction Ironhorse. Orr squeezed his cheek against his chew in a tight-jawed but affable smile. After Postell left, Orr said, "Kenny knows more about clearing these golf courses than I do, so I leave him alone. I'm just down here today so he knows somebody loves him—he don't need no help from me."

Orr's laissez-faire supervision was a benevolent variation of what Isakson called Muss's "mushroom theory" of management. "He keeps us in the dark, feeds us shit, and hopes we prosper."

POSTELL HAD A LOAD of tires in the back of his gray pickup. "Some guys," he said, "would use a tire to keep a green fire burning." I asked him if there was a fine if you did. "Hell, yeah," he said, "a five-hundred-dollar fine. That's why I don't do it. Do I?" He dropped the tires off by the canal along the sixth hole, not far from the property corner, where Ranger is going to dig the outfall lake that will hold the storm water before it runs off into the drainage canal. "Don't

want to make it too obvious and leave these too close to the brush,''
Postell said. It's okay to soak in a few gallons of diesel fuel to get a pile
started. A fire that's burning hot doesn't give off much smoke. A few
more days of burning on the north end and Ranger can start moving
dirt. Postell's burning permit requires that he call every time he's
ready to light a pile to see if it's allowed that day. When he called this
morning, they told him it was too windy.

I'm bareheaded, enjoying the breeze. "If you're gonna be a red-
neck," Postell says, "you've got to get you a hat. Roll the brim, too.
Don't try to wear it straight across. That ain't the right way. Then if
you just kind of tilt it to the side like this here"—and he demon-
strates, rolling his hat just a shade toward one ear—"you'll be a
right-of-way man one hundred percent."

Postell's eager to burn the accumulated piles, but P&J's got plenty
of clearing left in the meanwhile. They don't want to hold up Ranger,
which has to finish its work in 180 days or face penalties of $1,000
a day. After all the months of waiting, the vaguely disquieting lassi-
tude that gripped Ironhorse all summer and early fall, P&J's attack on
the clearing seemed prodigious, even though Postell and his hands
never seemed much in a rush. Within a couple of weeks they had the
first pass on four, five, six, seven, eight, and nine complete and a bit
done on one, two, ten, and twelve. They'd started burning up in the
northwest corner and were ready to torch more.

When Charles and Alonzo finished the first pass over the eighth
and ninth fairways they moved south to clear for the big lake between fourteen and seventeen. There's a pine and palm forest with a
heavy palmetto understory to eradicate there, near the favorite pasture for Carrie Reese's horses, who graze contentedly while the dozers attack the trees. Muss is a horseman himself, but has been after
Isakson since Thanksgiving to have Carrie cart this bunch away. They
spend their evenings in the barn, attracted by the sweet oats they're
fed, but after they're turned out from the barn in the morning they
spend their days wandering about the shrinking meadows. Now that
the chain-link fence around the house has been breached and the
gate left open, the horses saunter across the lawn like proprietors,
stopping for an occasional mouthful of grass.

Alonzo Wright runs the front-end loader with a root-rake attachment. As well as moving up and down, the root rake on the loader
pivots, giving it a scooping action, the sort of motion your hand
would make reaching in a barrel for grain. The dozer blades only go

up and down. The Cat's a lot more powerful than the loader, but it's not as versatile. Alonzo can maneuver the root rake with the dexterity of a pointing finger. The loader has big rubber tires and a much faster cruising speed than the dozer, but with its short wheel base it's a lousy ride, bouncy and jostling. Unlike a dozer, which the operator turns by slowing or stopping one track so the drive of the other pivots around it, a loader has a steering wheel. The controls for the bucket or rake are on the column.

Postell says Alonzo is a "real good hand." Kenny trusts Alonzo's skill enough to stick his head underneath a clearing blade weighing several tons while Alonzo holds it in place with the tiny point of the root rake's tine. Wright's the only operator on this job not from Robbinsville. A couple of weeks ago, after a heavy afternoon rain, Kenny sent "Lonzo," as his name's usually pronounced, over to pick up a length of reinforced concrete pipe left over from Ironhorse's ranching days. Postell thought he might be able to use the pipe to build a little culvert along the seepage canal so he could get his equipment back into the preserve without damming the ditch and flooding ground he had to clear. Alonzo wrapped a chain around the pipe, which was ten feet long and about two feet in diameter, and when he lifted the pipe it dangled beneath the rake like a spent yo-yo. Postell told him to carry it all the way up to the north end, where they were clearing for the fourth green, a trip about as long as you could make moving more or less on a straight line within Ironhorse's borders. Ernest and Kenny headed out from the house, where they'd waited out the storm, skirting the edge of the barn. Before the rain, passage was easy along this route, but now the muck swallowed the tires on Postell's truck. He locked the front hubs and put it into four-wheel drive, searching for traction. Mud flew up and caked the rearview mirrors. When I asked where Alonzo was from, Kenny said "Alabama" and went on jamming the clutch and sliding the gear lever from forward to reverse, trying to escape. A winch could pull him to dry ground, but crawling from the slime unaided was just enough of a challenge to keep him spinning toward solid ground.

"We ain't got no niggers up there where we come from," Ernest said, moving his knee so Kenny could grab the gear-shift knob. "Not a one. We got some Indians, but no niggers." Kenny had told me that the writer Peter Jenkins, in his *Walk Across America*, had stopped in Robbinsville, so I'd looked at what Jenkins had to say. He'd excoriated Robbinsville as the meanest place he ever had the misfortune to visit. All the friendly fellas like Postell, I figured, must have been out of town, but Kenny laughed and said, no, he remembered Jenkins's visit. Kenny was in high school then. "They thought he was some kind of hippie selling dope or something. Didn't much take to him."

Graham County was opened to white settlement in 1838, when General Winfield Scott gathered up the Cherokee farmers and their families and marched them to Oklahoma over the Trail of Tears. "The plans for the removal and reestablishment of these people," President Andrew Jackson told the Congress, "has been dictated by a spirit of benevolence and enlarged liberality." Jackson never forgot or forgave any of the scurrilous attacks against his wife hurled in the rough-and-tumble language of Tennessee politics, but that Junaluska, one of the victims of the forced march to Oklahoma, had saved his life at the Battle of Horseshoe Bend in 1814 slipped Old Hickory's mind. Junaluska later walked back to Graham County, reuniting with the relict of his people, the ones who had managed to hide in the folds of the Smokies from the 7,000 U.S. soldiers sent to fetch them. North Carolina, grateful still for Junaluska's loyal service in the wars against the Creeks even if Andrew Jackson wasn't, made him a citizen and gave him a hundred U.S. dollars and title to a tract of 337 acres near Robbinsville. Fifteen years later, a regiment of Graham County Cherokees fought for the Confederacy, but there were nearly as many volunteers for the Union among Graham County's whites as soldiers loyal to the Stars and Bars. Fifty years after the Civil War the Robbinsville chapter of the Daughters of the American Revolution raised a monument to Junaluska.

I'd heard about the hostility of some Graham County residents to the federal government, too, ancient antagonisms roused by the culture of moonshine and quickened by anger over the condemnation of land—a second and gentler episode of forced removal, this time mostly of white people—to create the Great Smoky Mountains National Park during the Depression. Graham County spawned a notorious band of bear poachers, caught by a U.S. Fish and Wildlife sting operation, who were selling the paws, gallbladders, and claws to Asian customers who believed, among other things, that ingesting the bear organs stimulated their sexual potency. I'd missed that hard edge in the operators at Ironhorse, so Ernest's remark startled me—especially so given that Ernest and Alonzo shared lodging. They cooked together, breathed the same midnight air, and shared an occasional bottle of whiskey. Later I heard Ernest condemn Charles

Best, whom he thought closefisted anyway, not for calling Alonzo a "nigger," but for doing it *behind his back*. "He won't call Lonzo a nigger to his face." In the moral economy of the lingering South, the statement suggested ethical depth, or perhaps was meant to convey, by the ease with which it was uttered, that *it wasn't personal*, that it was not a vicious epithet if you didn't hide it. Alonzo neither complained against this usage—and I heard it more than once uttered in his presence—nor acknowledged any harm in hearing it. Aside from the isolating solitude of that word, Alonzo seemed to me as much a part of P&J's itinerant company as the Robbinsville cohort. They worked together, rode together, laughed at the same angry jokes, inhaled the same smelly vapors. A quiet and composed man of middle age, Alonzo Wright went about his work and sent money home to Alabama.

THE LOADER CAN UPROOT light underbrush, like myrtles and peppers, but its real forte is picking up the debris the dozers leave and getting it on the burn piles. In Alonzo's hands, the loader herds a heap of palmettos with rhythmic assurance. Alonzo will back it up six to eight feet, stick the tines of the rake deep enough to catch the palmetto roots, and then move forward, lifting the rake to roll the roots up to the surface. When the roots are above ground, he backs up, then rolls forward for more, then back, then forward, a steady cadence. When he's accumulated a goodly batch he runs it over to the burn pile, curling the root rake under the roots and branches and lifting them in the cradle the rake makes when it's extended parallel to the ground. The loader, like all heavy equipment, sounds an alarm when it's in reverse. Its high-pitched "riiiing, riiiing, riiiing" is Alonzo's field signature, the music of his labor. Forward, backward, forward, backward, hour after hour, day after day. He must hear it in his dreams.

As with all the clearing, the idea is to keep the pile clean. Sometimes, when there is dirt clinging to the load, Alonzo will gather it in the root rake, scoop it up ten feet off the ground, and shake it by dropping the rake in quick spasms, raining the ground with a pale, gray dust.

Charles creates the piles, knocking down trees and pushing them into great jumbled heaps, long and narrow rather than round, while Alonzo works in his wake, tidying up. Charles gobbles the edges in the D8, pushing the trees back into the center, and every hundred yards or so in dense growth starts a new pile. He'll drive the dozer right up the sides of the jumbled rick to build it high, so the flames can peak. The dozer blade will point to the sky, the tracks spinning for traction, skinning the bark off pines, churning out palmetto roots, while Charles, motionless, the throttle wide open, deposits his prey. A temporary operator signed on the other day, and Postell didn't think he showed a whole lot of flair for clearing. Tentative, delicate, insufficiently fearless. "Don't never judge a man," Charles reminded him, "until you've burned one of his piles."

Cattle egrets flock to the clearing, a half a dozen working around Charles, four more hunting in Alonzo's wake. They're very brave around the dozer, running nearly underneath its tracks to snag a tidbit. "They'll eat anything," Postell says, "but they love those little lizards. I've never even knocked a feather off'en one of 'em. They got an instinct for staying away." They forage near the hooves of their companion beast, and the dozer is, from a cattle egret's point of view, a new and vastly improved breed of cattle. A grazing cow may scare up a tasty critter now and then for a vigilant egret, but a dozer delivers up everything in its territory and masticates it besides. For a cattle egret, a dozer is a great evolutionary leap forward from the placid ruminant. They love these funny-footed yellow beasts.

Best said, "I've seen them eat a snake two foot long, moving their heads this way and that to get them down. They'll eat rats and mice, grasshoppers. Only thing I've ever seen 'em turn down at all's a crawdad. They won't eat that crawdad. But they'll eat about anything else. You can throw 'em bread, and they won't eat that. But they'll eat about anything else out here. They just make sure it's dead. Poke at it first."

The cattle egret, *Bubulcus ibis,* is a newcomer to Florida, but unlike the exotic flora at Ironhorse, the cattle egret arrived without human assistance—if, that is, one discounts the amplifying effect of human intrusion on the niche where the egrets flourish. They like savannas, meadows, pastures, plains, the open tracts of the greensward—the same environment human beings prefer, according to the researches of John Falk. Falk, who now runs a store in suburban Maryland purveying scientific and educational games and toys, was formerly an ecologist with the Smithsonian, a specialist in the "anthropogenic grassland," that is, a grassland made by humans. An educator first, he studied the "energetics of lawns" as a way to teach ecology. He wondered why people kept lawns at all and discovered what he believes is a "hard-wired preference" among humans to live in grass-lands. All vertebrates, he says, have "habitat preferences," a predilection to recognize and seek safe and biologically secure environments. Falk discovered that no matter where they grew up, human beings shown a picture of a savanna side by side with a picture of another landscape, whether desert or tropical rain forest, mountainous terrain or coniferous woods, overwhelmingly said they'd rather live in the grassland. He hypothesizes that because humans evolved on the plains of Africa, emerging from the forests to pursue prey, an idea of the savanna as a succoring environment somehow persists in a deep, neurological way. That's why humans cultivate lawns—they're neo-savannas, private anthropogenic grass-lands.

Falk learned further that an image of water in the landscape almost always skewed the subject's choice. Human beings need water—we *are* mostly water—so if we *are* hard-wired for habitat preference, then loving water is a plausible corollary. If it's a leap from the necessary to the Beautiful, if an aesthetic based on genetic endowment seems contrary to a modern view of Art, Falk's views nonetheless go a long way in explaining golf's appeal. The romantic landscape evolved in England, to pursue the Falkian logic, as a kind of unconscious democratization of this biological ideal, which theretofore had been, like hunting wild game, fishing from the streams, and commanding a view, the prerogative of the landlord. The poor are not hungry because they'd rather not eat. The humble live wretchedly not because they prefer mean landscapes, but because there's nowhere else to go. When resources are limited, power and privilege control them. As the standard of living rose in the West, providing material comforts, it fostered a proliferation of aesthetic delights. That's what Frederick Law Olmsted, a fervent democrat, understood. The people needed parks, with their meadows and lakes and specimen woods. "Practically, what we want most," Olmsted wrote, "is a simple, broad, open space of clean greensward, with sufficient play of surface and a sufficient number of trees about it to supply a variety of light and shade." And because that is what people want, Falk says, "everybody loves the look of a golf course."

Falk says, "It took a millennium for its inhabitants to topple the forests and create savannas in Europe. The same process took two hundred years in the eastern United States. It may take fifty years in the Tropics." But as the forests fell to the woodsman's ax, people congregated in cities—for the "comforts, diversions, service, leisure, and intellectual opportunities." No longer able to walk out on the back forty and feast their eyes on a nourishing vista, city dwellers needed parks. The millions of American acres cleared for pastures and agriculture, much of the land so marginal for farming that woods eventually reclaimed it—there are more trees now in New England and the South than there were in 1900—lured the roving cattle egret.

The first cattle egret in Florida was spotted near Lake Okeechobee in 1953. After arriving in South America, probably blown across the Atlantic from west Africa in a storm, the cattle egret slowly colonized its way north. Now it stretches across the Sun Belt from Florida to California and as far north as southern Canada. I saw cattle egrets on Hilton Head.

Sometimes, Best says, an egret *will* pay for its daring, even if Postell's never managed to harm one. "I've killed a few of 'em," Best says. "Caught them with the blade. They don't weigh more'n an ounce or two, seems like."

With their elongated bodies, the egrets looked as if they weighed a couple of pounds. And, as Alonzo says, "They eat all day." When it's running after food, an egret's neck stays extended like a roadrunner's, but when it's walking, its head thrusts forward first, and then its body walks back under it, a gait that looks as if it was choreographed by Michael Jackson. Bright-white, they look like scaled-down versions of the great egrets native to south Florida. A smudge of pale orange feathers on its wings, breast, and crown declares an egret's readiness to court. Whatever their plumage, they seem never to blink, so intent are they on finding that next little thing to eat. So ubiquitous on a Florida clearing job, so indiscriminately ravenous, so omniverous—so like the clearing crew—is the cattle egret that the P&Jers have adopted it as a sort of unofficial mascot. "Florida chickens," they call it. I saw one eating a frog. It flew off when I approached, the frog's legs dangling from its beak.

At the end of the day the operators walk the equipment back to a staging area, which for P&J, whose byword is mobility, is a very casual stop. Ranger and Wadsworth set up job trailers with desks and phones, but P&J just finds an open spot where the equipment can link with the fuel truck and sets to work. Unless a dozer's snapped the buried phone cable, which happened a half a dozen times during the clearing, Postell uses the phone in the office. Isakson agitated for a cellular phone, but Muss kept the purse strings drawn tight. It usually took a day to get the cable repaired, hours that for Isakson were an exquisite torture, the lifeless phone an affront to his larger purposes, a symbol of the months of frustration he'd endured trying to get Ironhorse—Ironlungs, Ironballs—under way. Isakson without a phone was Ahab harpoonless, David slingless, Johnny without a gun.

First thing each morning P&J's operators check all the fluids and hydraulic connections, warm up the engines, and roll over to the clearing patch. Clearing's hard on equipment wherever it's done, but the sandy soil at Ironhorse abrades moving parts and clogs air filters. It shines the rusted tines on the root rakes so they look like polished silver, glaring in the sun, and it grinds the lugs off the dozer tracks. Tracks that survive a thousand hours elsewhere perish in half that time in Florida. P&J changes its blades and tracks in the field rather than haul the equipment to a shop. Postell chases parts, but P&J's mechanics—each clearing crew has a mechanic—invent solutions when the right part's not available. They carry cutting torches, welding machines, and an instinct for improvisation.

The smoke I saw through my Amtrak window coming down from Dasher's was the spoor of a fire that blew briefly out of control. It flashed across the patch of forest between the fourth and fifth holes. Dash wasn't surprised by the accident. "If some flame didn't get away on this job, that'd be the first time." When Harpman and Isakson came to look at the charred trunks of the Sabals and pines, their canopies drooping and seared, Postell explained with a straight face that it was really probably better to burn out the underbrush, especially at this time of year, with the sap falling. Postell says they could have stopped the flames with a tractor, building a fire break, but didn't want to take down any more trees. Ironhorse will lose some of these seared pines. The charred palm trunks one sees all around Ironhorse are evidence that these dense trees can survive fires. Pines can, too, but the accumulated native understory, the consequence of years without a smaller, prophylactic fire, combined with the combustible Brazilian peppers, made this fire hotter, with flames spotting higher than the ones the native species are genetically equipped to survive. The prognosis is guarded for the trees on the north side. Hills's plan was to save an exemplary woods here—part of that "preservation of mature plant material" theme whose realization seems in jeopardy.

By the middle of December, Ranger has two scrapers, or "pans," on the job, digging the first lake up by the construction entrance and

Knocking it down. (*Illustration by Michael Strantz*)

hauling the dirt over to the north side, where an operator on a high-track D6 dozer can push it into the old perimeter drainage canal. At the end of the first day of digging there's an outline of the lake, its broad contours visible as a slight depression, barely distinct from the extant ground. The excavated surface is smooth, and, while it's only eighteen or so inches deep, already slick with a coat of ground water. Each scraper can haul about 800 yards a day, harvesting twelve yards or so with each pass. The operator clicks off each load on a counter as a rough accounting of each day's haul. The closer the drop is to the dirt's source the more loads a pan can scrape and deposit each day.

These machines are the descendants of the little horse-pulled pans that were used to create the modest landscape effects of the earliest manufactured golf courses. One costs about a quarter of a million dollars and consumes eighty gallons of diesel fuel every day. Comprehending the ease with which these giant hydraulic scrapers can move and place dirt was liberating to golf course architects. Geoff Cornish, the historian of golf architecture, says Trent Jones was the first architect to appreciate the implications of heavy earth-moving equipment for golf architecture. By 1960, he says, the dozer and the scraper had "revolutionized" course building. It was not that large quantities of earth were never moved before the 1950s or so, but the sites golf architects had to work with were more readily adapted to golf and didn't require such formidable engineering. It wasn't until the 1980s that moving huge volumes of earth was commonplace, making the construction of "linkslike" courses, with their mounds and tumuli spilling across the ground, a cliché. When Wadsworth started building courses in Florida in the late sixties, an old Wadsworth hand remembers, "There'd be two hundred thousand yards of dirt" to move. Now it's not uncommon to move more than double Ironhorse's 600,000 yards, which is a lot of dirt.

When Charles Blair Macdonald, creator of the Cape hole, built a course called Lido on Long Island in 1914, he anticipated Ironhorse's construction, but his techniques were rarely imitated between then and the last two decades. When told that Lido "was to be built over 115 acres of marsh land and swamps, with a lake of considerable size in the middle," Macdonald recalled in his autobiography, "I refused to have anything to do with it, saying a first-class golf course could not be laid over a filled in marsh."

He relented when the owner told him he "could do anything I wanted in constructing holes, as in making the fill"—that is, in placing the dredged soil on the ground—"hills, hollows, mounds and lakes could be created at will and they would pump them up or out according to any contour map I might submit." Robert Hunter was perhaps thinking of Lido when he wrote that a flat site invited a course "without a flaw." Hunter had played Lido before writing *The Links* and recalled its "rugged terrors," a surprising description suggestive of boiling ground rather than placid flats of deposited fill.

Having exhausted the catalogue of ideas he accumulated studying Scottish courses in his design of the National Golf Links, Macdonald was looking for new sources of inspiration at Lido. He asked his friend Bernard Darwin, the golf writer for the British magazine *Country Life*, to "start a competition for . . . the best design of a two-shot hole." Of the eighty-one designs submitted to the magazine, the one Macdonald chose as the best was by Alister Mackenzie, who had gradually forsaken his medical practice over the previous half-dozen years to give a hand to another erstwhile professional, the barrister H. S. Colt, designing golf courses. Dozens were then springing up all around England, and a handful of gifted practioners—like Mackenzie and Colt, who later would finish the work on Pine Valley left undone when its creator died—found their callings designing golf courses. Hunter met Colt when he went to the British Isles to study golf architecture in 1912 and admired Colt's stoutly practical essays on the subject. Hunter probably met his future partner, Mackenzie, too, but there's no record of their meeting. Mackenzie hoped to adapt in his designs the camouflage techniques he had learned from the clever Boers during the war in South Africa. "It is an important thing in golf to make holes look much more difficult than they really are," he wrote, a principle some modern architects turn on its head, making holes that look merely fiendish impossibly hard. Mackenzie was an especially forceful advocate of the natural style, railing against the flat, square greens and industrial-look cross bunkers ubiquitous on lesser English inland courses.

Mackenzie's winning design for Lido was a complicated scheme. He wanted to reproduce, he wrote, "the old type of golf"—by which he meant St. Andrews—"in which a player has no fixed line to the hole." Mackenzie's hole had five distinct routes from tee to green, one of them across an island of turf set floating in a sea of sand. A spit of sand one hundred yards out from the tee created a cross bunker, the sort of hazard course designers were then and forevermore abandoning. The safest route to the green was the longest. A series of bunkers swept one's eye toward the green when viewed from the safety of the fairway, but hid from players taking the riskiest route. Along its entire left side the hole skirted the ocean, and to its right was nothing but "rough grass, rushes, whens [sic], &c." The green, tilted from back to front and right to left, was a plateau with grassy hollows running off below it and a raised mound behind. Across its length, Mackenzie's hole dropped more than twenty feet from tee to fairway and then rose as much again to the green. Mackenzie's design was much too busy for Macdonald, so he simplified it. Seventy years later, Desmond Muirhead resurrected Mackenzie's idea of an island fairway at courses in Florida and New Jersey.

Lido was built entirely on sand dredged from an ocean channel, the method Florida's pioneer land creator, Carl Fisher, was using at the same time to create Miami Beach. It had not yet occurred to anyone that the marshes Lido destroyed were valuable water-cleansing wetlands. "The acreage was filled with 2,000,000 cubic yards, at seven cents a yard," Macdonald wrote. Not believing that sand was a good medium for grass, Macdonald and his construction chief, Seth Raynor, a wonderfully talented young engineer whom Macdonald had first hired to work on the National Golf Links, "dressed heavily with muck," then top-dressed with lime. Raynor built Mid Ocean in Bermuda for Macdonald, and sixty courses of his own design. He died in West Palm Beach in 1926 while building a course for none other than Paris Singer, still pursuing his vision of Palm Beach as the winter capital of the Frolicsome Leisured.

In death Raynor was yoked once again to Mackenzie, whose prize-winning hole he built for Macdonald at Lido. Raynor had been the first choice of the tiny syndicate formed to create Cypress Point on the Monterey Peninsula. When he died Marion Hollins, Cypress Point's prime mover, who had already distinguished herself as a pioneer among woman golfers by building the Women's National Golf and Country Club on Long Island in 1924, chose Mackenzie to finish what Raynor could not. Hollins's choice brought Mackenzie to California and his eventual partnership with Robert Hunter, who helped him design and build Cypress Point. Cypress Point, in turn, persuaded Bobby Jones that Mackenzie was the right man to design Augusta National. "Narrow fairways bordered by long grass make bad golfers," Mackenzie had written a dozen years before he and Jones created Augusta National's famously commodious fairways. "They do so by destroying the harmony and continuity of the game, and in causing a stilted and cramped style by destroying all freedom of play."

Marion Hollins, who went on to develop another great California golf course with Mackenzie and Hunter called Pasatiempo, is remembered even less well than Hunter—despite the fact that she designed the sixteenth hole at Cypress Point, the most photographed if not the most famous golf hole. Cypress Point and Pasatiempo, unlike Macdonald's Lido or its descendants like Ironhorse, whose features are invented—Macdonald said building Lido made him "feel like a creator"—were built on land that really was, in the hoary architect's cliché, perfectly suited for golf.

THERE ARE TWO BASIC TYPES of scrapers—paddle pans, which lap up the dirt with a kind of conveyor belt and run it up into a hopper, and "push-pulls," the kind Ranger's using. Painted a pale lime green, the push-pulls have two large diesel engines, one up front and another in the rear. Both run wide-open, with a screaming intensity that resembles the eager purposefulness of colonizing insects. Scrapers steer hydraulically. Neophyte operators forget they can't turn when the throttle's down. When Wadsworth was building Hills's TPC course at Eagle Trace, an operator got too close to the edge of a lake, let off the throttle, and then couldn't turn the pan away from the crumbling bank. He rode his mount to the bottom before a startled audience. "After a while, he popped to the surface," Dasher remembered, "like a fishing float." Afraid he might sue, Wadsworth rewarded him for not abandoning ship with a cushier job. "I think we had him counting trucks," his boss recalls. It took two cranes to pull the scraper up.

They're called "push-pulls" because they can yoke together in tandem or in teams. Each has a large rigid steel loop on its front, called a bale, that the operator can raise or lower, and a fixed hook on back for the bale to snare. In dirt that's dry and easy to load a pan can work alone, but in heavy material the pans link up and roar across the ground in symphony to pick up their loads. Sometimes a dozer will push, too, its tracks getting a purchase on ground that makes the scrapers' big rubber tires spin.

The pans lower a blade onto the ground as they drive forward, scooping earth into the bowl. When it's loaded, the blade retracts and the bottom of the bowl slides shut. The bowl itself can be raised and lowered, so the machines will have clearance when they're hauling from the pickup site to the drop. The higher the load the more wear and tear on the machine, but the greater the ease for the operator. Running with the pan low dresses the haul roads, too, so deep ruts won't develop.

Running a pan is low on the earthwork status scale. It's bumpy and noisy and poorly paid. Most operators wear earplugs, but some prefer a Walkman. Several of Ranger's operators early on at Ironhorse were on work release from the county jail. Behind on child support, or convicted of drunk driving or involuntary manslaughter, they figured eight hours riding a scraper was better than a restless day in the jug. Ranger picked them up every morning in a company van while the brief experiment in creative corrections lasted. Pan-jockeying was a step up from breaking rocks.

One morning every week Ranger starts the day with a safety meeting. "I want you guys to look behind you when you're running those pans," Kevin Phillipson, the foreman, tells them. "We don't need any accidents." Besides Kevin there are eleven hands assembled, smoking eight cigarettes, drinking four cups of coffee, and one can of Coke. "Especially when you're push-pulling you need to look around and see where you are. You're running those things like drivers, not operators."

Eight pans, parked like the weekend specials at a used-car lot, await their commanders. Kevin asks the dozer hand if he has anything to say. "I've been working these jobs many years," he says in quiet tones, looking into the distance, "but it still tears me up to see somebody get hurt and be lying on the ground." Kevin says Ranger's lost three men in the last five years. "I just don't want to work anymore when I see somebody hurt bad. It can just happen so easy and so fast, and it just tears me up to see somebody lying out there."

Crazy Dave, a refugee from the sixties who dropped one too many tabs, his black ponytail hanging down behind his filthy black Cat cap, walks away from the meeting and climbs on his pan with a smile, settling in the black vinyl-covered seat and tightening a belt across his lap. Good vibrations, and lots of them. He likes the work, but maybe not as much as Kevin, who ran a pan for four years, a suspiciously long time for someone neither coerced by the law nor brain-damaged. "I loved every minute of it. When I told John Riley the pan was my favorite piece of equipment, he said, 'You're not wrapped too tight.' But you've got to understand, I *like* to work."

Phillipson signed on with Ranger over at PGA National, ten years before, as a flagman. Getting on a pan was a step up. A year on a pan is a long time—four years is monumental, an Everest of endurance. Kevin says he could shape a golf course with a pan if he had to. "A good operator can really lay down a good shape." But Ranger can't get good hands to stay on the pans, so the strategy now is "Get it out of the lake and slop it down and we'll dress it up later. You don't have time like we used to. You've gotta move the dirt."

Kevin went to heavy-equipment school at night for three years. His first supervisory job was night foreman on the excavation of South Florida's M-1 Canal, 7:00 P.M. to 7:00 A.M., seven days a week. "We drained all the wetlands in Royal Palm Beach."

Phillipson, a tall and earnest native of Buffalo, brings his dogs, a mixed-breed mother named Bandit and her daughter, Mandy, to work. They're staked, with food and water, in the grove of trees Dasher saved just off the sixth tee. Calm when the pans scream by, they jump up and strain against their leashes, clawing at a wall of air, if a person approaches on foot. Kevin drives a white company pickup. When he lets the dogs loose at the end of the day, they chase for the entry gate in front of the truck, barking like sentinels. Riley's comfortable leaving Kevin in charge of the job. He's a good dirt man.

IN THEIR FIRST FEW PASSES, the pans scrape dry dirt, but pretty quickly they're below the water table, in marl and shell that have the consistency of wet concrete. They're running in a rough circle of perhaps a quarter of a mile, taking no more than five minutes to pick up a load of dirt from the lake, run it over by the perimeter berm, dump it where the dozer can push it into the canal, and return to the lake. The shorter the haul, the more efficient the operation.

Once they've breached the water table, Ranger has to pump the water from the hole. On most jobs, where they're required to keep the water on the site, they'll throw up a little impoundment dike around a few acres and pump water into it and then when the lake's done pump the water back into the hole. Ironhorse, though, has the big pump over by the fifth tee, at the northwest corner, still connected to South Florida's drainage canals, so Ranger can excavate a temporary ditch over to one of Bob Grier's drainage canals, then set up a pump running off a diesel generator to keep the water down so the pans can run. The water flows far enough before it hits the outfall pump to let the sediment settle out. Turbid water is a no-no. As Bob

Isakson says, "We start sending murky water to South Florida and they'll be on our ass."

There was once a lot of life in the drainage ditches, fish, frogs, turtles, and an occasional alligator. It's hard to imagine much of it surviving the construction. The raccoons, deer, otters, and snakes can take refuge in SWA and the water-catchment basin, but the fish can't amble to safety. Some will endure a trip through the pump, and some will survive in the vestigial ditches, but most will perish under the dirt Ranger is scraping for the new lakes, which will in their turn one day be stocked with fish.

WHEN BY THE NEXT DAY the wind had calmed down enough to burn, Postell drove out to the sixth fairway, where Conward was waiting on a rented Case loader, ready to tend fires. The transmission was out on the Caterpillar loader. Conward was a dozer man and hated the loader's bumpy ride. Dozers shake and rattle, but they don't bump or bounce. What's worse, said Conward, is that on a loader, "You can't see the load in front of you."

The wind was coming from the east, off the ocean, so Postell sprayed some diesel on that side, let it soak a minute, and then knelt to ignite it. The pile was still a little green. The wetter the wood the more it would smoke. There were seven piles to burn, and the one farthest west had the unburned remnants from last weekend's fires on it, gathered by the loader for another trip through the inferno. Postell struck a match and touched it to the fuel-soaked limbs, igniting them in glisks of flame that captured the dance of the diesel vapors in the air. When the fronds caught, heavy smoke hugged the ground, like fog, drifting west. Postell says he's been on reservoir jobs where they'd get five D8s rolling side by side to create piles thirty feet high and ten times as big as what's burning at Ironhorse. "You get that going and it's like standing next to a freight train. I love the look of a big fire like that at night."

Once Postell gets the fires lit, Conward's job is to tend them, or "chunk" them, as they say. He'll keep the pile consolidated, make sure it doesn't spread, and lift the smoldering limbs to let the fire breathe. The fires on the sixth fairway are in the open, well away from the trees left on the northern perimeter. Postell would just as soon avoid a rerun of last weekend's exercise in escaped flames.

When Conward chunks the piles, he runs the root rake right into the flames, dropping the ends of pine logs whose middles are already ash back into the flames. The loader's big tires roll through red embers, while Conward sticks the rake into the fire and lifts the burning logs. Sometimes when a fire's slowing down, he'll back a dozer up against it and open the throttle wide so the radiator fan can bellow air across the flames. Once in a while a dozer ignites—another good reason for P&J to stick with well-worn equipment. Chunking involves more sitting around than any other part of a clearing operation.

William Bartram's *Travels*, in 1765-1766, took him, as the subtitle to the book he published on his journey said, "Through North & South Carolina, Georgia, East and West Florida, The Cherokee Country, The Extensive Territories of the Muscogulges, or Creek Confederacy, and the Country of the Chactaws." Graham County historians think he was the first white man to visit there. Bartram was a botanist, trained by his father, John Bartram, whom William had accompanied on an earlier collecting expedition along the southeast coast. Bartram *fils* had a grand head for facts, an acutely observing eye and ear, a sturdy disposition, and a capacity for physical bravery. He camped alone within yards of alligator-filled lagoons—sleeping fitfully, he acknowledged—and described a battle to gain the shore against an attacking legion of the reptiles in an adventuresome prose which would have done H. Rider Haggard proud. But mostly Bartram's tone is matter-of-fact, a calm recounting of his journey.

Floating along a river near the present-day boundary between Florida and Georgia, Bartram saw "rich, deep swamps, well timbered with Cypress, Ash, Elm, Oak, Hiccory, Scarlet Maple, Nyssa aquitica, Nyssa tupilo, Gordonia lasianthus, Corypha palma, Corypha pumila, Laurus Borbonia &c." His Latin cadences bounce, a botanical encyclopedia in verse. Further on, he saw a "loose black mould, very fertile, which naturally produces Orange groves, Live Oak, Laurus Borbonia, Palma elata, Carica papaya, Sapindus, Liquidambar, Fraxinus excelsior, Morus rubra, Ulmus, Tilia, Sambucus, Ptelea, Tallownut or Wild Lime, and many others." Bartram's lists rehearse the exuberant inventories of Walt Whitman, a celebration of abundance, an insatiable appetite for experience. "I see where the live-oak is growing, I see where the yellow-pine, the scented bay-tree, the lemon and orange, the cypress, the graceful palmetto."

Bartram's journal, published in 1791, found a wide audience. The Romantic poets were particularly taken with Bartram's lyricism, his

celebration not merely of nature but of the red men who lived har-
moniously amidst its bounty. Floating in a barque among the sea
islands, hugging the Atlantic shore, Bartram, sometimes accompanied by traders or slaves, saw not just the natural world, but the
people in it, the noble savage with the rambling bear. Once, while his
companions set up camp for the night, Bartram set out "reconnoi-
tering our ground":

> and taking my fusee with me, I penetrated the grove, and afterwards
> entered almost unlimited savannas and plains, which were absolutely
> enchanting; they had been lately burnt by the Indian hunters, and had
> just now recovered their vernal verdure and gaiety.
>
> How happily situated is this retired spot of earth! What an elysium it
> is! where the wandering Siminole, the naked red warrior, roams at
> large, and after the vigorous chase retires from the scorching heat of the
> meridian sun. Here he reclines, and reposes under the odiferous shades
> of Zanthoxylon, his verdant couch guarded by the Deity; Liberty, and
> the Muses, inspiring him with wisdom and valour, whilst the balmy
> zephrys fan him to sleep.

This stuff was a great hit with Samuel Taylor Coleridge and William
Wordsworth and grist for the Romantic gardener's mill. There is a
current of imagination that flows from William Bartram to Ironhorse,
the curious line of descent that runs through Frederick Law Olmsted.
It reminds me of the rock invasion of the sixties, when middle-class
English kids listened hard to African-American music, mostly elec-
trified blues, adapting a popular style in turn reexported to the States.
White American kids claimed this native-born music as their own
only after it was repackaged with a British accent. Bartram's view of
nature enthralled the Romantics, who in turn influenced the great
landscape designers, men such as Humphrey Repton and Joseph Paxton. Coleridge was inspired by Bartram to propose a utopian colony
on the Susquehanna, a society of equals he called Pantisocracy.
America has always entertained the dreams of utopians, from Coleridge to Koresh, and Ironhorse is their enfeebled descendant—
secularized, commercialized, deracinated.

The earliest parks, too, had a redemptive nub. In hopes of modi-
fying the effects of industrialization, the English gardeners created
public places with sporting fields and promenades among carefully
planted landscapes, with artificial lakes, hillocks, and mounds. Sometimes there was a fee for using the park—a green fee, as it were.

Olmsted is the bridge between Bartram's Florida, a world of fable and romance, and the landscape of golf.

Bartram saw and described scenes that read like passages from a landscaper's journal. Coming upon "a magnificent Indian mount," he followed

> a noble Indian highway, which led from the great mount, on a straight line, three quarters of a mile . . . terminated by palms and laurel magnolias, on the verge of an oblong artificial lake, which was on the edge of an extensive green level savanna. This grand highway was about fifty yards wide, sunk a little below the common level, and the earth thrown up on each side, making a bank of about two feet high. Neither nature nor art could any where present a more striking contrast, as you approached this savanna. The glittering water pond played on the sight, through the dark grove, like a brilliant diamond, on the bosom of the illuminated savanna, bordered with various flowery shrubs and plants; and as we advanced into the plains, the sight was agreeably relieved by a distant view of the forests, which partly environed the green expanse on the left hand, distant misty points of the surrounding forests, which projected into the plain, alternately appearing and disappearing, making a grand sweep round on the right, to the distant banks of the great lake.

Bartram saw a lot of "mounts" or mounds, "great tumuli" that spoke of the achievement of the ancestors of the "generous and true sons of liberty," the native Americans. Fifty years after Bartram's journey, settlers in the Midwest also came on earthworks of great size and power, like the enormous serpent mound in Ohio or the giant mounds at Cahokia, Illinois, but they refused to believe that ancestors of the native people whom the settlers had displaced under a banner of racial superiority could have created these great works. Bartram, no prisoner to racist hostility, accepted that the mounds he saw were built by ancient inhabitants of the region whose descendants he met.

> The pyramidal hills or artificial mounts, and highways, or avenues, leading from them to artificial lakes or ponds, vast tetragon terraces, chunk yards, and obelisks or pillars of wood, are the only monuments of labour, ingenuity and magnificence that I have seen worthy of notice, or remark . . . The mounts and cubical yards adjoining them, seem to have been raised in part for ornament and recreation, and likewise to serve some public purpose, since they are always so situated as to command the most extensive prospect over the town and country adjacent. The tetragon terraces seem to be the foundation of a fortress; and

perhaps the great pyramidal mounts, served the purpose of look out towers, and high places for sacrifice. The sunken area, called by white traders the chunk-yard, very likely served the same conveniency that it has been appropriated to, by the more modern and even present nations of Indians, that is, the place where they burnt and otherwise tortured the unhappy captives that were condemned to die; as the area is surrounded by a bank, and sometimes two of them, one behind and above the other, as seats, to accommodate the spectators at such tragical scenes, as well as the exhibition of games, shows, and dances.

The Cherokee played a game called *chungke* on these chunk yards, a sort of lacrosse. So golf was not the first game played in North America on fields prepared by moving earth. A piece of wood is called a "chunk," too, probably the true origin of the Robbinsvillians' use of "chunk" as a verb to describe what they do to keep the fires burning. But it's possible to suppose that for these North Carolinians, its roots reach to the chunk yards. When General Scott, following Andrew Jackson's orders, marched into the Smokies to deport the Cherokees, he built Fort Montgomery, where Robbinsville now sits. Fort Montgomery was built "on the Indians' ballground"—its chunk yard. At Ironhorse, the victims given up to flames are pines and palms, not men, but the fires burn hot and the ashes smolder, and another playground takes hold on the land.

As DUSK DESCENDS, Ironhorse looks like a Civil War battlefield after a long day of fighting. The noise of the fires crackling and the machinery tending them gives way to the peace of the evening as wisps of smoke rise from the embers. Ranger's pan operators—all "shorttimers," as Kevin calls them—scoot in a hurry at quitting time, but P&Jers tend to hang about at the end of the day, with the kind of patience that loneliness brings. Postell has his new wife with him out at Wildlife Safari, setting up housekeeping in a tiny nomadic bungalow, but most of the operators are batching it, billeted in motels. Rent on a mobile home pad is cheaper than a motel, but the quarters are close. Kevin lives in a trailer, too, even when he's home in West Palm. "You meet a nice class of people in trailer parks," he says. When Postell gets home, he sits in his patio chair, cooling down with a can of Bud, visiting with his temporary neighbors as if he's known them through three generations. His temperament is perfect for this life of casual association. One hundred percent.

11

Two Steps Forward, One Step Back

All this is, is a phone power business. He who screams the loudest gets the work.

—Bob Isakson

ALAN SHER CAME by Ironhorse almost every day, reaping images for his video chronicle, marveling at the transformation wrought by the heavy equipment, loitering and kibitzing and wondering aloud when Muss was going to perform his duty and hire Craig Shankland, Sher's choice as Ironhorse's golf pro. Sher would trail P&J's extirpating troops, squinting through the lens of the camera propped on his shoulder, recording sight and sound as trees shuddered and fell, narrating his excitement in exclamatory bursts. "Look at that tree! Smell that smoke! Whoa! Watch out for that big green thing!"

This was all new and delightful, even if the big show was no longer his to direct. For Muss, however, the clearing stirred no feeling. His companies had developed thousands of acres, built enough dwellings to house a good-sized city. Clearing was a dull preamble, quotidian, prosaic, a necessary shrug. "I only get emotionally involved," Muss said, "when the checks come in."

His dwindling toleration for Sher—whose easy communion with Ironhorse and pleasure in its transformation never wavered—was a measure of the seriousness with which Muss had staked his claim. Ironhorse was a chance to stretch his developer's legs, to soar above the starter market and loosen the purse strings of people who didn't have to worry about qualifying for an FHA loan. That Sher was still waiting for money—$2 million—was a subtext to Muss's grousing. The Ironhorse professionals had their hands out, too. It was February before the money spigot was finally turned back on.

The Water Control District hadn't yet sold any bonds when the clearing and excavating started, and the Gulfstream offering, aimed at raising $3,000,000 in equity, in the end attracted few takers and failed to float. The district had a letter of credit from Ironhorse equal to the bond sum and confidence that its bonds would, as always, find a ready market, so Pete Pimentel, its director, turned Ranger loose. Dash told Isakson that Wadsworth would need to sprig grass by July for Ironhorse to have any assurance that the course would grow in and be ready for play before the start of the next selling season. Muss was still hoping the course would be ready to play by August, but that prospect was fading if not gone. In the meantime, until he had all the financial elements in place, Muss was keeping expenses down, using what Isakson and Webber said was his time-honored method—aging accounts. Muss, Webber said, "never does things the conventional way if he can create a way he likes better."

Sher had hired good people for Ironhorse but tolerated a dilatory style uncongenial to Muss. It had taken forever, Bob Isakson said, to get things done, like the county approvals. "Alan paid everybody, too," Isakson said, frowning as he tidied the notes on his desk. "Josh doesn't pay, and he gets it all done. He's always been a believer, don't pay until it's all done the way you want." Isakson understood that rationale. Stay on the right side of the money. It was an axiom in the construction business that the general owned the subs he owed, especially if it was known that he was good for the money. Muss was definitely good pay, if an exacting ruler. The only person other than Sher unfazed by Muss's steely authority was Kenny Postell, who must have inherited from his bootlegging father whatever of his instinct for anarchy didn't just come naturally from growing up in the hills. Once he asked Muss, "You weren't named after old Uncle Josh, were you?" Muss no more knew what country music dobro player Postell was talking about than Postell could have dilated on the finer

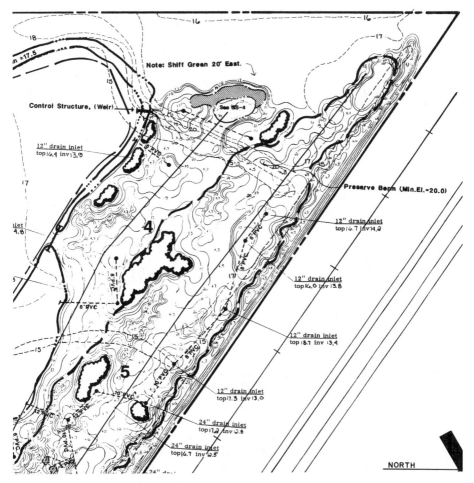

Detail of the grading and drainage plan. (*Courtesy Arthur Hills and Associates*)

points of equitation. They equally gave not a good goddamn what the
other thought of him and figured it was natural and good that no
messages crossed the borders between their worlds.

Hills had started calling Isakson about his bill in late November, but
didn't push it. Dash heard a rumor in January that unless some
remuneration passed their way soon the engineers were going to pull
their surveying crew, which was staking out the parcel boundaries,
off the job temporarily. "You move in a slow, precise, and careful
manner here," Dash observed to Isakson.

"Yes," he acknowledged, "we do."

"Is our check in the mail?" Dash pressed.

Isakson said he'd call D.C. "Art's worried about this more than I
am," Dash said.

Isakson, tired of playing the dunning target and passively angry
that Muss was keeping him in the dark about finances, suggested to
Hills that he get in touch with Muss directly if it was reliable information about money he was after. Isakson's stubborn loyalty to Muss
was not exactly obsequious, but he tolerated a lot of frustration.
"How can I get anything done if Muss won't look at anything I send
him?" Isakson would wonder. "Muss's got no more interest in this
job than the man in the moon." As Isakson headed out to Dallas for
a weekend of R and R in mid-January, he said, "I oughta just stay
home."

Would Muss try to talk him out of it if he did?

"Hell, no. He's too macho for that. Muss doesn't tell me anything
anymore," Isakson lamented. "I'm like Rodney Dangerfield."

The next time he came to Ironhorse on one of his infrequent,
usually unannounced visits, Muss complained to Isakson that Hills
had called him, and on a Saturday, no less, to ask for money. "That
pisses me off." If Hills refused to come on the job, Muss continued,
"we'll finish it ourselves—we can farm and garden it from this point."

Hills, Isakson said after Muss left, "has been owed twenty-two
thousand dollars plus interest since last May. Josh may be pissed, but
I told Art to do it. He shouldn't have to wait that long." But Isakson
didn't tell Muss that he was the instigator of Hills's weekend call.

Sher's fiscal style, like his reaction to the work commencing, had
been the opposite of Muss's. Not only had Sher always paid promptly,
he spent $23,000 to fix the outfall pump, which was useful in keep-
ing Ironhorse drained during construction but not an expense Muss
would have borne. Sher had kept the swimming pool at the ranch-

house in working order, even though no one lived there. Under the new regime its water cooked a scummy stew and the dark mosquito screen surrounding the pool was collapsing, torn from its frame by the accumulating weight of pine needles and palm fronds. Sher had installed an automatic gate opener at the entry, too, but like the pool it succumbed to abuse and neglect, and to get in or out a visitor had to park, walk to the hinged cattle gate, unwrap the chain, swing the metal gate open, get back in the car, drive through, then park and reverse the procedure. After Carrie Reese hauled the horses off, the gate was left open all day. When Muss first saw the opener he had laughed and said, "Alan sure knows how to spend money."

One of the paternal dictums Sher was fond of repeating, the sort of naive economic wisdom Muss found laughable, was "Spend a dollar to make a dollar." Sher courted the public, passed out *tchotchkes*, cruised the avenues of desire. He was a man of *fashion*, his whole being trained to sense style. Muss was more attuned to impersonal market forces, the stricter geometries of supply and demand. Sher preferred to tickle the coordinates of hope. He liked celebrations and partied on principle. Good times were his calling, the barometer of the possible. And of all the worlds available to him, in imagination, in memory, in dreams, none exceeded in its satisfactions what he had conjured at Ironhorse. Sher's was not an optimism easy to discourage. Still, that didn't keep Muss from trying.

Early in December, as Dave Webber and Matt Weeg were preparing to run the Gulfstream dog and pony show, Muss told Isakson to keep Sher and anyone else who might, according to his ample suspicions, muddle it, away from their presentation—but not before arranging to use the Sher family's two Range Rovers to drive the guests around. "He borrows the man's cars," Bobby Isakson said, "then doesn't want him there."

It was true that Sher was often stuck, even in the Rover, and would have to call for help on his cellular phone—*all* his cars had phones. He just couldn't subdue his affection for wandering over Ironhorse's inviting acres, especially if he could share the experience with a friend. Postell had to pull him out a time or two, and Isakson, in a venerable Jeep that Ironhorse, Ltd. bought from Muss, hauled Sher to dry ground now and then. Isakson, like Sher a patriot but without the Button King's cosmopolitan sensibility, appreciated the irony of basic Midwestern American iron—a venerable rig made in Toledo—pulling Sher's expensive and fashionable British buggy to safety.

Among the happy visitors on a Sher guided tour was Alan Dixon, the senior senator from Illinois and a friend since childhood of Ardus Sher's. They were both from Belleville. Dixon was a congressional friend of the MacArthur Foundation, proprietor of tens of thousands of Florida acres but, with headquarters in Chicago, a constituent of the senator. As they drove the course, Senator Dixon noted all the lakes, and another passenger said, "You'll need a lot of balls to play Ironhorse."

"If there's one thing a United States senator has," Dixon said, "it's lots of balls."

One Monday afternoon, as he was drawing a cup of water from the Deep Rock cooler in the kitchen—the well water that ran through the house pipes still pumped at a good volume but was no longer potable, and smelled of sulfur, fetid and vile, so drinking water was imported—Muss aimed his eyes around the corner and looked into the living room. "Isakson, you're a jerk."

Bobby, sitting at his desk, resting his elbows on its tidy top and herding the smoke from a Camel, looked up through his beefy hands in surprise and said, "What?"

"Why did you pull Sher out? I heard he got stuck again. Fuck him, he's a jerk. Let him call a tow truck. He's a three-year-old. I don't want him out here anymore."

The day before, Sunday, Sher had buried the Rover up to its axles showing a neighbor where, in six months or so, he'd want to aim his tee shot on the thirteenth hole. Sher was vague on the routing of the golf course, so when he called Isakson at home late in the afternoon, Sher guided Bob to a spot behind the ranch house, on the spoil pile from the old perimeter canal on the southern border, opposite the spot where the Solid Waste Authority planned to build its new headquarters. Isakson, master of every detail on land or paper, could have driven to the spot blindfolded. The cab of Isakson's Jeep was filled with combating odors, the sweet fragrance of an air freshener grappling with Camel smoke. And sometimes from Muss the scent of a cigar.

"I told Sher no more tours," Muss emphasized, as he and Isakson reviewed the clearing and excavation, just in case the railing from the kitchen hadn't sufficiently impaled Bobby on the point of his objection. "I don't want you to try to enforce it, Bobby," he said, softening, "but let me know. I'll talk to him."

Muss didn't want Sher taking up Isakson's time now that the

project manager finally had things to do, but he couldn't keep the limited partner away nor did he try. Sher organized fewer long lunches at Toojays—the distinguished local deli, caterer for the dog and pony show, purveyor of sandwiches whose vertical dimension slightly exceeded the opening capacity of the human mouth—for the crew that had sailed Ironhorse's ghost ship through the summer doldrums, but he was as convivially present as ever, and Isakson continued to treat him with respect.

Isakson's cycle of inconclusive stories, mostly illuminating the mysteries of construction in Chicago, had filled a lot of empty conversational space that summer, but were heard less frequently now. An occasional suburban cautionary tale, like the one about the homeowner who tied a rope around his waist and then anchored it to his car's bumper before climbing on his roof to clear it of snow, only to feel himself first tugged toward the eaves and then wrenched to the ground and then dragged, like a condemned Western outlaw, behind a bolting Chevrolet, screaming helplessly at his wife to *please* look in the rearview mirror, interrupted the construction cycle. What was most astonishing about Isakson's stories, apart from their oracular inconclusivity, was the accuracy with which their details were recalled. In another time, in a world without faxes and plastic folders, without copying machines and overnight mail, Isakson would have been Ironhorse's Homer, a guide to its scuffles and sorrows and the search for its tantalizing riches. He was instead the stalwart custodian of Muss's interests, his gifts of recall and stamina subservient to the routines of commerce. Details clung to Isakson like pox. He could never be rid of them. The tenacity of his memory comported well with his obstinacy. Where Muss had the reputation for juggling a thousand tasks, Isakson clamped down on a few and chewed them to death.

Sher, on the other hand, with his already marginal authority diminishing, made controlling the selection of the golf pro, the choice of the perfect person to teach Ironhorse's members the fine points of the swing, his winter obsession. That's why he was pestering Muss about Shankland, but the Button King's campaign to hire the golf pro sputtered from the start. Shankland, who had introduced Sher to Hills and was part of the team Muss agreed to inherit when he took over Ironhorse, proved a reluctant recruit.

Scheduled to start as the Director of Golf on January 1, 1989, Shankland canceled a meeting with Muss at the last minute in late

November so he could give an emergency lesson to an important client—rumor had it the pupil was a famous touring pro. This did not sit well with Muss, and embarrassed Sher, who recovered by telling everyone that the urgency of the lesson proved what a great teacher and how much in demand Shankland was. Muss by this time had his own candidate, Dick Lanscioni, the pro from his old club in Chicago, Green Acres. Muss told Ironhorse's lawyer, Mike Gordon, in a jesting tone but without quite enough frivolity to undercut its message, "I don't care if Sher ever gets his money—he's not getting it until he approves Lanscioni as the head pro."

Isakson relayed the message to Sher that he'd better have Shankland at Ironhorse on December fifth or Muss would hire Lanscioni on the sixth. Sher laughed, and in good humor replied, "The pro's mine. Josh knows that."

But when Shankland turned the job down flat Sher started an elaborate flanking maneuver to maintain the fiction that his opinions on the subject of the pro still mattered. His *real* first choice as pro, he said, had been a fellow at PGA National, "a friend of mine and the guy I wanted all along. But I figured it's better not to deal with a friend."

The unspoken implication was that Shankland, whose decision puzzled Sher—how could anyone turn down an invitation to direct Camp Paradise?—was *not* a friend. Sher's *real* choice—albeit the second chronologically—turned the job down, too, but not before recommending a young pro from Arizona, whose candidacy Sher then briefly sponsored. Sher also ran an ad in the *PGA* Magazine, and while many replied, none were chosen—there was plenty of talent, Sher was certain, to pluck off the grapevine. He'd rather depend on his friends. Then the pro from Arizona, leveraging Ironhorse's interest into a better deal where he was, declined even to interview. "That's it," Dave Webber said. "We're hiring Lanscioni."

He called Sher to tell him about the latest hitch.

"As your sole advocate here," Webber told Sher right before Christmas, "I've got to tell you we've got to get this settled. I'm your ally, but I'm getting pressure."

"Just trust me on this," Sher replied, turning up his salesman's amps. "Do you trust me? Trust me on this. I'm a club man, I know people, let me do this. Muss knows money, development, but he's not a club man."

While they were struggling over who would teach golf at Ironhorse, Muss and Sher agreed that Don Reese, Sher's son-in-law, would carry the banner as Ironhorse's *touring* pro. A couple of weeks before, Reese had finished third in qualifying for the right to play on the PGA Tour, shooting a sixty-one in the fourth round at La Quinta to guarantee his spot. Webber and Matt Weeg didn't think that Ironhorse's sponsorship of a touring pro would carry much marketing muscle, but Muss approved a request to help pay Reese's expenses, which on the Tour can run to $60,000 for a year's travel and lodging. Reese's golf bag would bear the Ironhorse logo.

During a hectic month for Reese, he won a pro-am at Bonita Bay, earned his Tour card, and got his walking papers from his wife. She was glad he got his card, Carrie said, so people wouldn't say she was leaving him because he was a loser and he wouldn't have personal bad news compounding the burden of a stalled career. They remained friends. Reese still came to the Shers' parties. Carrie soon moved into a house just a couple of miles west of Ironhorse, one with sufficient grounds for Honey, Charlie, and The Colonel to graze away in contented retirement. Reese sought solace in the grinding solitude of a life on the road and a chance at fame and glory. He was thirty-four and had never swung better.

The issue of Ironhorse's teaching pro simmered. Alan, convinced the choice was his, shrugged off the disappointment of three failed candidates and nominated a fourth, Brett Upper, a thirty-year-old native of Pennsylvania with several solid years of play on the PGA Tour under his belt. Upper was living near Orlando, working as a club pro. Alan invited him to Ironhorse in early January. This was not an "official" visit, but rather a casual invitation from Sher so he could meet Upper. Muss happened by, but completely ignored both Sher and Upper, who were talking to Isakson in his living room office. "Let's look at the site," Muss told Isakson, not even acknowledging Sher and Upper's presence, and walked out. Walking past his blue Ferrari 328 GTS—Muss could match Sher valve for valve, wheel for wheel, when it came to extravagant transportation—Muss climbed into Isakson's Jeep. Sher was flabbergasted. His face flushed, but he didn't move. Isakson thought Muss was punishing Sher for calling him every day about money. "Nobody," Isakson said, "can give a cold shoulder like Josh."

Rebounding from Muss's snub, Sher introduced Upper to Weeg and to Webber, who claimed he was still playing the role of Sher's "sole advocate" in this odd drama. Weeg liked Upper, but as he said later, when it comes to the choice of pro, "I really don't care. All I want is somebody who'll come with a cart and a smile on his face to drive my potential buyer around the course and show it off. I think Upper would do that. I'm not sure Dick Lanscioni would. Maybe he's too old to want to do that. So in that sense, I like Upper best."

Encouraged by Weeg's reaction, Sher asked Muss to meet with Upper in late January. Muss told Sher he thought Upper was too young. (Dash, who had met and played with Upper in Orlando, was surprised to learn that he was *only* thirty. "He's so solid and straight," Dash said, "he acts older.") Sher said, "Josh, what if someone had a chance to hire you when you were thirty, or if I'd have had a chance to hire me? Would we get a good man? Josh," he told him, "we need to have a younger man here."

A week after this conversation, Lanscioni, who like a lot of Midwestern golf pros spent his winters in Florida—he had a condo in Tequesta—pulled his waxed and tidy blue-striped van to a stop in front of the office. Graying and trim, he had a quiet and easy manner and a soft voice and a wardrobe that ran to pastels. A native Californian, he liked to draw as well as teach golf and had invented, patented, and unsuccessfully marketed a golf glove whose original feature was a little pouch on the back that carried a ball marker. Lanscioni's children were all nearly grown—one was still in high school—and he was ready to live in Florida year round. He felt comfortable at a place like Ironhorse, whose members, he assumed, would act pretty much as the members did at Green Acres. He got on well with Muss. Even Sher admitted after they met that Lanscioni was a pretty terrific candidate. But, he told Ardus, "I'm sticking to my guns. I still have veto. You can appreciate Muss's loyalty, but we need a younger guy. Muss says he's not gonna have anybody thirty years old. Upper's fresh, he's young, he's full of ideas."

Lanscioni was actually ten years younger than Sher, whose energy had summoned Ironhorse to life, but that irony was lost on the Button King. His turf had so diminished he could barely stand. Attenuated, embarrassed by Shankland's rebuff, this prince of the youthful spirit, gregarious, glib, and generous, was fighting a rearguard action. Muss was marching forward, and he'd found a good man, besides. Even Sher knew it, but wasn't yet ready to sue for peace. Just before Upper drove down with his wife for a formal interview with Muss in late January, Weeg said, "I hope Josh hires the pro pretty soon, 'cause Alan's driving me nuts with all this bullshit about young pro *versus* old pro.''

WHILE THE DISCORD over the pro stewed, the real work at Ironhorse proceeded. Ranger was steadily excavating, struggling with longer and longer runs and getting the perimeter berms ready for the tree spades. Ironhorse, along with the lands of the Solid Waste Authority, was annexed to West Palm Beach over the protestations of Riviera Beach. The services of neither city were particularly convenient, but West Palm was at least vaguely contiguous, as Ironhorse adjoined that city's water catchment basin. "Our main priority" in annexing Ironhorse, West Palm's mayor said, "is to protect the water catchment area. If we don't have control over that area, we have potentially disastrous scenarios."

Riviera Beach, saying it had spent a million dollars acquiring a water company after Ironhorse had requested services in 1985, threatened to sue. "Cities like mine are at a disadvantage," complained Riviera Beach's city manager. "My city is seventy percent black and low income." Without the tax base communities like Ironhorse provide, he continued, Riviera Beach would "be doomed to be that kind of city forever."

"West Palm Beach," one of West Palm's commissioners loftily replied, "has not conspired to cause anyone harm."

"It looks that way," was Riviera Beach's reply.

To connect itself to West Palm, Ironhorse would have to run a sewer line nearly seven miles long to a treatment plant. Getting it built and getting water supplied were two more small headaches for Isakson to order in his triage of Ironhorse's tasks. He had roads to build and a clubhouse to erect, and, in case anyone forgot, Ironhorse was still waiting for a permit from South Florida to build a golf course. "Our problems are with the bank, not permits," Webber said, summing up his view of the delays, but money was not in Isakson's purview, so he fussed over the permit. He tried to leave the supervision of the field details to Jon Harpman, but wasn't always confident that his assistant's nose was staying quite close enough to the ground. Harpman preferred to survey the work from the comfort of his air-conditioned Bronco, even if he did complain to Isakson, "I'm tired of being a walkie-talkie."

"What do you mean?"

"I go out into the field and walkie, and then come back to you and talkie. That's not exactly responsibility."

This was a month after Muss, cruising the site with Isakson, saw his nephew driving by. "Why isn't Jon walking," he asked.

"It's a lot quicker to drive," Isakson replied.

"Yeah," Muss said, riding, "but you can't see anything."

Another small worry for Isakson was the smoke fairy. In early January the fire marshal told P&J to douse its fires when a layer of smoke blew across the Beeline. Responding to a complaint, the marshal counted ten smoking fires at Ironhorse and told Isakson each one would cost him $500. Bobby assayed as how it was impossible to tell which fire actually contributed the offending smoke, why didn't he just assume there was a single culprit, consolidate the charges, and hold the fine to $500? The fire marshal said that seeing as how this was a first offense he reckoned he could. An "assistant," as Bobby called him, who'd been sitting in the truck while this discussion was going on, sauntered over to Isakson after the deal was struck and said, "Since we got the fine down to five hundred bucks, don't you think you could top it off with a bottle of Jack Daniels?"

"If you need a drink that bad," Bobby said, giving him a hard stare and remembering his building days in Chicago, where gratuities to officials were *de rigueur* and the first thing an apprentice learned was how to point out the liquor cache for the building inspector, "I'll get you a case."

A health inspector came by the next week to discuss burning. He wanted only two burn piles per machine, he said, so they could chunk the fires faster, keep them hotter, and improve their defense against escaped flames. No more green material, he said. Call for inspection before igniting. No more blanket permission to burn, either. Breaking up the offending fires on the previous Friday, scattering the smoldering trunks and covering them with dirt, was an affront to P&J's clearing decorum. "It was spread out like a week's washing," Charles Best said, giving his head a slow, sorrowful shake.

Postell had a tactic to circumvent the required ratio of machines to fires. For the four fires burning on the lake by the fourteenth hole, in the southeast corner, Kenny had Best chunking in a D8 with a D6 parked nearby. "I got a machine for every two fires," Postell observed. Best said if the smoke fairy asked him to put out a fire, he'd say, "Here's the dozer, have at it," and climb down. "They ain't any of 'em wants to climb up there."

A second ploy to outflank officialdom was burning on the weekends or a holiday. When Postell looked to the west and saw great clouds of smoke billowing up from cane-field fires, while he was nicked for smoke not much worse than the air on a still day, the injustice offended him. "You're all following the same rules," the fire marshal told him, but nobody believed that a little old clearing outfit like P&J was under the same regime as the subsidized sugar barons, who sweetened the Palm Beach economy with their annual millions. Postell resented the assumption that he was fool enough to swallow that line more than having to put the fires out.

The holiday to commemorate Martin Luther King's birthday provided a convenient opportunity to light up. Fires ringed the site, a mock celebration. Once a Ranger employee asked what the superintendent, John Riley, thought about him taking off on King's birthday. "We don't take Washington's birthday off, we don't take Lincoln's birthday off," Riley replied, "so if you take Martin Luther King's birthday off, take Tuesday off, and Wednesday off, and while you're at it Thursday and Friday, 'cause you ain't gonna have a job anymore."

At Dasher's request Ranger was pushing the topsoil aside so something better suited for growing grass on than the shell and marl coming out of the lakes would be on hand for Wadsworth to use in the final shaping. "They ought to pump that stuff," Dash said, watching a DJB dump truck's load slosh the goo it was hauling over its sides as it headed for the perimeter berm. The fill looked like wet concrete and dried almost as hard. It took a lot longer to dry than concrete, though, and was almost impossible to drive over as long as it was wet.

The good soil at Ironhorse was mostly right on top of the ground, so to stockpile it Riley had a D8 Cat blade off the tops of the lakes and the golf course corridors, piling the soil along the edges of the housing parcels. After filling and rough-shaping the golf course, the Cat could push the good material in a thin layer over the contours of the new topography. It was a technique Ranger had used to build the courses at PGA National. A good golf course superintendent could grow grass in a basement, but it was nice to have decent soil to work with, and easier on the golfers, too, who wouldn't have to contend with bruising their clubs on a concretelike surface hidden below the concealing grass. There was also good material in the lakes, Riley said, a nice clean sand buried so deep that when they reached it, it was time to stop digging.

P&J was pushing hard to finish the golf clearing. It had been un-

usually hot all winter, with daytime temperatures in January aver-
aging eighty degrees, so the burn piles were drying fast. Not fast
enough, however, for Postell. "I hate this golf course clearing," he
said. "Too picky. I'd like to get a few thousand acres and just knock
it down."

P&J HADN'T BEEN quite picky enough, though. Just north of the first
hole, in one of the wettest spots at Ironhorse, they cleared a cypress
hammock, small trees but healthy, a sturdy native counterpoint to
the Australian pines on the other side of the seepage canal, near the
site of the future second tee. When the engineer Howard Searcy had
negotiated the dimensions of the preserve with Debbie Goss, an environmentalist from South Florida, he agreed to jog its boundary to
include this hammock, which would otherwise have been in a housing parcel. They had walked the land together the previous July,
reviewing the plans for wetland mitigation. Peter Aquart, whose firm
worked out the details of Ironhorse's water-management plan and
was handling all its civil engineering, explained that no one had the
right to fill or drain wetlands. "Many developers think all you have
to do is mitigate," Aquart said, "but that's not how it works. What
they're really saying is, 'If we decide to let you fill, then you *must*
mitigate.' "
   Goss and Searcy worked together on the details of Ironhorse's
mitigation plan. "Mitigation" is not exactly a euphemism in this
context, but its use here gives a twist to its meaning. "Lightening the
burden of an evil of any kind," reads an *Oxford English Dictionary*
definition of "mitigate." As it's used in the context of the choreographed dance of development, "mitigate" is a neutral word, in the
technical lexicon taken to mean simply the trade-off of one good
thing for another. Give me an acre here, I'll mitigate you one there.
Fill that marsh, but mitigate me one to replace it. The inadvertent
eradication of the thirty-odd cypress trees required something closer
to mitigation in the old-fashioned sense. Knocking down those trees
was, if not an evil, at least not a good idea, and it was up to Searcy
to figure out how to lessen the burden of having done it.

THE ARMY CORPS OF ENGINEERS, which claimed jurisdiction over Ironhorse's shrinking wetlands, had issued a permit in May for a project

that "consists of placement of fill material over 47.2 acres of wetlands for the construction of a residential development known as Iron-horse." Having decided to allow Ironhorse to fill, the Corps—pursuing the logic Aquart had explained—then *required* that it "create a 10-foot-wide fringe along lake shorelines covering a total of 4.36 acres, create 6.38 acres of marsh"—that is, the littoral zones that Ranger was excavating, shallow flats extending from the deeper lakes—"and preserve and enhance a 54 acre buffer between the development and the Water Catchment Area."

The preserve boundary as approved by the Corps was not fully comprehended for some time in Hills's Toledo office, a failure that precipitated a couple of minor episodes of finger pointing, but the berm was clearly expressed on all the construction drawings for the "Bondable Water Management Facility," that is, Ironhorse's lakes, all of them, as Aquart said, "a function in the final analysis of the desire to build a golf course." The error in knocking down the cypress hammock was innocent, apart from the fact that cypresses in general are protected. No one was trying to get away with anything, but it aroused a suspicion of bad faith that plagued Debbie Goss when, six months later, she saw further despoilation of the preserve. P&J was just trying to get down the road.

Ranger was building the berm separating the preserve from the golf course as part of its contract with the Water Control District. All the land on the western side of the berm, including the golf holes, would belong to the district. The berm was designed with a plastic liner to serve as a kind of head wall to keep water in the preserve. Hills's office was slow to grasp this feature of the water-management plan, partly because it was hard to take seriously the inviolability of a preserve boundary when you knew there were half a dozen golf features in it.

From its origins on the north side of the property, just in front of the fifth tee, the berm would run along the edge of the old seepage canal, but at a point just north of the unfortunate cypress hammock it was supposed to turn abruptly east and loop around the trees. The old canal ran on south, down past where the first hole would go, then above the driving range and just below the tenth and eleventh greens, two more golf features countenanced in the preserve. It continued on clear over to the apple-snail pond adjacent to the twelfth tee—by this time running well within the preserve boundary and far from any golf construction—but the berm was going to bump below the canal in an arc that gathered about an acre, resume running parallel to the canal until it was past the eleventh green, then head south to form a boundary between the preserve and a large housing parcel.

When the chief of the Regulatory Division of the Corps issued Ironhorse's permit in May, his cover letter emphasized, in words underlined and typed in caps, carefully centered on the page just above his signature,

IT IS NOT LAWFUL TO DEVIATE FROM
THE APPROVED PLANS ENCLOSED.

The cypress trees were protected on the approved plans, but other trees along the line of the berm had to make way in order to build it. The grading plan Hills's office sent down from Toledo—a copy of which had been included in the bid package, each page stamped, in bright-red letters, BIDDERS COPY NOT FOR CONSTRUCTION—did not show the preserve boundary at all, one of several ways the golf course drawings deviated from the engineer's plans. Until P&J rolled over the cypress trees, the only effect of these discrepancies was on Bob Isakson's peace of mind. He professed "real shock" at discovering that none of the golf course drawings reflected the engineer's treatment of the berm, but then Ironhorse was the first golf course he'd ramrodded. He was accustomed to the stricter correspondence one expects between plans and product in, for example, building apartment houses.

When he discovered the problem, Isakson's first call was to Searcy, who in turn contacted the South Florida Water Management District and the Water Control District to see what they could do to recover, to mitigate. Muss wondered briefly, now that the damage was done, whether they couldn't just add the cleared ground to the housing parcels, but Isakson said that would open a can of worms he'd just as soon leave to wiggle in darkness. He'd rather avoid a review of the extent to which the golf course availed itself of the preserve.

"There was just one row of stakes out there," Kenny Postell said by way of exculpation, "and we've been clearing thirty-five feet on either side of the stake. Ranger or somebody fucked up. I've been doing this right-of-way work for fifteen years, and they always stake out the clearing for us."

More likely the operator had been following the old seepage canal, which was coterminous with much of the berm, and stopped looking for stakes. Isakson was past caring whose fault it was, he just wanted it fixed. Even the tiniest dangling detail bored into Isakson's serenity. This accidental clearing was an ache he was determined to cure.

Isakson asked Postell if there were any stumps left. "There ain't gonna be any trees grow up there if that's what you're thinking," Postell replied with a lame laugh.

"Last March," Isakson finished his thought, "back there by the twelfth tee, where a couple of cypresses were pushed over, there were small shoots coming off the trunks. Searcy remarked on that."

"Well, that ain't gonna be the case here. We got that all grubbed out. Only thing gonna be coming off those trunks is smoke."

The solution was simple, eased into place by Ironhorse's prompt attention. South Florida didn't even send anyone to look. Searcy arranged for Ranger, whose tree spades had finally started colonizing the tops of the perimeter berm—not to be confused with the *preservation* berm—to transplant cypresses to the desolated ground. As long as the trees were moved before the middle of March they would survive. Ranger would also transplant, on instructions from Hills, small groups of cypresses along the fringes of four lakes—by the fourth tee, behind the third green, and near the sixth and ninth greens.

These trees had a remarkable effect on the lakes and the golf course, like adding a painted backdrop to a stage. The lakes are to a golf course what windows are to a building's exterior, a flat reflective surface that casts no shadows but gathers up the images of the trees and the sky and tosses them back up to the eye. The cypresses looked, from the moment the tree spade tucked them onto the lake edge, as if they had grown there from seed. The land around them was shaking and quaking in the agonies of its transformation, but the elegant cypresses looked undisturbed, anchoring their domain, untroubled by the turmoil around them. They were as contrived as the berms and the lakes, as the trees marching on the crest of the berms, as the greens and tees and traps and grass, all of which would, in the long run, echo the cypresses' tranquillity and share in its deceptions. That was the art of building a golf course, a product of the learning and intuition that guided Hills's choice in placing the transplanted trees. As long as the fairways were gray with dust and mud and the greens shapeless mounds, as long as the lakes were sterile containers, it was the cypresses alone that gave to the golf course the illusion of nature, sturdy and perdurable.

Dash thought there was something about the cypresses that acted as a natural algicide. "It turns [the lake] that Coca-Cola color. It's kinda long-range, I think. Like thirty years." As the litter of a cypress decomposes, organic acids stain the water around it a characteristic reddish brown. Chlorophyll-producing phytoplankton can't flourish in the dark water, so in that way Dash is right, but the cypress does not, in the manner of the Australian pines, produce a phytotoxin to actually kill the algae.

Except for the cypresses by the sixth green, later suffocated by fill dumped around their trunks, the trees Ranger transplanted would survive at a high rate—even those eventually sent in to replace their accidentally eradicated cousins in the preserve. Still, the replacements looked forlorn standing in the open, an odd contrast to the assimilated effect of the lakeside trees.

With the cypress problem solved, Isakson had only the tree planting on the perimeter berm to worry about—*and* getting his permit to build the golf course so that as soon as Ranger was ready Wadsworth could start drainage and installation of the irrigation system and the fine-shaping of the golf course. The actual *use* of the water was yet another permit, one the Water *Control* District had to solicit from the Water *Management* District.

Isakson had a clubhouse to build, too, but that was straightforward, with prints that told the tradesmen exactly what to do. He wasn't worried about the clubhouse. He knew how to build *buildings*. The golf course was more loosely conceived, a child as much of "field adjustments" as of planning, of Hills's "arm waving," as Isakson saw it. Isakson preferred certainties over improvisations, and, until Hills and Dasher began to suggest improvements to the golf course that were nowhere to be seen on any drawing, aimed his discontent at Jay Bridge, the landscape architect with Urban Design Studio in charge of the plantings on the perimeter berm. Isakson called him in for a consultation in the middle of January, soon after the tree spades made their first stab at rearranging Ironhorse's still luxuriant flora.

12

The Ever Popular Field Adjustment

Four days before Christmas, in the early afternoon, Hills had come for his first look at Ironhorse's clearing. He, Jon Harpman, and Bob Isakson met at the third green, not far from the old entry gate. Two pairs of Ranger's screaming green scrapers were shaping the shallow outlines of the lakes on either side of the third green. Ranger's digging had so far created only the hint of a lake, a barely perceptible depression, but a surprisingly large volume of dirt along the northern perimeter was its consequence. The excavated dirt fluffed up, as if proud to be above ground at last, but rain and heavy equipment trampling over it would compact the soil.

Hills, in chinos and a madras shirt, white dollops of sunscreen drying on his nose, unfolded the drawing he'd had tucked under his arm to study the formal proximity of the third hole to the lakes, the parcels, and the fourth tee. He wanted at least one hundred feet from the center point of the third green to the parcel property line south of it. "Even a hundred and fifty feet is narrow," he said. Hills wondered, too, if they couldn't move the fourth tee ten feet north, along the lake edge, and while doing that also push the adjacent fifth green thirty to forty feet farther north, closer to the perimeter berm. Then a slight reconfiguration of the lake edge would create a little maneuvering

229

room for the third green . . . Jon Harpman was scribbling notes as Hills spoke. When Hills suggested reshaping the lake, Isakson whispered to Harpman, "That's a fucking change order, you know."

What for Hills is merely a simple instance of the ever popular field adjustment is an assault on Isakson's highly developed sense of order. "I'll tell you how I feel about changes after being at this place for nine months," Isakson had said a couple of days before. "Like I told Webber when he started talking about moving the housing parcels a little bit. Art Hills and Webber and everybody's had plenty of time to think about changes and now that we're moving dirt I don't want any messing with plans."

The first 180 yards or so of the fourth hole skirt the edge of the larger and most westerly of the two lakes the scrapers are digging. Then the fairway doglegs back to the right along the stand of trees that caught on fire the weekend I was in Orlando with Dash. Many of these trees surely will die, but Hills notes them only in passing. He's focused on the routing and the clearing, the fit of the tees and greens. The fourth green, playing to the west, is in the preserve, with a beautiful backdrop of Sabal palms. Hills wants to shift it just a little east, shortening by a few meaningless yards what looks as if it will be a long and difficult par four.

"This is a good place for a low-profile green," Hills said, looking at the palms rising like a wall behind the green. He also thought a wide, flat bunker behind it would keep balls from bouncing off its sloped side into the trees.

The wind blew smoke in a low tumble across the fifth fairway from fires on the eighth and ninth holes. The burned trees separating the fourth and fifth holes looked forlorn, the huddled remnant of a stand of pines and palms that once spanned more than 500 feet, but Hills wanted still more clearing to assure an adequate landing space for drives off the fifth tee. "We need to take out that nearest palm," Hills pointed out to Harpman, "and these pines on the left."

The perimeter berm Ranger was building along the left side of the fifth fairway had a uniformity about it that worried Hills. Ranger has to make the berm flat enough for the tree spades to work along its crest, but Hills wants the top to undulate and the slopes toward the fairway to fall away from the crown with the indifference of eroded hills. An engineered perfection, Hills thinks, is fatal to his aesthetic. His goal is a mock-tectonics, an artful, miniaturized geology, a way to trick the eye into believing that the thrusts and billows of the earth's

A lake cut. (*Illustration by Michael Strantz*)

restless crust conspired in these shapes, scouring ice and desolating floods or windstorms and deluges. Something orogenic, but in scale. The biggest design problem is figuring out how to soften the edges, create rolls, imitate the angle of repose. Manufacturing these touches with earth-moving equipment, which is designed for sharp angles and uniform surfaces, is like slicing roast beef with a chain saw.

"When you're on the tee," Hills explained to Harpman, "we like you to see face and shadow—not in an orderly rhythm but in an irregular way."

Dash had left a lot of trees on the sixth hole on his last visit, creating a narrow clearing through tall pines about 300 yards off the tee. One side would have to yield for an adequate playing corridor, which meant that P&J would be back on this fairway for another clearing pass. Hills, walking back and forth to sight down the line of play, moved the clearing line out to the left. The print showed the sixth fairway protected along its entire right side by an open canal connecting the lake by the ninth tee—the same lake that is *behind* the third hole—to the lake by the sixth green. Hills wanted water in play in front of the sixth green and hoped he could pull the littoral zone of the lake around enough to give pause to any player bold enough to go for the green in two.

Five and six, the consecutive par fives, play in the same easterly direction. The perimeter berm flanks their left sides, well beyond the fairways and out of play but sufficiently massive, given the scale of the landscape, to loom. The holes are of roughly similar lengths—506 yards for five and 526 yards for six were the designed yardages at this stage in Ironhorse's evolution. Varying their difficulty was Hills's solution to the problem of differentiation. Five was very straight-ahead, with nary a kink in the fairway. In the earliest drawings, Hills had placed a couple of fairway bunkers on the right side at the landing area, but by clearing fewer trees he could tighten the target from the tee without building bunkers. Eliminating them lightened the architect's touch by preserving an existing feature, a choice Hills always preferred. At Ironhorse, about the only natural feature he had to work with, he said, was the trees. Ironhorse needed few bunkers anyway, Hills decided, and discarding the fairway bunkers left the fifth hole with only a couple of target bunkers about sixty yards short of the green. Keeping them well away from the green would create an illusion for a player standing 200 or so yards away, compressing foreground and background to make the green appear nearer than it actually was, the sort of camouflaging trick Alister Mackenzie favored. Bunkering is a powerful weapon in the golf course architect's arsenal, one Hills had chosen at Ironhorse, again in imitation of Mackenzie, to use sparingly. "All bunkers are eliminated," Mackenzie had once written to Herb Graffis, "that do not add materially to the pleasure of my courses. As my courses have only a quarter of the usual number of sand traps, the cost of maintenance is correspondingly reduced."

These holes play into the prevailing wind, which blows off the ocean, but even in a breeze five will be reachable in two shots. By making its green small and elevated—a tiny mesa, almost flat, especially compared to the dramatic slopes of some of the greens on Ironhorse's back nine—Hills made it strategically more sensible for a player to lay up either just in front of or just over those foreshortened fairway bunkers with his second shot and then lay a wedge shot up on the small green. The green will crown at the center and run off gently to either side, contours which effectively eliminate cupping areas from its heart and shrink the available targets. Its crown turns what was already a small green into two vest pockets. A player who aims at the center of the green risks catching the slope running away from the cupped side, while a bolder player who misses or flies over the green will end up in tall rough. The rough also discourages attempts to bomb the green from a long distance. Mackenzie abhorred rough. "No rough," he said, "no lost balls." Hills used a lot of artifice to make what is essentially a straight, not very long par five into a hole that at least *looks* hard.

I THOUGHT THE biggest problem with five was that its commodious fairway offered too inviting an alternative route for playing the *fourth* hole. Played as designed, four was going to require a very difficult drive over water. A player trying to avoid the lake risked hitting into the burned forest. As I surveyed the clearing on four and five, I thought the best place to aim one's tee shot on four was down the *fifth* fairway. Robert Hunter pointed out in *The Links* seventy years ago that at the Old Course at St. Andrews, "play to the seventeenth is often safest along the fairway of the second, and nearly all the canny golfers will use the fairway of the fifth when playing their second shots to the fourteenth. Play to the superb eleventh is across the fairway of the seventh."

But just as there are ancient precedents for finding routes the designer didn't intend, the architect has remedies, the simplest among them planting a tree or two near the tee, cutting off the angle like a hockey goalie coming out of the crease to smother an attack. Hills thought that's what he'd do at the fourth tee.

Playing the fourth hole down the fifth fairway will put players coming up five at risk of walking—or, more likely, given the ubiquity of golf carts—*riding* right into a tee shot. Courtesy might suggest not playing the hole this way, but while golfers in general adhere to the game's rules with the rigid devotion of penitents, righteously adding a stroke to their scores when detecting a movement of the ball no one else has seen, there is no dishonor in seeking an advantage—acting cannily—within the rules. Unless Ironhorse pitifully evaded this problem by declaring the fifth fairway *out of bounds* for players on the fourth hole—an admission that there really wasn't room on the course to *play golf*—people would go that way, either on purpose or because of a bad slice. Mounding between the holes, which the plan called for, was not going to provide sufficient separation.

There was a lot more room around the sixth green than the fifth, and as it was truly a three-shot hole for most players, Hills made its green larger. The third shot would come from farther away and therefore deserved a larger target. The fifth green had an area of 4,250 square feet, while the sixth green was a third again as large at 6,125 square feet. The sixth green was also much deeper than the fifth, and that, too, could make the hole longer. The sixth green was tucked tightly against the edge of a lake—Hills had cypresses transplanted there—and sloped toward the water. Unlike the fifth hole, which was on a dead straight line from tee to green, the sixth hole doglegged slightly to the right. The first two shots were straight, but the angle of the third shot depended entirely on the length and direction of the second. The lake guarded the right side, but there was a lot of room out to the left. A bunker on the left side well away from the green was a target more than a hazard, while a smaller bunker protected the green's front left side. Hills had set up at six what golf architects like to call a "risk-reward situation." If the water on the right made you swallow hard and bail out to the left, there was plenty of landing room and very little trouble.

There will be mounding on that side, but no severe stances, no difficulty with the ball above or below your feet, unless the shot is pulled well left, up into the berm. The green will slope *away* from the left side, making it very hard to hit a ball from that angle that won't roll toward the lake. At the same time, that innocuous little bunker will forestall a run-up shot. Those are among the choices—the "strategy," as golf architects like to say—Hills has fused into the design of the sixth hole. At this stage, though, it's all still theoretical. Ranger has yet to start the big lake—the one Isakson will take to calling "Kennicott" because without water, in its pumped-dry construction phase, it will look like a refugee from Montana, a gaping mining pit torn to the depths for mineral riches—along which this sixth green sits and on whose opposite shore the seventh green will beckon, across 200 and more aqueous yards.

JAY BRIDGE FROM Urban Design joined Hills and Isakson on the eighth tee. Bridge is slender, with thinning reddish-blond hair and an abrupt style of speech, like someone perpetually late hurrying to catch up. He smokes nervously—unlike Isakson, whose habit has a contemplative, grave, and considered quality about it, as if it's not an addiction but a ritual—and sometimes in his eagerness to speak Bridge takes such a quick drag on his cigarette that it makes a slight popping noise, like a feigned kiss, when he jerks it from his lips. He'd been looking for donor areas that day, especially places that could contribute pines to the perimeter berm. Isakson wanted the tree spades to harvest from the lakes and roads and try to avoid the parcels. He wanted to keep the house lots as intact as possible. Muss planned to let the builders bring in their own fill, too, rather than build the lots up to a specified grade, and that would save trees. P&J had held off clearing the eighteenth fairway, which was thick with donor plants.

"Those pines are all dead," Bridge said, pointing in the direction of trees that Ranger's scrapers had rolled near. Dash had already told Harpman to wrap surveyor's tape out to the driplines of the trees he wanted to save near the greens and tees. Between the fourth tee and the fifth green and behind the eighth green, lime-colored ribbons wrapped around the pines like a parody of Christo. Bridge started to tell Hills how to protect the pines.

"We've only done it on fifty courses," Hills said, cutting off Bridge's tutorial. "I know you don't water or fertilize pines."

"What I'm worried about is them ending up in the low spots after the course is graded," Bridge emphasized.

"We know what we're doing," Hills assured him, and headed on down the fairway, looking at the trees between the eighth and ninth holes. "We can make sort of a sunken garden here," he told Isakson, as if in refutation of Bridge's fear. None of the surviving grades, Hills knew, were within two feet of the lake elevations, which meant that Wadsworth could—planned to, in fact—drain any of them with the simple installation of a pipe or two. Hills's office had prepared a drainage plan for Wadsworth to follow, showing all the low spots and the locations of drainage basins. Hills, who knew nothing was more important to the quality of a golf course than good drainage, was plainly offended by Bridge's style. Isakson wasn't happy with Bridge either.

Hills took most of two days to review the course and was generally pleased with what he saw. Most of his clearing suggestions were minor. A two-page letter a few days later summed up what he'd seen. He wanted a little more clearing by the eighth tee and the green a little lower than what his plans showed at nine, and he was worried about the lake by the practice range. "Most of the lakes are pretty tightly located," he had said, "and if they move them thirty or forty feet it really screws up things."

When he spoke, Hills had no way of knowing that the lake by the practice range was going to double in size in an effort to find enough dirt to finish grading the golf course. Hills also admired the tall pines at the clubhouse site and wished there was a way to save them. "We've got a clubhouse at The Wilderness," he told Isakson, "that we set in among native material, and it almost all survived—and the people who bought there recognized a kind of low-keyed elegance, a comfort level that doesn't require contrived plantings."

"We don't want our clearing guys coming back three or four or five times," Harpman interjected.

"Well, Jon," Hills replied, "in some places we're going to have to. Usually, the clearing operation ends after the first mowing."

They discussed the clearing at each hole, trying to find the balance that would yield enough room for golf without denuding the landscape or intruding on the housing parcels. Hills, feeling squeezed, was asking for thirty feet here and twenty feet there and worrying that the green "complexes," as he called them, were too small. "We've been pretty exacting in creating these spaces," he said, as they looked at the clearing on the back nine. "Maybe we should have asked for more latitude. We kept squeezing the course to enlarge the parcels."

"My uncle wants the most lots," Harpman said.

"If the golf course doesn't have the quality of the developments you're competing with you're in big trouble. Maybe I'm being overly defensive," Hills concluded, "but I feel I'm getting imposed upon and losing my golf course."

Dash said that at least until clearing's complete, and sometimes right up until the courses are grassed, Hills tends to worry that nothing's going to work out and takes a tormentedly vigilant attitude toward his work. He frets about his authority and what might go wrong. When they were building Willoughby, Dash said, "Art kept telling me, 'If we can't do better than this, we're never gonna get another job on the East Coast.' Then the job was done and the course was great and Art acted mildly surprised, like 'I guess this turned out pretty good after all, huh?' Like it was a shock."

We slogged across the muck on the range, which sucked at our boots like quicksand, and left dark, permanent stains on any fabric it touched. At ten and eleven Art thought the greens—both tucked into the preserve—had wonderful settings. The old power line to the house ran in front of the tenth green. When he was clearing there Postell knocked a tree into the wires and shorted out the power to the house. The new electrical service to Ironhorse was coming in along Jog Road, at the new entry.

The clearing for the preservation berm, along which the cart path leading to the twelfth hole would run, opened onto the prettiest stretch of holes on the golf course, and I suspected also the most challenging. The long haul between eleven and twelve, though, like the march between seven and eight, discouraged walking at Ironhorse. It was a rider's course. Hills complained, as he looked back from his grading plan to the stakes set out to describe the engineered boundaries of the lakes, that the greens at twelve and thirteen looked closer to the water than he wanted, a plaint that echoed over Ironhorse for the next few weeks like the moan of a murdered ancestor. It was the theme of the unresolved discrepancy.

"If the engineers say, 'We need more water,'" Hills said, "I'd like to make suggestions about where we make the adjustments."

But it wasn't more water Ironhorse would need, it was more dirt, and the suggestions Hills would have to attend with care came not from the engineers but from Muss. Already, on his first look at the clearing, Hills voiced the fear that his golf course was under siege. The beauty of the twelfth hole, however, even in the primitive condition of the first clearing, reassured him. If they were able to keep alive the two large pines that looked from the tee as if they stood dead center in the fairway about 200 yards out, the twelfth hole could be special. The trees created, in the Mackenzie manner, another deception. They were well to the left of the line of play, but they sure looked as if they owned the middle.

Dash had told Harpman that Hills wanted some "aerial hazards" at Ironhorse. What, Harpman wanted to know, was that?

"That's a biomass characterized by a root system, dense fibrous material ascending from the ground and a photosynthesizing mechanism on top to knock your ball down if you get behind it. A tree, son."

Hills built a course in Naples called Imperial "that had a huge pine that lasted about five years. Sam Snead came to play there," Hills remembered, "hit a drive into that tree, and said, 'What the *hell's* that doing there!?' It was nice while it lasted."

Pete Dye won't build a hole around a tree. "On opening day guaranteed it gets hit by lightning," he says, and then you've lost the hole.

Hills doesn't think the strategy of twelve is compromised by the pines, that if they do succumb the hole will play the same but won't be as pretty or as capricious. On fifteen, ultimately Hills's favorite hole at Ironhorse, there was also a tree jutting into the fairway and a pair of aerial hazards on one.

Hills directed more clearing around the greens and asked Harpman to make sure the carries—the tee shots—across the lake at fourteen weren't too long. "We don't want it two hundred and twenty yards instead of two hundred." He also told him to clear the myrtles from behind the fourteenth green. Later, when Harpman pointed out the clearing Hills had ordered at fourteen, Dash said, "Art must have felt pretty important when he left the job that day."

At the end of the walk-through Hills lamented again the destruction of the trees around the clubhouse and thought an informal landscape style would best suit Ironhorse, because it's an isolated development and because it's small. "You don't need," he said, "any razzle-dazzle."

Razzle-dazzle has come to mean showy and diverting, but it was coined to describe a style of camouflage invented by Britain's Royal Navy during World War I. Painting odd geometrical patterns on the sides of ships hid them on the horizon, just as the green-and-tan muddle of conventional camouflage hid objects in foliage. While Alister Mackenzie was in the British army teaching the camouflage idiom he'd learned from the Boers and wondering how he could adapt it to golf courses, his naval colleagues were developing the radical disguises of razzle-dazzle, made obsolete by radar. Mackenzie was working on a book on camouflage when he died, hoping to prove "that the peace of the world would be assured if all nations were taught to camouflage their defenses." Razzle-dazzle camouflage survives only as a name for vapid display.

Hills thought a simple entry—he again brought up The Wilderness for comparison—would harmonize best with the look of the golf course. He emphasized these feelings in a letter to Muss. "The introduction of outside landscape materials would immediately downgrade, by inference, all of the beautiful native material. It will be contrary to the effect of the course preservation effort." And then he added, "Some of the most beautiful, largest pines and other plant material on the site is within the area designated as clubhouse site. The opportunity exists to beautifully and carefully fit an elegant building into the native site . . . The opportunity to do this rarely exists in south Florida."

The palmettos behind the sixteenth tee had been cleared to the entry road, which meant there would be no buffer between golfers and traffic there. Hills thought that, too, was a mistake and suggested plantings as a screen. "We urge you," he wrote Muss, "to limit the width of clearing to that necessary for a 24' road and utilities." Overall, he expressed himself satisfied with the progress, praised Isakson and Harpman, and hoped Ironhorse would honor the preservation-of-mature-plant-material theme.

THE DISCREPANCY BETWEEN the engineered drawings and Hills's grading plan nagged at Isakson, and by Dash's next site visit, at about the time the tree spades finally came on the job in mid-January, his distress had sharpened. When he realized after Hills's previous walk-through that Art hadn't been aware of the difference between the demarcation of the lakes' edges and the tops of their banks, he relieved part of his worry. The top-of-banks stakes were as much as twenty-five feet from the waterline. On Dash's next visit, though, they all realized that the corridor on the sixth hole really was too tight. "We're showing a corridor going two hundred and forty feet over to that canal"—Dash pointed to stakes marking what amounted to a ditch between the golf course and a housing parcel—"and that's what we need to get."

Dash also wanted to make sure that Ranger didn't dig the canal as a straight line, as it was staked. He wanted them to dig a meandering creek. Harpman and Isakson came out after Dash left and "farm and gardened it," setting out stakes for the excavator to follow that echoed the sinuous wanderings of an old stream. Fake waterways are nearly as common in south Florida as artificial lakes. Hills had not only designed a pair of golf courses around an artificial creek on a development near Naples, but had done it so successfully that the place was called Quail Creek and players remarked on how well he'd shoehorned the golf courses around the coursing water.

After a meeting with Peter Aquart, Isakson called Harpman into the dining room to explain why the sixth hole seemed so tight. "Urban Design, when they were involved in the site planning, had a Mylar to stretch over this aerial"—and he gestured to the one hanging on the wall—"showing the boundaries"—drawn in a thick broken line—"that didn't quite line up with *another* Mylar from the engineers showing the lakes and the utilities. They printed both over the aerial, but these Mylars tend to stretch, so you've got this narrow line"—he pointed it out on the photo—"and this wide line *off the property* that they probably used to draw the grading plan."

Once the horizontal controls were fixed, Isakson said, it was "Art Hills's responsibility to use that and get the course to fit. Everybody's got to use that, all the subs and everybody. Hell, if they didn't, my utility contractor would have fire hydrants sitting on my lots."

Isakson said he was going to get an official, computer-drawn Mylar from Aquart, and "You can bet your sweet ass I'm gonna keep that baby locked up." The Ironhorse Rosetta stone.

"Nothing against Art Hills," Isakson wound down, "but somebody's got to know where exactly to put the golf course."

A WEEK AFTER Isakson's oration, about the time Dash and Harpman were scratching their heads over the narrowness of the sixth fairway, Brian Huntley in Hills's Toledo office was reading a letter from Aquart itemizing variations he'd discovered between the engineer's horizontal control and Hills's golf course plans. Most of them were minor encroachments of the golf course onto the parcels, or tees and greens set too close to lakes. The course wandered thirty-five feet this way or that, nothing of great consequence. Aquart enclosed a print of the horizontal control plot.

"It's very routine and very frustrating" was Huntley's reaction to what Isakson had taken to calling the case of the stretched Mylars. "We rarely get to start working on the grading or routing from a truly accurate survey. Our baseline may be a fence you can see on the aerial or rough points plotted on a map. By the time they do the actual survey and get actual lines, the fence we've been working off of may be three feet off.

"Then the engineer gets everything described and surveyed," as Aquart had done, "gets it back to us, and we're not the same. Over the course of a mile you can be off thirty or forty feet—then you end up compromising either the residential parcels or the golf course. But if you keep the corridors wide enough you can usually work things out pretty easily.

"We're working off a different base than the engineers usually do until about halfway through the project. But if we didn't do some work early, then the project would end up being six months behind. Golf course architecture isn't like rocket-scientist work. It's easy for us to adapt as long as we don't lose fifty feet in the driving area."

Dash wanted to avoid a repeat of Willoughby, where, as Huntley remembered, "everything lined up on one side, but the further away from our base the more it stretched until finally there was a tee in a road. We straightened everything out."

Part of the problem was that Hills's office was so busy—too busy, Brent Wadsworth thought. There were twenty-five Arthur Hills courses at some stage of construction, with Art doing all the design and most of the fieldwork and his five draftsmen in Toledo cranking out plans. I'd once gone to a meeting with Hills where he was scheduled to present the routing for a new course to the developers, who were gathered in a hopeful crowd to meet and see the wonderful new work, and he didn't have anything to show them. He'd forgotten to bring the drawings, which may not have quite been done besides. Almost at the door, he realized he couldn't recall the developer's name, so he drove around looking for a phone booth to call his office and update his mental file. That made him a little late for the meeting. He winged a marginally convincing description of the new course, but he was even more self-conscious than usual. When he wondered if they could change the wetland boundaries—this was another Florida project—they told him no, the Water District had cast those in stone. When we left, Art said, "They were nice not to say, 'Why haven't you done any work on this thing?' "

Stories like this about Hills drove Wadsworth crazy, perhaps because Hills seemed always to escape their consequences. At Ironhorse, too, the discrepancies in the grading plan occasioned a brief
moment of turmoil, then receded in the face of new crises of the sort
endemic to any construction job, whether it's remodeling your bath-
room or damming the Nile. Wadsworth was chagrined that if his
company left out a sprinkler head or misgraded a green the error had
to be remedied—not that he minded fixing mistakes, it was just that
the architects could do anything short of designing only seventeen
holes and get away with it. Sometimes he wondered if they really did
think through their designs or if they waited to see what happened on
the ground and then adjusted as the mood struck them. Only a pro-
pensity both personal and philosophical to look on the bright side
kept Wadsworth from descending into cynicism. Muss was a thorn in
Hills's side at times, but he sure as hell was going to know what he
paid for, and that was something Wadsworth could understand and
even admire.

Despite Hills's fears that he was losing control of the course, the dirt
Ranger was spreading started to look remarkably like what was
drawn on his grading plan. When Wadsworth's company finally was
able to start, it found the rough contours very much to its liking.
Wadsworth's superintendent said Ranger was doing a great job, he
just hoped they could pick up the pace.

Muss, much to Dasher's and Isakson's surprise, agreed that if the
golf course had to have it he'd shrink the housing parcel along the
sixth fairway. Hills's suggestion to simplify the plantings at the entry
also earned Muss's approval. "I don't think we should screw up the
golf course. I don't mind giving up some backyard as long as we don't
lose anything from the zero lot lines. We've hired the experts. We
should listen to what they say."

Dash received a report of Muss's assent to his professional recommendations with skepticism. "I've heard that before. 'The golf course
is our first priority, but I've got to have fifty feet for my lots off that
fourth tee.' "

When Isakson pulled out his cherished Mylar to drop over the
grading plan, Dash studied it a bit and then said except for the sixth
fairway, he didn't see any problems. "In fact," he said, "I think I can
give you a little on the zeros."

Six was, of all the holes, the most fussed over. The canal that was
going to run along the north side migrated to the south side. Then it

was eliminated, and an underground pipe was put in its place to connect the lake by its tee to the lake by its green. (All of Ironhorse's lakes were connected by large underground pipes, creating a single drainage basin.) Next, what Isakson called the "old-timey creek" that he and Harpman had farm and gardened was supposed to replace the straight ditch that in turn had replaced the buried pipe. Muss then decided that where the old-timey creek ran into the lake the fairway was too confined, making the hole too hard for weaker players, and suggested putting the water there back in pipe. He paced it off one day, while Dash, Webber, and Isakson looked on. Dash thought that would work fine. Besides, he'd rather the owner nibble at the course from the edges than start suggesting new green locations or better places for bunkers. He could live with simplifying a hole or two. Ironhorse had plenty of challenges. The hole following six, after all, was a 235-yard carry over water—Isakson's Lake Kennicott—to a green tucked right down on the water's edge behind a timber bulkhead.

Between the flawed drawings and what Isakson regarded as a vague concept for the plantings on the perimeter berm, he was mired in pessimism, about to conclude that Ironhorse really had no plans, or at least none he could depend on. It was Jay Bridge's misfortune to come by Ironhorse to explain and organize the planting on the perimeter berm just when Isakson's frustrations were at their thickest. Isakson jumped on Bridge as soon as he walked through the door. "Your drawings don't show me what I'm supposed to do on these berms," Isakson began. "That's what I call farm-and-garden engineering. How am I supposed to figure out what it costs?"

"That's how I've always done it," Bridge said, and if he was startled he hid it well. He looked away from Isakson as he spoke, out the living room window. A clutter of cars in the front yard blocked his view. A drawing of the berm was tacked to the wall, illustrating its typical shape and plantings. Bridge was borrowing a technique at least as old as Birkenhead Park, mounting trees on top of the high spots to emphasize their majesty. In the Ironhorse context, this method stressed a decidedly attenuated grandeur. Still, the rise of a dozen feet on an otherwise flat landscape creates a plausible acme.

"I've done golf courses where I just ordered a thousand Sabals and planted them. Do you want to see some of that work?"

In a voice tingling with hostility, ratcheted up to drill-instructor intensity, Isakson served up a message he'd been waiting months to

deliver, either to Bridge or to Hills or one of these loose constructionists whose maunderings he found so disconcerting. "I don't think
that's very professional. I need a drawing! What if Muss comes out
and says, 'I hate that design. Who *approved* that design?' And I say,
'Oh, we didn't have a design, Josh, we had Jay Bridge out here
waving his arms!' "

Bridge turned in a half circle where he stood but never wavered.
The smoke from his cigarette mingled with Isakson's cloudy exhalations. He looked back out the window, avoiding Isakson's glare, and
flipped him his reply: "If you want a plan, I'll draw you up one, but
what we're trying to get here is a natural look and you've got to figure
that out in the field."

Bridge finally looked Isakson's way, and written on his face was
the tired suffering of the *Übermensch*. *"That's why I'm here."*

They drove together to look at the berm, conciliatory but bristling.
Isakson, about to leave for a weekend of R and R, knew he was wired
pretty tight. "Everything's going too slow for me," he said before
Bridge wandered into his force field. "I've got to get out of here."

As they walked onto the berm, Bridge said, "Can I explain what
we're trying to do here?"

The tree spades had not made an auspicious beginning. One was
stuck atop the flat shelf the dozer had bladed across the crown, riding
in muck Ranger brought over to give the new trees a nourishing
foundation. It was perfect material, Dash had told Ranger, to dress
the mounds—not too peaty, he said, you can't roll a snake out of it
with your hands. They had to get the muck off the golf course, so now
the berms were thick with it. The tree spade had captured a tiny pine,
the pioneer of its race in this new land, the first to ride the high
ground—assuming the spade was able to free itself to plant it. The
foreman on the tree-spade crew told Bridge, "We need some dry
material up here." A dozer was just then crawling over to push some
of the shell rock from the fairways up the slope to give the tree spade
something solid to ride over.

"We've told the tree-spade crew from the beginning," Bridge said
to Isakson, " 'Look from the Beeline, see where there's a pine head
in the background, and fill in between.' It's a natural, random mix,
it's not a *design*. We'll use the saw palmetto on the understory as a
design element, but what we're trying for is a natural look."

Isakson circled out to the Beeline to take a look. Bridge expected
the transplanting crew to move mostly single pines, Sabals in clusters
of three, then myrtles, gums, and the odd dahoon holly. On the outer

slope, they'd plant palmettos, which would form a thick barricade to discourage trespassing and also hide the chain-link fence wrapping the perimeter. Hills wanted to keep all the planting on the outside of the berm to preserve the inside slopes for grass alone. "Put everything at least three feet back of the ridge," he said.

Ranger planned to drop a temporary well point to irrigate the trees for a year, giving them time to establish, but then the berm plantings would be on their own, to flourish or perish as the weather dictated. This was the technique all the environmentally correct water managers were advocating these days, calling it "xeriscape." Dash was asked to give a lecture at a big xeriscape conference the South Florida Water Management District organized. Could he speak on "golf courses and xeriscape"? Sure, he said, be happy to. About a mile from the conference hall it occurred to him to wonder, "What in the hell *is* xeriscape?"

At Ironhorse, not only would a berm planted in the xeriscape fashion Bridge prescribed look great, it would be cheap—free, really—to maintain. Isakson liked that part, but it was driving him crazy that he didn't know exactly what the plantings would cost. Well, Bridge said, each tree-spade unit was $125, and he guessed there would be about 150 TSUs along the fifth fairway. It wouldn't be hard to figure.

The tree spades, from that day onward, worked at a deliberate pace. It was important for them to finish as quickly as possible because they were too heavy to run over the golf course after Wadsworth had installed drainage pipe. If they crushed a drainpipe it might not be discovered until after the irrigation was in, and repairs would then not only be expensive, there wouldn't be anyone left around to blame.

Nothing, however, could light a fire under the tree spades. It was slow work—finding the right tree in the right place to move, picking it up, hauling it over a route firm enough to bear the truck's weight. Another company came along later with a technique of digging up Sabals with a backhoe a dozen or more at a time, hauling them to the berm on a flatbed trailer, and heeling them in, and that accelerated the process of planting the berms. But the spades were slow by nature. Isakson said later, "They could plant a seed and it'd be quicker'n what they're doing."

"They're so slow," Charles Best agreed, "they dig a hole and a bird could fill it with shit before they could get a tree in it."

The pace of tree transplanting was only one of the problems on the berm. Over the first hundred yards or so, despite Bridge's commands and in confirmation of Hills's fears, the trees looked as if they had been installed by a team of German engineers, precision horticulturists. The pines marched in perfect regularity, like soldiers, their tops at uniform height, on the top of a berm whose crown had none of the uneven wave the drawings called for. Instead of imitating the profile of the canopy that Ironhorse's woods drew against the sky, the transplanted crown looked as if it took its inspiration from a roof. Harpman struggled to get this resolved, and at about the time the berm began to acquire a natural look, Muss finally hired the pro.

Sher was still on about his money. The owners of Frenchman's Creek, whose success inspired such high financial hopes for Ironhorse, decided to sell an undeveloped property of just over 600 acres that they'd bought from the MacArthur Foundation as a part of the Frenchman's Creek purchase. A firm in which Jack Nicklaus has an interest bought it for $63 million, or more than Frenchman's owners had paid for both it *and* the developed land a few years earlier. Reporting this to Isakson and Weeg, Sher said, "Ironhorse is worth a fortune. They're buying undeveloped property for one hundred thousand dollars an acre. I'm foreclosing."

Everyone laughed. "I know what I'm saying," Sher insisted. "That's the price now." The dirt at Ironhorse may have sold for $15,000 an acre, but then it was not across the street from the hottest development in Palm Beach County.

Sher had butted in too many times for Muss's satisfaction. When Roger Whitford, whom Hills had recommended for the golf course superintendent's job, came to visit Ironhorse, Sher told Weeg, according to Isakson, "that he'd have to hire Whitford's wife to sell real estate, as a package deal. When Webber heard that, he was livid. Alan's just getting into stuff he shouldn't, taking away Josh's negotiating power. Alan may have some role here, but this is too early and out of line. I *want* the superintendent here when Wadsworth starts putting in irrigation. I *want* him to help on the maintenance building. Josh isn't hearing me on that now, but this is not Alan's business."

Muss didn't want Sher presuming to exercise any authority. He agreed to hire Shankland, but if Shankland didn't want the job the choice was Muss's. Sher wanted to hire his pro.

Brett Upper, Sher's final candidate, drove down with his wife to Ironhorse expecting to meet Muss at ten in the morning. At eleven, as they sat in Isakson's office, nervously making idle conversation,

Muss called. "I heard Isakson say, 'Well, what do you want me to do with Upper?' It was sort of humiliating," Upper said.

"I told Muss Brett was waiting," Isakson said, "and he said he couldn't make it. I think that's a discourtesy to the guy. Josh may have had his mind made up, but he should at least meet with the guy. But," he then hedged, "I'm not saying anything to Muss."

Sher didn't feel the same constraint. "I can't believe Josh," he said. "Why would a guy with all his money treat people like that? It's disgusting. No wonder Art Hills doesn't want to come here any-more."

Hills had not been back since his first look at the clearing nearly six weeks before, but Dash had made one inspection visit. He heard about Upper's travails and called to commiserate. Upper said he sort of wandered around his house in a daze when he got home, so disturbed was he by Muss's second snub. Webber and Weeg both thought Upper would bring exactly the "energy and willingness to promote the project" that Sher longed for, but Muss, confirming what had long ceased to be a mystery, soon after offered the job to Lanscioni, who immediately accepted. In a conciliatory gesture to Sher, he also offered Upper a job, as Head Pro to Lanscioni's Director of Golf. Upper, though he was grateful that Muss did finally meet with him, treat him decently, and tender employment, wanted more authority than he believed he would have under Lanscioni and de-clined the honor.

RANGER HAD A discrepancy to deal with, too, but it had no one to blame for it but itself. Ranger's bid for the bond work had been so much lower than its closest competitor that Isakson figured the company had either made a pact with the devil to learn the secret of moving earth cheaply or somebody had miscalculated. When Ranger started hauling dirt from the lake by the seventh hole all the way over to the eighth fairway, a run of nearly half a mile, Isakson knew for sure it was going to have trouble making money at the price it had bid. By the time he saw the trucks dragging dirt from a lake at the south end of the property clear up to the ninth hole, at the north end, he knew Ranger was struggling to balance the fill. The fact that the lakes were sloughing, that their banks weren't holding, and Ranger was digging some of them repeatedly compounded Ranger's woes, but it was a big and reputable company with the resources to finish the job. Isakson wasn't worried about Ranger taking a hike, but he tired pretty quickly of what he called "Ranger's crybaby attitude." Once he said he didn't want to hear any more complaints along that line, they stopped. Isakson recognized that Ranger's John Riley and Kevin Phillipson were eventually going to get the dirt where it belonged.

Phillips and Jordan finished the golf course clearing at the end of January. It came back to clear for the model-house lots later, but it was done with all the golf course work a little over two months after it started. As P&J was finishing, Kenny Postell said, "Well, we'll just have to go fuck up some other state when we're done here, won't we, Charles?"

And Best, recognizing a good straight line when he heard one, answered, "Shit, when we're done it'll look like a nuclear explosion—just little brown smoking stumps sticking up," and off they rattled, another good day's work dispatched.

Ranger wasn't having such an easy time. Between the long hauls and the pokiness of the tree spades, Isakson didn't know when he could turn Wadsworth loose. Then Jon Harpman called Pat Painter, who was in charge of Ranger's tree spades and by all lights the most experienced tree transplanter in south Florida, to complain that he had transplanted a dead tree on him and had better get it out. "You've got to get that snag out of the berm," Harpman told him.

"We call those hawk roosts, not snags," Painter said. This was a fight he'd had before. "Nobody really knows how those things are created." It looked like a dead pine. "I've studied the tree rings," Painter said, "and it looks like they follow a certain natural history. Seven years of drought, then a couple of years of good growth, then seven more years of drought. Then they're completely dehydrated, the cambium sloughs off and they stand there, basic cellulose with nothing really alive on them, nothing to rot. Nobody knows how old they are."

Well, Harpman said, it still looks like firewood to me and I want it out. Painter smiled and nodded. He'd done what he could.

Harpman told Riley that he was sympathetic to Ranger's problem with long hauls, too, but he was worried more about timing than anything. Wadsworth was waiting to go—it set up a job trailer the first week of February, right after P&J pulled off the job—and hoped for a run of at least nine holes to turn its crews loose on. Ranger was still looking for enough dirt to finish the holes at the north end, where Wadsworth would set up its irrigation trailer, stockpile its pipe, and prepare its greens mix.

"It seems to me," Harpman told Riley, "that somebody on the estimating screwed up."

"Big time," Riley said, folding his long arms in front of him. He had an easy way about him, but was big enough to be the boss. It took his sense of humor a little while to catch on at Ironhorse. One morning the word on everyone's lips was that Riley was dying. Had a year to live, Isakson heard.

I put on a long face and asked Kevin Phillipson, Riley's foreman how ol' John was doing. He laughed. "John's always saying Ranger has this policy that you've got to give two weeks' notice if you're planning to die. He's such a good company man he went to the doctor to see if he should be giving notice. Doctor says he's healthy as a horse. He's gonna have to keep moving dirt a few more years."

Once, after one of the regular Friday morning construction meetings, everybody was talking about a giant lottery payoff. "I know what I'd do if I won," Riley said. He'd go to his boss and say, " 'How much for this Bronco I'm driving?' And I'd peel off however much he wanted. Then I'd say, 'How much you charge me to use that loader over there?' And I'd peel off some more. Then I'd climb on that loader, run her over to that Bronco, lift that bucket, and BAM! drive that son of a bitch flat into the ground. Flatten it! Then I'd climb down and How! De! DO!"

Riley said they're having to haul some dirt from the lake by the seventeenth hole clear over to the perimeter berm on the north side. But in any case, he assured Harpman, "We'll get her done when the district's contract says 'cause there's no way we're gonna pay those penalties."

"Well," Harpman said, "you-all just bid this wrong."

"Don't say 'you-all!' We didn't bid it."

"Yeah," Kevin pitched in. "They're gonna have to sell the helicopter to pay for this one."

Jon then said Muss was demanding three more tree spades. "What's he gonna do if we don't get 'em, fire us?" Riley asked. Then he reached in his pocket, pulled out all his money, and handed it to Harpman. "Run me off right now and I'll pay you this, 'cause with all the money we're gonna lose here it's gonna be my ass. I'm better off gone now."

13

Mixing All Day

BY THE MIDDLE OF MARCH, Ranger was still excavating lakes and placing dirt, working its way south. The accreting layers Ranger's scrapers were depositing built a dusty, embryonic version of the golf course grading plan. Truckloads of sand for the greens mix rolled in at irregular intervals every day, adding to a small mountain at Wadsworth's staging ground just west of the ninth fairway. The sand came from a quarry west of Lake Okeechobee. What was left of the old entry road was covered with a thick layer of dirt, the droppings from hundreds of truckloads and scraper loads of fill. "We'll be mixing all day, every day, till we're done," Stu Britton, the Wadsworth superintendent, had said about his greens mix when the first load of sand arrived.

"It's an eighty-twenty greens mix," Britton explained. "Four loads of sand to one load of peat." Britton started looking for his peat the day he set up shop at Ironhorse, in early February. "We'll get seven truckloads of that Canadian peat in here," he said. "Somewhere around three thousand bundles. That'll be frozen when it gets here. Weighs about eighty pounds a bag thawed, but it'll go about a hundred and thirty frozen."

Stu's peat finally arrived at the end of the month, on the same day his shaper, Willie Owsley, checked in from Atlanta. "It was too cold up there," Owsley said, turning his face to the sun. "I need to be where it's warm."

Owsley had done the shaping at Willoughby, and then, waiting for Ironhorse to start, spent two months in Georgia. His dad was a Wadsworth mechanic, so Willie, almost thirty, had been around the company all his life. He had seven years in and dreamed of the day it was ten so he could claim his vested pension and find something easier to do. Willie was famous for his malaise—"Willie's always bitching about something" was the way his boss put it—but prized by the company because he was not only a good shaper, he was a *fast* shaper and complained on his own time. Wadsworth paid for his moves and provided a housing allowance, so Owsley was well compensated. Still, sometimes he got so worried he would hyperventilate and have to climb down from the Cat and find his breath. He was tired of swallowing dust.

Willie and Wanda Owsley have five children, and the three oldest, all boys, are in school. Moving's hard on the family, so Owsley was grateful Wadsworth had successive jobs—Ironhorse and Willoughby—near enough together for the Owsleys to stay in one place. It's about a forty-minute drive down from Stuart for Willie, but he doesn't mind. He's got so many watts of sound power in his Mustang that if he boosted it to the max his windows would shatter. It soothes him to ride with the sheet metal throbbing. A thousand watts. Thirty-five hundred bucks. The Mustang has 165,000 miles on it and still purrs. When Willie drives by a heavy cloud of sonic dust rumbles in his wake. Finding the perfect phonic balance inside the Mustang is Owsley's hobby. He installed all the equipment himself. "I like this Mustang," Willie said later, "like Alan likes this golf course. I'm gonna tinker with it the rest of my life."

Without good shapers Wadsworth might as well be bidding on road jobs. A fast good hand—an "A" shaper like Owsley—makes money for the company. He runs his Cat like his Mustang, with a roar. He's partial to machines named after animals. "Anybody runs in first gear and takes three days on a green," Willie says, "you know something's wrong." Shapers are golf construction's *primo uomos*. Willie started out "pan riding, but I'll never get on another one."

"Remember how they pushed us like hell to get done up at Willoughby so we could be at Ironhorse by October first?" Stu asked Willie with a laugh. Now Stu had his expensive shaper here, the highest-paid hand in the company—the shapers made twice as much as the supers and with overtime, which was common, pulled down $60,000 or more a year—with nothing more for him to do than run the little tractor with the front-end loader to help shag the peat when it finally showed up.

The drivers hauling the peat were paid by the bundle for their delivery. "They'll get a load of tomatoes or something to haul back. Peat," Stu said, squinting from under his short-brimmed hat, "is just like that tundra up there, that's all. I think it's about halfway to being coal."

Wearing green overalls to ward off the morning chill, a cigarette stuck like a prop in the corner of his mouth, Britton wanted desperately to get his part of Ironhorse under way. Slightly stooped, he looked older than he was—it surprised and pleased him, he said, to think that he and Brent Wadsworth were exactly the same age—and seemed ominously thin. But he was durable and tireless and, except for the wheeze induced by his smoking, in good health. He was also hard to discourage. The cluster headaches he suffered from made him withdraw for a few minutes into his job trailer every once in a while, where he could sit in quiet solitude, but with his medication he never had to miss a day's work. "You've heard of migraine headaches?" he asked. "Well, if you've got a cluster headache, you *wish* you had a migraine."

Britton was intensely loyal to "Wads," as he called both the company and its founder, and hated to think that a job he was in charge of might lose money. "Wads don't make a profit, at some point we don't work."

Britton's devotion was not lightly given. How he came to work for Wadsworth was proof of that. About ten years ago, Britton was sipping a cup of coffee in a little greasy spoon over on the gulf coast, nursing his anger. He'd just quit his job running pipe, the kind of hard labor he'd done all his life. A native of upstate New York, he'd been a sandhog and a union laborer, migrating to Florida in the late seventies when the northeastern economy took a tumble. Now he was out of work again. A couple of months before he'd been promised a raise, but the extra money hadn't shown up on his next paycheck. When he asked why, the boss just said, "Next time. We'll make it up on your next check." But they hadn't. Where principles were concerned, Britton was not a man to waffle. When he asked a second time what happened to his raise, he got the same dilatorily casual answer. Next time. In the matter of his earnings, he expected a dollop of urgency. "I'll show you next time," he told his boss, heading for his truck. That's how he came to be drinking coffee on a Friday morning in Fort Myers when Wayne Ragsdale walked through the restaurant door.

Ragsdale worked for Wadsworth. Looking for hands to start a new project, he saw a middle-aged man with mud on his boots, dust behind his ears, and fingers thick from labor wrapped around a mug and figured this was someone who knew how to work. Ragsdale struck up a conversation with Britton, hired him to install drainage pipe, and nine years later Stu was running the Ironhorse job.

If the fidelity of its employees and the longevity of their service are any measure of how well a company's run, Wadsworth stakes out a pretty good claim for itself. Brent Wadsworth is the company's chairman. (Wadsworth is also the sole proprietor of the Wadsworth Company, which operates as "a personal investment, equipment, and real estate company" and was the first incarnation of his golf construction business.) He is also the major stockholder of the Wadsworth Golf Construction Company of the Southeast, the Wadsworth Golf Construction Company of the Midwest, and the Wadsworth Golf Construction Company of the Southwest, owning 51 percent of those companies, while "key employees"—like Wayne Ragsdale—own the remainder. When I write of Wadsworth here, I mean the Southeast Company, which is building Ironhorse. The three golf construction companies have combined annual revenues of $50,000,000. Brent Wadsworth also runs Golf Hosts, Inc., which owns and operates two golf resorts—Innisbrook in Florida and Tamarron in Colorado. Hills designed the Tamarron course.

The first person Wadsworth hired when he started in the golf-construction business was a young fellow originally from rural Arkansas who'd just been laid off at a Caterpillar plant near Chicago and was looking for temporary work. Wadsworth had a little seeding contract up near Joliet. John Cotter ran equipment for the next six years—mostly farm tractors, as the use of big earth-moving equipment wasn't yet the norm in the course-building business—and was then made superintendent. For the next fifteen years Wadsworth's work was mostly seasonal—"you worked hard from spring until about the end of October"—but since 1980 it's been year round. Now Cotter, the quiet man in the coveralls who hired Mike Dasher, is Brent Wadsworth's second in command.

Wadsworth, like a Japanese company, provides lifelong employment. Jon Shapland, who presides over the Southeast office, went to work for Wadsworth as a teenaged rock picker on a course Shapland's father owned near Champaign, Illinois. He joined Wadsworth full-time in 1970 with a fresh degree in civil engineering from the University of Illinois. "Brent let me do everything right from the start," Shapland says, and by the age of twenty-four he was a vice president. "Brent just made sure I knew that didn't mean much."

When he was not much past thirty, Shapland was made president of the newly formed Southeast Company, and that did mean something. Shapland is one of the reasons Dasher decided there was too little room at the top with Wadsworth and cast his lot instead with Hills. By 1973, Wadsworth had enough work in Florida to open its office in Oldsmar, not far from Innisbrook. Innisbrook has sixty-three holes—two eighteen-hole courses and a twenty-seven-hole course—designed by Larry Packard, Wadsworth's former partner. Hills counts it as a great disappointment that he didn't get to design the Innisbrook courses.

Shapland worked on Hills's first Florida course, Palmetto Pine in Cape Coral, finished in 1970. It was this course that Jack Nicklaus visited in 1971 when Hills sought a design partnership with him. "I certainly enjoyed seeing the golf course," Nicklaus wrote Hills. "You should have a great future in the golf course business." Just not with me.

Wadsworth, on the other hand, did forge a link with Nicklaus, building more than twenty Nicklaus designs. In 1988 and 1989, of the forty courses the Wadsworth companies built, seven were by Nicklaus, nine by Art Hills, and others were by Tom Fazio, Robert Trent Jones, Jr., and the team of Tom Weiskopf and Jay Morrish, a former chief designer for Nicklaus. The golf business is very cozy. Brent's heard it whispered recently, as he had for years about Hills, "You made Jack Nicklaus"—as a designer, that is. He dismisses any such notion, but there is hardly a course designer of note whose reputation hasn't been made, saved, or polished by Wadsworth.

"When the pros came along," an old Wadsworth hand says, "Nicklaus, Arnold Palmer, they only gave you a concept—a cut-and-fill plan. Then they'd come in and tune it according to their game. It was—still is—frustrating. We weren't sure that they were sure what they were after."

The designers get the fame, but all of them know that without a good builder their jobs would be tougher. That truth would be underscored for Hills later that summer at a course called Old Trail, in Jupiter, a half an hour north of Ironhorse.

*   *   *

ED HARBAUER, who is Britton's boss and the formal liaison between Wadsworth and Ironhorse, the guy who's supposed to smooth over any tension between the owner, the excavation contractor, and the golf architect to make sure the job runs smoothly for Wadsworth, also joined the company straight out of college. He ran scrapers, jostling his kidneys so much they rang off his vertebrae like castanets, fetched pipe into the ground, and learned to operate a dozer. Then he was a superintendent, the job Britton has now, the job Mike Dasher once held. Harbauer built Hills's original course at Pelican Bay—nine holes · were added in 1989—and was the construction superintendent at Wyndemere, another of Hills's Naples courses.

What unites all these Wadsworth employees is their adherence to the chairman's principles, which he's somehow convinced them to believe, or at least not to loudly dispute. Hills is a devotee of inspirational tapes and a reader of collections of managerial wisdom, but Wadsworth avoids any such exhortation or instruction. Hills says, "Brent's just always known what he wanted done."

On the second course Wadsworth built for Hills, a municipal course on wetlands and fill in Toledo, he lost $100,000 on a $400,000 contract. Wadsworth was still a small company in the late sixties, and $100,000 was way more than it could afford to lose. Had Wadsworth walked, the city of Toledo might have lost its whole investment in a course that has been one of the most popular in northern Ohio for twenty-five years. But Wadsworth stuck it out, "just kept going and going until they got it all right," as Hills remembers. It almost did in his company, but Wadsworth would rather fail trying to do his best, hackneyed as it seems, than avoid it by cutting corners. Hills occasionally runs into the fellow who was Toledo's city manager at the time the course called Detweiler was built, and twenty-five years later he still remarks about Wadsworth's willingness to finish that job.

Unlike Muss's employees, who apart from David Webber are afraid to make any claim on his attention or time, Wadsworth's employees—several part owners of the company—work with a sense of larger purpose. At the office in Oldsmar, a clean, new wooden building that looks as if it would be at home in the Northwest, no one is looking over his shoulder.

When Brent plays golf with Harbauer, for example, there is an ease passing between them, teasing about bets—Brent's are always small—or errant shots, an ordinary camaraderie. Wadsworth's golf swing and his game are neat and tidy, like everything he does. He doesn't hit the ball a long way, but he rarely gets in trouble and has no illusions about what he can and cannot do. Brent Wadsworth's touch massages everything that goes on in his company.

"He can ream you a new asshole if he doesn't think something's right," Shapland says. Superintendents dread his spotting a bend in a cart path where it doesn't belong or a break in a green that's too severe. As the company shares profits, if Brent decides on one of his rare visits to a job that something needs fixing, there will be less to share, an incentive to get it right the first time. Hills says Brent's punch list, his compilation of little errors and unfinished details, is always "about three times as long as the owner's."

When he does spot a flaw, he'll say, "We have to fix that," looking grief-stricken, his shoulders slumping, less over the money it will cost than at the presumption of the imperfection, the realization that he cannot forestall every inevitable bungle. Looking at Brent now, small and at sixty still youthfully handsome, it's not hard to imagine why a pioneering Midwestern golf course builder, a rough-hewn fellow who made his bones greasing the palms of county pols to get contracts for road work, took one look at him thirty years ago and said, "Brent's a nice kid, but this business is a little too tough for him."

When Wadsworth sets his face in a deliberate frown, the signal that he's serious, it looks studied, as if he's fighting an inclination to grin. His diffident manner sets off his occasionally tumid speech. A conversation with Brent can plunge into rhetorical depths, as if the diction of Don King were flowing from the lips of Bob Newhart. He once wrote a letter to Hills after Art had called his office to complain about Wadsworth's supposed failure to keep to its schedule on a job. The call made Wadsworth very angry—that Hills had called him to complain, that Hills had already carried his complaint to the client, that what he was complaining about might be true were all wrenching to contemplate. A little taste of his reply to Hills gives a good flavor of the Wadsworth verbal style.

"The call came as a surprise and was accepted with a great amount of concern. Certainly without reasonable understanding and thorough analysis of scheduling programs, disputes may arise. In that particular case, a more thorough review of the matter might have been made before taking the chance of stirring up emotions to the point of impeding advancement, rather than nurturing and encouraging progress." And on and on.

Brent was hurt by Art's suggestion that after thirty years of building courses, not a few of them designed by Hills, Wadsworth's company had somehow lost its ability to perform. Wadsworth's letter went on for three pages, anger squeezed out of every line. "While it has been difficult to overcome your mode of operation," he concluded, rubbing salt in an old wound, "we have somehow always found a way to deliver projects of exceptional value."

Wadsworth's passion was lost on Hills, who has a temper but not much heart for conflict. He knows Brent thinks he sometimes spends too little time designing his greens and has heard Wadsworth more than once, in his convoluted way, take him to task. He just chooses not to listen.

"Dear Brent," he wrote in a sort of reply to Wadsworth's scold, which he cut off at the pass. "With all due respect, after reading the first paragraph or so I could tell I didn't want to go on. That brief perusal told me there was nothing but pain ahead so I laid your lengthy reflections aside."

Their friendship was too ancient and durable to shatter on this shoal, so they agreed without speaking any further about it to set their one-sided conflict aside. Brent tried to moderate his criticisms of Art, knowing how sensitive he was, but still wished Hills would do fewer jobs so he could concentrate better on each. This was not an argument Wadsworth was going to win.

I visited Wadsworth at Innisbrook. He spends most of the winter in Florida, summer and fall in Illinois, and the Christmas holidays in Colorado. He invited me to dinner with his wife, Jean, at one of Innisbrook's golf course dining rooms. Each of the resort's three courses has a dining room with a theme. We ate at the most formal one. Wadsworth had made early reservations, a chance to eat without bustle before the resort's guests crowded in.

"Welcome, Mister Wadsworth," the host said, clearly innocent of who he was greeting. *All* the guests at Innisbrook are welcomed by name. "Have you been with us before?"

Wadsworth answered with a shrug and a nod, speaking almost in a whisper, that yes, he had been there before, but not recently. The setting sun was shining in Mrs. Wadsworth's eyes, and while there were many empty tables in shadow around us, he asked if we could move with great reluctance, evading even the tiniest fuss. It would never have occurred to him to say, "I *own* this place! Can't I even get a decent table?"

The Wadsworths don't live at Innisbrook when they're in Florida, either, but instead have a modest condo nearby. They rarely dine out, and retire and rise early. A big night out is dinner at Sonny's Barbecue, where they share a senior special. Jean eats the slaw, Brent the beans, and each has a taste of brisket. They can both eat for $6.95 as long as Brent lays off the iced tea.

There was such an affecting modesty about Wadsworth that I could understand Britton's devotion to him. But as the old rival in Chicago who predicted a grim future for the sweet kid running pipe would have discovered had he lived long enough, Wadsworth's humility made him easy to underestimate.

Hills wrote a poem for Wadsworth's sixtieth birthday, but didn't finish it in time to deliver it at a party thrown for him in Chicago. Hills had it printed on parchment and framed when it was finally ready:

> Let's delve into this gentle man of mystery.
> Talk of the times when he would embarrass
> Larry Packard and Robert Bruce Harris.
> His crazy designs with short doglegs and backward bunkers
> Made some think he might do better as a spelunker.
> Alas, work got slow
> And Packard said, "Brent my lad you'll have to go."
> Off they went over hill and dale,
> Building a mound and cutting a swale.
> The word did spread and wealth amassed.
> And along the way every time he stepped to the tee he got gassed.
> "I'll fix that," he said
> "I'll build a course that will fill the long hitter with dread."
> And so he built a place where golfers went gaga!
> Innisbrook, its beauty captured all.
> As Brent and his friends walked to the tee he said: "See, I gotcha."
> For on every hole he had a trap or a tree.
> And if that wasn't enough there was some water for you and me.

Wadsworth's company brochure, heavy on philosophy, quotes Saint Thomas Aquinas: "A small error in the beginning is a great one in the end." It also borrows from Joseph Wood Krutch—"We put survival first. But when we have a margin of safety left over, we expend it in the search for beauty. Who can say that nature does not do the same?"—the anthropologist Loren Eisley, John Ruskin, Ralph Waldo Emerson, and, rather more eccentrically amid this frothy eclecticism, Wernher von Braun. Wadsworth has a company policy, obviously written by Brent, that is so high-minded it reads as if it were a government protocol. "It is the purpose of this company to serve those who have so trustingly put their faith and confidence into our hands in a manner which will produce, under all circumstances, a product of the highest quality and excellence attainable. This belief, while maybe not producing the highest monetary return, does render other far greater rewards—the experience of devotion to duty, proudness, and extraordinary satisfaction."

Beneath this earnest effusion is a credo Stu Britton knows and accepts, even if his version is a little more to the point. "If I can't do it right and make Wads some money, I'm gone. Don't want to be here."

STU'S GETTING ANXIOUS. He's got a short crew here ready to start laying pipe, but until Ironhorse gets its permit from the South Florida Water Management District he can't start. He'd hired a crew of Haitian laborers for the Willoughby job and liked their work well enough to want to keep them busy on Ironhorse. They lived in Fort Pierce, about seventy miles north of Ironhorse, and rode to the job together in a van, leaving at 5:30 A.M. to be on the job by 7:00. Wilmon Laguerre was Britton's ace greens mixer, a thin and affable man whose kind smile communicated the feelings his limited English could not. My Creole, of course, was more greatly lacking than his English.

WADSWORTH'S CONTRACT, for $1,700,000, requires it to build an "eighteen-hole golf course and practice range, including the shaping, fairway drainage, irrigation, greens construction, grassing and cart path installation." The irrigation is the most expensive part of Wadsworth's work, more than half a million dollars. The company figures it costs $30.30 to prepare and spread a cubic yard—that is, twenty-seven cubic feet—of greens mix. The mix is the pricey part of the green, and the green in turn is the most expensive feature of the course to build. Ironhorse's greens mix is costing almost $160,000—that's for 5,250 cubic yards. Spread out all in one place, that's a beach.

The peat arrived on the last day of February, an overcast Tuesday. A Gershman Produce tractor and trailer from Winnipeg, Manitoba, driven by Albert and Lisa Peters, pulled up next to Wadsworth's sandpile at 8:00 A.M. The Kenilworth truck, painted black with gold stripes, was so clean it glowed in the morning sun. Everything else at Ironhorse was by now covered with dust. The fifty-three-foot-long trailer carried a load of Fison's peat. The Peters are in their midtwenties. They've been driving their truck, which has a commodious cab-over sleeper, for five years. Before they bought the truck they worked their prairie farm 150 miles north of Winnipeg. Now Albert's dad is running it for them, farming and putting together a little beef herd. The tractor cost $104,000, and it is their home as well as their office. In the last three months they've only been to their farm once, for two days right before Christmas. They're hoping for a slow turnaround at Ironhorse so they can get a little sun. On a typical day they roll out in the morning at 4:00 or 5:00 A.M., then drive until midnight. They stop every day for a shower. "Albert likes to get an early start," Lisa says. "He'll drive until six or seven, then we switch."

Lisa, a pretty blonde with milkmaid skin, and Albert, short and handsome, with hair parted down the middle and a winning smile, defy pretty much every stereotype of the trucker. They left Winnipeg on Friday, drove down through Minneapolis, on down through Madison, Wisconsin, then south through Illinois, "taking some two-lane for a while on 51," barreling past Centralia, my hometown. They caught Interstate 57 near Salem, the birthplace of the Boy Orator of the Platte, William Jennings Bryan, presidential candidate and secretary of state, who concluded a life of public service by putting his great rhetorical gifts in the service of selling south Florida real estate, peddling lots in Coral Gables for $100,000 a year. Near the southern tip of Illinois they veered left, onto Interstate 24, which took them through Nashville and Chattanooga, then 75 through Atlanta and on down to Tampa, where they dropped off a small load of furniture that rode south tucked behind frozen bundles of peat. The Florida Turnpike brought them right by Ironhorse, but it was too late to deliver their load, so they treated themselves to a motel and brought Britton's devoutly hoped for "frozen tundra"—really decomposed sphagnum moss—over first thing in the morning. Stu had some temporary laborers, small Hispanic men—Stu malaproped them as "Gualamalians"—waiting to unload the peat. They grabbed the large cold bundles in their small brown arms and stacked them in neat rows.

The peat had not been harvested in a gelid state, but froze in storage at the factory. The Peters were hauling a short load—only 430 bundles, as opposed to the 750 they could carry—because the peat was so wet and heavy, like blocks of ice. They usually get paid by the bundle, as Britton said, but because this was a short load they were collecting on the weight. Even with fewer bundles, they were 1,400 pounds heavy on a Georgia scale, so they enriched the state's highway fund by $14. Their pay is 78 percent of the cost of hauling, so Albert figures this trip grossed $2,600. When they leave Ironhorse, they'll call the home office to learn where and when to pick up their return load. Their trailer isn't refrigerated, so they can't follow Britton's prescription and bring home perishable produce.

Strung out in rows north of the sandpile, the peat—rectangular bundles wrapped in white plastic—was mobilized in orderly rows a hundred feet long, like arctic gabions. Over the next three months, a few bundles at a time, they were hauled to the mix pile, torn open, and spread in a thin layer. Then sand, in an amount equal to four times the volume of peat, was dumped on the pile, and the tractor, trailing a disk, was driven back and forth, churning the mix like a giant recipe. Some contractors cut corners by dumping the sand and peat into the hole at the green and mixing it there, but that never produces the exact proportions good greens require. Wadsworth did not cut corners. Every once in a while Britton sent a sample of his greens mix to a lab to make sure his peat and sand were mingling in the proper proportions.

WHILE BRITTON'S MIXING he's also waiting, both for Ranger to get ahead of him and for Isakson to produce the permit from South Florida. Stu was happy in general with the grades Ranger was laying down, but asked for more dirt on his greens. Kevin Phillipson had been putting in dirt to subgrade, but Britton told him, "I need final grade so I'll have something for the collars."

"No problem," Kevin said, pulling off his sunglasses.

"The fairways, we shot them, Kevin, and they're beautiful, right where we want it within a few inches," Britton said.

They were in the office for the regular Friday morning construction meeting, and Pete Aquart was dropping by to catch Isakson up on the South Florida permit. The phones were down again.

"It'll be two to three weeks before I can start with the underdrainage," Stu told Isakson.

Aquart explained to everyone—but especially for Britton's sake, since he was the new member of the Ironhorse cast—the process of getting approval for building a golf course from South Florida. "First you get conceptual approval, so that the idea is accepted." Ironhorse was conceptually approved a year ago, which paved the way for the bondable work.

"Then you submit for the pieces—the roads, the utilities, the golf course. You don't want to do all the engineering and design before you get conceptual approval, or you might have to change things before you get started. So you get a series of permits. It used to be free to do this, but now it's on a scale based on type of construction. The golf course permit is costing $1,475. Before last January first it was free."

"Like I said," Isakson noted. "You've got to figure a year down here. Figure a year. Save the alligators. Save the snakes. Save this. Save that. Like with that snail kite monitoring. It's like having the fucking CIA on you. Environmentally, they're very sound down here."

"In other words, what you're saying," Britton said, with typical concision, "in Florida you need a permit to get a permit."

14

Desperate for Dirt

I don't build a course once, I build it three times.

—Stu Britton

WILLIE OWSLEY was waiting for his dozer, killing time on a little tractor helping with the greens mix until Howard Stevens delivered his Cat from Oldsmar, Wadsworth's Southeast headquarters and its equipment depot. Having Willie on a tractor fiddling with the greens mix was like putting Nolan Ryan to work pitching batting practice. There are not more than a couple of dozen good and proficient golf course shapers in the country, and if Willie isn't leading off he's on deck. He learned from a Hall of Famer—the Pete Rose of shaping, a Wadsworth hand who tried to turn his pension into a fortune in a cocaine deal and instead bought a stretch in the state pen. There were rumors that he'd shot somebody, but no could say exactly what David Thomas—as I'll call him—had done to land him in Raiford.

"Thomas always said he could do more with a grain of sand than a monkey could do with a peanut," Owsley said. "And he could, by God. He was *fast*. I learned from the best. He could shape swales that would make water *think*."

Thomas had a speech impediment, but according to the old Wadsworth hands was so quiet you didn't much notice it. Once a trench collapsed on a pipe crew, burying a laborer. Thomas jumped on a backhoe and tried to free him. "When I pulled up the bucket," as he described it later, "I had Wuffer's weg"—that is, "Luther's leg"— "but that's okay. Wuffer was alweady dead."

If the "Wuffer" story isn't apocryphal, it's at least the cousin to a story the Ranger hands tell about an operator ordered to pull a horse stuck in a marsh to safety. It was up to its belly in ground that gripped like guilt. This part I believed. I once sank up to my knees in mud that wouldn't let go. There was nothing around me to pull against, and I swayed and tried to lift, but it was like willing myself to rise, like trying to levitate. Muscles weren't doing the job. It was an odd sensation, echoing the fears aroused in childhood by movie scenes of quicksand swallowing explorers, pith-helmeted victims gobbled by tropical quagmires—Conradian metaphors for imperialism, of course, but who knew? I tried to lean over and spread myself on the surface, the technique inspired no doubt by a matinee memory, but I couldn't get loose. I was like an inflatable doll with a weighted bottom—I could sway but never fall. Britton came over and broke the surface tension or whatever the physical force was holding me by jamming a stick in next to my leg, and I was able to lurch out. Anyway, in the Ranger tale the horse must have wandered into something similar. The operator sent to save the horse wrapped a cable around its neck, attached the cable to a dozer, and pulled away, jerking the horse's head off. I was grateful Britton didn't have a cable handy when he noticed my distress.

Owsley operated a D5 Cat with a six-way blade, or would when one finally got to Ironhorse. "That's the finest finish dozer there is," he says.

The blade goes up and down, as on a conventional dozer, but it can also tilt forward and backward and even rotate over a small arc. Owsley calls the D5 his "chunk of iron." Even though Ironhorse didn't have its South Florida permit, and wouldn't get it until the end of March, as soon as a dozer arrived Britton would set Owsley to shaping. Wadsworth wouldn't take the risk of installing any drainpipes without a permit, but didn't mind doing a little grading. Compared to running pipe, shaping was cheap.

Once Ranger had the dirt down—and where it *was* in place Britton was happy with the grades—Wadsworth would work the shapes, getting them closer to the details Hills was after, contouring mounds, roughing in fairway bunkers, getting the slopes right on the tees so they'd drain but not make a player struggle for balance. Most of the shaper's attention, though, was on the green complexes. In the typical foursome, golfers approach the green from every direction, congregate at the hole, walk together—or, shamefully, ride—to the next tee, then disperse again in pursuit of their drives. The greens focus the course, have the best-maintained and most delicate turf, and demand the most attention from the golfers. The part of the job Owsley does is called "artwork and contouring." At Ironhorse there was $182,000 worth of it.

Installation of the drainage followed the grading, but tended to tear up the work, so before the next stage—irrigation—Britton would have to shape the course again. After the irrigation, he'd rake and clean the ground so the sprigging contractor could put the grass down. In an ideal world, all this could be done in four months once the course was rough-graded, once the dirt was down, but Ironhorse was not an ideal world, so it took closer to twice that time.

RANGER WAS STRUGGLING with long hauls, bad soils, and then, just when they were least needed, heavy rains. Rain is a special devil for a course builder, whether in the clayey soils of Georgia or Florida's sands. After a visit to the course Wadsworth was building in Atlanta, where Owsley worked during his exile from south Florida, Hills and Dasher would come to Ironhorse with traces of red mud on their boots, the residue of clinging soil that accumulates with every step, so that after a few yards your feet are so heavy with mud it feels like you've got tombstones lashed to your soles. In Florida, rain washes away the shapes in the sandy soil exactly as a wave eradicates a sand castle. Until there is grass anchoring it, Ironhorse's golf course will be vulnerable to heavy rains. If the shapes wash away after pipe's in, the repairs are very expensive. Ranger's problem with the rain was severalfold—the course could lose the shapes Ranger had already placed, and where the contours held, the finer sands might wash from the soil, leaving a dense, calcareous residue of the sort that was collecting on parts of the perimeter berm. Beyond that, it was difficult operating equipment over the wet ground. Scrapers sank and got stuck, especially in the old muck pockets that a foot or so of fill was able to bridge in dry weather.

When Ranger was hooking up the interconnects, the big pipes that would let the water flow freely among Ironhorse's lakes, it had to temporarily shut off access to the old outfall canal. Then the heavy rains came and water stood in deep puddles around the site, proof enough that without the big pump—or the water-management plan designed to replace it, with its own outfall pump pushing the water east—Ironhorse would drown. Ranger lost a couple of days, but John Riley called the men back to work even though it was hard to get much done in the mire. "Hey," he said, "my guys can't go to the grocery store and say, 'That dirt was too wet to move. Can I have a discount on that loaf of bread?' I got to keep them on that equipment, not at home."

Ranger by this time was running dirt from the lake behind the old ranch house all the way over to the second hole, hauling along the path of the preserve berm. "I've got three trucks, two hoes, and six pans running," Riley said, "and I can't move five thousand yards a day. Hell, I can't pay for the fuel."

When Jon Harpman asked him why Ranger was making such long runs, he said, "You wanted the golf course done first."

Another problem for Ranger was the tendency of the soil to slough, especially along the lake banks. Ranger would excavate the lakes to the surveyed dimension, then lose the edge. The banks would crumble and the fractured soil would fill the lake bottom, which meant that it couldn't hold the volume of water required for flood control. Ranger had to bring in a dragline to dress the banks, an expensive method. The dragline is a crane with a cable-controlled bucket hanging from its boom. It walks—very slowly—on dozer tracks. Its operator swings the boom out over the water, releases the cable, and lets the bucket drop like the cast of a mighty robot fisherman. As the winches wind the cables up, the bucket gathers soil, then breaks free of the lake's surface in a burst. Water spills from holes in its side like the draining of a great colander, and the operator swings the boom back toward the shore, lifts the rear of the bucket, and dumps its load. Then a front-end loader can scoop the soil into the hopper of a dumpster. This is a lot more complicated than running a pan across the ground, but it was the only way Ranger could get the dirt out of the slumping lakes. If a scraper is a home run, the dragline is a bunt. Even with the dragline, Ranger was running short on its quantities.

In some places at Ironhorse, as Kevin Phillipson, the Ranger foreman, described it, "The soil won't let the water loose. You know how if you pick up a handful of wet sand to build a sand castle the water sort of stays in it? That's kind of how this material works. A rim ditch won't do any good. The water just won't come out."

A rim ditch is a simple idea, and variations of it helped Ranger get at Ironhorse's dirt. At its most basic, a rim ditch is a kind of moat around the spot you want to excavate. In theory, pumping water out of the ditch dries out the surrounding soil. When Ranger was trying to dig a big hole in wet material, it first pumped water out and over a temporary dike, then excavated a deeper trench down the middle of the hole to pump from, creating a kind of inverse well point. Then the pans could scrape reasonably dry soil. When the soil wouldn't give up the water, it was a fight to dig it. At a certain level, the lake by the seventeenth hole stayed wet and the pan hands started burying themselves there with enough frequency to make Phillipson start talking to himself. "As long as I spent on one, I shouldn't say anything, but these scraper hands don't have a reputation in general for being too swift."

Phillipson spends his mornings shooting grades so the pans will know where to drop their loads. He sets up a simple little builder's level, then walks off the distances and the design elevations on Hills's grading plan. Next, he'll drive a stake into the ground showing the operator where and how much fill to drop. He rechecks the grades afterward, a conscientious regime that earned Britton's admiration. He's followed some dirt contractors, he said, who leave the site looking like a bomb hit, like the earth just blew out of a crater and landed willy-nilly. Phillipson trusts his long-legged gait to measure distance for rough grades. His biggest fear is that the operators will bury or miss the stake. "You know what they say about how a lost surveyor finds his way out of the woods in Florida, don't you? He drives a stake in the ground, puts a grade mark on it, and then sits down to wait. In a few minutes a pan will come by and knock the stake over, and the surveyor follows him out."

At the lake on seventeen, the pans were getting stuck so often that Phillipson put a dozer operator on a D6 there to help push them out. "I've explained to the scraper hands," Phillipson said, with some exasperation, "that since that rear engine runs off an air throttle it's either wide open or it's not, so when you sit there with your foot barely on the peddle you might as well have it on the floor. The rear wheels only push, so if you get in soft material and bury and keep the rear wheels running you just bury it more."

The dragline was pulling dirt from a rim ditch, tossing it up where the D6 could spread it for the pans to pick up. They were running it over to the eighth fairway, where Phillipson was shooting grades. After a bit he noticed—the silence was the clue—that no pans had

arrived in the last ten minutes. There were two pans seriously stuck
in the lake when Phillipson arrived, and two more were idling at the
edge wondering what to do. The surface of this soil would pulse—
Isakson said it looked like a water bed—when a pan ran over it. The
motion reminded me of the undulations the passage of a heavy truck
sets off on the ice roads on Lake Superior. Phillipson waved the
operator down from one of the waiting pans and positioned it in front
of the two that were stuck, signaling the operator of the nearest one
to throw his bale over Phillipson's hook. He then started working the
front wheels back and forth, like a bull pawing the dirt, pulling his fist
in the air as a signal to the others to crank up the rpms. The dozer was
pushing against the pan on the end, the caboose to this little train.
They were out in minutes. The dozer hand told Phillipson that the
two pans idling on the bank had been stuck in exactly the same deep
ruts, but no sooner had he pushed them out than he saw the two
Phillipson had just extricated blithely motoring toward the same trap.
He just shook his head. Pans run to mud like lemmings to a cliff. The
most scrapers he's ever seen stuck at one time, Phillipson said, was
nine.

Phillipson was inspired to his current diligence, he says, by once
having moved 25,000 yards to the wrong place. Not at Ironhorse, but
on an earlier job. "I wasn't paying attention," he confesses. Even at
the $1.38 a cubic yard Ranger's getting for Ironhorse's dirt, that
would be a pricey error. No wonder Britton's found the rough grades
at Ironhorse so to his liking.

"All things being equal," Phillipson said, "we can make money at
$1.30 a yard—we're making thirteen cents or so at that rate, so our
cost is $1.17. I have moved it as cheap as thirty-eight cents. We hit a
dry lake once and moved thirty-eight thousand yards in three days.
Sometimes you get one that just digs.

"If this was good material there wouldn't be any water trapped out
there. It's been a tough job because it's bad material. It's wetlands,
really. When you're two feet above the water table, it's like you need
scuba pans. When you're only two feet above the water table, you're
just dumping the water you pump onto more water, but the point is
to dig dry dirt. We haven't been able to work with any normal
sequence on this job, either.

"Our biggest problem is having to have dozers with the equipment
so much. We dig, and dump, then have the dozer strike it off, spread
it, let it dry, then dump more on top. Slow."

Aside from the pans and the dragline, Ranger brought a couple of big track hoes—backhoes mounted above dozer tracks—to Ironhorse. They can fill a twelve-yard dumpster with a few loads from their huge buckets, and the dump trucks—the DJBs—are a lot faster between the pickup and the drop than the pans.

Another problem Ranger's run into is shelly material that won't hold the equipment. Once again, Phillipson has to call the dragline into action. More slow digging. "We've talked to Wadsworth," Phillipson said, "and they think they'll work this shelly material enough shaping it to get the shell and topsoil mixed up anyway," so it's just the pace that's frustrating.

All this in league with Ranger's unit price for the dirt and the terms of the Water District's contract for the bond work conspires to create a dirt shortage. The surveyors staked the lakes' boundaries and then, superimposing a grid or a series of imaginary points over the surface, shot elevations of the existing grade. At Ironhorse this was easy work, since it's so flat. Then, after Ranger has finished digging a lake, the surveyors come back out with a little flat-bottomed boat, row it out to locate the same imaginary points, and measure the elevation at each one along what's now the bottom of the lake. This is called "sectioning the lake." When it's done, the surveyor calculates the volume of earth removed. Ranger gets paid $1.38 for every cubic yard excavated *up to the engineered quantity*. Beyond that they're digging for free. Or as Phillipson said, "We don't get paid to overdig."

Most of the 606,000 yards they're supposed to get out of the lakes they'll put where the golf course needs it. Some is needed for the roadbeds and the clubhouse pad. What the course builder dreads—and the owner, too—is too little dirt. As Britton put it, in one of his favorite aphorisms, "I can always lose dirt, but I can't make dirt. I can always lose it."

It's no big deal to add six inches to a mound or lay a few more inches of fill across a fairway—to lose dirt—but if there's not enough to shape with the golf course will suffer. As soon as Hills started suggesting bigger or taller tees or raised greens, he bumped into the limits Ranger's problems digging the lakes were imposing. Dash, worried about this problem from the start, said in a letter to Isakson months before, "In our grading specifications, we have wording to the effect that we have the right to raise or lower elevations plus or minus 1 and ½ feet anywhere on the course . . . to be able to fine tune the design of some features. We don't intend to be capriciously

changing elevations anywhere on the course," but he was concerned
that since Ranger was moving the dirt but Wadsworth was building
the course, there might be reluctance on Ranger's part to place additional dirt not specified on the grading plan. Nine months later,
Dash's worries proved prescient.

THE TREE SPADES had moved around to the Jog Road side of the perimeter berm by early spring, trying to get enough ahead of Wadsworth
so Britton could turn his drainage crew loose. P&J was back to clear
some roads and lots. The tree-spade crew was picking over P&J's
newly created burn piles for Sabals, the most durable of Florida's
trees. They'd pull them out of the rubble, lop off the fronds, dig a
hole, and plant them. Earlier in the job, Ironhorse had rejected shade-
grown Sabals on the berm, trees whose life under the canopy of pines
made them grow great wings of fronds searching for light. These trees
would fry in the sun unless their fronds were clipped, but Muss
hadn't liked that look, so there were no shade-grown palms along the
Beeline berm. Now with speed of the essence to complete the course
before the next selling season, standards were adjusted. In the long
run, all the transplanted palms would look the same anyway.

Fronds on all the Sabals were trimmed during transplantation as a
way to reduce stress on the plants, slow down their growth, as it
were. The procedure was more radical on the ones bred in shadows.
With the palm lying on the ground, the tree-spade operators would
lash the fronds at the very tops of the palms into a hemp-bound
bundle, trim off the remaining fronds with a chain saw, and stick the
tree in the ground. The tops thus prepared made the trees appear as
if a horticultural stylist trained in a Soho hair salon had contrived
their look. Eventually, the hemp rots and the fronds spread. "It's like
a turtle pulling its head in," said Norris Lindsey, the superintendent
for Ranger's tree-spade operation. "It'll come back out. The ones we
planted three weeks ago are already showing green."

Lindsey is a handsome, strong man in his middle forties who,
much to his surprise, loves his work. When Pat Painter, the restoration biologist who set up Ranger's tree-spade operation and pioneered the plantings at the Dyer Landfill, quit Ranger a few weeks
earlier Lindsey, whom Painter had trained as his assistant, took over.
It was his idea to salvage Sabals from the burn piles. "I seen that D8
crashing through there knocking those Sabals down," he said, smil-

ing, his gold tooth glinting. "I know those guys get their rocks off knocking all that down. I remember when I was running a dozer, I'd really get my nuts off on clearing, too. I'd be sweating and going hard and knocking trees down everywhere so the boss could come out there and see me and say, 'Norris, you're the best clearing man I got.' And I *never* guessed that some day I'd be saving trees, not knocking 'em down."

Now Lindsey, inspired by Painter, spreads the gospel of transplantation. He's proud of the work he did on the Dyer Landfill, the astonishment visitors express when they learn that all of the "native" ponds and forests were created by Painter, Lindsey, and their crews. He knows the berm will look great soon and screen Ironhorse exactly as Jay Bridge planned.

The Sabal crew with the fast technique, the backhoe bunch, is laying in palms in quantity along the Jog Road berm. The rubber-tired hoe digs a hole, then runs over to a trailer, where the Sabals are stacked like carrots on a grocer's shelf, wraps a chain around a cabbage palm, and lifts it with the bucket. The palm swings and knocks against the ground on its short ride to the hole. The operator sets it in the ground and holds it up straight until two guys waiting on the berm can lock it in place with shovelfuls of dirt. As soon as it's upright they drench the ground around it, pumping up water from the canal with a little portable pump fired by a gasoline engine.

One of the guys with a shovel is Collie Gordon, whose white hair and beard wrap his face like an aura and make him look much older than a man in his late forties. Born and raised in Florida, he was one of fourteen brothers. His parents also had two girls. His seventy-year-old father is still alive. Gordon's separated from his wife, but says, "I'd do anything for her and she'd do anything for me."

Gordon's job on the tree-spade crew is trimming the smaller plants, the myrtles and cocoa plums, and keeping everything well watered. Holding the thick red hose as it poured a stream of murky water on a palm, he said, in a quiet voice, "These aren't man's plants, these are God's. That's why I love them so. These aren't ours. We couldn't make one of these."

Muss's acceptance of Hills's suggestion to avoid formal plantings at the entry doesn't sit well with Matt Weeg, the sales manager, who says, "You've got one chance to make a first impression, so you've got to make the best of it. That's where you've got to massage them."

He's also wondering what strategy to use to overcome whatever fears people may have about the Solid Waste Authority. David Webber, he says, wants to keep quiet about it unless someone asks. Weeg thinks they ought to say there is a resource recovery unit nearby and let it go at that. "Seven out of ten people will be too embarrassed to admit they don't know what a resource recovery unit is, so that'll cover me there. If they say later, 'You didn't tell me about the waste recovery,' I'll say, 'I did,' and that'll be true. It doesn't make good marketing sense to dwell on it, but you've got to talk about it. Any wise buyer is going to drive around the neighborhood to see what's here anyway, and it's hard to hide that stack."

Weeg's also a little worried about the "window" leading to Ironhorse. "You get off the freeway, there's a Denny's and a Burger King and a cheap motel. Then there's a trailer park, which normally you could look on as a good source of domestic help. Ironhorse's buyers are not gonna be people who do housework. But it's a retirement-type mobile home park, so that doesn't help. Then you've got gas stations and a couple of produce stands. Then, if your view isn't blocked by an SWA truck, you see boxcars sitting on a siding and birds circling over the dump. Of course, the dump and the birds are going away soon, so I don't worry about that, but that leaves the rest of that lovely drive up. That's my window."

That Webber could even suggest clamming up about SWA, Weeg thinks, "shows nerves. David's got an interest in this from Josh, not just salary."

Before Muss decided to accept Hills's suggestion for the simplified entry, to stick with native plant material, Ironhorse hired a landscape architect known for his elaborate formal entries to design Ironhorse's gate. He proposed a lighted sign in the lake by the seventh green that Muss figured out was pretty much invisible from the road. Still, Weeg was cheered by what he had to say about Ironhorse. "If you fly a helicopter from Lauderdale to Stuart, you can see why Ironhorse is going to be such a success," he said, bracing Weeg. "You've got space to sell, privacy, and a sense of security. There aren't that many places around here that can offer that. And with the combination of environmental restraints and long-term planning goals, you're not going to find many places to develop."

There was also some talk of putting up a billboard on the berm near the sixth hole. Weeg wondered who would see it. "You know who uses this road? Guys making twenty thousand dollars a year on their way to Lake Okeechobee."

*　　*　　*

HOWARD STEVENS SHOWED up with Owsley's dozer, pulling it on a trailer behind his $99,000 Peterbilt. "That's the tractor, not the trailer. Bought it in nineteen eighty-six."

Stevens is a stickler for dates and a hound on details. Sixty-one years old, he went to work for Wadsworth on August 11, 1975. Way back when, he says, he was driving equipment for a tunnel job under Lake Ontario while Britton was working there as a sand hog. They didn't know one another. When he went to work for Wadsworth, the company had enough equipment to keep him busy moving it from job to job, but not nearly as fine a rig to haul it with. His Peterbilt has a hydraulic seat, a console with enough instruments to play a symphony, and a three-spoked steering wheel almost parallel to the ground. It has a sleeper Stevens rarely uses. Wadsworth never puts air conditioning in its superintendents' trucks, which is why Britton is always driving around Ironhorse with an arm propped on the window. "We got that two-seventy air conditioning," Britton says. "Roll two windows down, go seventy miles an hour."

There is nothing worse, says Jon Shapland, the head of Wadsworth's Southeast office, "than busting your butt laying pipe or spreading a gravel blanket, sweating under a hot sun, drenched and dry at the same time, and looking over at the boss sitting in his air-conditioned truck wiggling his finger at you. So you walk over and he cracks the window a quarter of an inch and you stick your ear close enough to hear, catching the tiniest whiff of that cool air, and he says, 'Don't forget to catch that basin by fourteen on your way in,' then closes the window and drives away, cool as ice. Makes you want to kill. That's why our supers drive with the windows down."

Stevens's Peterbilt is another story. "You think we wouldn't put air in a ninety-nine-thousand-dollar truck? We got *two* air conditioners—one for the cab, one for the sleeper."

There's the obligatory CB and an electric cooler rated at eight bottles of Gatorade. "Bought that myself."

Stevens moves all Wadsworth's equipment in the Southeast, from North Carolina to Louisiana to all over Florida. "I have fun loading this stuff myself. Dozers that won't start, I have to jump 'em. Big-wheeled pans. Do it all by myself."

When he's not hauling, he's "the Japanese gardener" on the grounds at the Oldsmar office. He rides a little mower, chopping down the Saint Augustine grass, skirting the beds full of the annuals he's planted. The mower doesn't have enough power to start the Peterbilt, but Stevens rides them both with equal aplomb. He shares with Britton a tendency to operate without his upper plate, which collapses his smile and loads his speech with sibilants. He's much too happy for Owsley, who was at least glad to see him when Stevens delivered Owsley's D5. Phillipson says, "Willie's a great operator, but he's got the black ass."

It was nearly three months after his first visit before Hills made it back to Ironhorse, for the second of six site visits he made during the year it took to build the golf course. Dasher, who meanwhile had walked the course twice between Hills's first two visits, joined him on a walk-through in early March, three weeks before South Florida issued the permit that finally turned Stu Britton lose. Dasher came three times as often as Hills, sometimes as frequently as four times in a month. Ed Harbauer, who was Wadsworth's big boss on the Iron-horse job, drove over from Oldsmar to meet with Hills and Dasher and review the rough shaping on the first few holes Owsley had managed to put his touch on. Britton was in charge of shaping, drainage, and coordination with the grassing contractor. Wadsworth would also send an irrigation superintendent, who was Britton's equal in the Wadsworth hierarchy and would, like Britton, report to Harbauer. Harbauer ordered material, managed the contracts with subcontractors, and negotiated with the owners.

Harbauer left Oldsmar at 3:30 A.M. in a company Oldsmobile to make it to the site in time to meet Art and Mike. Harbauer has a round, friendly face that turns red in the sun and a dry wit. His laugh is loud and quick, and when he's upset he chokes it into a reluctant smile. He loves the Tampa Bay Buccaneers but shows no other signs of mental fatigue. Owsley's been working on four, five, seven, and eight, the only holes Wadsworth's managed to get anything done on. The company building the outfall pump—also part of the bond work for the Northern Palm Beach County Water Control District—at the corner of Jog and the Beeline has been using the sixth fairway as a haul road. The dirt's not all down yet anywhere on the back nine.

Britton wants most of all to find some order according to which he can work. The overall sequence is simple: rough-shape the fairways, build the tees and greens, put in drainage, install the irrigation, run the cart paths, clean it all up, and grass. There's nothing complicated about any of these tasks, which tend to repetition, unless they're out of sequence or have to be redone. Once the shaping's done the work has to be protected, either by prayer to forestall rain or barricades to keep trucks off the finished work.

"These guys are just like dairy cows," Britton said, roping off the sixth tee. "One of 'em gets started on a path and they all use it. Then you get compacted ruts, and when you go to finishing your tee and grassing it the rest of the dirt isn't compacted as much, even after you regrade it, and you get puddles of water standing in the ruts. I've seen it too many times, and I don't want to build that tee more than once."

HILLS WANTED TO start at the fourth tee. Wearing a pink Eagle Trace shirt and a white Windward hat, he looked down the fairway past a lake that was new since his last visit. A tiny tern fluttered above the lake. As the tern whirled and plunged toward the water, Hills looked off to the west, settling the scale of the hole in his mind. The tees, he decides, are too far from the water. "We can move 'em," Britton says.

Hills wants more drama at the edge, more height and a steeper slope. "You'd rather have the two-to-one slope right into the water?" Harbauer asks.

"If we can do it," Hills replies. He wants the side slopes of the tees tied together, even if they're at different elevations, to give them a feeling of continuity. The dirt's roughly piled on the tee, not shaped. "We need to be up another foot, foot and a half."

Britton slumps, and looks at Jon Harpman, who's joined the assembly on the fourth tee. With resigned solemnity, he intones the phrase whose implications he dreads. "More dirt."

Ironhorse has plenty of trees, lakes, sunshine, and breezes, but this struggle over dirt at the moment overshadows them all. There's just not enough dirt to build higher tees or more dramatic mounds. Hills doesn't want to compromise the golf course. Britton wants to get it built.

A single great egret worked the opposite shore, looking for lunch in the infant lake. Aquatic survivors from the old drainage canal were migrating to the new lakes, small fish, frogs, and tadpoles scurrying just below the surface of the warm, brown-tinted water. At the preserve boundary, Ranger unrolled a thick gray plastic vertical barrier in the large trench, about four feet deep and six feet across, it had dug along the length of the preserve berm to limit the flow of water. High water—water above seventeen feet—would spill over weirs at either end of the preserve and flow into Ironhorse's lakes. Once the plastic liner was in place, dirt was piled on top of the berm to elevation twenty, a fact that Hills's grading plan had been slow to grasp. The flip side of getting to put golf holes into the preserve was a grapple with the implications of the berm. It would look like a roadbed when Ranger was through. It was great for the cart path between the eleventh and twelfth holes and between the first and second holes, but where it ran in front of greens it had that deliberate, fabricated look Hills loathed on a golf course.

Back behind the twelfth tee, near its southern terminus, the preserve berm wrapped around the old apple-snail pond. Right after Ranger cut the sheer-walled trench, I saw a large turtle crawling along its bottom. Thinking it was trapped within this small canyon, I jumped in the ditch behind the turtle. I'd seen turtles sunning along the seepage canal and remembered one of the clearing hands saying the safest way to handle a big soft-shell like this one was to grab it by the very back of the shell, at the tail. Whether this was a big turtle or not I cannot say, but it looked formidable to me, with the approximate dimensions of a curled-up, sleeping springer spaniel. As I approached it, the turtle settled, so I squatted down and reached out to seize it. It swung its rear feet in a great vigorous thrust, and I pulled my arms back so fast my elbows cracked into my kneecaps. The pain was so intense I couldn't rise and stood bent over behind the turtle, which had resumed its amble. I climbed out of the trench and pulled up one of the stakes set out to mark the berm, thinking perhaps I could use it as a lever to flip the turtle on its back. Then I could lift it over the wall of the trench. Sliding the stake, which was about the length of a yardstick, under the turtle's side, I levered it over. The turtle's head came out, and out, and out, its neck like the foot of a giant clam or a stallion's calling card. With a quick thrust of its head against the ground, the turtle righted itself. It happened very quickly. Out of curiosity, and with no intent to harm it, I waved the stake in front of the turtle's mouth. Biting so quickly I saw the results more than the action, the turtle severed the wood as easily as if it had been a noodle.

The Florida soft-shell, *Trionyx ferox,* has legs powerfully adapted for digging. Its snout, which gives the soft-shell an almost mammalian-looking head—William Bartram thought its "proboscis," as he called it, looked like a pig's nose—lets it breach the water's surface for air without creating a ripple. Bartram made a wonderful sketch of a soft-shelled turtle lying on its back that's reproduced in his *Travels*. It was surely dead when he drew it. "They are very large when full grown," he wrote, "from twenty to thirty and forty pounds weight, extremely fat and delicious, but if eaten to excess"—one guesses Bartram wrote here from experience—"are apt to purge people not accustomed to their meat."

My turtle crawled on to the end of the trench, in the direction of the water catchment basin, and sank below the grimy surface of shallow water accumulated there. A couple of charred pine limbs, the debris of an old burn pile, probably from Ironhorse's ranching days, floated over the turtle's wake. "They bury themselves in the slushy bottoms of rivers and ponds," Bartram wrote, "under the roots of flags and other aquatic herbage."

The berm ran in front of the first, fourth, tenth, and eleventh greens, all of them in the preserve. Looking at the berm from the fairway of the fourth hole, Hills wondered, "Can we pull it back toward the dogleg?" The berm made it harder to see the green, and the uniformity of its shape contrasted with the subtler forms Hills wanted on the golf course. Raising the green, Hills thought, would perch it too high above the surrounding ground. There was a similar problem at the eleventh hole, where the height of the berm made it almost impossible for a golfer standing on the tee to see the little pond in front of the green.

Harpman said Peter Aquart's advice was not to approach the Water District about moving the berm. "We're going to leave it where it is," he said.

Owsley was shaping on the fourth green. He turned off the machine as the entourage approached and climbed down. Art told him he wanted steeper slopes on the backs and side of the green. "I want at least three-to-one," he said, meaning for every foot down the slope went out three feet.

As he listened to Hills, Owsley collected dirt with his booted foot and began to work it into tiny bumps and hollows, creating miniature contours, as if the work had become so much a part of him that even at rest, without thinking, he was shaping. Hills wanted him to mold a grassy hollow into the front of the green and "pull the mass at the front of the green out toward the fairway," so the green would look as if it were part of a larger land form instead of sitting up, isolated

and contrived. Hills also asked Owsley for "more accent in the cupping areas." A couple of weeks before, Hills said, the Senior PGA
Tour players complained about the severity of some of the undulations on the greens at Hills's course at Pelican Bay, a tournament site.
Hills said he didn't mind the undulations as long as the cupping areas
themselves were fair.

THE FIRST STEP in shaping a green, once the dirt's laid in at rough grade,
is to locate its center. A green is three-dimensional, but the drawing
has only two dimensions. The green at the fourth hole has the footprint, or profile, of a potato—but then most greens that aren't kidney-
shaped look like potatoes. There are only so many ways to distort a
circle while keeping a shape where a straight line can be drawn
between any two points within it. A "C"-shaped green, for example,
even if it were designed with radical slopes to guide the ball from one
side to the other like a banked track steers a race car, wouldn't make
sense. While there may be a theoretically infinite number of green
shapes, as a practical matter there are only a few that work, and
they're all arbitrary distortions of a circle. It's their slopes, their undulations, their settings, and the orientation of the greens to the
fairway that give them interest.

Britton spreads the green sheet on the ground and looks back
down the fairway to locate the line of play. The surveyors have staked
the tees, doglegs, and greens. There's a two-inch plastic pipe with a
green ribbon hanging on it marking the center of the fourth green.
The axis of the line of play on the green sheet is labeled "AB" and
runs from the front to the back of the green. Britton and Owsley pull
a tape to measure the distance from the center to the front and back
edges and drive a stake at each point. They measure along the other
three axes, whose effect on the drawing is to create a series of uneven,
pie-shaped wedges, and drive six more stakes. Looking at the grid on
which the green shape is drawn, they can fill in the dots between
stakes, as it were, to outline the green. They can tell at a glance from
the contour lines how high the green sits and how steep its sides are.
The green sheet also shows the pattern for the drainage tile and its
connection to the overall drainage system. Little numbers covering
the green like a pox tell the shaper what the slopes are from front to
back and side to side. The highest contour line on the fourth green,
for example, is at elevation twenty-six. Near it is the notation " + 2"—

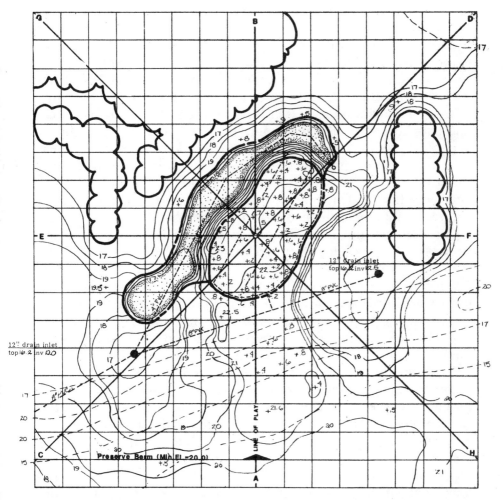

Detail of the green sheet for the fourth hole. (*Courtesy Arthur Hills and Associates*)

so Owsley knows there is a slight rise there. After all the stakes are set, Britton will mark them with the finish elevations of the green.

Architects have struggled with ways to communicate green shapes to the operators. Geoff Cornish in Massachusetts says Stanley Thompson and Robert Trent Jones sometimes built clay models so the operators could see the shapes they were after. Cornish still has thirty-year-old Plasticine models that his wife molded on Masonite bases and painted green. He saved some of Jones's models, too. They're very plain, with none of the commotion of the contemporary green. Pete Dye, the most intuitive and instinctive golf architect, will flop to the ground, gather up an armful of loose sand, and shape what he's after with his hands for the operator to see. He has a plastic imagination. Computer-generated drawings that boost the topographic representations into three dimensions are the latest thing, but few golf architects have adopted the technology. Before long, optical scanners will read the contour lines on a topo map and translate them to a video screen, where the designer will be able to manipulate the images with the same easy control word processing offers to writers. Two-dimensional drawings are hard for many people, like Alan Sher, to read. The computer won't enhance the design, it will simply make the ideas in the architect's mind more accessible.

Hills's green sheets carry plenty of information for Owsley. In addition to the plan view and the topo lines, Hills draws sections through the green, so Owsley can see the major slopes at a quick glance. When he's creating a green, Owsley folds the green sheet so only the outline of the shape is visible and attaches it to the roof on the dozer operator's cage, just above his eyes. As he runs the Cat over the ground, shaping it, he looks up at the drawing. He *feels* the contours as the dozer rolls over them, sensitive, even sitting above tons of steel, to the subtlest movements in the ground. He does a lot of back-blading, running the Cat in reverse with the blade down to smooth the surface and erase his own tracks. Forward or backward, Owsley runs quick. Owsley shapes the greens at subgrade, or sixteen inches *below* the finished surface of the green. A recently shaped green is a hole in the ground, as if the green itself had been extracted by a giant cookie cutter plunged into the earth. A freshly shaped green is a little disconcerting, like something undone. Shaping at subgrade leaves room for a four-inch blanket of gravel over the drainage pipe and for a foot of greens mix. Owsley makes it two feet wider around the edges, a way to add extra greens mix and plant a margin of Tifdwarf to ward off the more aggressive grass planted on the fairways and collars.

After he's shaped the green itself, Owsley works the dirt around it, contouring mounds and molding bunkers. The bunkers are also shaped below finish grade—they'll be filled with a half a foot or so of sand. All of this work is described on the green sheet, but it too is subject to the ever popular field adjustment. Owsley doesn't outline the bunkers with the same precision used on the greens or build them with quite the finesse. To outline a bunker, he'll grab the green sheet from the cage, climb off the dozer, and find the bunker location, looking back and forth from the green to the drawing until he has a good fix on where he is. Then, looking at the drawing as he walks, he'll drag a foot to scrape an outline of the bunker in the dirt.

Hills has to approve all the shapes before Britton runs the drainage pipe and approve them again before Wadsworth sprigs. Britton likes to have a half-dozen holes or so for Hills to look at each time he comes, a wish hard to fulfill at Ironhorse. When Hills came to look at the shaping in March, Owsley had worked on parts of five holes, all of them at the north end, near the construction entry—four, five, six, eight, and nine. There was nothing to do on seven, the par three over Lake Kennicott, until the tie wall at the green was built. On the other holes, when Hills pointed out something he didn't like, Britton would say, "Willie hasn't been on that yet, Art."

Dash followed up the visits with a letter summarizing what he and Hills wanted. A typical paragraph reads: "Hole #5: Keep tee as far left as possible. Expand landing area to right by clearing dead trees and adding fill. Grade in ledge definition in front of green."

At the sixth hole he wanted to change a fairway bunker and at nine a higher tee. There was too much dirt along the right side of the fairway and a crown between the dogleg and the green Hills wanted cut down to achieve a "sort of downhill feeling to the green."

Hills asked Britton to cut "shadow faces" into the mounds behind green nine. Even though the green is low, the small lakes on either side of it—visible but not in play—give it an illusion of height. "Cutting it down low in front of the green," he said to Britton, "gives a nice contrast from back in the landing area."

"This is a pretty plain hole," Hills reflected. "I kind of eased up here. My thinking was, they've had plenty of tough shots to this point, so I'd give them a little respite. I don't know if I should have, but that's how I saw it. A basic hole."

At the eighth tee, Hills asked not only to raise the tee but to build screening mounds behind it to baffle noise from the entry road. "You'd need a lot of dirt in here to do that," Ed Harbauer observed.

"We'd have a definite lowering of quality," Hills responded, "if we don't block that traffic."

At green eight, which Owsley had already shaped, Hills said, "This is a short hole with a small green. It ought to be perched. It should be two feet higher."

Britton, Harpman, and Owsley all stopped dead in their tracks at Hills's words. Noticing the reaction, Hills said, evenly, "It's a short little hole. That's what it needs."

Harbauer smiled at Hills and said, "I guess we just get paid too much for our shaping. Boy, that's a tough one, Art. This other stuff we're doing on the fairways, I don't mind, but this, this is a lot of work."

Hills, listening calmly, signaled Dash with his eyes and started walking back down the fairway. From fifty yards out he studied the green. "The bunkers and the green shape and the faces are good," he said. "Just cut down the green, from the front to the back."

Britton's shoulders slumped, and his head lowered. "Everything I'm doing now is just free gratis," he said. "That's just the way it works. Free gratis."

15

The Bunker Imbroglio

The designer should not be tied down too closely to his original plan. Mature consideration may make a modification in the plan necessary to get better results.

—Alister Mackenzie

AFTER HILLS AND DASHER LEFT, off to visit a job in Jupiter, the Wadsworth and Ranger groups met with Bob Isakson and Jon Harpman at the office. Who, they all wondered, was going to pay for moving the dirt Hills's new instructions required? Ed Harbauer also expressed concern about the quality of the dirt on several fairways. Some of that shelly material was sterile and hard to work, and it washed badly when it rained.

"When we get to the elevation where we're supposed to stop digging," Ranger's John Riley, who was at the meeting with Kevin Phillipson, said, "We hit the prettiest sand you've ever seen. But we don't get a dime to dig deeper than design elevation."

Britton told Phillipson he'd need 800 more yards to build up the eighth green by two feet. "Why does Hills want to do that," Isakson demanded. He'd never be reconciled to field adjustments. To him, working this way was like sending men into battle without orders. Isakson liked a chain of command.

"That's what golf course architects *do*," Harbauer said, leaning against the door jamb with his arms folded over his chest, speaking through a pained smile.

"How much dirt do we need for these changes Hills wants?" Isakson continued.

"My guess," replied Phillipson, "is that we'll need close to seven thousand yards."

Harbauer nodded in agreement. "Kevin's right. But we're done here if we don't get some dirt moved."

Phillipson aimed his dark glasses in Harbauer's direction. It was disarming not to see his eyes. "The problem," Phillipson said, repeating a phrase frequently rehearsed by the Ranger employees, "is that the dirt's at the south end and the golf course is at the north."

Riley, pulling on a toothpick, loomed over the table where Isakson and Harpman sat. "We'll work together to get this done," he assured them, and Phillipson, as he often did, picked up the thought. Phillipson operated out of such a supportive frame of mind that he often finished sentences started by someone else. "It'll take a week to get squared around," he interjected, "but I can move a couple of scrapers to nine and get that high stuff moved for you."

"Good," said Harbauer. "That'll give Willie something to do. He can shape nine, redo eight the way Hills wants. We're lucky we've *only* got Willie on this job."

"We'll be out of here June first," Riley announced. It's the middle of March, and they don't have nine consecutive holes rough-shaped. Muss wants nine playable holes by the end of September.

Harbauer leads the laughter. "What'll we do if Hills comes back after June first?"

THE NEXT TIME Hills and Dasher came to Ironhorse, in early April, Dasher "thought it looked real good, a lot of potential." Even Hills thought it had possibilities. "Usually at this point in a job Hills is thinking, 'Oh, God, did we screw this one up!' " Dasher says. "He's pretty excited about Ironhorse, thinks maybe we've got something here. He's not totally negative like he was up at Willoughby. Near the end up there you'd have thought the course was going to be an embarrassment to him, to his firm, to his family—and hey, that course is not half bad. At Ironhorse, we may end up with a Seville or a Bonita Bay."

After the April walk-through, Hills and Dasher joined Wadsworth's Harbauer and Ranger's Phillipson for a meeting with Jon Harpman. Harpman said that from now on every change Hills wanted was subject to approval by Joshua Muss. In fact, Harpman explained, Muss didn't want *any* changes. Harpman had written as much to Hills at the end of March: "All further changes to the grading plan will be reviewed and evaluated by Josh Muss for approval. There is a cost concern with the major changes, even with the small changes that will add up very quickly."

"Art," as Dasher recalled, "got a little exasperated. Every change we'd talked about making that day, Ed or Kevin would say, 'We can take care of that,' or 'We can handle that.' We weren't talking about spending much money.

"Art said to Harpman, 'Josh has just got to loosen up. If he doesn't spend money now to get it right he's just going to lose money at the other end.'

"Harpman said, 'Well, Josh got to where he is acting the way he does.'

"Later, Art said to me, 'Where is Josh? He's miserable, that's where he is.' "

Harbauer felt the same frustration Hills expressed. Wadsworth bid on the retaining wall at the seventh green, but as Harbauer said, "They'll dick around a month on that 'cause Josh doesn't want to pay the fifty dollars a foot that Wadsworth quoted him. After he delays the project a month he saves four bucks a foot on the wall but instead of having a nice, green golf course at the start of the next selling season, he's got to decide whether he can open one nine, or should he overseed the rest because it wasn't planted in time to grow in. Wasting time and money, as I see it. It's a false economy, penny wise and pound foolish."

Hills's frustration would come to a head in June, not long before Wadsworth was finally able to start sprigging. Meanwhile, Britton was attacking the drainage. Rod Lucks, his young assistant, was directing a crew of Haitian laborers running pipe and setting basins. These were all men who migrated to south Florida from Cap Haitien, on Hispaniola's northern coast, not far from the Ile de la Tortue. Not all spoke English, and their ages ranged from the early twenties to late fifties. They worked very hard. Britton liked their gentle ways. Sometimes language difficulties stymied communication, but the work was plain enough not to require a rich vocabulary. Lucks would point to something and ask "What?" and in that way learned the Creole words for shovel, rake, level, grass, dirt, and water. "If I want them to shovel dirt, I say, *'Nevel tierra.'* "

"Pipe" was part of the lingua franca. Lucks learned what's called "golf course Spanish" the same practical way, so he could direct the Guatemalan laborers placing sod on the lake banks and vulnerable slopes. Sometimes one of the Haitians would work wearing only thongs on his feet. They formed their hats into imaginative shapes and wore tattered shirts. The work was hot and tiring. They liked Britton. Wilmon Laguerre, Britton feared, was *too* devoted to him. Britton thought his eagerness offended his countrymen. "Wilmon can't swim," Britton said, "but if I told him to cross that lake he'd dive right in the water." They were eager to learn how to operate equipment, so Britton was breaking them in on the little utility tractors, hauling pipe and fittings. "Stu good man," Rolland Charles said, "good, good man."

Once, as I talked with Paul Filus, a muscular man with strong features and large teeth who jumped at the chance to run irrigation pipe when the drainage work was done, a deerfly landed on my cheek. I couldn't feel it at first, but would as soon as it bit. Paul reached toward me with an almost maternal gentleness and brushed the fly off my face. He smiled at my surprise. The Haitians are collectively the nicest people I've ever met.

The drainage inlets ran wild above the ground when they were first placed, so after final grades were established someone could cut the tops off exactly flush with—or slightly below—the grass line. The location, direction of flow, and length for every basin was marked on Hills's print, but as each was installed Britton carefully recorded its exact location on his "as-built" drawing. These as-builts recorded the anatomy of Ironhorse's subterranean fixtures, its drainage and irrigation, so if Wadsworth ever needed to come back and repair a damaged pipe, or if the superintendent needed to replace a sprinkler head, they'd know exactly where the pipe ran and wouldn't inadvertently cut into it. Sometimes a superintendent will place white paper plates over every sprinkler head and have an aerial photograph made, but that's not as informative as Wadsworth's technique because it only records what's on the surface.

Wadsworth installed 134 drainage basins at Ironhorse, all draining into the lakes. "12 inch drain inlet," the print would say, "top 16.2, inv 12.5." "Inv" means invert, or in plain language the depth of the hole. "Tie into storm water system," the drawing instructs. The smallest drainage pipes at Ironhorse, other than those on the greens, were six inches in diameter, the largest fifteen inches. The inlets ranged in size from twelve to twenty-four inches. Lucks and his crew ran nearly three miles of pipe, all of it at least two and a half feet below grade. The irrigation pipes run above the drainage lines, at least in principle—but at least once on every job the irrigation crew will accidentally chew through a drainage pipe. That and their tendency to dishevel the shaping earned the irrigators their nickname—the *irritation* crew.

Installing drainage is a simple operation. The pipe men dig out for the basin with the backhoe and set the corrugated steel inlet pipe in the ground vertically. Then they excavate a trench over to the nearest lake's edge, make sure they have a little fall from the outlet to the lake according to "the water don't run uphill rule," and connect the two. Usually, the basins are in series, so as it neared the lakes the water from several basins would flow into progressively larger pipes. "Water should never run more than one hundred feet to a basin," Britton says.

Except for the inlets, the drainpipe is plastic. It comes in ten- to twenty-foot lengths and is not heavy. After the inlets are installed, they are wrapped with a cloth cover to keep out debris. After the course is ready to grass and they are cut to length a green plastic grate is fitted over the top.

The green drainage is a variation on the fairway technique, once again designed by Hills's office. Hills prefers what's called a gridiron green drainage pattern, as opposed to a herringbone style. A series of parallel trenches, eight inches wide and eight inches deep, is cut with a small trencher across the bottom of the freshly shaped green, and a similar trench is dug around its lower perimeter. These trenches are no more than twenty feet apart. Within each trench, surrounded by pea gravel, a four-inch perforated PVC pipe runs. The fairway pipe is solid-wall because it's draining the surface. The greens use perforated pipe because they're collecting underground water. Above the tops of the pipe trenches is a four-inch layer of pea gravel and on top of the gravel twelve inches of the greens mix Britton's been concocting for the last two months. The blanket of pea gravel, like the greens mix, has to imitate the undulations in the green, so when they're spreading it the workmen paw at it with their feet as a rough gauge to check the depth of each layer. On the greens mix, they use a thin steel rod to measure, skewering the sand every few feet to match the surface contour with its base.

A USGA green holds water where the grass needs it—in the root zone—but is designed so that in a deluge water will flow through the pea gravel and into the drainpipes. Standing water on a green is a sign of poor design and construction.

Ironhorse's greens are *almost* USGA greens. The USGA method calls for a thin layer of coarse sand between the gravel and the greens mix. Hills recommends eliminating this sand, a technique called the "Improved Approach." What greens mix promises is a uniform growing medium for the grass on the greens, but not everyone believes it's necessary. Roger Whitford, who signed on as Ironhorse's superintendent early in the summer, would have preferred a little more native material in his greens to firm them up. USGA greens, he says, are soggy. Paul Frank, developer of The Wilderness Club and, according to Whitford, one of the best grass growers in Florida, likes "a little more organics" in his greens than the USGA's recommended ratio of one part peat to four parts sand. On the greens at his Innisbrook courses, Brent Wadsworth uses straight native sugar sand, with no peat, and a lot of people think Innisbrook has the best greens in Florida.

THROUGH THE REST of the spring and into the early summer, Wadsworth was struggling to keep busy, trying to find the sequence of holes that would let it work without a lot of wandering. Ranger scrambled to find enough dirt to accommodate Wadsworth. Britton knew this was standard Florida building, this battle over dirt, but he was chafing anyway. "Trying to get dirt," he'd say, "is like beating my head against the wall."

By the middle of May, despite Britton's pessimism, Owsley had pretty much finished the shaping on ten holes, and the forms he'd created were beautiful. In the mysterious manner of construction projects big or small, the work unfolded with a logic of its own, a kind of wondrous persistence, and almost without knowing how—even though you knew there were lots of people out there working every day—new objects, new forms, a new physical reality appeared. Alligators were starting to claim the ponds, and a big one floated up not far from where Owsley was having lunch in the shade of pines behind the fourteenth green. Owsley tossed a couple of rocks its way, "hitting that sombitch between the eyes." The gator accepted the blow as an act of God.

Kevin Phillipson had to watch where he staked his dogs, too, after Bob Isakson saw a gator moseying their way. "Those dogs would make a nice snack for that old gator," he said.

By the time he got to Ironhorse on the afternoon of Thursday, June 1, Art Hills had already had a bad day. He and Dasher had flown in late the night before from Richmond and crashed at an airport hotel, then left at 5:30 A.M. for the Old Trail project west of Jupiter. Hills had designed a companion for Old Trail's Tom Fazio course, built in 1986, and the progress of its construction was roughly paralleling Ironhorse's. Hills and Dasher usually visited both jobs on their trips to West Palm.

Hills drove a mile past the turnoff to Old Trail, but getting a little bit lost was routine. Hills and Dasher weren't even late for their 7:00 A.M. meeting. Their morning started well.

Fazio's Old Trail course was built to handle the overflow from its parent project's main course at Jonathan's Landing, in Jupiter. Jonathan's Landing's director of golf said, "We told Fazio we wanted a course the members could play with a putter if they wanted to. There's a straight, solid line on every hole from tee to green. No cross hazards."

Waiting at Old Trail to meet Hills and Dasher were the contractor and his superintendent, the project manager for the owner and his engineer. Also along were the golf course superintendent who will maintain both the Fazio course and Hills's new course and the golf professional. After Hills and Dasher slathered on sunscreen, they walked to the tee of the new driving range, the part of the work nearest completion. The sun was hidden behind a small cluster of clouds, disguising the promise of heat the day held. A moderating breeze blew in from the east. Hills suggested some modifications in the practice chipping area, but praised the look of the range. East of the driving range, the first hole was rough-shaped. That's where the bad day began.

Curling down the first fairway in perfect symmetry, not so much serpentine as mathematical, like a sine wave, ran a uniformly rounded mound of dirt, its only break with perfection a subtle rise over the 300 or so yards from tee to green. It looked like an abbreviated imitation of the Great Serpent Mound in Hills's native Ohio, but it had as much affinity to the flowing sinuosity of the Hopewellian original as AstroTurf has to grass. Approaching the carefully raked curves, Hills let his eyes drift toward the green. The diffidence with which he began each site visit fell away, the shy mask effaced by an amalgam of stupefaction and grief. "This," he said quietly, barely able to squeeze out the words, "doesn't look like anything I've ever seen in twenty-five years. It doesn't look like a golf course at all."

A snake defiled *this* Eden. The Old Trail crew kept a respectful distance while Hills tried to fathom how the course builder could have translated his suggestions from the last visit into this curious form. "It may be like giving me plans for a house," he began, sympathetically. "No matter how good the plans were, I couldn't build the house. I guess I don't know how to describe what we want to do here. Maybe you don't have the people to do what I want. I'm stumped."

While Hills huddled with the course builder and his superintendent, the Old Trail crew shuffled about in a quiet huddle, the way kids do around trouble, fearful of blame, pretty sure they're innocent but not quite confident enough of the rules to proclaim it. They were conversing in whispers. "I knew this wasn't right," said the project manager. "We all knew it."

Hills sent for a spray gun, a rolling wand that holds a cylinder of spray paint. When you pull the trigger in its handle, it paints a line on the ground. Dasher bummed a smoke from the golf course superintendent. Working back from the green, Hills painted lines in the dirt, describing what he wanted. "We've got to earn our money here," he told Dasher, essaying a crooked smile, counseling a cautious optimism while his instincts screamed despair. Dasher walked toward the green to get a better look.

"What Art wanted was for them to mound up to the fairway side of those palmettos," Dasher said, pointing to the stand of pine and palmettos separating the first hole's fairway from the range, "and then let it work back across the fairway tailing off into some gentle undulations, and then pick up a similar mound on the other side up closer toward the green. On the back side they'd just kinda fall off into the pines and palms. So he drew a rough line in plan view the last time we were here that squiggled up toward the green, but they took that sketch literally, I guess, and built this snake."

As Hills walked the reptile's back, painting long, broken red lines

on the brown, sandy ground, the golf course superintendent came by
to plead for patience, a big man towering over Hills, leaning down to
make his case, quietly, pausing first to draw smoke into his lungs.
"This is the only hole like this," he promised.

"Yes. Uh-huh. Uh-huh. Yes," Hills said in his distracted way, looking back along the red arc he had just limned on the earthen canvas.
He told the builder to cut a convex face in the mound where he'd
drawn the line to let the back of the slope "work down into those
palmettos."

"Ah, I love the smell of spray paint in the morning," Dasher said.
"Damn, I love it." He fixed Hills with a grin. Hills wanted to know
why the hell Dasher was smoking. Hills wasn't quite ready to relin-
quish his frustration, but Dasher had decided that this problem was
an easy fix. "They can redo it in a day."

But for Hills it was a crisis of confidence, fear that he couldn't make
himself understood, that short of camping on the site he couldn't
explain exactly what he imagined for this golf course. It was why he
liked having Wadsworth build his courses—Britton and Owsley knew
the meanings contained in the dance of Hills's hands as they drew in
the air. They knew how to build the shapes he wanted.

After the shock of the fairway, Hills didn't have much to say about
the green, a conventional-looking shape, deeper than it was wide. He
saw a large pile of dirt piled at the base of a couple of pines he'd left
behind the green to give some visual depth for a player standing on
the fairway. The dirt was strangling the pines, suffocating them.
"Those trees are dead," he said. His voice took on the tone of a
Puritan divine who had discovered his congregation at an orgy. "That
should never happen. That's the worst thing that could happen on a
construction site."

The second hole was different, but no better. The tees, plateaus set
above the fairway grade, had square corners, an abrupt, industrial
appearance, as if inspired by the Nash Rambler. Mounds banked
against a stand of trees 250 yards from the tees had the serrated look
of eroded peaks, tropical badlands. Their skyline—the profile at the
ridge—was forlorn, with none of the curving grace or gentle motion
that Hills had hoped for and that Dasher, on his last visit to the
course, had seen in the very mounds that now looked like a brigand's
redoubt. "Hell, this looked pretty good when I saw it," Dasher told
Hills. "I just wanted them to take a little out of the face of those
mounds. At least they head back into the trees the way we wanted."

The second fairway, echoing the uniformity of the first hole, had several rows of low mounds cut across it, fifty yards or so apart. It looked vaguely agricultural, an experimental plot for growing giant hybrid pumpkins perhaps, or dikes for rice paddies. "How can we solve this?" Hills wondered. "I'll rant and rave and make a fool of myself if it'll do any good, but I don't know if I'm making any headway."

He looked across a dry marsh to the green, squinting under the brim of his cap. Standing atop a pile of Old Trail's dry, sandy dirt, Hills was "under a deep exercise and concernment," to borrow a phrase from Jonathan Dickinson, the Quaker merchant who washed ashore near Jupiter after his ship wrecked there late in the seventeenth century. Dickinson's name was appropriated for Jonathan's Landing.

It was still early in the morning, but the sun, risen from behind shallow clouds, drove the temperature up in an instant. Hills told Dasher as they walked across the washboardlike mounds of the second fairway, "I did the last one, you do this one."

Dasher fell in beside the construction superintendent and explained how he wanted restored what he'd approved two weeks ago. "The fella that ruined all this was just helping us out," the super warranted. "He's not shaping here anymore."

"Must have been a road man," Dasher offered. "He got all these lines awful straight and clean. Thing is we're not building a road."

Hills, halfway through his second can of paint by the time he had finished with his suggestions on the second green, was starting to feel a little better. Beyond the dogleg at the second hole, the shaping finally had begun to resemble what was drawn on his green sheets and grading plan, as modified by the ever popular field adjustment. Hills extended a bunker in front of the green out into the fairway by thirty yards to create a target. Thereafter the fiddling was routine. The remaining dirt work looked unremarkable, a soothing contrast to the first two holes. By noon the walk-through was over, but the encounter with the first two holes left Hills with an emotional hangover. The leave-taking was polite, even convivial, but Hills couldn't push the first two holes from his mind.

"That was the second worst shaping work I've ever seen," Hills said five minutes later as he pulled into a quick-stop deli to browse, hungry and dry after five hours in nearly tropical sun on a day that would hit ninety degrees. "The worst was on a public course I did in

Cincinnati, quite a while ago, I don't know. They had some guy in there to do the first nine who didn't know what he was doing. Terrible. But they got rid of him, and the course turned out well."

Hills grabbed down a big grapefruit juice and a salad, let Dasher pay the tab, and then aimed the maroon rented Olds toward Ironhorse. Dasher ate as Hills wheeled south. He had told Ed Harbauer of Wadsworth that they'd be there shortly after one o'clock.

Dasher had been to Ironhorse the previous week, trying to allay the increasingly burdensome frustration the Wadsworth crew felt about not having any sequence of completed holes it could work on. Britton was feeling the squeeze of Muss's pressure to get nine holes in play by the end of September.

By one-thirty Hills was devouring his salad, sitting on the marble window ledge in Bob Isakson's office. Isakson was in Dallas, finally getting his family moved to Florida, where he'd been living by himself for a year and a half. Selling a house in North Texas's flat economy was harder than waterskiing on snowshoes, but Isakson had finally managed. Jon Harpman was the man in charge at Ironhorse.

Harbauer leaned against the cabinet wall behind Bob's desk. Dasher was using the phone, checking with his service in Orlando and returning calls. There were always fires to put out. After spending the afternoon at Ironhorse, Hills and Dasher would go to Jacksonville for a walk-through at yet another new course, Windsor Park. By Friday afternoon, Hills hoped to be home in Toledo. But if he was looking to improve his mood, Ironhorse was not the right place. He was about to have a bad day in earnest.

Harbauer asked if Hills could talk while he was eating. Chewing, Hills nodded assent. "Tell him what the problem is with this pump house," Harbauer said, nodding at Harpman.

"As far as we're concerned," Harpman said, "Wadsworth agreed to build the pump house as part of the irrigation system. The city won't accept the drawing you sent for a permit without an engineer's stamp. That's going to cost six hundred dollars, which Josh says he won't pay."

Ed, with a slight smile, shook his head. "*We're* not buying permits for this job. It's not any different for the pump station than for the roads or the golf course or anything else. The owner provides the drawing and permits. We'll build it, just like we said we would, and we'll put in the irrigation, just like we said we would, but it's not our job to pull permits."

Jon wouldn't back down. "Josh doesn't want to pay for any engineering."

Hills looked up from his salad. "Okay. We'll do a drawing, but we'll send the bill to Josh."

"But they need a Florida engineer's stamp," Ed said. "It's not the drawing, it's the engineering. This equipment can survive without a building, and I don't know how much calculating you've got to do to build a twelve-foot-square pad with four sides and a roof, but Jon says the cheapest price he's been able to find is six hundred dollars."

"That's fine," Hills replied, putting down the empty clear-plastic container that had held his salad. "We'll just send Josh the bill."

It was, finally, a matter of taste, of judgment. Hills had designed and built more than fifty courses. He was the *golf course architect*. If they didn't want to build the golf course he could give them, why was he there?

Muss had paid for a design, Harpman said, the best design presumably that Hills could create for his site, and he intended to see built what he bought. Same with the irrigation system. Wadsworth bid it from the original print, then when it came time to install the system told Ironhorse it was going to cost $50,000 more. How, Muss wondered, if you had enough irrigation in there in the first place to water the course, could you raise the price at all? Wasn't the original price to *irrigate the course*? This question had come up, rather heatedly, a few weeks before and was still nagging at Harbauer. It was straightforward to him. Wadsworth bid a print that showed a certain number of irrigation heads and then was presented with a print to build from showing *more* heads. The company had to charge for the difference. If bunkers had been added, or greens moved, the problem would be the same. As Harpman had explained then, Muss wanted to know exactly why each head had to go where it was going. This was typically Mussian, in Isakson's view. "Muss's value engineering," he called it. Muss had to know what he was getting and paid only for what he agreed to buy. That was one of the issues Harbauer hoped Hills and Harpman could resolve today.

Dasher looked over from the phone to reply to Jon's insistence that they stick with the original grading plan. "That's going to cost you in the long run, Jon. We're trying to give you a better treatment of the site. Improve the drainage, improve the playability, improve the look."

"I'm telling you what Josh wants," Harpman said.

Britton had come in with Owsley. Stu stood near the doorway, slightly hunched, his cigarette perched in the left corner of his mouth, his chin tilted slightly up toward his shoulder to aim the smoke away from his eyes. His white cotton shirt, the mandatory Wadsworth logo stitched on the sleeve, hung loosely on his shoulders. His khakis bunched around his boots. Owsley, nearly a head taller than Stu, wore a black baseball cap with a Caterpillar insignia on the front, his dark, wiry hair pulled back over his ears and bushing out behind his cap like the neck flap of a foreign legionnaire. He said "Hello" to Hills and Dasher and then stood quietly next to Britton.

"Art, I thought we'd best start down at six," Britton said. The issue of the irrigation pump house drawing was left dangling inconclusively, another scab ready to pick. It was the *scale* of the quarrels that so amazed Harbauer, that on a project costing millions they were fighting for what amounted to pennies. But it was hard to argue with Muss's track record. All decisions came from D.C., from Muss's office, and Ironhorse's issues seemed never to have the urgency for him that was felt by the people in the field, unless he was on the job, in which case his demands had the potency of ultimatums. As for the pump house, as things stood, Wadsworth wasn't going to pay for it, Arthur Hills and Associates wasn't going to pay for it, and Josh Muss in his incarnation as Ironhorse, Ltd., was not going to pay for it, either. A lot of tension massed over a very small dispute. A few days later Harbauer, rather than risk more delays, decided to let Wadsworth swallow the $600.

Britton's pickup was parked by his job trailer, just north of the house. Hills climbed up front with Stu; Ed, Dasher, Willie, and Jon got in the back, heaving up over the tailgate, and sat on the tops of the toolboxes fixed along the top rail of the truck bed. A broken bundle of stakes, a pitchfork, a spate of crumpled-up cone water cups, and a couple of shovels littered the bed. Two plastic drinking coolers, the kind Britton filled every morning with a bag of ice as company policy required so the men would have plenty of water, knocked against the tailgate. Stu drove slowly, his arm laid out the window over the edge of the door, watching the work in front of him. He collected air in short, deliberate breaths, his thin chest rising against the cigarette pack riding in his breast pocket.

Phillips and Jordan's dozers were back, clearing the land where the sales center and the model homes would go, getting out all the Brazilian pepper, myrtle, and underbrush, leaving only the pines and palms. The clubhouse site had long since been stripped of vegetation, and Isakson had had P&J clear the zero-lot-line parcel up near the construction entry, where Wadsworth's irrigation trailer and staging areas were set up. The model sites were being selectively cleared, but on the zeros Bobby had P&J take out everything. When Ed saw the tractors working along the sixteenth fairway, which could be seen for the first time all the way from the clubhouse site, he asked Jon, "Wouldn't an air strike have been easier?"

"Yeah," Dasher added, "a little Agent Orange could have done the trick."

Hills had worried on the way over that "Alan's Garden of Eden had pretty much been done away with." Hills and Dasher had never liked the way the clubhouse was sited and planned. Hills's letter to Muss urging the preservation of the big pines around the clubhouse in hopes of maintaining the "tropical look" his original course design for Sher emphasized had been to no avail.

Six was the hole closest to the construction entry, the long par five running parallel to the railroad tracks. Its green was near the property corner where the Beeline Highway would intersect with Jog Road. Left of the fairway ran the perimeter berm on which hundreds of pines and palms had been transplanted. Some of the pines were succumbing to the elongated dry winter, their needles turning a rusty brown. Ranger had a subcontractor installing a security fence on the outside slope of the berm. Britton had a couple of the Haitian laborers driving little farm tractors, one pulling a harrow whose tines were raking small debris to the surface, the other pulling a weighted section of chain-length fence to dress it.

The ground was sandy and dry, impossible to work. It wouldn't hold a shape, it had no body. Not far below the powdered surface a layer of excavated shell rock bridged the primordial muck where scrappers had sunk up past their bowls in the dark, slippery soil five months before. Harbauer said cleaning and dressing the fairways before the irrigation was installed was a waste of Wadsworth's time, a show for the customer, a way to keep the troops busy. "We just don't have much to do until Ranger finishes some more holes."

Britton said he'd told his men, "If those tractors break down, boys, we pick stones. They heard that pretty good. Since then, they go through that equipment every morning with a fine-tooth comb. 'If I find a dry fitting,' I told them, 'your next job is picking sticks.' "

There was plenty of small debris on the course, but little rock.

There were black charred vestiges of palmetto roots, the odd remnant of a plastic bucket, larger bits of shell. None of the great acres of rock that have to be gathered in New England, for example, or blasted away in the arid Southwest. There was some rock underground that the irrigation crews would have to contend with, mostly where pines and palms had grown, the upland or mesic areas. As the course traveled mainly over former wetlands, it pretty much avoided rock.

"Cleaning" and "dressing" seemed appropriate words to describe the work the tractors were doing on the fairways. When a hunter kills game, he cleans and dresses it. A rough-shaped fairway without grass on it looks like the carcass of an animal whose skin has been peeled off, and in a way the grass—the turf—is the golf course's skin, its protection against the elements, the erosive power of wind and rain. The grass collects the sun's energy, it breathes, it fixes the soil. But until the irrigation system was in, no grass would grow at Ironhorse. The discussion of the irrigation system resumed on the walk down the sixth fairway.

Hills told Mike he needed to write to Muss, explaining "hole by hole, head by head," what the irrigation system would do. Using only full heads—ones that sprayed water in a full circle—in double rows would create dry scallops along the edges of the course, along the parcel lines, while a row of half heads along the perimeter, while costing more, would cover the lacunae. Hills said Dasher and Wadsworth needed to stake out the location of every irrigation head on every hole, get them all approved by Ironhorse, price them, and then do the installation.

"What if we get to eighteen and we're out of heads?" wondered Harbauer. "I'm willing to stake this out, but we have to figure out what we're selling and what Josh is willing to buy."

"But we can't know exactly how many heads we'll need until we stake it out."

Harpman says Muss just wants to know why the new plan is going to cost more, why instead of two rows of full heads the new plan shows a single row of full heads sandwiched between two rows of half heads? Hills was getting weary of the discussion. "This wouldn't need to be done if Josh let the professionals do the work," he started. "We're out here *in* his interests, not contrary to them. He keeps fighting us. He's the one who's going to lose hundreds of thousands potentially, not us."

They hadn't finished walking down the fairway of the first hole

Hills had come to inspect, and they were already skirting the edge of "The Quarrel." Hills wanted to make Ironhorse the best golf course he could, and that meant fine-tuning it along the way as he awakened to new potential at the site. Muss, for whom Jon spoke with an increasingly confident voice, wanted to get the job done as cheaply as possible, a reasonable approach, but one that Hills regarded as too inflexible. As Muss saw it, the minor changes Hills made on each visit were like the interest on a bad debt. Hills was sensitive to commerce—lifetime subscribers to *The National Review* are not typically indifferent to the allure of profit—and he was devoted to building golf courses, proud of his service to developers, his ability to deliver the goods that would help sell dirt. Somebody had figured, he had said recently, that his courses around Naples, Florida, had sold 7,000 lots. How could Muss not see his true interests?

Harpman, hearing Hills's complaint, adopted a conciliatory tone. "I know you don't want to have to go through this, but that's Josh."

Keeping the other guy on the defensive was part of the way Muss stayed in control. Knowing that, Hills agreed to march forward under Harpman's white flag. "I guess if somebody told me I'd have to spend an extra fifty thousand dollars, I'd want to know why," Hills said. "But," he added, taking on a hectoring tone, "you've got to explain to Josh that Wadsworth needs to get done so he can sell his lots. If we keep going like this he could lose another selling season and that could mean millions, not the thousands we're talking about spending to do the job."

Dasher said he'd send Muss a letter to explain all that and come back the next week to walk through the irrigation plan with Jon and Wadsworth's irrigation man, Tim Wilson, who was scheduled to start the next Monday. They were finally ready to look at the golf course.

OWSLEY HAD DONE a beautiful job of shaping the mounds behind the sixth green, Hills thought, but now he had to find a way to run the cart path up into them, hiding it without disturbing the shaping. Britton got a bundle of small green flags, about the size of a man's hand, their flagpoles pieces of thin rigid wire about two feet long, to mark the route of the cart path. It was going to run to the left of the green, picking up the carts as they approached, then sending them around it to the left with a place to park so the players could leave the carts to putt and return to them in position to drive to the next tee, a piece of the gray asphalt ribbon tucked into Ironhorse's folds.

Standing in the bunker in front of the sixth green, Hills told Stu, "We need to get this shaved back thirty feet so we can see this sand." He also wanted the edges cut down in front of the bunkers so they could be seen from the fairway. "We want four inches of sand," he told Stu, "and five inches of containment."

Lumber was stacked for the bulkhead around the green at number seven, but until it was in place Stu couldn't build the green. Willie had shaped the tees for seven, the par three with nothing between the tee shot and the green but water. Hills complimented Willie for his work on the tees.

The entry road will run behind the seventh green. Opposite it—across the road—were the fifteenth green and the sixteenth tee. Since there was not much to look at yet at seven, Hills led the pack to the sixteenth tee. Kevin Phillipson, who was trying to figure out where the rest of the dirt Ironhorse needed would come from, drove up in his white pickup.

When I talked to Kevin a couple of days ago, he told me he thought Ironhorse might be shy as much as 250,000 yards of dirt, an estimate that proved wildly inflated. That was at least a million bucks' worth. Even the 70,000 or so yards they really were short was a serious amount. Harpman, feeling the heat of the miscalculation on the dirt, passed the flame to Hills.

Standing on the sixteenth tee, SWA's great smokestack rising in the background, Hills looked at the tight corridor under the pine left standing to the right of the tee. "We'll have to limb that," he told Jon. He also said he needed more tee.

"I don't know where we'll get the dirt," Jon said.

Hills's bad day was coming to a head. Hills didn't want to hear any more about what he couldn't do. "If you expect to get fifty thousand dollars for a membership in this course," he said, "you need the dirt."

Phillipson, always accommodating, guessed at the quantity required—a few truckloads—and told Hills and Jon, "I can get this for you."

On every other visit, the right side of the sixteenth fairway had been defined by the vegetation on the housing parcel, but since Jon had had Kenny Postell clear it—the "air strike"—the fairway seemed to melt away into somebody's backyard. Kevin suggested putting rye grass on the clearings, "so they'll look like meadows instead of borrow pits." This was where Matt Weeg's sales office would go, his model row, the engine to move all this dirt. It looked a bit forlorn with the brush gone.

Hills didn't spend a lot of time on sixteen and seventeen. He thought the mounding to the right of the approach to sixteen, part of whose purpose is to hide the seventeenth tee, was "nondescript." But, he said, "The key thing as far as the green area is concerned is what you look at from the landing area, and that works pretty well."

We stopped by the house to get a drink on the way to twelve, but with Hills you never tarry. Tee twelve was cut back into the preserve, near the southwest corner of Ironhorse. A large stand of Australian pines cut off visual access to the catchment area. Hills would like to see them removed to give the preserve a chance to recover its original look, but Jon told him there was no requirement to move them, so as far as he was concerned they were going to stay. This was an issue that would, in the weeks ahead, lock Ironhorse into a serious conflict with the South Florida Water Management District's environmentalists.

Hills looked at the large pines on the twelfth fairway, about which Dash had said a couple of months before, "We'll leave them in there long enough to drive everybody nuts, and then we'll probably take them out," but Hills decided he still liked them. "I know it's irrational," he said, shrugging his shoulders. He did want some changes in the fairway, though, particularly having Ranger push the dirt mounded on the right side of the fairway even farther to the right to open up the hole a bit.

Jon explained his plan to dredge a canal to connect the lake by twelve over to the lake by thirteen to get more fill. Hills, designing with his waving arms, suggested a meander for the canal. Then he looked further east to the thirteenth green, a strong par three whose tee shot resembles the approach shot on twelve. He was concerned that the knob to the right of the green was "kinda weak." He wanted a bigger bunker. There was a small gator in the lake by the thirteenth tee. Because of the long dry spring, gators were coming out of the catchment area looking for food.

Hills wanted to get the trap and sand "in scale" to the big mounds to the right of the green. He told Willie to cut an area in front of the green down lower for emphasis. "It sets up the green. It's a one-shot hole. If it was a long par four, you might want to let it just run into the green, but on this hole we want to separate them."

At fourteen, though, the modus vivendi reached on the previous holes evaporated, swiftly and angrily. On a previous visit Hills had added a large bunker to keep errant approach shots from running into the water, but this time decided it was "really redundant." Hills looked up toward the green. The bunker was well out of the line of play. "It looks kind of dumb," he said.

"I'm not in love with it," Dasher agreed.

"Then we ought to get rid of it."

As Hills started describing to Willie how he'd like the bunker filled in, with a two-degree slope down to the water and a small mound along the water's edge, Jon approached him. "We're not going to get rid of this bunker. It's already got the drainage in, and we've bought the sand."

Hills snapped. "I'll pay for the fucking thing!" Turning to Harbauer, he said, "Let me know how much the fucking thing costs!"

Jon stood his ground, calm and quiet. "Josh is going to want to know why you keep changing this."

"If Josh is just going to be an asshole about everything while I'm trying to make him a better course I don't know what's the point."

Jon stayed close to Hills, not frightened by his fury. Everybody else was drifting away, getting out of the force field of the argument. Owsley had his back turned, stifling a smirk. "Hell," he said later, "I thought I'd bust out laughing."

Hills turned to Harbauer again. "If I pay to regrade this goddamn bunker, I want credit for the cost of the sand." Turning to Jon, who was standing on the upper edge of what might be a bunker, he concluded; "I'm so goddamned tired of hearing this nickel-dime shit."

Britton drove around with the truck to ferry everyone to fifteen. The bridge over the canal from green fourteen to tee fifteen hadn't been built. "I got an idea for saving Josh a few bucks," Dasher said to Harbauer, out of Hills's hearing range in the back of the truck. "Let's eliminate a couple of greens. Might affect the course a little, but sure as hell save some money."

Fifteen had a small circular green hidden behind tall mounds, among Owsley's best work at Ironhorse, and a tight driving corridor with trees standing like goalies between the tee and the fairway. It was Harbauer's and Hills's favorite hole. The pleasure in seeing it wasn't enough to restore harmony. The rest of the walk-through was perfunctory. The tension never entirely dissipated. Hills looked at four more holes without much enthusiasm, suggesting only minor changes.

When Matt Weeg heard about Hills's tantrum, he was surprised at his naiveté. "Wouldn't a professional know that Muss is a guy who's not going to spend a dime he doesn't have to spend? My feeling is, Hills is here to make *recommendations*. If the guy paying the freight doesn't like your recommendations, or says to you, 'You wanted that another way before and I paid for it, I'm not paying to do it again,' you might have to accept that. My feeling."

HILLS'S FIT OVER the bunker was, in a curious way, a sort of denouement in the making of Ironhorse. "After going over the site," Hills wrote to Muss, "it looks like the course will be a darned good one. It's pretty, it's playable, and it's challenging. We will continue to work to make the course as good as we can."

Muss called Hills and told him, respectfully, not to castigate Harpman for decisions Muss had made. Muss wasn't angry, Hills said, but he was firm. Hills was embarrassed anyway and wrote an apology to Harpman. "My outburst," he said, "was uncalled for and certainly you are only relaying Josh's concerns in a proper manner. I will try to express my concerns in a more rational manner in the future."

A month later the offending bunker was still in place. "We're leaving that bunker," Isakson said. "It's *on the print*."

Hills tried another letter to Muss. "On fourteen fairway," he wrote, "I asked that a fairway bunker be wiped out. The net result will be less cost and a better hole. My request was vetoed because tile was in the bunker already. I hope you will concur with my request."

Muss did as Hills hoped. Owsley bladed dirt over the bunker manqué. Ironhorse was steaming toward the station now. Sher dreamed of playing before Christmas. Hills just hoped Ironhorse didn't run out of track. The track, of course, was dirt. The search for it led to one more flash of tension, and then the final glide to the depot.

16

An Exotic Impasse

EYEING A STAND of Australian pines rooted in the preserve, Jon Harpman said, "They're trying to get us to do an exotic removal program, but that ain't gonna happen, I guarantee."

"They" were the South Florida Water Management District. Despite Harpman's bravado, there was absolutely no doubt that the district's environmentalist expected Ironhorse to rid itself of Australian pines, Brazilian peppers, and melaleucas. Palm Beach County had imposed the same condition when it issued a clearing permit in February 1988, two weeks after I first saw Ironhorse and walked the site with Hills, Dasher, and Debbie Allen of Urban Design. "The issue of exotics was mentioned," Allen wrote in a memo about a meeting held then with the county's clearing inspector. "A comment to remove all exotics from the site was reaffirmed . . . Concern about removal of exotics from the preserve areas was expressed due to limited access by heavy equipment. Some method of removal will have to be devised."

Then Ironhorse was annexed to the City of West Palm Beach, and the county's jurisdiction waned. South Florida's authority, though, was unabated, and its desires unambiguous. In August of 1988, almost a year before Harpman's defiant guarantee, the district sent a certified letter to Ironhorse, Ltd., addressed to Muss's office in Washington. "Enclosed is a copy of this District's staff report," it began. "It is requested that you read this staff report thoroughly and understand its contents."

Its recommendations, the letter continued, would likely determine the action of South Florida's governing board, required by law to approve any project with a potential effect on water quality. Pretty much anything that could get rained on fell under South Florida's rubric—farms, shopping centers, housing developments, golf courses.

The district foresaw "no significant adverse environmental impacts" from building Ironhorse. "A strip of land adjacent to the water catchment area on the western property boundary will remain as a conservation area and act as a buffer to the wetlands in the catchment area," its staff reported. "This area will encompass approximately 54 acres of a mixed assemblage of communities including; mesic hammock, graminoid marsh, slash pine, Sabal palm hammock, transitional pine and cypress and disturbed areas containing Australian pine. *An enhancement plan within the conservation area,*" the report concluded, "*will be undertaken to eliminate the areas of exotic invasion and to create new wetland habitat*" (author's italics).

There was no ambiguity in the district's review and recommendations. It expected at some point to see detailed plans for the mitigated wetlands—the littoral zones in the lakes—and for the preserve, and it agreed in principle to let the golf course breech the preserve boundary. The district reaffirmed its botanical xenophobia—the exotics had to go.

The district's biologists, like their counterparts in the U.S. Fish and Wildlife Service, had a sort of hangdog resignation. Powerless, overworked, they licked when they wanted to bark. Debbie Goss, South Florida's environmentalist in charge of reviewing Ironhorse's plans, now wanted to make sure that what she had approved was implemented. She wasn't convinced the mitigated wetlands would have much of an ameliorative effect on the recovery of the wading bird populations, but thought it was an experiment worth trying. The littoral shelves planted with native grasses were, like the Dyer Landfill's re-created uplands and wetlands, attractive examples of commerce wedded to conservation, but bereft of a breeding bird population to serve, Goss feared they were little more than dioramas, nature captured and confined.

Ironhorse's preserve was a pretty standard case of the trade-offs negotiated between developers and regulators, but instead of emphasizing the "natural" beauty of the site, as Bonita Bay on Florida's gulf

The fifth hole at Ironhorse. (*Illustration by Michael Strantz*)

coast had done, Ironhorse concentrated its aesthetic emphasis on the golf course. Ironhorse might have chosen to emphasize the vistas across the water catchment basin, perhaps negotiating for the installation of bird-watching blinds or an unobtrusive nature walk along the boundary between Ironhorse and the Loxahatchee Slough. It had, after all, managed to get golf greens and tees onto the preserve, so a place to sit and watch the birds, deer, and alligators would hardly have been a more formidable intrusion.

The great English landscape gardeners of the eighteenth century discovered a way to hide boundaries, to open a bound landscape to the horizon, as it were, and draw in distant vistas. Their innovation supposedly derived its name from the unexpected delight it aroused, the visual trick of opening the garden to the outside without relinquishing control over the inside. The "ha-ha" was a moat or ditch, with a fence hidden along its bottom to keep livestock from straying. The eye could pass over the ha-ha oblivious to any boundary. Ironhorse wanted to create a sense of isolation, of privilege and privacy, but in doing so its planners abandoned any visual claim to the slough, with its panoramas and wading birds. Because the catchment dike stood ten feet or so above the preserve, it obstructed views to the west, but had the planners chosen to blend the slough into Ironhorse's vistas, they might have achieved a ha-ha effect. After all, acres of lakes and hundreds of thousands of yards of dirt were moved to create the golf course.

Once the South Florida Water Management District agreed to the land plan and its water-management scheme, there was little inclination to alter it. Harpman's confidence that Ironhorse was not in the exotic-removal business was based on his knowledge of the convoluted jurisdictional lines running between South Florida and the Northern Palm Beach County Water Control District. Northern had, in essence, bought Ironhorse's lakes, the outfall pump station, and the preserve with its bonds. If it was anybody's job, Harpman was saying, exotic removal was a chore for Northern, not Ironhorse. Same with the snail kite monitoring. Ironhorse was an innocent bystander. Harpman shrugged.

Debbie Goss believed that the boundary described by the preserve, and all the work done in it—the greens, tees, and cart paths—were not what she and Howard Searcy, the consulting engineer who designed the water-management plan, had agreed to. They'd walked the ground along the preserve in the late summer of 1988, before construction started, and Goss had formed a pretty clear idea in her mind of what the preserve would look like. She remembered large stands of cabbage palms dead in its center and an expanded boundary at the north end. Then, when she flew over Ironhorse in the district's helicopter nine months later, "It didn't look like they followed the preserve alignment they said they were going to." Besides, she said, "The greens look really tiny on the plan. The plan shows each green as a little thing, but they have to be big to hit to, I guess. In that way, I think, they deceived."

By the time Goss discovered what she believed was a discrepancy in the preserve boundary—not in its size, but in its alignment—Ranger had the berm cleared and graded and its plastic liner installed and was about to plant grass on the dike. Ranger was also digging three shallow lakes in the preserve that the Army Corps of Engineers asked Ironhorse to excavate as habitat for the apple snail. Ironhorse, desperate for dirt, 10,000 or so yards short on the golf course and thousands more shy on the range, was happy to get whatever little bit the preserve ponds could supply. Ironhorse thought it was simply following the Corps' directive, but when Goss, looking down from South Florida's helicopter, saw the ponds, she was shocked. They were, to her, large and violent intrusions on the preserve.

"I hear you're mad at me," Searcy said when she called. They should have "coordinated better," he acknowledged. Searcy said the change in developer, from Alan Sher to Ironhorse, Ltd., had led to a redesign in the site plan, and that somehow the changes had not been adequately conveyed to South Florida. Goss didn't care how the problem came about. She wanted it fixed.

"Being an environmentalist," Goss said when she came back from flying over Ironhorse, "it looked like a tragedy. Because I don't know golf I saw the greens as tiny, but they're *huge*!"

She was sure Searcy, the master of the environmental compromise—the "developer's environmental guru," she called him—would manage a solution, but in the meanwhile she was frustrated. Harpman and Isakson, too, felt caught.

"Nobody knows who's responsible for anything," Goss lamented, but the words could just as easily have come from Isakson. "This deal was made in nineteen eighty-five, before I was involved in it. I don't think that's acceptable. The golf holes got grandfathered because things were a lot looser then.

"The developer makes the deal and passes it on to Northern. Then South Florida makes an agreement, but ours may not agree with the deal Northern thinks it has. So we call Searcy. He says call Northern.

Northern says call Joyce Environmental which does Northern's mon-itoring, and they say they haven't heard anything. Northern's build-ing an empire, and often it gets in the way of what we want to do."

Goss rarely looks at jobs on the ground. "You can knock off ten inspections in an afternoon in a helicopter," she says. "When you have an aerial to compare you can pretty much see from a helicopter what you need to."

What she saw from the air at Ironhorse, though, convinced Goss to make a closer inspection. Standing near the second tee on a June afternoon, she saw what to her was a large excavation under way in the preserve. "We consider this pond part of the enhancement pro-gram," Harpman said.

"Just digging a big deep hole isn't my idea of enhancement," Goss said. "Maybe the Corps likes a hole, but I don't."

Harpman leaned against his Bronco.

"What about exotic removal?" Goss wanted to know.

"I talked to Howard Searcy recently, and he didn't say anything about it," Harpman replied.

A track hoe was loading fill from the preserve a hundred yards from where Goss stood. Dressed in a tan shirt, jeans, and boots, she seemed determined to persuade someone that Ironhorse had derailed. Her proximity to the cypress hammock P&J inadvertently cleared wasn't any comfort. "I'm upset with how we've done this. I thought Howard was going to work with me on a plan."

"That got lost somewhere," Harpman replied in his literal way. He was not very flexible. "Howard told me all I needed to do was notify you when we started construction."

"We'd talked about exotic removal," Goss pursued.

"Well, maybe Northern covered it in the bonds. You're saying now you need someone to pick it up off the floor."

Harpman's every gesture, had the words not sufficiently clarified his meaning, shouted, "This Is Not My Problem."

PERMITS, GOSS REFLECTED later, are "all just paper up front. There's no compliance. When I was out at Ironhorse, there was a guy sleeping in the truck. He's enforcement. They all have bad attitudes because they can't do anything. This whole project has me very irritated.

"Howard's excuse wasn't really clear. I told him how uncoopera-tive Jon was. He said he'd talk to them and get it all into agreement on the preserve and restoration. When the Corps said they wanted lakes, he should have come to us and said, 'They want lakes,' so we could review. I told him if we couldn't agree we'd come up with some enforcement.

"These Ironhorse guys are fairly near the bottom—the agriculture people don't even want to let you step foot on their property. These guys don't rate high, but they're not the worst.

"Howard's done his superb job of complicating everything. They submit half of this, and then wait to the last minute with other things, and it all kind of falls through the cracks. I want to see now if he reconciles us versus them and still looks like he's the master. He's made his way pulling this kind of stuff off."

"I don't think South Florida's got a problem in the first place," Isakson told Harpman. "They don't know what the Corps wants, and they can't read their own goddamn documents. The Corps designed the depths of those ponds. I'm getting tired of paying the consultants to keep dealing with these problems. Debbie Goss doesn't know what the hell she's doing. We don't have a problem with South Florida. Searcy and Pete Pimentel have got to get Goss back in line. I'm staying out of that one."

Muss had another idea for finding more fill, and Harpman brought it to Hills's attention at the end of June, just about the time the flap over the ponds in the preserve was irresolutely dropping from consciousness. Goss's complaint was there, then it was gone, buried under a glacier of reassurance. She never set foot on Ironhorse again. A year later, without fanfare, Northern started to eradicate exotics.

Ironhorse still needed fill. There was a small lake next to the first tee, in front of the practice range. By expanding it toward the first tee and into the range, Muss figured Ironhorse could excavate another 10,000 yards. Also, by demucking the range and exchanging the muck for the soils in the toes of the lakes—easy to get to with a track hoe—and by burying trees in demucked areas rather than burning them, they could pick up even more yards. The only place on the golf course still needing fill was along the old construction road behind the third and fifth greens. Fifteen thousand yards or more were needed on the range and a lot more than that on the roads and house pads.

"Josh wants to dig a lake in back of the range," Harpman told Hills, the vapors of their earlier battle dissipated. The whole job, in fact, had slowly smoothed out. Harbauer and Dasher reviewed all the irrigation, and the net effect was an addition of barely $13,000 to the irrigation tab, a nifty reduction from the $55,000 once estimated for the extra heads. Tim Wilson, the irrigation super, was optimistic enough to think that his crews could finish two or three holes a week. "But," said Stu Britton, as Hills listened to Harpman, "they don't have dirt enough to complete the range."

They'd lose a practice putting green, too, if they dug a larger lake, and that bothered Hills. "I was at Pelican Bay," he said, "and they've got a six-thousand-foot putting green and it's too small."

Instead of two putting greens, Ironhorse would have a single one on the opposite side of the lake from the first tee. Hills made a few tentative sketches and said he'd have his office work on the shapes for a revised lake, practice tee, and putting green. The revisions later sent from Toledo reflected Hills's suspicion of the whole scheme. His were modest alterations that wouldn't yield much dirt.

Dash came down to meet with Harpman and take a hard look at Muss's proposal in mid-July. Standing in Harpman's office, Dash looked over a sketch Jon had drawn that angled the water in front of the first tee. "I think that's an awful tough deal on the first hole, Jon," Dash said, "to have water coming across the line of play like this."

Isakson, who was making a pot of coffee, called out from the kitchen, "We need seventy thousand yards, Mike."

"Absolutely the worst place to dig that dirt from's in front of the first hole. You want to start off in a good frame of mind."

A larger lake would also foreshorten the range. "Two hundred and fifty yards is tight," Dash said. "You want three hundred. Besides, the evening sun reflecting off that lake is gonna double the amount of sunlight and make it awful hot in that clubhouse."

"We'll put in heavy landscaping," Harpman responded.

"Then you'll block out your views from the clubhouse."

Dash pulled a pen from his pocket and changed the profile on the lake, pulling its edge closer to being parallel with the line of play on the first hole. "That's more what it would look like," Harpman confirmed.

"Well, I'm not crazy about it. Screws up the range, screws up the first hole, makes it hard to get from the clubhouse to the range and then to the first tee. You're backtracking all the way back around this lake. Puts you right by the entry road, too."

"We gotta have some dirt to finish your golf course," Isakson reiterated. "And now you're talking costs that aren't Northern's costs anymore. Muss doesn't get reimbursed for this."

Muss also suggested switching the nines, Harpman said. What about that?

"Nine is not a strong finishing hole. You'd have a par three for your second hole, which is gonna slow down play, and lose your good view of the last hole from the clubhouse. You need to send this up to Art."

Looking back at the drawing, Dash cringed. "What does Dick Lanscioni think?"

"He doesn't like it much," Harpman said.

"Yeah," Dash said, "there's just too many chances to go splash already, and if you dump it on the first tee, you're talking misery. But if that's where that lake has got to go, we'll work with it."

When they walked the course later that morning, Dash found another source of fill. "Why don't you widen this pond here in front of the eleventh green?" he asked Harpman. "Hell, there may be ten thousand yards here."

He paced off fifty-five steps, did a quick calculation. "Well, you'll generate four or five thousand anyway."

Hills continued his resistance to a larger lake at the first hole, twice writing Muss urging him to buy fill off-site rather than modify the plans for the golf course and the range, but his advice was ignored. The odd thing was, the new lake looked great, and even with its expanded dimensions, despite Dash's dire prophecies, there was not a forced carry over water from the tee. They pushed the tee a little north, slightly altering the angle of the dogleg, but its effect was minor. They needed to transplant some trees to separate the first hole from the range, but that was simply done. One problem remained.

"Bob," Dash wrote to Isakson, "we understand there is an extremely steep slope below the waterline in the lake behind the driving range tee. This goes against safety standards. We don't accept any responsibility for loss of life or property due to this deviation."

ROGER WHITFORD, Ironhorse's superintendent, came aboard in time to witness and advise on the installation of the irrigation. The standard

wisdom said to hire the superintendent during the course's construction, so he'd know where all the ghosts were, the bad soils and buried
trees, and where all the pipes ran. He could advise on the irrigation
and the grasses. Whitford, who once worked for Wadsworth installing irrigation, was known as a great grow-in man—and it was said
growing in a course and maintaining it were two different skills—and
as a man with little capacity for idle chatter. Isakson thought it a
marvel if he could cajole from Whitford a morning "hello." Whitford
was more than taciturn, he was curmudgeonly, but he could whisper
to the little blades of Bermuda grass turning toward the sun and get
them marching in orderly procession. As Dash said, "Rog can flat
grow grass."

Whitford grew up in Ohio, in the very town where Florida developer Henry Flagler first made money. He learned about grass at Penn
State, an academic leader in turf science. He met Hills more than
twenty years ago, working as an assistant superintendent on Hills's
first course, Brandywine in Toledo. He spent two years in the Peace
Corps in Colombia, the first year working with coffee growers, the
second helping farmers improve pasture grasses. Whitford came to
Florida in 1972 and was struck from the first by the difference between growing grass up north and in Florida. "Here," he says, "we're
working all daylight hours twelve months of the year. Growing grass
here is like hydroponics—it's a different science altogether."

The problem at Ironhorse, he says, is the jumble of native soils and
the mixture of the three basic types—sand, shell, and muck. The
greens are no problem, since they have a uniform growing medium.

Part of Whitford's attitude comes from the knowledge that in Florida, "You can wake up and your greens are gone. Literally overnight."

The Bermuda grasses are subject to root-and-crown rot diseases
"that slowly weaken the plant and then BOOM!" There's also something called "Bermuda grass decline" that the plant pathologists can't
tell much about. There are beetles and bugs, webworms and army
worms and mole crickets, nymphs and larvae and mites and flies, an
endless list of pests, most of which are chemically controlled.

Too many young supers, Whitford thinks, start "spraying seven
hundred dollars' worth of pesticides every weekend, taking a shotgun approach" to the threat of blight, fearful for their jobs. "They
can all grow grass," he says, "but they spend a lot more money
than necessary. I guess they're probably trying to get some sleep.

Really, the only people who know what a super goes through are other supers.''

Driving Ironhorse's new red Ford pickup, wearing a stiff Panama hat, a plaid shirt, and khakis, with his bristly steel-gray mustache and ramrod posture, Whitford looks like a refugee from a tough batallion of English fusiliers or a gamekeeper conjured up by D. H. Lawrence. Whitford conveys a sense of injury or injustice without saying a word.

Whitford was Hills's choice to grow in Ironhorse from the start. Whitford had grown in The Standard Club in Atlanta and for a time considered setting himself up exclusively as a growing-in specialist. Whitford's knowledge of Hills's preferred use of grasses would help achieve the look Hills was after at Ironhorse. On steep-sided tees and lake banks, behind greens or on the crests of mounds, areas out of play, Hills wanted Bahia grass, left unmowed for its contrast to the manicured Bermuda. The lake edges, too, were seeded with Bahia, a thick-bladed, slow-growing, drought-tolerant grass. On the lake banks, and along the preserve berm, the Bahia was seeded in a mix with millet. Mulch was spread along with the seed and then disked to cut the seed into the soil. The millet pushed up fast, straight-stemmed and bright, a quick green miracle. It was months before the Bahia germinated, but in the meanwhile the roots of the millet, its leaves long since turned to brown, helped hold the soil. Until the grass was established, Whitford worried about rain, just as Stu Britton had.

Ironhorse had only a small budget for sod. Hills was doing a course in Atlanta where whole *fairways* were sodded, and Dash figured that the cost to sod an entire course would add "only eight hundred thousand to a million bucks to the budget." Maybe that was the New Wave. The Old Trail course, set back on track by its new shapers, was using hundreds of thousands of dollars' worth of sod to boost its chances of opening on schedule. It was startling to see the rapid transformation wrought by sod. Within days, or even hours, bare ground turned into lawn. In Ironhorse's course-construction budget, there was just over $22,000 committed to bunker sod, mostly Bermuda grass, to secure the banks until the sprigged grass was established.

Bahia sod, with its thick roots, is heavy, but cheaper than the Bermuda sods. Whitford told Dash, as they surveyed the placement of irrigation heads, that Ironhorse was going to hydromulch—blow down the mulch, millet, and Bahia seed mix—"and then come back after it rains and sod the washouts."

Wadsworth argued against this technique, believing the repairs would cost more than the additional sod, but that was a calculation of risk Muss had to make. If it didn't rain hard, Ironhorse might save a lot on sod. Wadsworth also worried about the heavy sod trucks running down finished fairways, especially after the irrigation was in. Not only did the trucks make ruts, the drivers sometimes failed to notice the sprinkler heads, no matter how carefully marked. There was a lot of sod on the perimeter berm, too, and on the steeper slopes of the bondable work, like along the canal near the weir by the twelfth tee.

THE IRRIGATION SYSTEM was hydraulically controlled, which meant that a little plastic tube ran to each head alongside the larger white plastic pipe supplying the irrigation water. Ironhorse was installing what's called an "open head system." Unless pressure from the little tube held its valve shut, the sprinkler head would run all the time. The sprinkler head was always under pressure. Ironhorse also looped the system at the greens and installed a gate valve so if a sprinkler head failed Whitford could turn off the irrigation just at the affected green. Wadsworth put a quick coupler—a device for attaching a hose—on the upstream side of the gate valve, so if a sprinkler head at the green malfunctioned Whitford could still water the grass while he was making repairs.

The sprinkler heads were designed to "break the water," to disperse it into droplets that would cover the ground like rain rather than simply shoot it in a stream to the perimeter. Running pipe, the irrigation crew first laid the supply lines alongside the ditch, which was usually cut by a trenching machine, but sometimes by a backhoe. The trenching machines were always breaking down, even in Ironhorse's soft soils. A trencher works sort of like a chain saw. As it crawls forward, the trencher claws the ground and throws the dirt to either side of the ditch it's digging. The effect is like watching a really big dog trying to bury a bone. There are usually two lines running down each fairway, and off each main line are regularly spaced lateral lines, each running to a sprinkler head. The crews run the main lines first, installing "T"'s at their junctions with the lateral lines. None of the waterlines are glued, but instead have pressure fittings, tight rubber gaskets at the female end of the pipe. When they're running the pipe, the installers clean each end, then lubricate the inserted pipe with a soapy, water-soluble kind of grease. After the main line is in, but before the lateral ditches are dug, they attach the first lengths of pipe ready to head off to either side. It's easy then to see where the lateral runs go, and the pipes sticking up in the air won't fill with dirt that might clog the sprinkler heads. The long pipes sticking in the air make an odd sculpture, a field planted with drunken flagpoles.

The control tubes unwrap from spools, each tube marked with a number so when it's connected to the control box hidden somewhere along the fairway it will operate the proper head. A simple frame on wheels with space for twenty-four spools, called the "tube wagon," trails the installers. Each crew has a tube man or, as he's called on systems with electrical controls, a "wire man."

Irrigation superintendent Tim Wilson worked with Dash on a course up on Dataw a decade ago. A few minutes after Dash and Whitford started looking over the grassing patterns and the sprinkler head locations, Wilson, with his Viking beard and his perpetual grin, drove up to join them. Wilson drove a white Wadsworth pickup, just like Britton's. Wadsworth recycled its pickups. When a superintendent got a new truck he'd pass the old one down to his foreman. The trucks ran until they died. You could see the evolution of Wadsworth's logo on the doors of its pickup trucks.

Wilson is a funny guy, full of banter. His chief pipe man, Jerry Banks, is as taciturn among strangers as Wilson is lively. For at least the last ten years, Wilson says, every job Banks has done he swears, "This is the last piece of pipe I'll ever lay."

Like a lot of Wadsworth employees, neither Wilson nor Banks joined the company expecting to make it a career. Wilson was working as a union laborer in Minnesota in the midseventies, making $8.50 an hour putting up fences and highway guardrails. When work slowed down in the winter, like a Midwestern golf pro he'd come to Florida, where he'd sort of grown up. His dad flew planes in the air force, and Wilson graduated from high school in Jacksonville. He spent a year at Florida State in an ROTC program that would have led to a stint as a navy pilot, but, abuzz with the sixties' Zeitgeist, he dropped out. When his lottery number came up 357 and he skated on the Vietnam draft, Wilson set off on what he remembers as "my wandering, hippie days."

His folks, whom he would visit during the winters, retired to a place in the woods up in the Florida panhandle. His beard, which looks full enough now to hide whole families of small rodents, used to be "*real* long." One winter Wilson wandered down to Tampa to catch a Jackson Browne concert. No prisoner of schedules, he was a week early. With nothing to do, he accepted when a friend who worked for Wadsworth asked him to come down to Naples for a week and run a little irrigation pipe. It was for a remodel on an Art Hills course.

When Wadsworth asked him to stay for another small job, he did, "wondering why the hell I was in Florida working for $3.75 an hour when I had that job in Minnesota paying $8.50."

Beyond the wages, Wadsworth's crews were "working five tens and eight on Saturday, and I just wasn't driven enough by money to work that hard."

But for reasons not entirely accessible to consciousness, Wilson stuck with it. By the time the company asked him to do some remodeling at John D. MacArthur's JDM Country Club, Ironhorse's neighbor on the east side of the turnpike, Wilson was feeling a certain kinship with his Wadsworth comrades. Banks worked at JDM, too, and hit it off with MacArthur, "who liked to hang out with the men. Offered me a job, too," Banks says, "but I turned him down."

Wilson decided to throw in his lot full-time with Wadsworth after the JDM job. He had a motorcycle in Minnesota that he wanted to bring to Florida, so he bet his next paycheck that he could get there and back in five days without any time in the air. But the train was late getting to Minneapolis, so he was half a day late arriving back to Oldsmar. The winners, in a fit of generosity, invited him along to the Bloody Duck Tavern to watch them spend his paycheck. "At $3.75 an hour," he remembers, "you could drink up a week pretty quick."

Now the last vestiges of his wandering days are the beard and high-top canvas Converse All-Stars stained the color of burnt butter. Wilson's been a Wadsworth irrigation superintendent for the last eleven years. In his tan Wadsworth shirt, walking to his truck, he looks like a cross between a small professional wrestler and an ambitious but still unpublished poet with an affection for blank verse.

Banks wears a battered straw hat and a long-sleeved blue shirt, buttoned to the wrist, protecting his fair skin. Even in the hottest weather, his outfit is unvarying. He says it doesn't bother him to work in the rain, he's already wet from sweat anyway. Banks is by far the oldest hand doing hard labor at Ironhorse. Britton works hard, but he's not down in a ditch with a shovel pushing pipe. Banks is wiry, but not as thin as Britton. Banks has the strong-chinned, rural gumper's look in common with Britton, too. Banks went to work for Wadsworth nearly twenty years ago in Ohio, on another Hills job. He'd been working in Oklahoma and had come to Dayton for a vacation. The business agent at the union hall kept after him to take a temporary job he was having trouble getting a local to fill, so "I finally agreed to give him three weeks."

Banks moved to Florida with Wadsworth seventeen years ago. None of the work here is unionized, "but I still get union wages."

A husband for thirty-eight years, Banks was nineteen and his wife "one month shy of her sixteenth birthday when I married her."

Just as at JDM, he hints that Ironhorse may be his last job. "My health ain't too good," he says. "I got to go to the doctor every six months. The bottom of my heart muscle doesn't work right, and a while back I had to pass a kidney stone."

Still a smoker, Banks works hard every day, and if his pace has slowed only he knows the standard unmet. Banks grew up poor in rural Kentucky and has never known not working hard for a living. His parents had eight sons in the service during World War II. Two were wounded and one, a sailor, was killed. "On one day they got a telegram that my brother'd been killed, and on the next day a letter came from him. My dad was out walking down the railroad tracks, reading that letter, and got hit by the train. I was eleven years old.

"When that ditch out there is open," Banks says, "it's my job to set the pipe in. If I can't make money for the company, I'll quit. I want to get this pipe in the ground. That's just the way I feel about it."

DESPITE THE HAND clearing and underbrushing Whitford has had a crew of laborers working on all summer, there are still a lot of palmettos around Ironhorse. The housing parcel along the seventeenth hole displays the mix of pines, cabbage palms, and palmettos characteristic of the mesic uplands once covering parts of the fourteenth, fifteenth, sixteenth, and seventeenth holes and the lakes around them. Along the trees left to separate the fifteenth and sixteenth holes, and behind the green at sixteen, laborers have trimmed the palmetto rhizomes, the plants' thick trunklike roots, of their lower fronds, leaving a crown of leaves perched like blossoms. The effect is of a shorn poodle. You know there's a dog there but not why it has that shape. The palmetto, tough as the cabbage palms, can survive this indecorous modification. The trimming makes it easier to find a lost golf ball, but the look of a flourishing stand of palmettos is gone. Whitford's crew is also cutting down the last of the Brazilian peppers and tidying up all the plantings around the course.

THE CARPENTERS BUILDING the bridges and the bulkhead at the seventh hole—the par three over water, where Muss thought Wadsworth was changing too much for the retaining work—stand waist-deep in water to do their work. All three are young and strong, with plenty of bulk to wrestle the heavy, pressure-treated timbers into place and drive thick spikes through them. They use a water jet to wash away the sand on the lake's floor as they wiggle the vertical timbers into place. They anchor them under the green with steel cables connected to dead men, weighted anchors buried under the green. The soil flows back around the post and fixes it in place as soon as the jet's removed. The splashing, blowing, and sucking of the work sound to alligator ears like an invitation to prey, and several show up to keep the carpenters company. South Florida has been in a drought, record temperatures following one day after another like raises in a poker game, and the alligator holes are drying up.

The speed with which alligators moved into Ironhorse's new lakes had surprised me. They arrived within days after the lakes filled with water. Perhaps they were claiming territory. The local newspapers were publishing warnings from wildlife biologists that the drought had made the alligators more aggressive and peripatetic, but the carpenters working on the bulkhead were unconcerned. They carried a pistol to fire at the water when the alligators were near, and that worked as long as the alligators associated the noise with danger. Alligators are not easy to discourage in any case, their dim wits so focused on food that few distractions penetrate. Once Dash saw a big gator sunning on a bank and tossed a large rock beside it: "It heard the rock land, reached over, and clamped its jaws on it. Kind of shook its head, like, 'Nah, this ain't food.' I tossed a couple of more rocks, and it kept doing the same thing. Flat learning curve on your gator."

The second day they worked on the timber wall, the carpenters spotted a gator. The foreman, a powerfully built guy in his early twenties, flopped on it from atop the completed wall, a drop of four or five feet. He wrestled it to shore and wrapped a rope around its snout and over and under its belly to make a carrying handle. The alligator's legs were free beneath its shackles. He tossed it in the back of his pickup and drove over to the office. The hero sprained his ankle in the struggle and was still wet and splattered with sand, mud in his hair and water sparkling off his chest hair, when they roared to a stop behind Isakson's Jeep.

The gator had a malevolent look in her eye. The experts were sure of her sex because her abdomen, they said, was swollen with eggs. Nearly six feet from tip to tail, the gator weighed perhaps seventy pounds. She was a great photo op, so everyone posed with her hanging beneath her rope handle, a living reminder of the luggage once made from her ancestors' skins. Hissing, she tried to back away in an angry scurry, but her custodian, painful ankle and all, was vigilant. When she moved, everyone but he jumped back. Calls to kill the beast were overruled. They tossed her back on the truck and carted her down near the seventeenth green, carrying her to the lake edge. A foot bore down on her great upper jaw while her bonds were loosened. Free of the rope, she flexed slightly, lifting as if poked from below, and then sprang into the water, breaching the surface and staying under until she was hundreds of feet from shore.

A couple of days before, Britton, who's been feeding a little alligator by the twelfth tee for weeks, dropping it scraps of bread and bologna every day—a practice that may lead to a surprise for a foursome there some day—saw why the gators were so quick to occupy the lakes. Alligators subsist mainly on fish and turtles, but they'll eat anything that smells of flesh. A little armadillo, one of the few to survive P&J's invasion, was lapping its morning water from the lake in front of the eighteenth tee. There was a furious splash, Britton said, and when the droplets cleared only the back third of the armadillo, its feet still gripping the bank, remained, an armored table scrap. Later that day, a buzzard spotted the hindquarters and dropped down to investigate. Its eyes tiny bubbles on the water's surface, the gator watched the buzzard, who hopped warily toward the armadillo's rump. The buzzard took several quick pecks, then pulled away. Sensing the alligator, the buzzard jumped in the air with a squawk and flapped heavily away, as the alligator rose briefly and ominously, then slid back into its dark, still bunker. It was as if the gator had left the armadillo remnant for bait.

If he catches that old bird, Britton says, he swallows him feathers and all.

Late in the summer, as Ironhorse heaved toward completion, heavy rain washed sand over the rock blanket on the third green. Britton had six laborers—his "Gualamalians"—shoveling the blanket clean so he could put greens mix down. The laborers are small men, none of whom speaks English. They've spent most of the last month laying Bahia sod, trying to secure the ground. They arrive on the job early every morning, riding in the back of a small pickup, under a canopy, driven over from Jupiter by the labor contractor who sells their muscle power. I've noticed one very young man in this group who smiles whenever I approach. Rod Lucks, who pushes this crew, says he is a very hard worker, even though he's only sixteen or seventeen years old. I asked him to sit with me at lunch one day so I could hear his story.

EMILIO MENDOZA QUINONES was frightened when I called him aside. He looked fearfully to Lucks for reassurance. Like all the laborers, he has no papers, and suspects I am the law. No, I said, I am a writer, I want to know about you. He hunkered in the shade of a pine, just off the fourth tee, and picked at its bark, looking carefully at the ground. He wore a brown shirt, its long sleeves buttoned at the wrists, and a red bandanna around his neck. His skin glistened with sweat, dark brown from long days under the summer sun. His eyelashes were long and fine, his dark eyes guileless, struggling to hide his discomfort. He was hungry and asked if he could eat while we spoke. He recovered a paper bag from the crotch of a tree and washed his hands in the murky water of the lake, under the small cypresses transplanted beside the fourth tee. He ate a bologna sandwich—white bread and bologna, neat.

Emilio grew up in a pueblo in Huehuetenango State, working on his father's farm, the youngest of six children. He went to elementary school, where he learned Spanish, but "I didn't obey, so I didn't stay." The language of his pueblo is Jakalteko, he said, "a sacred tongue spoken in a sacred town." Jakalteko, the words of his town of Jacaltenango, is a Mayan language.

Emilio left home to escape the violence of the guerrilla war. The men of his pueblo were impressed by the army and forced to chase the guerrillas into the mountains. They were given two guns for ten men and no provisions, no pay. Once they went three days without food. They dug roots to boil.

"Since 1982," a wire service story datelined Guatemala reported in 1990, "the Guatemalan army has incorporated about half a million Indians into unpaid, often arduous service as a way of patrolling against guerilla activity and spying on the Indians."

Emilio's father didn't want him to come north. Two days before he left home, he told his parents he was going and they cried, so when he left, late in the night, he didn't say good-bye. Hitchhiking, walking, and riding buses, he crossed Mexico in ten days, arriving at the border in Nogales, a town straddling the line between Sonora and Arizona. A coyote—a crossing guide—wanted $500 to bring him over the border and transport him to either California or Florida. He had little money, so he crossed alone at night. He brought with him 1,000 pesos.

Immigration caught him the first morning. He convinced them he was Mexican, so they sent him back to Nogales. He was very scared because he knew "my mother and father couldn't help me."

EMILIO CONTINUED TO pick at the bark of a pine, tossing pieces on the ground, shielding his eyes. He rolled up his shirtsleeves, and showed me on his left arm, in capital letters, the initials "JDR" tattooed in plain black, done with a needle and ink. J for his father, José, D for his mother, Dori, and R for Rosalie, his sister who died. He left Arizona on April 25 and arrived in West Palm on May 15. It took three months to pay for his passage. People told him it was easy in America, but it's not true. It's very hard to be illegal. Sometimes they steal from him. His last job they didn't pay him his last week's wages—$200. Who can he turn to?

He doesn't eat breakfast, instead "holds his hunger." His stomach hurts a lot, and he thinks he may have an ulcer. He can't go to the doctor, though: "If a Latino comes in with an illness they operate and put him on the street the same day." He has no money for medicine.

Twenty days ago he sent a money order for $400 and a letter home: "I didn't buy my words from anybody. They were all my own."

There is such a great flow of cash to Central America and Mexico, delivered in the small sums of Emilio and his countrymen, that American Express announced in 1990 its plan to compete with Western Union for control of the business. Perhaps a thousand people from Emilio's part of the highlands now live in Palm Beach County, most of them in Indiantown, just twenty miles from Ironhorse on the Beeline toward Okeechobee.

Emilio came to Florida willing to do any job, hard or soft. If the job was so hard that it killed him he would do it. "I didn't buy my life. God could take me any time He wanted."

He lives with six men, none of whom he really knows, in a rented house in Jupiter. The first time he went to the labor center in West Palm he walked, a trip of thirty miles. The house in Jupiter has two bedrooms, a living room, and a kitchen. There's a TV in the living room, with a VCR. They watch karate movies. Emilio thinks about his life and cannot sleep. He watches the TV until 1:00 A.M. On Sunday he sleeps until ten, then shops for his weekly lunches. He gets up at six to meet the labor boss, who charges $8.95 an hour for his work and pays him $32.50 a day. He's been working five days a week at Ironhorse for the last month and a half and sometimes on Saturday at other jobs.

As lunch ends, Emilio's comrades pick up their rakes and shovels and turn back to cleaning and spreading the gravel blanket over the third green. Emilio asks if he can go back to work. What is golf? I ask him.

"I once saw a course in Guatemala," he said. "It's just, put a ball in a hole." He gestures, with the gentle motions of a shepherd. "They make the lagoons and the mountains here to make it harder. They use a hook—*gancho*—to strike the ball over the mountains. The lagoons make it beautiful."

Who will come to this *campos de golf*? "Rich people," he imagines.

Who is rich in the United States?

"Students, professionals, bosses, teachers—somebody who can eat breakfast, lunch, and dinner. Somebody who has an air conditioner and doesn't have to work the fields.

"We are all slaves of life. When we are hungry we must think of what we must do to feed ourselves, when we are cold we must clothe ourselves." He pauses, looks away. The work beckons, he fears isolation.

Sometimes, he says as he rises, eyes still averted, he gets homesick, and that makes him feel defeated, and he doesn't want to get up in the morning. But then he remembers, no one made him come here, and he laughs, and rises. I offer my hand. He lays his small, rough palm in mine, and smiles. He's barely five feet tall.

The other Guatemalans relax as Emilio rejoins them. Lucks motions them back to the raking. They pull at the tiny rocks, dreaming of mountains.

17

Green at Last

There is not a sprig of grass that shoots uninteresting to me.

—Thomas Jefferson to his daughter, Martha Randolph, 1790

FIRST P&J HAD LEFT, and then Ranger's trailers came to haul its equipment away, and finally Wadsworth was down to fine-tuning the details, finishing the cart paths—built to "DOT specs," Britton said, his way of complimenting the contractor for the path's quality while still nagging about how long it was taking to get it done—installing the last sprinkler heads, dressing the fairways, and loading and spreading the greens mix. It seemed symbolically appropriate to Britton somehow, a sort of monument to his frustration, that at Ironhorse "my biggest green was the one farthest from my mix pile."

At last Hills had approved the contours on all the greens and the course was shaped to his satisfaction—a "bolder" transition accomplished here, a "calmer" ledge there, this bunker bulked, supporting that carved face. There was dirt enough on the golf course, plucked from here, borrowed from there. Whatever wasn't done as he might have liked—a higher tee on the eleventh hole, perhaps, or more volume in the mounding by the first hole—was close enough to assuage Hills's worries. Britton wanted most of all to "close the gate."

His grading plan was so wrinkled and ragged by now that Dasher said you couldn't even get a measurement off it.

"It got wet," Britton sniffed.

Not that he cared. As soon as the course was grassed, he said, "Ironhorse owns it and I'm gone. The only satisfaction there is on this job is seeing it done, and I really don't get to see it."

Owsley, too, was ready for a new assignment. This job was too many nibbles and not enough bites. "If I needed a blade," Britton said, "I had to get Willie. If I needed to rake a green, I had to get Willie. If I needed to spread fertilizer, Willie. I been running him to death."

Dick Lanscioni, busy designing the scorecard, a bag tag, and signage for the tees, was not the first to notice that "Art Hills doesn't use many bunkers."

"Art would rather make the strategy with the shaping," Dash said. "Have you figure out it's better to be here than there instead of aiming you with bunkers."

Finishing the course resurrected Hills's optimism. He sounded again like the person who had brought such earnest hopes and high expectations to his meeting with Alan Sher in 1985. "With good care," Hills wrote Isakson, after his penultimate site visit in late August, "Ironhorse is going to be an attractive, challenging course."

Ed Harbauer, when he saw the final shaping on the eighteenth fairway, said, "Wow, does this look good! Boy, boy. It's nice to see something exciting."

Harbauer laughed. "I've got to look for defects, so I'm pissed off the whole time I'm here—I mean, I *do* find defects. But boy, Ironhorse does look good."

Dasher concurred. "I think this course is looking real good," he told Britton.

"Damn good," Britton said, "for the money they spent."

THE GRASSES SPECIFIED for Ironhorse are all hybrid Bermudas bred by Dr. Glenn Burton in Tifton, Georgia, at the United States Department of Agriculture's Coastal Plains Research Station. "419" is the name of the hybrid used on the fairways. Its creator called it Tifway, but that didn't take. Everybody calls it 419, its test plot number. It's the fastest growing—"most aggressive," as the supers say—of the hybrid Bermudas. "328" is a finer-bladed grass used on the tees, and until

The first hole at Ironhorse. (*Illustration by Michael Strantz*)

Tifdwarf, an even finer and slower-growing Bermuda hybrid came along, 328 was often planted on greens. Now it's used mostly for contrast—it has a sort of apple-green color to set against 419's darker hue.

In 1946 the USGA told Burton, who had by then developed new strains of Bermuda grass for forage, that if he'd "be willing to add turf research to [his] job description" it would give him five hundred dollars a year. The USGA wanted better grasses for Southern golf courses. "Many courses had sand greens and carpet grass fairways," Burton remembered. "The better golf courses had common Bermuda grass established from seed on the greens that were overseeded with annual ryegrass for winter play." Even discounting for inflation, the USGA cut a great deal.

Leonard Tufts, the founder of Pinehurst, said the first thing he discovered there was that "our wretchedly poor sandhill land," as he called it, "was not made for growing turf grasses." This would seem an astonishing claim to anyone who's seen the quality of the turf on Pinehurst Number Two. Supers now love to grow grass on sand, and they have the grass for it. A hundred years ago, though, when Tufts created Pinehurst, greenkeepers didn't have Glenn Burton's grasses. Tufts asked his landscape architect, none other than his friend Frederick Law Olmsted, then nearing the end of his long career, what to do. Olmsted—making another contribution to golf, whose modern settings and landscaping style he so influenced, however indirectly—advised Tufts to engage the services of a "scientific German experimenter from the Emperor's gardens in Berlin." Over "a good many years," Tufts recalled, his German experimenter learned that "Bermuda grass and Texas bluegrass were the only grasses that would live through our summers."

Armed with their expensively acquired Continental knowledge, the fellows at Pinehurst *still* had a lousy time growing grass. Imitating Charles Blair Macdonald's strategy at the Lido Club, Tufts's greenkeeper spread "six inches of muck on some of our holes"—the same sort of stuff Ranger and Wadsworth struggled to keep off the course at Ironhorse—and managed to grow a tolerable stand of common Bermuda, a grass modern supers regard as obscenely pestiferous, a leggy thug trying to insinuate itself into the company of their elegant hybrids. They treat common as a weed.

By the time Burton started his work for the USGA, Southern turf grass knowledge hadn't progressed much beyond Tufts's troubled understanding. There were still a lot of sand greens in Florida and various coarse-bladed grasses, among them Bahia, growing on fairways. Southern courses took a decided backseat to the creeping bentgrass-covered greens and fairways of the North. South Florida had great winter weather, but without improved grasses the golf it provided was barely better than no golf at all. Burton changed all that. Turf aficionados may still prefer creeping bentgrass on greens—Jack Nicklaus even tried to grow it in Florida, way south of its comfort zone, where it destroyed the sanity of the supers trying to maintain it—but anyone who can't enjoy putting on a good Tifdwarf green probably wouldn't enjoy flying coach, either. A dwarf green tended by someone as skillful as Roger Whitford—who knows how to keep the little rascals cut down to within a hairsbreath of oblivion, fighting to find the sun—putts truer than the carpet on your living room floor. Burton thinks the pros demand greens cut *too* short. "You're destroying the factory that manufactures the food," he says. "The plant's near death all the time."

The turf work was always a small sideline for Burton. In addition to forage grasses, he bred millets widely used in tropical Asia and Africa. Still, his turf discoveries were enough to change the face of Southern golf.

Burton started out collecting plugs from the best turf he could find on Southern golf courses. These were all *Cynodon dactylon*, or common Bermuda. He made some crosses between these samples and selections from his pasture-grass breeding program. One he named Tiflawn—test plot number 57—was the first turf grass Burton released. Then came the big step, a cross with another species.

The person who recruited Burton for the USGA, himself a plant breeder specializing in Northern grasses, sent Burton a plug of grass he found on a golf course in Cairo, Egypt. This was a *Cynodon transvaalensis*, a grass originally, as the name suggests, found in South Africa. Cecil Rhodes, in fact, sent the first sample of this grass to the United States, where it was adapted to pasture in Texas. Surviving passage through quarantine in Washington, D.C.—near, incidentally, Arlington, Virginia, where on the spot the Pentagon now sits the USGA had established its first turf test plot right after the War to End All Wars—the Egyptian plug made it to Tifton.

Armed with the germ plasm of the *C. transvaalensis*, Burton launched the breeding program that produced Ironhorse's grasses. Tifton 328 was a cross between the Egyptian and a plug of common from the fourth green at the Charlotte Country Club. The 328, like all such crosses, was sterile. One of its folks had thirty-six chromosomes, the other eighteen, and that left little Tifgreen with twenty-seven. The common Bermuda contributed hardiness and durability to its pollen-less offspring, and the *transvaalensis* gave it its fine-textured leaf. Hybrid Bermudas can only be propagated vegetatively. They don't even make seed. But if you pull a handful from the ground and jam a piece of it in bare dirt, grass will grow. That's why truckloads of sprigs rather than bags of seed showed up at Ironhorse to plant its fairways.

The 328 was released in 1956, the 419 in 1960. Burton went on to experiment with other hybrids, as well as with mutations he created by radiation, and he searched around the world for new sources of Bermuda germ plasm. He found Bermuda grasses growing in Italy and Germany. He helped the Chinese stabilize thousands of acres of riverbanks by sprigging Bermuda grass. 328 and 419, though, are his great contributions to turf grass and to golf. Tifdwarf, too, was a Burton discovery, but "dwarf" is a more complicated story. I'll tell a condensed version.

Most golf course superintendents will tell you that "dwarf sports." What they mean is that it mutates, or "goes off," another phrase meant to describe the same process. Some supers insist they need to resprig their greens every so often to eradicate the mutations. Some claim they're growing a "good dwarf," while others complain they have a "weak dwarf."

What's more likely is that they have contamination, an invasion of 328 carried on the green by a golf shoe, perhaps, or by a mower. There is *some* mutation in Tifdwarf, but Burton says Tifdwarf "mutates at such a low frequency that new mutants would rarely make more than one small spot on one golf course."

Some of the superintendents' confusion lies in Tifdwarf's origins. According to Burton, Tifdwarf was first discovered by a USGA agronomist on a green in South Carolina. Soon after, another small stand of dwarf was discovered at another nearby course. Both were found on greens planted with 328 that came from Tifton, directly from Burton. After extensive testing, Burton was convinced that Tifdwarf *was* a natural mutant of 328, and that it was in the batch of sprigs he sent to the courses where it was found. It didn't mutate there, it was in the sprigs they received.

Earl Elsner, who worked with Burton on Tifdwarf, now maintains the pure strain of Tifdwarf in Athens, Georgia, where he's the director of the Georgia Seed Development Commission. If a nursery wants to start growing Tifdwarf, Elsner will send them starter sprigs. He wants to see the pure strain propagated. Given the wonderful workings of the geometric progression, it doesn't take long to go from a little plug to a nursery flat to an acre. Ironhorse's dwarf, though, did not come from sprigs sent from Elsner's pure stock, or at least not by any direct route. Ironhorse's dwarf had a more complicated provenance.

Tifdwarf is not a protected variety. If I can convince you to buy Bahia by calling it "dwarf," *caveat emptor*. Elsner has been trying to establish a certification program, similar to that used by patented seed growers—the best-known certified seed in the golf world is Penncross, a creeping bentgrass developed at Penn State and grown exclusively by Oregon seedmen—but it's tough when there's no penalty for selling bogus goods. Penncross is protected, and its producers go to court frequently to protect their rights. You can't just package any old seed lying around the warehouse and call it Penncross, but you can call anything you want "dwarf." Tifdwarf is in the public domain because Burton felt that's where it belonged. He's a public employee, he says, and tax dollars support his work. Besides, he says, if money drives your research you may be less careful and push a variety on the market before its characteristics are fully known. Even though the USGA's contribution to his research now is ten times greater than it was forty years ago—though in purchasing power about the same—Burton still won't agree to patenting plants developed with its help.

Ironhorse's dwarf came originally from a commercial turf farm in Georgia, carried to Quality Turf, the grassing contractor hired by Wadsworth to sprig Ironhorse, by a fellow named Ralph White. I'd heard Quality Turf had a "really good dwarf," but from what Earl Elsner told me that was like claiming to have a *really wet* drink of water. Tifdwarf is Tifdwarf is Tifdwarf. This was cloned grass, more of the same, over and over and over again, unless it mutated, and that was an unlikely occurrence. Tifdwarf is or it isn't, that's all.

Some supers, including the head of all of Brent Wadsworth's courses at Innisbrook, told me what Quality Turf was planting on greens was a selected and improved grass called "Classic Dwarf." "Better than the old Tifdwarf," they said.

Someone else said, no, Classic Dwarf was a grass developed by a turf man named Granville Horn, *not* the grass Quality Turf had. Paul Frank, Hills's old friend, the superintendent at The Wilderness Club, thought there was a real good chance Horn's Classic Dwarf was a mutant Frank had discovered on one of his greens, a rare, true sport from 328. Frank called his selection PF-11, after his initials and the green he found it on. Horn, whom Frank had known for thirty years, took a plug of PF-11 to study, but when Frank called to ask him about it, Horn said it had died. Not long afterward, Horn was trumpeting a new dwarf he had discovered, called "Classic Dwarf." Frank was suspicious, but Horn died in an automobile accident, "carrying," as a friend of his said, "the secret of Classic Dwarf to his grave."

Ralph White, on the other hand, said Classic Dwarf had nothing to do with Granny Horn or Paul Frank, it was just a marketing name he used for "the really good dwarf" he brought to Quality Turf from Georgia. "It's like Classic Coke," he said, "that's all. Classic Dwarf's just a name I gave it. We're not using that name anymore. It confuses people."

Horn's son was still growing a grass *he* called "Classic Dwarf," using it in his green-sprigging business, but he didn't know where his dad had found the original stock—he thought maybe somewhere down near Naples. White was right. It was all very confusing. Roger Whitford said he sure as hell didn't want an experimental grass on his course. Quality Turf said absolutely that its dwarf was only the finest *pure* Tifdwarf, even if Elsner hadn't supplied the sprigs. Wherever it came from, when Elsner got a look at a sample of Ironhorse's putting grass, he was sure it was Tifdwarf—the real McCoy. Whitford, too, once the grass established itself, had no doubts. Dwarf was a grass he knew how to grow. He didn't give a damn where it came from, he just wanted it green and healthy.

QUALITY PLANTED THE GREENS FIRST. Isakson persuaded Muss to invest in more sod as protection against washouts, so Britton had to wait on sprigging his fairways until the sod was down. He couldn't risk a sod truck running over a fairway. The first batch of sprigs came over from Quality Turf in August, and the company finished planting the last fairway six weeks later.

Quality Turf was doing all of Wadsworth's grassing in Florida. Its work was good, Harbauer said, but its honesty won Wadsworth's trust. Quality Turf sprigged a course for Wadsworth that called for 400 bushels an acre on the fairways. It grew in beautifully. But when he was preparing the bill, Howard Barnes, one of the little turf company's owners, realized, "We grassed that at three hundred."

"There was no way we would have known," Jon Shapland said, unless Barnes had told them, as he did. His honesty saved Wadsworth $15,000 and won Quality an important customer.

Quality Turf's nursery is an ordinarily flat sixty-acre field near Tampa. Its crop, except for the dwarf sod, which is carefully mowed, looks like a large untended lawn or an especially lush pasture. Howard Barnes's brother, Calvin, manages the nursery. There were 300 cattle egrets working the field for worms the August day I stopped by. A sprig harvestor, which looks and works like a potato chain, sits near each field. The harvestor knocks up hunks of grass, roots, blades, and bits of dirt, about like what you'd get if you attacked your lawn with a small hoe, and runs the sprigs up a conveyor to a hopper. Then they're loaded onto a truck and covered with a tarp for the journey to their new home. Barnes can harvest 2,000 bushels in forty-five minutes. Quality is careful not to contaminate the fields, to let the hybrids mix or allow any common Bermuda in: That's why there is more than one harvestor. Contamination is the worst sin for a Bermuda turf nursery. Quality grows twelve and a half acres of dwarf, three acres of 328, and about forty-five acres of 419. There's a fence around the dwarf. A small job trailer near the dwarf is the office. It's a young company. Calvin Barnes says a turf nursery is like a prostitute—"you get to sell what you got and keep it, too."

Ironhorse is the fourth course Quality has done for Wadsworth. It did Seville and is planting Hills's Old Trail course at the same time it's doing Ironhorse. Old Trail, like Ironhorse, has conquered its construction bogeys and is gearing up for a winter opening.

Calvin Barnes patrols the fields for weeds and pests and uses herbicides lightly. Courses are never sprigged on Monday because the nursery has to harvest in advance to get the sprigs to the job, and since Quality takes Sunday off, it would have to harvest a Monday job on Saturday. Then if it rained on Monday, the company would be stuck with a truck full of expensive lawn clippings.

"If you keep it in the shade, keep water on, it'll keep—we've gone as long as two days. Then you start hitting PR problems. Sometimes you plant it and it looks green all the time, other times it's strawlike, and they think it's dead. Then it takes off."

The dwarf sprigs for the greens fill a small truck. The hands sent to spread the sprigs fork them into big red plastic buckets and then walk across the green, casting them to either side, shaking the pieces loose, kicking them into a reasonably thorough coverage. They put out fifteen bushels for every thousand square feet of green, so the average green at Ironhorse gets about eighty bushels. Once the sprigs are spread, a little tractor runs back and forth across the green, pulling a harrow to disk the sprigs into the ground. When they're done, Britton turns on the water for a few minutes to prove that it runs, and then, as he says, "Roger owns it."

Before any grass is placed on the greens, Britton has the mix fumigated with methyl bromide, which kills anything that might be growing in or near the greens mix. The fumigator covers the green with clear plastic and injects the gas. "This puts it on the grassing contractor," Britton says. If the grass doesn't grow, or if it's contaminated, Wadsworth is blameless. "Fumigation provides that separation of responsibility."

The fairways are sprigged mechanically by a machine that looks a lot like a Zamboni, the contraption that dresses the ice at a hockey game. Ironhorse started sprigging fairways at 300 bushels an acre, but increased the rate to 600 bushels. The days were shorter, the growing time shrinking. There was talk now of playing by December. The more sprigs, the faster they establish. The heaviest concentration Quality ever spread was a thousand bushels an acre. "That grows 'em in quick."

LANSCIONI'S OLD CLUB in Chicago presented him with a beautiful watch. When he returned to Ironhorse, he held out his arm to show it off. "That's it," Muss said, "for twenty-three *years*?"

"FOR EVERY HALF HOUR you don't water," Whitford said, "you lose ten percent of your sprigs."

Once Whitford had grass to tend, talking to him was like interrupting a woman in labor. He flew around Ironhorse on his green Cushman cart, running from hole to hole, from green to green, fighting washouts, stabilizing soil, checking for disease. Small showers started little gullies, so he'd set small rubber dams in the soil to hold the grass. Trying to keep grass growing on the edges of the course and on the mounds soaked the center of the fairway. You could never let the water run too long. It was a constant vigil. "I'm not one to set the irrigation on auto and then sit back," Whitford said. "I pride myself on growing grass for less than my neighbor. I'm seven days a week now, seven to seven. Maybe on Sunday if everything's working right I may run home for lunch."

His crewmen worked six days—everyone Monday through Friday, then half came in on Saturday, the other half Sunday. "This is not a job you can ever completely forget on Sunday and go fishing," Whitford said. "You're always worried about the course."

He was poised against winter. "As soon as we get temperatures below seventy degrees at night you start losing Bermuda grass growth. Below forty-five degrees and it just stops. I always figure about thirteen frosts a year. Most golfers don't see that. You try to wash it off before the sun hits it."

A webworm moth laid its larvae on the ninth green. It and the moth that lays the army worm—"it flies over the grass and bombs it"—are the main pests this time of year.

"These little moths are smart," Whitford said. "It's their evolution, I guess. They know the greens are a good feeding area—they eat the blade all the way to the soil."

He sprays to kill the worms. Several dozen cattle egrets congregate on the green to eat the dying worms. They poke their beaks into the ground looking for mole crickets, a delicacy armadillos also favor. There are several clumps of regurgitated larvae lying on the green.

"People ask me, 'Will that kill the birds?' I don't know. But I'm not gonna keep a job with wormy greens. I know I've never seen a bird keel over."

Whitford confined himself to growing grass. "I'm not gonna tamper with an Art Hills course," he said. "He's an artist."

Muss, he said, had everybody afraid. Whitford wished his maintenance building was done. His workers didn't even have a place to wash their hands. "How can they eat," he said, "after they've handled fertilizer?"

He erected a tent near the clubhouse site so he'd have someplace under cover to store his equipment and his chemicals. Harpman was in charge of the maintenance building, a metal-roofed structure under construction near the fourteenth tee. Whitford had no time for small talk. Like Harbauer, he was an official pessimist on the job. I thought the course was a miracle. After so much wailing and bashing and worrying, there it was. The days were quiet. Birds trooped to the lakes, even a flock of wood storks. A pair of sandhill cranes nested in the preserve, yards away from the pond ordered dredged by the Army Corps of Engineers. By spring they were tending a pair of chicks.

Within three weeks of the first sprigging, Whitford started to mow. There were small setbacks in the grow-in, but the movement overall was to green. He was going to have a golf course soon.

There was always something to contend with, but Whitford was a good and observant husbandman. After the worms, he said, "the weeds would come on next—and herbicides will affect the Bermuda. You're pretty reckless if you spray in November and stun the Bermuda."

A newly sprigged green, or a fairway for that matter, is a homely thing, with raggedy, weedy-looking, tired clumps of grass spread across it. Then, as the turf forms, as "profusely branching" rhizomes search below the ground and busy stolons creep across it, the course fills in, its green lawn erasing all traces of its origins.

In the stillness, it's hard to remember the dozers, and the fires, and the scream of the pans. This looks right, you think. These greens belong. This *is* a good place for a golf course. The Button King, wide-awake, stands on the first tee. He unsheathes his driver and surveys his conjured kingdom. He smiles. Life is good, he says. Life is very good.

18

A View of Ironhorse
from Arthur Hills

IN EARLY DECEMBER, Hills wrote a commentary on Ironhorse. "It is well balanced," he observed, "as one reviews what is in place." Ironhorse through Hills's eyes looked like this:

#1—A moderate length Par 4 (404 yards) dogleg right. One must hit the ball far enough to clear the corner or play over or around large trees. A gentle beginning.

#2—A strong though not long (374 yards) demanding Par 4. Play is to a plateau and then to a beautifully elevated green. With wetlands, a grassy waste bunker and native vegetation behind the green, #2 is a beauty.

#3—A straightforward Par 3, no water in the way but plenty of interesting rolls around the green, and yes, there is water on the left. 157 yards.

#4—At 410 yards #4 is a strong Par 4. Water left and trees right create a definite target area. There is plenty of space around the green and the green is large.

#5—This narrow Par 5 at 530 yards calls for accuracy. The shot onto the elevated green must be precise. The green is small and its surface is surrounded by grassy hollows and sand.

#6—The 2nd Par 5 at 532 yards is a beautiful hole. The tee shot plays off a sloping fairway. The shot to the green is made interesting by the water bordering the right side of the green and extending back down the fairway.

#7—All over water, #7 demands a very fine effort. The green area is not large so the shot to it needs to be accurate. There are several tees each playing over water. The distances range from 100 to 220 yards. No one in his right mind will play this hole from 220 yards!

#8—This very pleasant hole medium length at 354 yards plays among trees to an elevated green. The landing area is broad but a shot too far right will wind up with trees between it and the green.

#9—At 441 yards this is the one long Par 4 on the front nine. There is a good carry to the landing area from the tee. The shot to the green is fairly open as befits a hole of this length.

#10—#10 is also very long at 441 yards. These are two very strong Par 4s back to back. #10 is a long straightaway hole to a big green.

#11—A very pretty Par 3 hole, playing over water to a green surrounded by cypress trees and other wetland type vegetation. At 180 yards from the back the hole is a challenge.

#12—After a ride along the dike through untouched tropical growth the player arrives at the 12th tee. The view from the tee, with a giant pine in the fairway and a big lake bordering the left side of the hole, is beautiful. At 392 yards to a green which stands at the end of a long rise, the 12th hole is one of the best.

#13—A dramatic Par 3 with water on the left and a mass of rising and falling, steeply contoured hollows on the right side. #13 is a picturesque hole to say the least. At 181 yards into the prevailing easterly winds it is a very strong hole from the back tee.

#14—This beautiful Par 5 features a big carry across water to the fairway and then a 2nd shot where water can come into play. The green is guarded by sand and grassy hollows. One of the prettiest Par 5s to be seen anywhere. Not long at 501 yards.

#15—Our favorite hole. Only 317 yards from the middle tee but quite an exhilarating little beauty! It's narrow off the tee but what makes the hole is the green setting. The green surface is a simple, little circle of about 3500 square feet, raised above the fairway several feet and partially hidden by a steep mound which rises 6'-8' above the green. From the right side of the fairway the player is challenged to lift a shot high and arching to clear the mound and stay on the green. In any case the player must play the shot up into the air and drop it onto the elevated green.

#16—Another short narrow Par 4. At 361 yards from the back the hole calls for a straight tee shot and a short or medium iron to the gently contoured green surface. #16 is another very pretty hole, framed by trees.

#17—This is the long, long Par 4 on the back side. It is a big open hole calling for length and power. There is water along part of the right side but it comes into play only for the very errant shot. #17 is a beautiful complement to #15 and #16 as it calls for the fairway wood or long iron. 445 yards.

#18—A moderate length Par 5 at 531 yards. #18 is a strategic hole with water on the right off the tee and on the left at the second landing area and at the green. It can be not too tough or tough depending on the wind and your game today.

"Ironhorse," Hills concluded, "is interesting, challenging and at times demanding. It has balance and variety. It has beauty. It provides the opportunity to play every kind of shot. It is a course which every person who loves golf will enjoy and want to play again."

A Dedication

To the memory of Bill Mabry, a great dentist and an avid golfer, and vice versa

AFTER MY UNCLE BILL won the Big War he hurried home from the Pacific to go to dental school on the GI Bill. Setting up his practice in a tiny Illinois town surrounded by cornfields, Uncle Bill ground on molars and cast gold crowns, keeping farmers' hours, working from dawn to dusk and sometimes into the night to accommodate patients who wouldn't climb off their tractors in daylight for something as trivial as a toothache. Bill and Aunt Margaret Nell, fertile like the black prairie soil, had five babies. Themselves children of the Depression, Bill and Margaret Nell had no trouble remembering when farmers poured milk on the ground and plowed crops under and cash was as scarce as whiskey at a Protestant picnic, but given a chance to share in prosperity and peace, they never looked back. They'd accepted their duty in war without complaint, and now welcomed its aftermath, confident and composed and ready for a better life.

Where once idleness was proof that someone was either very rich or broke, in the postwar world there was not only spare change, there was *spare time*. A new siren, something called leisure, was whispering down from the cultural ramparts. That, as Margaret Nell told me years later, made possible my Uncle Bill's great discovery.

"A couple of Bill's friends heard about a golf course that had just been built and they all wanted to go visit it," Aunt Margaret Nell remembered. "None of them had actually *played* golf yet. I think they just wanted to see what one hundred acres without corn on it would look like. So they picked up Bill and took off one afternoon to drive out there. Then about suppertime his friends came back by the house without Bill. They told me they just couldn't get Doc—that's what they all called Bill—to leave.

"So I told your cousin, Jane, to watch the little ones and headed off to get him. When I finally got there, I saw this dim light off in the distance. Bill had somebody holding his cigarette lighter by the hole while he was putting. Getting him to come home was as hard as talking a scared cat out of a tree. I'll never forget the day your Uncle Billy found golf."

Golf seized Uncle Billy, squeezed him in its tight embrace. It struck some ancient Celtic nerve that vibrated for three decades. In its grip he built a beautifully sloped little practice green near the alley on the vacant lot next door. A backyard green in Piper City, Illinois, was an unlikely indulgence. It was Bill's devotional object, like a concrete Madonna, which one would also not see in Piper City. Bill tended his green with priestly ardor, cutting it by hand every day in the crisscrossing pattern that makes the grass look like a checkerboard dyed in muted shades of green. He dispatched weeds with a hangman's solemnity so that the surface on which he cultivated the touch that is to a golfer what pitch is to a musician was smooth and unblemished. He could aim away from his green and drive old balls across the street into a sea of corn. He owned a hundred putters.

The summer after my dad died, more than thirty years ago, Bill and Margaret Nell had me up for a month to hang out with my cousins and caddy for Bill. I knew nothing about golf, but I loved the manicured lawns, the cool morning dew polished by the low shine of the rising sun, the rich expanses of fairway. I had a professional interest, too, in figuring out how they cut the putting grass so short without killing it. I was wearing out a twenty-one-inch Western Auto rotary mower every summer in my own lawn-tending business, but I cut the grass high, as I had been taught, to keep it from browning out during Illinois' glowing summers. On the golf course the grass was low *and* green. The secret, Uncle Billy told me, was water. The greenkeeper, trailing a thick red hose behind his Cushman cart as he ran from green to green in those primitive days before wall-to-wall irrigation and automatic controls, bathed the turf with a cooling spray several times a day and let it drink its fill at night. The pampered blades put down deep roots and churned out chlorophyll, gathering the strength to survive the mower's daily attack.

I liked carrying Uncle Billy's clubs, listening to the banter, being a useful boy. The dramatic trajectory of the ball driven off the tee, the long, sudden elliptical trace of its flight, sucked a universe of energy right out of the ground that left me slack-jawed. I'd never seen an object so emphatically in motion. When Bill gathered some old clubs and set up a game for me with his best friend's son, whose swing had the easy grace of one to the fairway born, I even played a handful of rounds. Golf succored me that summer while I grieved for my dad, but back in my hometown in southern Illinois there was no place for me to play.

Centralia had a country club course, laid out in the early twenties by the Scotsman Tom Bendelow. We used to ride our bikes by Green-view Country Club on the way to the reservoir to catch the big carp under the spillway, loading a hook with dough balls made from old bread that the fish would suck down through their tiny round mouths. Golf was for old men. I heard that some of the boys from St. Mary's and Franklin schools caddied, but that work had a servile quality that didn't appeal to me. I'd do it gladly for Uncle Bill, but not for money. I'd rather mow grass. My folks were Democrats.

There was a tale still current in my youth about Al Capone stopping to play at Greenview on his way south through The Gateway to Little Egypt, as Centralia styled itself. The main highway from Chicago to the South was a narrow two-lane street that ran by fifty yards from my back door. Perhaps Capone was on his way to Miami Beach, where, between federal prison terms, he lived in his Palm Island mansion. I imagined gangsters with tommy guns guarding the green as Capone, a cigar clinched between his teeth, urged his putt toward the hole. That was as close as golf came to having romance for me.

Bendelow was credited with designing over 400 American courses—among them Dasher's Dubsdread—an estimate that strikes me as generous. Until 1920 he was employed by A. G. Spalding, who understood clearly that to sell the balls and clubs he manufactured there had to be golfers, and the best way to create golfers was to give them a place to play. He was a kind of one-man National Golf Foundation. Spalding sent Bendelow from coast to coast on a colonizing mission for golf. Bendelow's technique was later disparaged as "eighteen stakes on a Sunday afternoon," even though Bendelow, a devout Calvinist, never worked on the Sabbath. But on any other day, he could for $25 find a basic route for a golf course across your stubbled fields, performing a simplified artisan's version of the job that today can command a fee of more than a million dollars. I never set foot on the grounds Bendelow helped Centralia's burghers cultivate. It was the only playing field in Centralia I didn't muddy my jeans on. My folks had neither the temperament nor the means for the country club life, preferring the socializing at church potlucks and Little League games.

In the evening on the long summer days that are golf's true season, my parents sat with the other grown-ups in our backyard, chairs drawn into a circle around the old well, talking, the men smoking and the women tending infants while the older kids played hide-and-seek and kick-the-can, chased lightning bugs, and tried to stretch bedtime deep into the warm, humid dusk. If it seems idyllic in memory—when I talk about it now one of my friends says it sounds like "my wee timorous mouse was more tremblin' than your wee timorous mouse"—it's because I think it was. I inherited a dog I loved when the people across the street moved, but I was grown before I learned the reason for their departure—a divorce. Other people might not remember it so fondly, and after I became a teenager and began to see the viciousness in the town's racism, I didn't think it was so all-fired fine either. But for a boy it was grand, with woods and wild places nearby and grown-ups who encouraged kids to love sports.

Nobody ever talked about golf unless Uncle Bill came by to visit. Bill's courtship of the game was admired for its social daring, but he was a professional man, after all, entitled to a little reach. Golf was as foreign to the railroaders and paper hangers and carpenters gathered in my backyard as yoga. It was nearly as alien to me, too, as the years passed and the memory of my summer of golf receded, a tiny pleasant cluster of associations packed behind recollections of college and marriage, births and deaths.

Then, in the spring before I turned forty, a year after Uncle Bill died, I felt a surge of that ancient Scottish instinct to hit a golf ball that must have grabbed him. It was a primordial, somatic urge, a cellular destiny calling—its lure was identity, not recreation. I was Ishmael on the bowsprit, Houdini in chains. I could feel the smooth release of the sword sliding from the stone. There was a power and a conviction in this obsession. I played before work, after work, and best of all, instead of work. I played in rain, in snow, in any inclemency. Traveling to strange and perplexing psychic realms, I spent a lot of time on the mental part of my game. I wondered about the origins of this obsession, tried to link it to something I knew. Vigorous memories of Uncle Billy, whom I had hardly seen since childhood, flashed back, detailed images fueled by my passion for golf.

Uncle Billy was rarely without a club in his hands. Once, staying with us to comfort my mom, his sister, as her husband drew his last breaths, Bill fetched his five iron from the BelAir wagon and carefully measured off the arc of his swing in the living room, checking his setup in the mirror over the couch. At the top of his takeaway the club caught the ceiling fixture, which fell around him in a shower of frosted glass. His face blazed. He must have set up to hit a fade and come over the top. It wouldn't have been as funny if Bill hadn't insisted so to his skeptical sis that there was *no way* he could hit that chandelier. It was our only laugh that winter.

The golf lore in our family was decidedly peripheral, the mythology of Bill's obsession. I don't know if Bill could break ninety or if in his thousands of rounds he ever made a hole in one. But I knew about 200-mile round trips he'd make in an afternoon, pushing his Chevy wagon over narrow bands of baking asphalt at a hundred miles an hour to get in eighteen holes before dark. If Margaret Nell or the kids were along she'd get on him about the speed, so he'd notch it back to ninety mph in the interest of family harmony. He'd borrow my aunt's nail polish to paint balls red so he could play in the snow.

My guess is that Bill had a tendency to hit snap hooks. When you hit a nasty hook, the ball runs out to trouble in a tight arc, like suppressed ambition. It's the Type A trajectory. Bill would not have been charmed by the wisdom of Shivas Irons, the guru of Michael Murphy's *Golf in the Kingdom.* He lived to conquer, not endure. Bill loved the boldness golf inspired. The challenge of the long carry blended with his eagerness. He was wild about Arnold Palmer, and if he were alive today Bill would surely place Greg Norman beside Palmer in his pantheon. There was a joy in his mad pursuit, an unself-conscious zeal. He loved the game so purely that even Bill's fatal heart attack was a sentimental triumph. He died napping between the morning and afternoon rounds on his annual gulf coast golfing holiday, dreaming, I liked to imagine, of a long birdie putt nestling in the cup as his spirit fled. That helped me accept the mysterious act of inheritance through which his madness passed on to me.

So this is my thanks to Bill Mabry for giving me golf and showing me passion. Wherever you are, I hope the putts are falling. And say hello to my folks.

Love, John.

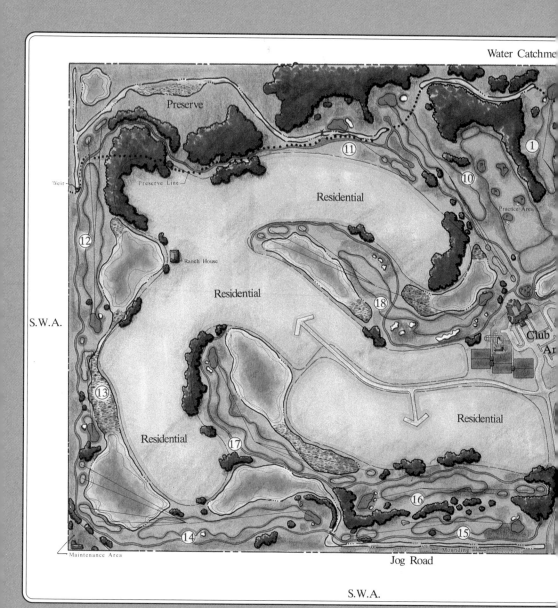